REINVENTING "THE PEOPLE"

Reinventing "The People"

THE PROGRESSIVE MOVEMENT, THE CLASS PROBLEM, AND THE ORIGINS OF MODERN LIBERALISM

SHELTON STROMQUIST

UNIVERSITY OF ILLINOIS PRESS

Urbana and Chicago

Front matter illustration: The "Capital and Labor" image appeared repeatedly in *Survey* magazine in 1912 and 1913, reflecting reformers' deepening perception that the interests of the two must be balanced, or they would lead, alternatively, to anarchy or tyranny.

Library of Congress Cataloging-in-Publication Data
Stromquist, Shelton, 1943–
Reinventing "The People" : the progressive movement, the class
problem, and the origins of modern liberalism / Shelton Stromquist.
p.   cm. — (The working class in American history)
Includes bibliographical references and index.
ISBN-13: 978-0-252-03026-0 (isbn 13 cloth : alk. paper)
ISBN-10: 0-252-03026-5 (isbn 10 cloth : alk. paper)
ISBN-13: 978-0-252-07269-7 (isbn 13 paper : alk. paper)
ISBN-10: 0-252-07269-3 (isbn 10 paper : alk. paper)
1. Working class—United States—Political activity. 2. Social
reformers—United States. 3. Social classes—United States.
4. Progressivism (United States politics) I. Title. II. Series.
HD8076.S77   2006
303.48′4′097309041—dc22   2005017136

Contents

Preface

Books often come to be written by circuitous paths. This one is no exception. It began as an offshoot of a larger project on the transformation of working-class political culture in the Progressive Era. In the course of that research, I confronted what appeared to be an inescapable conclusion: not only had a "Progressive movement" existed, despite claims by some historians to the contrary, but its identity seemed tied to the question of whether class conflict was an irreducible feature of American society. As I looked deeper, I realized how central the "class problem" had been to the discourse and reform program the Progressives crafted. It seemed that even as they denied the centrality of class, they could not stop talking about it.

This effort to locate and map the Progressive movement and to explain its distinctive identity might seem redundant, given the extraordinary attention progressivism has received. It appeared necessary for three reasons. First, since 1970, when historian Peter Filene provocatively questioned the very existence of such a movement, and subsequently, historians have to a large extent skirted the question, we have been left with a void of attention to the movement dimension of progressivism. This study argues for the existence of such a movement. It does so by focusing on the common ideological and rhetorical ground Progressives claimed.

The second reason for undertaking such a study ultimately proved more important. While synthetic work on progressivism atrophied after the mid-1970s, historians probing specific aspects of Progressive Era history have revisited the archives, brought new approaches to bear on the study of older questions, and drawn on creative scholarship in a number of related fields to reconceive certain aspects of progressivism's landscape. New syntheses of the period, its reform movements and politics, are now possible.

Third, and most consequentially, the interpretive direction this book took came from my own research and a growing conviction that the "class problem" was critical to the way Progressive reformers looked at the world. I saw through their writings and public speech a movement profoundly shaped by the common experience of social crisis in the late nineteenth century. Those in Progressive reform's predominant wing may have emphasized different programs and diverged at times in their analyses of the underlying causes of the problems they confronted, but they nonetheless crafted a common language that stressed the paramount need for social reconciliation in the service of democratic renewal. They convinced themselves that class conflict and the "parochial" class loyalties that bred it could be transcended. They imagined "the people" as a civic community in which class would lose its meaning. They reinvented a broad notion of citizenship and civic responsibility drained of nineteenth-century producerist class partisanship. But in their programmatic efforts to constitute an imagined people, they failed to come to terms with the structures of class power and domination that shaped "public" interest and over time undermined their quest for democratic community. Other reformers—outside the mainstream of the movement—believed only a mobilized and politicized working class was capable of challenging the entrenched class power that perpetually stifled real reform.

As I began to understand the perspective of Progressive reformers better and recognized how pervasive that perspective was within their movement, I also realized the powerful influence Progressives had exerted on twentieth-century liberalism. Liberal reform in this century sprang from the agenda and world view of the Progressives. And like their Progressive forebears, liberals have largely continued to deny the relevance of class to reform. Unable or unwilling to recognize and confront the sources of class power in American life, they have pursued a politics of amelioration. Enlisting the state, they nevertheless sought to limit the scope of its initiative, circumscribe its power, and leave in place the structures of corporate property and influence that continue to reproduce inequality and dominate American life.

Although this book offers a different angle of vision on progressivism, it is fundamentally a work of synthesis that builds in its particulars on the scholarship of others. As subjects of historical interpretation go, progressivism has seen its ups and downs. Every generation, it seems, must come to grips anew with this profoundly transformative period in American history. I am convinced that we are in the midst of a new interpretive upswing in the study of progressivism, and I am deeply impressed and influenced by the wave of new scholarship in a variety of fields that is refiguring what we thought we knew about the subject. Historians of women and reform have reasserted the pivotal and contested role women played in defining progressivism. The work of Kathryn Kish Sklar, Robyn Muncy, Mina Carson, Ellen DuBois, Paula Baker, Melanie Gustafson, Maureen Flanagan, Linda Kerber, and Sarah Deutsch is especially noteworthy. New critical perspectives on the settlement houses have been offered by Rivka Lissak, Elisabeth Lasch-Quinn, Thomas Philpott, and Ruth Crocker. And building on the important work of Alice Kessler-Harris and Nancy Schrom Dye, historians Annalise Orleck, Ardis Cameron, Linda Gordon, Gail Bederman, and Louise Michele Newman have continued to explore the intersections of race, ethnicity, and class with women's reform activity. Labor historians have brought serious consideration of workers' collective action and politics into the sphere of Progressive reform, building on an earlier generation of scholarship pioneered by Irwin Yellowitz, Melvyn Dubofsky, and, most important, David Montgomery. Especially noteworthy in this newer scholarship is the work of Steve Fraser, James Barrett, Joseph McCartin, Julia Greene, and Leon Fink. The centrality of race to Progressive reform, demonstrated so powerfully by George Frederickson, has been buttressed in recent studies by David Levering Lewis, Ralph Luker, Kevin Gaines, Patricia Schechter, Michael Perman, and Bryant Simon. The powerful role played by progressivism's intellectual allies is explored with subtlety by Robert Westbrook, Dorothy Ross, Mary Furner, John L. Thomas, Clarence Wunderlin, James Livingston, and Andrew Pfeffer. Any consideration of progressivism as a movement must build on the important work of an earlier generation of historians whose pioneering studies of reform remain an essential starting point, notably J. Joseph Huthmacher, John Buenker, Allen F. Davis, Clarke Chambers, Robert Crunden, Walter Trattner, and Robert Bremner. Finally, others have taken different tacks in trying to synthesize the reform impulses of this era. Important recent efforts include those of Alan Dawley, Stephen Diner, Robert D. Johnston, Kevin Mattson, Michael McGerr, Richard L. McCormick, Daniel Rodgers, and Theda Skocpol. I have been led by this exciting new scholarship to try my hand at considering what gave unity and coherence to this movement of diverse partisans and arenas of reform activity.

I have labored with this project for several years and, in doing so, put on hold my own study of working-class politics in the Progressive Era. Many colleagues and friends have listened with patience and insight to my ideas as they evolved and read pieces of the project as it materialized in one form or another. I am especially grateful to my colleagues at Iowa, Ken Cmiel, Linda Kerber, Colin Gordon, Jeff Cox, and Allen Steinberg. I deeply appreciate the insightful criticism and shrewd editorial suggestions that Julie Greene provided for a portion of this work. Joseph McCartin and Nelson Lichtenstein read the work in its entirety and provided absolutely invaluable guidance for its improvement. Matt Stromquist patiently read and commented insightfully on the chapters in their penultimate form. Others generously read or listened to parts of the book as it took shape in conference papers and made very helpful suggestions for revision. Bruce Laurie, Eric Foner, Paula Baker, Bob Cherney, Elisabeth Perry, Joe McCartin, Roger Horowitz, Eric Arnesen, Ron Schatz, Eric Fure-Slocum, and Steve Rosswurm deserve particular mention. Over many years I have treasured my friendship with the late Steve Sapolsky and our discussions of urban working-class politics. How I wish this work in its final form could have benefited from his critical reading. I have been blessed with a wonderful group of graduate research assistants who, over a number of years, have contributed to this book in many ways. They include David Lewis-Colman, Crystal Bailey, Dana Quartana, Yucheng Qin, Mark Stemen, Patricia Reid, Shannon Fogg, Bob Bionaz, Mike Innis-Jimenez, and Matt Mettler.

I spent very productive semesters at the University of Iowa's Obermann Center for Advanced Study and am deeply grateful to Jay Semel, Lorna Olson, Carolyn Frisbie, and Karla Tonella for their support and encouragement. And without research leaves funded by the University of Iowa and its College of Liberal Arts and Sciences, I could not have written this book.

I owe a deep debt of gratitude, as always, to librarians and archivists who helped me make my way through the rich collections at the State Historical Society of Wisconsin, the State Historical Society of Iowa, the Western Reserve Historical Society, the University of Iowa Libraries, the New York Public Library, the Chicago Historical Society, the University of Illinois at Chicago Library, the Milwaukee Area Research Center, the Milwaukee Historical Society, the Milwaukee Public Library, and the Smith College Library. In particular, I want to thank Harry Miller, Mary Bennett, Karin Mason, and Bob McCown.

Finally, on a more personal level, I have had the good fortune of having three extraordinary teachers who guided me through different stages of my formal education: at Rich Township High School, Stan Moore; during my undergraduate years at Yale, Staughton Lynd; and in my graduate training at the University of Pittsburgh, David Montgomery. I continue to reap the benefits of their guidance.

Despite having written a rather long book, I hardly have words enough to express my wonderment at the generous love my children, Chris, Matt, and Elizabeth, and my soul mate, Ann Stromquist, have bestowed on me. As always, Ann's shrewd editorial advice has proved invaluable. None of this would have been possible without them.

INTRODUCTION

Progressives and
the Problem of Class

We are not willing, openly and professedly, to assume
that American citizens are broken up into classes, even if
we make that assumption the preface to a plea that the
superior class has duties to the inferior. Our democracy is
still our most precious possession, and we do well to resent
any inroads upon it, even though they may be made
in the name of philanthropy.

—Jane Addams, *Twenty Years at Hull-House,* 1910

With the outbreak of the Pullman car shopworkers' strike in 1894, Jane Addams faced a formidable challenge. She felt torn between sympathy for the strikers and her own desire to bridge the class divisions that the strike revealed. She was frustrated that the arbitration efforts of the Chicago Civic Federation had not borne fruit. As the only member of the arbitration committee to have met with the striking Pullman employees and listened to their grievances, she had also dutifully listened to the official pronouncement of the Pullman managers, who "insisted there was nothing to arbitrate."[1] With that pronouncement, the arbitration effort effectively ended and, to her dismay, class war once again loomed on the horizon.

Preoccupied as she was with her sister's terminal illness that summer, she later recalled her absence from the city during critical parts of that conflict-torn time. But she also vividly remembered the several-mile pilgrimage she took in the midst of the strike to the newly erected statue of Abraham Lincoln near the lakefront:

I walked the wearisome way from Hull-House to Lincoln Park—for no cars were running regularly at that moment of sympathetic strikes—in order to look at and gain magnanimous counsel, if I might, from the marvelous St.

Gaudens statue. . . . Some of Lincoln's immortal words were cut into the stone at his feet, and never did a distracted town more sorely need the healing of "with charity towards all" than did Chicago at that moment, and the tolerance of the man who had won charity for those on both sides of "an irrepressible conflict."[2]

Like her fellow reformers, Addams had come of age in an era of profound labor conflict. Solving the "class problem" became the preoccupation of her generation. In trying to do so, they looked unflinchingly at the social inequity that surrounded them and the conditions that thwarted individual opportunity and threatened democratic institutions. They devised methods and programs they hoped would overcome barriers to individual opportunity. And they reinvented for their own conflict-torn times the idea that "the people" were capable of self-government. In so doing, they hoped to consign the embers of class conflict to the ashcan of history. Addams had warned in an essay written just before the Pullman strike of a "constant temptation towards class warfare in the labor movement." She perceived the settlement houses and the reform movement in general to be working not for the betterment of "one kind of people or class of people but for the common good." By encouraging the organization of labor, she hoped to foster the development of "the ethical aims of the movement." In words that echoed the views of many fellow Progressives, she worried that "any class or set of men deprived of the companionship of the whole, become correspondingly decivilized and crippled."[3]

* * *

For a social movement that was palpably real to its contemporaries, the Progressive movement has been surprisingly elusive for historians writing since World War II. The spreading virus of McCarthyism after the war bred a skepticism toward reform that infected the scholarship of a generation. In the view of some historians, Progressives were members of a displaced middle class driven to reform by their own status anxiety.[4] The 1960s witnessed a different variety of skepticism toward progressive reform. Some argued that Progressives, in the name of reform, had promoted a corporate ideal that promised social stability while protecting the interests of large businesses. Still other historians saw the reformers as the progeny of an organizational revolution, a new middle class that had promised efficiency, professional expertise, and bureaucratic solutions to society's pressing problems. These shifting tides of interpretation made the reform rhetoric of the Progressives themselves seem naïve, archaic, and vague. Historians' attention became riveted on the question of who these so-called Progressives were and what sort of movement they constituted. While the social identities of reformers and Progressive Party politicians could be readily discerned, what distinguished them from their stalwart competitors became less apparent. Although historians might cast nets that would ensnare many varieties of Progressives, how these individual reformers became a movement and what ideology they shared was no longer obvious.[5] Some even professed skepticism that a Progressive movement had existed at all.[6]

In this book, I argue that a Progressive movement constituted itself in response to the mounting social crisis of the late nineteenth century that was most clearly revealed in the battles between labor and capital and in the campaigns to save the wasted lives produced by industrial growth. Through diverse and overlapping networks intellectuals, social gospel reformers, young educated women, labor activists, and insurgent politicians developed over time a sense of participating in what they came to call a "movement." They drew inspiration from older traditions of reform, from the legacy of the abolitionists' campaign against chattel slavery, and from seemingly more advanced reform movements that sprang up alongside or in competition with social democratic political movements across Europe.[7] But fundamentally, the Progressive movement was created by a new generation, born and reared since the Civil War and steeped in the labor and social conflict of the late nineteenth century.

To assert the existence of a Progressive movement is not to deny the diversity of perspectives and interests from which it sprang. Nor is it to underestimate the conflicted and discontinuous course of its evolution. Only by charting its history and core ideology and documenting its internal conflicts can we discern the shape and character of the Progressives' movement. I have found it useful to distinguish between a dominant "meliorist" wing of the movement and a vigorous but smaller group of reformers who identified with the class partisan perspective associated with the nineteenth-century producers movement or in the early twentieth century with socialist or syndicalist tendencies. Between these two wings lay a group of reformers whose ideology and organizational commitments fluctuated and overlapped the two. Henry Demarest Lloyd, Vida Scudder, and Florence Kelley might best represent this group.

Progressivism spawned a new language of reform. Embracing neither older varieties of republicanism nor a newer nationalistic Americanism, these self-styled reformers arrayed themselves in the universalistic garb of what they termed "the people," a social category broadly conceived and undifferentiated by class interests. Their "rhetoric of the moral whole," as historian Daniel Rodgers termed it, promised restoration of the common good as a social ideal. The movement defined its enemies, by contrast, as parochial, corrupt, and antisocial "interests" that bred the twin evils of greed and inefficiency. The corrupting influences, represented by urban boss rule and corporate "robber barons," threatened democratic institutions and the expansion of economic opportunity. These interests conspired to produce a dysfunctional industrial society that eroded public virtue. By consigning "the other half" to squalid, less-than-human conditions, the "interests" undermined social order and stability.[8]

This new language of reform circulated through popular journals and in the public speech of reformers and politicians. The promise of "reknitting the social body into wholeness blossomed," according to Rodgers, "in new and inventive forms."[9] Progressive reformers seized a political middle ground to speak for the broad "public" that stood apart from contending, parochial class interests.[10] As Kansas editor William Allen White noted, after watching both Greenbackers and Populists, who appealed to what he called "the ne'er-do-wells" and the "misfits," the Progressives were different: "Here were the successful middle-class country-town citizens, the farmer whose barn was painted, the well paid railroad engineer, and the country editor. It was a well-dressed crowd. . . . Proletarian and plutocrat were absent."[11]

The Progressive movement banished the language of class from the vocabulary of reform. By focusing on the individual and by attacking the environment that limited individual opportunity, Progressives promoted the idea that social differences based on structural inequality could be ameliorated through voluntary action and enlightened governmental social policy. In their view, however, neither individuals acting collectively nor the government acting through "class legislation" should alter the fundamental structures of social power and property. By seeking to reinvent a society in which class had no enduring place, Progressives, sometimes intentionally, sometimes inadvertently, lay the foundation for twentieth-century liberals' inability to see the world around them in class terms or conceive of social remedies that altered the social structure of class power.[12]

Progressives did not invent the idea of class harmony. In one variant or another since the American Revolution, that ideal figured in republican social thought.[13] Historian Edmund Morgan called "the sovereignty of the people" a "dynamic fiction" in republican thought, "a goal to be sought" but "never attainable, always receding." And Arthur Mann argued that in the view of the founders, "the people . . . were unfettered and dynamic, endowed with the power to choose and to change, to break the crust of custom if need be and to shape the future."[14] The elimination of property qualifications for white male voters had made citizenship classless while still excluding African Americans, nonnaturalized immigrants, and women. After the Civil War, a liberal "free labor ideology" promised universal access to opportunity through a capitalist marketplace and a bountiful frontier. But as the industrial revolution advanced in the late nineteenth century and class conflict erupted on an unprecedented scale, a *working-class* republican critique of acquisitive individualism gained wide support within a self-styled class of "producers."[15] If day-to-day poverty, long working hours, and economic oppression effectively denied the rights of citizenship to a large portion of the population, and if the resulting "wage slavery" placed them in a position analogous to chattel slaves, then the universalizing claims of republican citizenship lost meaning. An alternative strand of progressivism rooted in the producers' movement of the late nineteenth century ebbed and flowed in the new century. Its class-partisan perspective found expression in local labor and socialist parties, in the industrial unionism of the Industrial Workers of the World (IWW) and some affiliates of the American Federation of Labor (AFL), and among labor Progressives committed to a radical vision of "industrial democracy" that flowered in wartime and postwar Left-labor organizing.[16]

Progressive reformers at the turn of the century undertook the project of reclaiming citizens from the "human junk" produced by industrialization.[17] Unlike the more radical producerist movement of the 1880s and 1890s, they saw harm, not virtue, in a dispossessed class empowered to reclaim the wealth it created and to realign the structures of power that produced inequality. The reformers embraced the idea that industrial progress, organized by capitalist property holders, would produce prosperity and alleviate misery. Economist Simon Patten's optimism about the liberating effects of increased consumption through economic growth inspired a whole generation of reformers. For journalist Walter Weyl, a Patten student, this vision lessened the prospect of class warfare. "Where wealth is growing at a rapid rate," he noted, "the multitude may be fed without breaking into the rich man's granary."[18] That prescription has remained at the heart of liberal thought throughout the twentieth century.

In the face of rapid urbanization and new, massive immigration spawned by the "second industrial revolution," early-twentieth-century reformers worked determinedly to produce an enlightened citizenry. Placing stock in new educational techniques and the socializing influence of settlement houses, they also insisted on socially responsible behavior by capital, enforced where necessary through legislation and state regulation. Democracy, they believed, would humanize industrial society. Assisted by enlightened business leaders, the reform movement hoped to rationalize the processes of production and reengineer a safer, more healthful, and more socially productive environment at home, in the community, and at work. Edward Devine and the editors of *Charities and the Commons* argued that the problem was a set of "more or less isolated . . . conquerable evils," not a "bad system." Reformers should mount an "attack on insanitary tenements, tuberculosis, and child labor . . . as if it were worth while to overcome them even while private property and wages and profits remain in evidence as essential features of our industrial system."[19] In 1908, Chicago reformer Graham Taylor worried that some signs pointed to an "awakening of the wage earners of our country to the consciousness of their class interest." But he also professed to see a more widespread "awakening of the mass to move together to claim and conserve the rights and interests common to the whole community." And Progressive journalist John Graham Brooks called on organized labor to "enter upon its heavy task of leading the fight against a party tyranny." He noted that "no class (if the word must be used) has so much at stake in all this as the wage-earner."[20] Purged of corrupting influences, democratic politics could be a vehicle for building social solidarity and community responsibility.

The inability or unwillingness of Progressive reformers to accept a world indelibly demarcated by classes shaped their approach to reform. The "working class" as a social category lost its salience. The settlement houses addressed instead the problems of what educator Vida Scudder termed "the submerged tenth."[21] This population, largely immigrant or nonwhite, disorganized and destitute, required the ministrations of those possessed by a "crusading spirit." But for the most part they stood outside the circle of "the people." Political reforms designed to purify and protect the democratic process—personal registration, at-large elections, direct primaries, and initiatives and referenda—would ensure, they hoped, a democratically inclined polity and a disinterested body of voters capable of putting social good above personal interest.[22]

Progressive democrats, such as John Dewey, imagined a society of citizens whose equality was guaranteed by their "direct and active participation" in the democratic process. "Political freedom and responsibility," according to Dewey, "express an individual's power and obligation to make effective all his other capacities by fixing the social conditions of their exercise."[23] In Dewey-esque tones, historian Mary Ryan has celebrated "as an essential feature of modern democracy" the "civic wars" of nineteenth-century cities, with their "indelicate balance between civility and belligerence."[24]

While some democratically inclined Progressives saw citizenship as an expansive category, "citizen" was, in fact, a term of more restricted meaning for many in Progressive Era America. A very large proportion of what nineteenth-century Americans termed the "producing classes" was excluded. Most Progressives regarded the vast majority of new immigrants and African Americans as unprepared to join the political community of voters.[25]

In the short run, as many historians have shown, Progressive reform of the political process narrowed rather than expanded the circle of citizenship. Dewey and most Progressives not only failed to acknowledge this process of exclusion but also underestimated the continuing influence of class power within a democratic polity. In this respect, they shared with antebellum abolitionists and the Radical Republicans of the immediate post–Civil War period an inability to look "beyond equality" and see, as historian David Montgomery noted, that propertyless "wage earners were effectively denied meaningful participation in the Republic."[26]

An unwillingness to acknowledge the enduring fact of class divisions was not unique to the Progressive reformers' imagination. But they embraced the ideal of classless social harmony with an earnest conviction that transcended that of their reforming forebears. By pursuing that ideal, the Progressives hoped to marginalize and disarm an alternative politics of class.[27]

While reformers constructed a common language and a network of social ties that bound them to one another, their movement nonetheless consisted of diverse and discrete communities whose ideological differences were often profound. Two dynamics are worth noting. First, on important occasions or at critical moments, a broad constellation of self-proclaimed reformers gathered despite their differences to reconsecrate progressivism as a social movement. Such moments included the Chicago Civic Federation's Conference on Industrial Arbitration and Conciliation, held shortly after the Pullman strike in 1894, the Civic Federation Conference on Trusts in 1899, the National Conference on Social and Political Reforms in 1899 at Buffalo, and the annual conventions of the National Conference of Charities and Corrections (NCCC), the National Child Labor Committee (NCLC), the Mothers' Congresses, and the American Association for Labor Legislation, especially from 1909 to 1912. The reformers also reaffirmed the movement when many of them gathered to support formation of the National Association for the Advancement of Colored People (NAACP) in 1910 and to petition in early 1912 for a government investigation of the "causes of industrial unrest."

The movement crested at the nominating convention of the Progressive Party in 1912. Jane Addams later recalled, "In the five years before the outbreak of the world war . . . our general efforts were more and more interrelated with many other movements." And of the convention itself, she remembered, "Suddenly, as if by magic, the city of Chicago became filled with men and women from every state in the Union who were evidently haunted by the same social compunctions and animated by like hopes; they revealed to each other mutual sympathies and memories. . . . For three days together they defined their purposes and harmonized their wills into gigantic cooperation."[28] These moments affirmed the reality of a Progressive movement for many of its participants.

A second set of influences that shaped the Progressive movement arose with the pressure of continued popular insurgency outside the movement itself. "As I lived through the *fin de siècle* and the ensuing years," Vida Scudder recalled, "I found society aquiver with vague social idealisms, while a sense of conflict, ominous if not clearly defined, moved everywhere below the surface."[29] That conflict periodically broke the surface of reform, produced a sense of crisis, and precipitated political and social realignments that reshaped the terrain on which the reform community worked. Whether in the form of violent streetcar strikes in Cleveland or Philadelphia, third-party insurgencies erupting in San Francisco or Oklahoma, all-out class war in the coalfields of Colorado or West Virginia, or a mind-numbing tragedy like the Triangle shirtwaist fire, the orderliness and efficiency of managed reform and the sense of a "moral whole" shattered periodically and alternative pathways to reform appeared. These events and their consequences were, for the most part, absorbed by the movement, generating a different spin or direction to reform initiatives and realigning the political field of battle on which reformers fought for the implementation of new public policies that might restore social peace. Reformers came to view the state as a useful, even necessary, instrument for reform but also a filter for parochial concerns. Vida Scudder, again, astutely noted the way reform refashioned politics. "Proposed reforms have entered practical politics, to a degree unimagined in the last century," she wrote. "Even in that last refuge of rugged individualism, the U.S.A., conceptions of the sphere of government have slowly and irresistibly changed, to include the social services, and coquette with more searching reforms."[30]

To reconstruct progressivism as a movement, we need to distinguish levels and degrees of connection between its functioning parts. But to make sense of the conflict, contention, and ideological differences within the movement, we need something more than Daniel Rodgers's notion of a sea of contending interest groups within a pluralized polity.[31] More useful might be the concept of a core movement that emerged in the early to middle 1890s, shattered existing alliances, spawning a host of ideologically related but discrete reform initiatives.[32] But counterposed to that core movement was a more radical, if episodic, movement determined to realign in fundamental ways the power of labor and capital. Reformers in the core movement acted on many fronts to purify democratic institutions, attack organized greed in business and public life, celebrate and guide the "public's" interest, design measures to enhance efficient and humane treatment of the submerged tenth, and defuse social conflict. By welcoming, within limits, expanded state power and harnessing expertise, these reformers believed they could reconstruct society. This dynamic core of the reform movement precipitated responses from large corporations and the major political parties as well as their more radical reform competitors. Those radicals revealed their alternative reform vision in an aggressive western working-class movement, in a new urban politics where battles for municipal ownership took center stage, in a Socialist Party that claimed impressive local and regional pockets of strength, and among an increasingly vocal group of labor Progressives who stood outside both the narrow trade unionism of the AFL leadership and the professional proponents of labor arbitration. The reform impulse found itself continually absorbed, reshaped, and redirected as crises came and went. Some specific reform initiatives—the hygiene and housing movements, for instance—in time took on a life and ideological cast of their own. The core Progressive movement may have lost its initial coherence but not its identity. What we have understood as "progressive" was to a very large degree still shaped by a common vision of cross-class reform. In recent decades, some historians of progressivism lost sight of this core vision amid the whirl of reform activity, functional organization, and interest-group mobilization.[33]

The Progressive movement carried with it the cultural baggage of the middle class and segments of the native-born working class from which it sprang. It drew powerfully on the cross-class model of reform pioneered by women on behalf of a gendered, maternalist reform agenda.[34] Its vision of the people, although universal in its claims, was in fact more limited and culturally bounded. New immigrants and African Americans were consigned to the margins, their capacity for assimilation dependent on their slow social progress, their citizenship claims always contingent. As dependent peoples, they merited charitable attention, even concerted education, but Progressives deemed them incapable of constructive group activity on their own behalf. When ethnic or race leaders arose to represent new immigrants or African Americans, settlement workers regarded them with suspicion. When, as workers, they struck on their own behalf, many charity reformers thought them dangerous.[35]

While a broad cross-section of Progressive reformers came to believe that class conflict could be transcended, the resurgence of class warfare between 1909 and 1914 shook their faith. Stunned by the unprecedented labor violence, they pressured the Taft and Wilson administrations to create an expert commission, their favored remedy, to investigate anew the causes of industrial unrest. To their dismay, the contentious U.S. Commission on Industrial Relations (USCIR), chaired by Frank Walsh, turned its considerable scientific and public relations guns on corporate tyranny and the allied "charity trusts." The shrapnel hit many of the Progressives who had lobbied so strenuously for a commission of experts in the first place.[36] When the smoke had cleared, the reformers' confidence in their ability to sustain a movement committed to industrial peace and class reconciliation had been profoundly shaken but not abandoned.

As the guns of a distant war in Europe grew ever louder and the appeals for American military preparedness became more insistent, the reformers reassembled their fractured legions, minus those who objected on principle to the war, to undertake a new national mission on behalf of democracy. But with the rest of the world as their field, they found the campaign for democratic reform at home absorbed into the wartime agenda of a broad patriotic coalition that included many of their erstwhile corporate enemies. Beyond their ranks moved other legions—African Americans migrating north to join the industrial working class, restive immigrant workers tasting the first fruits of "industrial democracy" in strikes made possible by wartime labor scarcity, and a socialist movement increasingly fractured and isolated because of opposition to the war and poised on the precipice of political exile from which it would not return until the Great Depression.[37]

Progressivism figured into the reform equations of succeeding decades in ambiguous ways. A legacy of voluntarism mingled with the propensity of reformers to look to the state and dispassionate experts for the solutions to social problems. That tension between voluntarism and statism animated the reform undertakings of the next generation, but in the context of the Great Depression, the New Deal bolstered confidence in state-orchestrated solutions to economic and social dislocation in ways the Progressives had only begun to imagine.[38] Despite another wave of reform—President Lyndon Johnson's "war on poverty"—the Progressive tradition had run its course by the end of the 1960s. However, those waves of reform left a legacy. "Protean" liberals may have shifted their focus to accommodating racial equality, but they continued, for the most part, to deny that class matters in American society.[39]

Whether from an exceptionalist disposition rooted in the American republican tradition or from the profound imprint of Progressive reform itself, most American liberals in the late twentieth century continued to believe that solutions to problems of poverty, the environment, corporate irresponsibility, and political corruption lay in cross-class coalitions acting in the broad public interest. Much as their forebears did one hundred years earlier, late-twentieth-century reformers largely denied the reality of class-constituted power and the possibility of political mobilization around class interests.

But in a supremely ironic twist of historical fate, these very liberals now stand accused by their New Right adversaries of preaching "class warfare."[40] The language of class has reappeared, charged with political and social meaning. Republicans accuse Democrats of preaching "class warfare" when they note the benefits accruing disproportionately to the wealthy or the harm done to the working poor through tax cuts, budget belt tightening, or limitations on unemployment compensation. What is lost in the new debate about the relevance of class in American life is the role played by liberal reformers of the Progressive Era in constructing a discourse and a set of social policies that they hoped might enable American society to transcend its "class problem." By promoting social policies and political action that mobilized the people with a promise of class reconciliation and reform, Progressives had hoped to make the class problem a thing of the past. This book examines the origins of this Progressive project and the liberal discourse it spawned.

1

The Labor Problem and
the Crisis of the Old Order

We declare that there is an inevitable and irresistible conflict between the wage-system of labor and the
republican system of government. . . . It is war—war against
the divine rights of humanity; war against the principles of
our government. There is no mutuality of interests, no cooperative union of labor and capital. It is the iron heel of a
soulless monopoly, crushing the manhood out of sovereign
citizens. . . . The mob can be put down for a while;
but the spirit of hate that now centres upon the
great monopolies will soon extend to the government
that acts as their protector.

—George McNeill, *The Labor Movement:*
The Problem of Today, 1886

Stalwart labor reformer George McNeill spoke for a growing segment
of working-class partisans in the 1880s who believed class conflict had become
an endemic feature of industrial society and saw a war of seemingly irreconcilable class interests as inevitable. Nearly a year after the great railroad strikes
of 1877, McNeill addressed a grand labor parade and picnic in Chicago on July
4, 1878, and railed against what he called "a serious and bloody communis-
tic conspiracy" of "railroad kings, merchant princes and cotton lords" who
"proposed to reduce workmen to the level of paupers and take from them the
elective franchise." He claimed that "there is a war between capital and
labor . . . a war that we don't like, and which is the result of the separate and
distinct interests of the two classes." He preferred the cooperation that would
result from the "perfect organization of the working classes," but he knew
that "strikes are justifiable as a means." Even though he had on occasion coun-
seled against them, he advocated strikes rather than "submission."[1]

McNeill's talk of a war of classes resonated with particular force among members of a generation that had experienced firsthand a different civil war of unprecedented dimensions. As the wounds of that war healed and the aftermath of the secession crisis receded, Americans found themselves in the throes of industrial changes that again tore at the social fabric. Industrial change had spawned conflict that touched the lives of ordinary citizens, and Americans of all stations worried about what their futures might hold.

The language of class permeated late-nineteenth-century America. The years of economic expansion following the Civil War had produced new hierarchies of power and privilege that seemed to threaten the virtuous republican commonwealth. Amid the frenzy of railroad speculation, the machinations of western land speculators, and the cost cutting of a new breed of manufacturing entrepreneurs, self-described producers confronted what they perceived to be a dangerous new parasitic class of nonproducers. The fact that these "robber barons" benefited directly from government policies that financed railroad development, regulated land sales, and deflated the value of paper currency confirmed suspicions that undemocratic influences had already gained control of the political process. In the face of such threats, a class appeal to join in defense of the sanctity of republican institutions and the egalitarian ideals of the American revolution resonated powerfully.

Antebellum conceptions of a society divided between virtuous artisan republicans and parasitic masters took on new meaning in the post–Civil War era. New conceptions of class difference drew on several sources of inspiration. First, the rhetoric of "wage slavery" acquired renewed power to evoke both the onerous dependency bred by the "wages system" and the prospect that, like chattel slavery, it too might be abolished. In a nation where more than two-thirds of the working population had become "hirelings for life," the vast majority of people experienced the wages system on a daily basis.[2] Yet industrial capitalism as a system for organizing the labor of a large, propertyless population was new enough that many Americans could plausibly imagine alternative, cooperative arrangements by which labor might be organized and deployed.[3] Second, the state had acquired new functions and unimagined powers during the Civil War crisis. Government became not simply an instrument of total war but also the vehicle for confiscating illegitimate property (slaves) and reconstructing a morally and economically bankrupt society (the South).[4] Members of the producing classes began to conceive a state that might acquire and operate railroads, telephones and telegraphs, coal mines, and even manufacturing monopolies, or that might construct and finance a vast network of cooperative warehouses and granaries. Third, new organizations embodying producerist values and fostering a "movement culture" gained legions of adherents and expanded influence. This organizational ferment testified to the existence of a society divided into warring classes. The Knights of Labor (KOL) and Farmers' Alliance became powerful national organizations in the 1880s and influenced a generation of workers, farmers, and their reform allies to believe in the possibility that through their leadership the producing classes might reconstruct American society.[5]

But the producers' language actually spoke for a narrower class than their rhetoric implied. Social boundaries defined by masculinity and whiteness in most circumstances shut out women, African Americans, and Chinese immigrants from what has been called the "lodge democracy" of white men.[6] On occasion, a dispossessed working class struggled with some success to transcend those divisive boundaries of race and gender. In Richmond, Virginia, during the heyday of the Knights of Labor, on the New Orleans docks in the early 1890s, among black and white sharecroppers in Oklahoma and Texas, in some locals of the fledgling United Mine Workers of America, or in the ranks of the United Garment Workers, tenuous alliances joined white and black producers or led male workers to support the organizing of women.[7] But to a significant degree, race and gender—whiteness and masculinity— functioned in ways that privileged white male workers and excluded others from the benefits of collective organization.[8]

By any measure, the last decades of the late nineteenth century witnessed unprecedented social turmoil. With unrelenting labor strife, a population in perpetual motion, deepening urban social problems, legions of new arrivals joining an already swollen immigrant working class, and parasitical politicians who fed at the troughs of corporate franchise holders, society's middle seemed incapable of holding together. The middling classes had formed a self-conscious presence in American society at least since the 1840s. As proponents of common school education, middle-brow cultural respectability, and an ideology of separate spheres of the sexes, they viewed themselves as apostles of measured economic growth, social stability, and republican national purpose.[9] But in the contentious environment of the late nineteenth century, their reform efforts achieved only limited success. Elite "mugwump" reformers challenged urban boss rule in cities and states with only limited success. Christian social gospel reformers addressed the proliferating problems of industrial society but with marginal influence. Proponents of economic fairness, conciliation, and government regulation of corporate excess won few, largely ephemeral victories. Middle-class women focused their considerable reform energies on the liquor question and the campaign to police the social behavior of the immigrant working class. But there, too, victories were few.[10] When Minneapolis editor Ignatius Donnelley spoke to the Populists' Omaha convention in 1892 of the "two great classes—tramps and millionaires," he described a social order in which the middle had given way to a contention of opposing classes. Middle-class reformers of a new generation would take up the task of restoring and enlarging the social middle in the name of the people.[11]

Class conflict lay at the heart of the social crisis of the late nineteenth century and reformers' preoccupation with the class problem. At stake was what kind of industrial society America would become. Reformers brought different prescriptions to the table. Some argued for an aggressive and fundamental redistribution of social and economic power; others sought to create social machinery that could reconcile the interests of antagonistic classes and promote social harmony. Both groups foresaw the use of state power to curtail the excesses of corporations but in different measures. While at times overlapping, these perspectives represented distinct and often conflicting tendencies. In the last decade of the century, a discernible group of Progressive reformers emerged to claim space for their social vision and leadership in the project of social reconstruction. By claiming their own organizational and ideological space, they challenged the producers' conception of a society divided along class lines. This Progressive movement articulated with increasing confidence the proposition that class conflict could be transcended, social harmony between classes orchestrated, and a classless citizenry—the people—made the agents of democratic renewal. But the problem of reconstructing society along such lines remained formidable in the face of the massive social crisis unleashed by industrialization.

Encountering the Labor Problem

Reformers had made tentative first steps in the 1870s and 1880s to come to grips with the spreading class antagonism that confronted them on all sides. Their task was to master the "labor problem." By doing so, they believed they could restore the conditions under which a truly democratic people might flourish.

By the early 1880s, the labor problem had grown to formidable proportions. A young economist, Richard T. Ely, returned from Europe in 1880 to find the country in upheaval. Like many of his generation, he had acquired at European centers of learning theoretical tools that led him to question the laissez-faire orthodoxy that reigned in America. Confronted with the seething conflict between labor and capital that had erupted in the railroad strikes of 1877 and continued to unsettle the surface of economic prosperity, Ely identified a set of problems that would shape his life as a reformer and educator. As he walked the streets of New York, seeking to make sense of what he encountered, he later recalled, "I took upon myself a vow to write in behalf of the laboring classes."[12] His Christian values, more than his training in political economy, suggested the posture he initially would adopt.

Ely and his fellow academic "young rebels" gathered ample evidence of labor's rising strength in the mid-1880s.[13] In one report, he celebrated the ascending fortunes of the Knights of Labor: "Keep off the track! The train of progress is coming! Prepare the way! It rests with us so to direct inevitable changes that we may be brought nearer that kingdom of righteousness for which all good Christians long and pray."[14] Ely's relationship to the labor movement would be more complicated than these euphoric comments, penned in the midst of the "great upheaval," suggest. As the costs of identification with labor rose for members of the academic community in the early 1890s, and as the limits of their intellectual commitment to collectivist reforms surfaced, they would join a growing movement of reformers seeking a middle ground in a class-torn society.

But the society rent by class conflict that Ely and his fellow young political economists encountered had roots in the harsh depression conditions of the 1870s. A rapidly deflating economy following the panic of 1873 and the massive unemployment, wage cuts, and social dislocation that came in its wake produced disorientation, fear, and mounting anger among workers. The railroad strikes of 1877 served as a detonator for their accumulating discontents.[15]

The railroad strikes seemed to sweep across the country like wildfire, jumping from one railroad center to another. In some places—mostly the smaller railroad towns of the East and Midwest—workers enlisted their communities in a battle that they understood to be part of a larger campaign against monopoly's strangulation of the economy. In the larger cities—Baltimore, Pittsburgh, Chicago, St. Louis—the specter of a war between the classes loomed. "Mobs" comprising a cross-section of urban workers responded with vengeance to police and military intervention and the bloodshed it precipitated. As casualties mounted and flames engulfed railroad property, respectable opinion called for massive intervention by the authorities and the liberal use of force to stem the rebellion. And as the railroads tallied their losses in smoldering freight yards, they also debated new measures for avoiding or controlling such conflict in the future.[16]

After the 1877 strikes, a cacophony of reform proposals rose from a chorus of voices. Some, such as Robert Harris, president of the Chicago, Burlington & Quincy Railroad, called for conciliation and welfare measures that would cultivate loyalty and concede the legitimate grievances of valued employees. Others, such as his own vice president, Charles Perkins, warned against coddling workers or in any way disguising the harsh and rigorous lessons of the iron law of supply and demand.[17]

Strike activity after 1877 did not subside, nor did it appear that labor conflict might easily be resolved.[18] By virtually every measure, strikes increased in number and magnitude. Of particular note, strikes over "control issues" rose sharply. With more workers organized in unions, the discipline of organization produced more, not fewer, strikes.[19]

Strikes against the Gould lines in 1884–86, the wave of strikes by workers newly affiliated with the Knights of Labor in 1885–86, and the eight-hour general strike of May 1886 were unprecedented. The numbers of workers engaged in sympathy strikes rose dramatically. The spread of a "contagious" class feeling infected large segments of the working class, especially in the early 1890s. On the railroads, the proportion of strikers involved in sympathetic actions rose from 11 percent in 1885 to 45 percent in 1887. In 1894, the year of the Pullman boycott, 85 percent of all railroad strikers participated in sympathy strikes.[20] The strikes of workers in other sectors of the economy paralleled those of the railroads.

Taken together, these patterns of collective action suggest that an "audacious" spirit of resistance during these years took hold of large segments of the American working class and transcended incremental calculations of costs and benefits. They fought not simply to improve their working conditions but also to assert more fundamental rights. At stake were their dignity and their right to imagine a future for themselves different from the one employers prescribed.[21] These developments deeply troubled would-be reformers, who saw little common ground for class reconciliation in this deepening chasm of conflict.

Employers and Workers Organize

Against the backdrop of the deepening labor crisis, employers as well as workers girded for battle. Despite the factionalism that infected both camps between 1885 and 1895, each experienced significant organizational growth. Few employers had yet mastered the "science" of managing large firms and armies of employees. Beyond a few sectors—railroads, textiles, iron and steel, and machinery manufacture—small, locally owned firms continued to dominate the industrial landscape. A social Darwinian model of competition fit the world of business under conditions of price deflation. Survival, let alone expansion, required ruthlessness and luck, even in a bounteous continental economy with rapidly expanding markets and abundant resources.[22]

Where large-scale firms predominated and bureaucratic management first appeared, attention to labor matters remained casual. Despite the strong impulse among railroads and other firms to limit competition through pools and trusts, competitive pressures shattered efforts at consolidation until the 1890s. Only the outright acquisition of competitors reduced competition.[23] In iron and steel, Andrew Carnegie led the way by introducing new technology, slashing prices, and devouring his competitors while forming what would eventually be the nation's preeminent holding company, the United States Steel Corporation.[24]

Even in the railroad industry after 1877, impassioned debate about remedies for the "labor problem" subsided as prosperity returned and attention focused again on competitive expansion. Amid mounting strikes by lumber shovers, warehousemen, and switchmen in May 1886, railroad general managers convened in Chicago for an intense series of daily meetings with the object of forming a durable employers' association. But the collapse of strikes after the Haymarket bombing brought another wave of complacency and competitive throat cutting among managers. Only in 1894 did the impulse to cooperate again overcome divisions in the ranks of railroad managers. They revived and fine tuned the General Managers' Association (GMA) to meet the unprecedented crisis posed by the Pullman boycott in June 1894. By that time, the consolidation of railroads into a handful of major systems and belated improvements in personnel administration produced more lasting and effective cooperation.[25]

Businessmen in other sectors of the economy were not idle during this period. They created associations designed to strengthen management's position and coordinate responses to an increasingly aggressive labor movement. Early combative associations gave way temporarily in the late 1890s to "an era of good feeling" that saw some firms in a variety of industries pursue strategies of conciliation and mediation. At the national level, the National Civic Federation (NCF) incorporated labor's top echelon into its tripartite structure. But an open-shop campaign led by a revitalized National Association of Manufacturers (NAM) in 1902–3 shattered what labor-management conciliation the first years of the new century had seen. As local open-shop campaigns spread, the NCF and its corporate allies, despite some reservations, joined the anti-union efforts.[26]

Employers' efforts to enhance their competitive position and thwart unionization fueled the labor wars of the late nineteenth century. Conflict intensified in response to government use of injunctions and troops on behalf of capital. But the great upheaval in labor relations also resulted from workers' own activism, spontaneous as well as organized.

Terence Powderly and other labor leaders believed the propensity of American workers to strike undermined organization.[27] But, in fact, late-nineteenth-century workers joined unions in unprecedented numbers. Membership may have risen and fallen with the tides of the economy and the effectiveness of specific unions and their leaders, but overall more workers, by a wide margin, came to be represented by unions. Membership in the KOL soared in the mid-1880s as the "Noble and Holy Order," stripped of its secrecy and elaborate ritual, became the central arena within which workers—skilled and unskilled, black and white, male and female—constructed a "culture of opposition" to the "wages system."[28] At its peak in 1886, estimates put the Knights' membership at 700,000 to 1 million. Together with scattered trade unions comprising another 100,000 to 200,000, organized labor represented as much as 20 percent of the nonagricultural wage labor force. American workers would not again achieve this level of unionization until the World War II era.[29]

An abundance of evidence testifies to the distinctive class culture workers forged in the heat of late-nineteenth-century labor conflict. Depression era pressures bridged the worlds of skilled and unskilled, diminishing differences in status and income and fostering a degree of cooperation and interdependence rarely witnessed in the decades before or after. In battles over the use of public space and in contests over control of local government and police, workers made common cause despite ethnic differences or level of skill. Studies of communities as diverse as Worcester, Massachusetts; Pittsburgh; Detroit; Homestead, Pennsylvania; and Dubuque and Creston, Iowa, suggest a high degree of class bonding. Such tendencies raised alarms among middle-class observers. Jonathan Baxter Harrison believed after visiting New England mill towns that the United States was "in the earlier stages of a war on property." He reported in his 1880 tract *Certain Dangerous Tendencies in American Life,* widespread "distrust, suspicion, and hostility regarding all who do not belong to their class" among the mill hands.[30] The language of producerism and the image of a society divided into classes of producers and parasites had gained wide currency by the end of the nineteenth century.[31]

Seeking Remedies for Class War

After the 1877 railroad strikes, public authorities and many company officials called for the vigorous prosecution of law breakers, the construction of
armories in industrial districts, and the modernization of state militia. While
Joseph Medill, publisher of the *Chicago Tribune,* railed against "Communist
gentry" and the "Dangerous Classes" and appealed for a larger standing army
and strict enforcement of vagrancy laws, his own financial editor, Henry Demarest Lloyd, offered a different set of proposals. Lloyd, who had immersed
himself in railroad problems during the 1870s, criticized the administrative
and financial management of the great rail lines. He had come to support
greater government oversight of railroad operations and the prevention of
railroad pooling. The strikes of 1877 led him to attack the companies' "cut-
throat and starvation policies" that lay behind the strikes. He called for arbitration of disputes and noted that railroad workers' real wages had fallen from
an index of 196 to 106 between 1868 and 1877.[32] The 1877 strikes profoundly
redirected Lloyd's life. Over the next fifteen years he came to believe strongly
that fundamental reform was needed.[33]

Lloyd was not alone. Growing public awareness of "the labor problem"
manifested itself in a number of ways. A new political climate in many industrial states supported "scientific" investigation of the conditions workers
faced. On the model of the pioneering Bureau of Labor Statistics in Massachusetts and in response to the labor movement's demand for investigatory
bodies, a large number of states created labor bureaus between 1881 and 1886.
The U.S. commissioner of labor, appointed at the federal level in 1883, began
systematically gathering and publishing annual data on labor. The third annual report (1886) provided for the years 1881 to 1886 the first comprehensive,
national accounting of strike activity. A comparable volume covering the years
1887 to 1894 followed in 1895. These data confirmed a "labor problem" of staggering proportions.[34]

Faced with intractable labor conflict, public authorities turned to the appointment of state and federal investigatory commissions. The state of Pennsylvania held extensive hearings on the 1877 strikes, and at the federal level,
hearings conducted in 1878 examined the causes and consequences of the depression of the 1870s.[35] But the most ambitious effort to document the national scale of conflict between labor and capital came in hearings conducted
during 1883 and 1884 by the U.S. Senate's Committee on Labor and Education in New York, Chicago, and other sites of labor conflict. The hearings con-

firmed that the labor crisis had spread and that a new, robust organization capable of mobilizing workers regardless of skill or industry was assuming leadership of the working class. The comments of workers like New York trucker Thomas Maguire bore home the depth of class alienation workers felt: "I live in a tenement house, three stories up, where the water comes in through the roof, and I cannot better myself. My little children will have to go to work before they are able to work. Why? Simply because this present system under which we are living is all for self, all for the privileged classes, nothing for the man who produces all the wealth." Telegrapher John McClelland warned the committee that a revolt was near: "I will say this, that there is a considerable undercurrent among the laboring classes of this country, which would require only a certain amount of agitation to set it into practical operation, and there is no telling to what extremes it might go if it was only started."[36]

Public hearings and the appointment of investigatory commissions, staffed by elected officials or public-spirited experts, would remain an important device to which the state repeatedly turned as conflict flared. Public authorities undertook such investigations after the Gould Southwestern railroad strikes in 1886, a Pennsylvania miners' strike in 1887, the Homestead strike in 1892, and the Pullman strike in 1894. A broadly mandated investigation by the U.S. Industrial Commission in 1900–1901 and an inquiry into the "causes of industrial unrest" by the U.S. Commission on Industrial Relations in 1913–15 constituted the most visible and wide-ranging public examinations of the labor problem in the early twentieth century.[37]

Such investigations mixed condemnation of violence with very modest proposals for ameliorating the conditions that produced labor discontent. At least in the nineteenth century, the idea that the government should intercede in strikes as a neutral party, let alone guarantee the recognition of labor's right to organize, fell far beyond the bounds of what the public conceived to be the proper domain for state action. Such bounds did not, of course, preclude the state's use of military force or judicial authority to restrain labor's activity in economically disruptive and sometimes violent strikes.[38]

Producerist and socialist ideology had some influence in academic and reform circles in the 1880s and 1890s. But advocacy of such principles drew the fire of conservative academic administrators, businessmen, philanthropists, and politicians. Young political economists such as John Bates Clark, Henry C. Adams, and Richard T. Ely may initially have found labor's critique of the "wages system" and the vision of a producers' cooperative commonwealth an appealing alternative to the existing, crisis-ridden economic system, but after the Haymarket incident in 1886, these reform-minded intellectuals "retreated from socialism." In retreat, Adams offered a liberal alternative to "constructive socialism," justified because "our entire juridical structure is against it, and it is easier to bring our industries into harmony with the spirit of our law than to re-organize our society from top to bottom, industries included."[39]

Even in retreat, Adams lost his appointment at Cornell for advocating labor's cause and nearly missed being hired at the University of Michigan. In subsequent statements, he abandoned his defense of the "proprietary rights" of labor and assured his academic superiors that his views were based on a commitment to individualism. Ely survived at Johns Hopkins, but some years later, after moving to the University of Wisconsin, he was brought before the board of regents on charges of "economic heresy." By distancing himself from positions he had once openly advocated, Ely, too, maintained his academic position.[40]

In place of labor's proprietary claims to the wealth it created, John Bates Clark and other economists began to define the value of goods as deriving from their marketplace utility. This "marginalist" theory made the competitive market, responding to consumer tastes, the engine of social harmony and progress.[41] Defense of the market and personal liberty would be an important liberal principle initially confounding reformers' deeper critiques of an industrial system, the excesses of which they nevertheless abhorred.

By such a route, the new political economists joined an expanding community of liberal reformers. They envisioned a moderately expanded role for the state. They pursued an ideal of social harmony in which the interests of labor and capital would be reconciled. And they believed such harmony would be the product of properly regulated "natural" laws that promoted a virtuous democratic society of freely competing individuals. The reformers jettisoned the producerist commitment to a fundamental reordering of social power and the reconstruction of society along cooperative lines. As historian Dorothy Ross has noted in the case of this generation of American social scientists, they had to "contend with the power of respectable opinion, and behind it, the power of the capitalist class to enforce its will."[42]

Ely and the new political economists formed one wing of a widening circle of middle-class reformers deeply affected by the class conflict of the late nineteenth century. Attracted to their ranks were Christian socialists, such as Rev. W. D. P. Bliss of Boston and George D. Herron, president in the 1890s of Grinnell College in Iowa, as well as settlement house workers from Hull-House in Chicago and other cities. Jane Addams and Florence Kelley exerted a powerful influence over a whole generation of activist-intellectuals. Henry

George's single-tax ideas and his Union Labor Party candidacy for mayor of New York in 1886 captivated other members of this loose-knit reform-oriented middle class, as did Edward Bellamy's nationalism.

No member of this constellation of reformers seemed for a time more pivotal than Henry Demarest Lloyd. He and his wife, Jessie Bross Lloyd, facilitated the social and intellectual mingling of widening circles of reformers at "The Wayside," their comfortable Winnetka home, and at their "Watch House" on Cape Cod, which they occupied for three months a year and which Chicago attorney Clarence Darrow called "Mrs. Lloyd's summer boarding house." There on a summer evening might be found the likes of Ely, William Dean Howells, Edward Bemis, Willis Abbott, editor of the *Arena,* and a variety of New England social gospelers. During the remaining months of the year, the Wayside became "the social mecca of transoceanic reform." The Lloyds gathered "a unique circle" that included "ethical leaders, socialites, slum-dwellers, clergy, businessmen, liberal and radical politicians, enlightened lawyers, labor leaders, Socialists, Single-Taxers, Bellamy's lieutenants, newspaper editors, British Fabians and Liberals, and Negro leaders."[43]

Even as the reformers strengthened their ties among themselves, some, such as Lloyd, moved toward political coalition with Populists and socialists. Between the fall of 1893 and the end of 1894, they witnessed another period of intense class polarization. Lloyd at times occupied a middle ideological ground between producerist and meliorist reformers. Others in the community of reform—Vida Scudder, Florence Kelley, William English Walling, Robert Hunter, and eventually Frederic Howe—would at times stake out a similar position. Lloyd lectured the AFL in late 1893 on the need to use the "power of organized labour as a stepping-stone to the greater power of organized citizenship."[44] In the heat of the Pullman boycott, Lloyd wrote from his retreat on Cape Cod urging Samuel Gompers to write his name "by the side of our greatest patriots" by assuming leadership of the movement that "would revolutionise the politics of this country." He observed that "the people are scattered, distracted, leaderless, waiting for just such guidance."[45] Lloyd may have moved in a more radical direction than some reformers, but like them, he never wholly abandoned his commitment to social harmony, class reconciliation, and state intervention to resolve the social crisis.

The Pullman Strike and the Reformers

If the labor problem of the late nineteenth century exerted a formative influence on the consciousness and outlook of a generation of reformers, the Pullman boycott and strike of 1894 seemed a magnifying glass that concentrated and inflamed that problem in ways that demanded the reformers' attention. Progressive reformers recalled the events of that summer with a clarity that suggests their enormous influence.

The Pullman strike became the quintessential strike of the period. Like the railroad strikes of 1877, which in the eyes of many Americans had inaugurated the period of crisis, the Pullman strike, played out on a national stage, involved the railroads and their employees as central actors. The boycott and strike saw considerable destruction of life and property and brought the massive intervention of the federal government. But unlike any other mass strike of the era, the Pullman strike manifested a degree of central organization and national coordination not seen before. Pullman car shop employees had struck in early May 1894 to restore a wage cut imposed by George M. Pullman. As members of the fledgling American Railway Union (ARU), the Pullman employees called on their union and its members for support. At the union's first annual convention in Chicago in June, the ARU attempted to intercede on behalf of the Pullman workers, but Pullman rebuffed any mediation effort. Although the leadership of the union, including its president, Eugene V. Debs, discouraged the convention from issuing a call for sympathetic action, the delegates voted and the members ratified a boycott of all trains carrying Pullman cars. As the boycott began, the General Managers Association, representing all of the major transcontinental lines, decided on a showdown with the ARU and, as their own act of sympathy with the Pullman Palace Car Company, encouraged GMA members to attach sleeping cars to all trains, including freights.

Within a matter of days, the strike and boycott effectively shut down all rail service west of Chicago and a good deal of traffic on eastern lines as well. At the behest of the GMA, the federal government, over the objections of Illinois governor John Peter Altgeld, deployed federal troops and issued injunctions forbidding interference with rail traffic and prohibiting union leaders from acting in their official capacity to direct the strike. Violence in Chicago and other rail centers followed the introduction of troops and the arrest of the union leaders. With the union's internal communications disrupted, federal authorities and company officials gradually restored order and increased rail traffic. Nearly a month after its beginning, the boycott had all but collapsed, and in early August the leaders of the ARU officially called it off.[46] But the strike had left an indelible mark on a generation of reformers, none more so than Jane Addams, John Dewey, Edward Bemis, and Ray Stannard Baker.

JANE ADDAMS

For Jane Addams, whose Hull-House had opened its doors five years earlier to serve myriad human needs in a poor and densely crowded immigrant district of Chicago, the Pullman strike brought enormous distress. Although dependent on the good will and financial support of Chicago's elite, the settlement house could not ignore the tribulations of the strikers and their families. Addams recalled in her autobiography that because "the Settlement maintained avenues of intercourse with both sides," it had "the opportunity for nothing but a realization of the bitterness and division along class lines." She recalled an encounter with an elite acquaintance, as she left a "futile" meeting of the arbitration committee on which she served, who declaimed that "the strikers ought all to be shot." But she also remembered the broken, blacklisted English worker of "a superior type" who "seemed to me an epitome of the wretched human waste such a strike implies." The strike and its poignant human consequences intensified Addams's "constant dread of spreading ill will."[47]

Through her membership on the "Board of Conciliation" of the newly formed Civic Federation of Chicago, she played an active if ultimately ineffectual role in the attempts to arbitrate a settlement of the strike. She recounted for the U.S. Strike Commission the efforts to resolve some of the issues at the heart of the conflict. She found Debs "eager to have the matter arbitrated." And as the sole member of the board who ventured to meet with the strike committee in the town of Pullman, she overcame the initial suspicions of the men, who declared themselves "ready to arbitrate any and all points." The Pullman Company, although "always very courteous," told Addams and the committee that "there was nothing to arbitrate." In the end, she noted, "we considered the effort a failure."[48]

During the strike, Addams found herself distracted by the personal crisis of her older sister's illness and death. Her reflections on the meaning of the strike—in particular, its ethical dimension—came in succeeding months and years. The most poignant may have been an essay, "A Modern Lear," presented as a talk to a number of audiences in Chicago and elsewhere. She subsequently sought its publication but faced rejections from editors at major national publications who found it either too personal or too unsympathetic to George M. Pullman. In January 1896, the editor of the *Review of Reviews* wrote that he did not believe "anything relating to the Pullman strike would be admissible." The journal had a practical obligation "to look forward rather than backward." John Dewey, however, found it "one of the greatest things we have read both as to its form and its ethical philosophy." He believed that Addams had said "exactly the things that must be realized if the affair is going to be anything more than a brutal and disgusting memory."[49]

Not until 1912, on the eve of the presidential election, did Addams publish the essay at the behest of editor Paul Kellogg in the *Survey*. In a new period of industrial turmoil marked by mass strikes and violence, he found the essay enduringly relevant. "There is a message for today in its powerful analysis of the human equation in industry," Kellogg wrote in his brief introduction. Addams drew the analogy between the personal tragedy of Shakespeare's King Lear and what she termed "this great social disaster" and "industrial tragedy" embodied in the strike against Pullman. She asked rhetorically, "What can be done to prevent such outrageous manifestations of ill-will?" Her analysis focused on the roots of the employees' rebellion under Pullman's well-intentioned but suffocating paternalism. "He had power with which to build this town, but he did not appeal to nor obtain the consent of the men who were living in it." Pullman had missed altogether the "Zeitgeist" that drove his men: "Outside the ken of this philanthropist, the proletariat had learned to say in many languages that 'the injury to one is the concern of all.' Their watchwords were brotherhood, sacrifice, the subordination of individual and trade interests to the good of the working class; and their persistent strivings were toward the ultimate freedom of that class from the conditions under which they now labor."

Addams also cited a "fatal lack of generosity in the attitude of workmen toward the company" and worried over a movement "ill-directed, ill-timed" and "disastrous in results." She urged reconciliation, pursuit of the common good, and a practical sense of what progress is possible in the circumstances. She held up the ideal of a man who seeks "consent," who does not teach "his contemporaries to climb mountains" but persuades "the villagers to move up a few feet higher." The lesson for reformers was unmistakable: "Progress has been slower perpendicularly, but incomparably greater because lateral."[50]

Addams also contributed an essay to *Hull-House Maps and Papers,* a volume published by Hull-House residents the year after the Pullman strike. Although she made few direct references to the strike, she shaped her essay around the problem of class conflict and its resolution. She proceeded from the premise that the labor movement must evolve from organizations focused on resistance and warfare toward institutions that "promote peaceful industrial progress." While "older unions" had already reached that plateau, "unions among the less intelligent and less skilled workmen are still belligerent and organized on a military basis and unfortunately give color to the entire movement." To the settlement, then, fell the duty of "keeping the movement from becoming in any sense a class warfare." The great danger to society lay in the isolation of any class. Deprived of the "companionship of the whole," they "become correspondingly decivilized and crippled." By the same token, she viewed the "powerholding classes—capitalists, as we call them just now," increasingly subject to "the disintegrating influence of the immense fund of altruistic feeling with which society has become equipped." That altruism was embodied in the constructive work of the settlements. This "fund of altruism," she insisted, was "slowly enfranchising all classes" and demanding "equality of conditions and opportunity."

Speaking more directly of Pullman, she argued for an abandonment of "sides" and "battle array." She viewed the sympathy strike, however noble in sentiment, as "too narrow" because "the strike is a wasteful and negative demonstration of ethical fellowship." Like the settlements, the labor movement, she believed, "must have the communion of universal fellowship. Any drop of gall within its cup is fatal."[51] In that view, she prefigured the vision of social harmony that fundamentally marked the Progressive movement.

JOHN DEWEY

The Pullman strike occurred at a critical turning point in John Dewey's professional life. Just taking up a new, prestigious position as chairman of the Philosophy Department at the University of Chicago, he brought with him the sensibilities of a "radical democrat." In his private correspondence, he recorded his strong support for the strikers and their cause. He wrote to his wife of meeting an impressive ARU organizer in Durand, Michigan, en route from Ann Arbor to Chicago: "One lost all sense of the right or wrong of things in admiration of his absolute, almost fanatic, sincerity and earnestness, and in admiration of the magnificent combination that was going on. Simply as an aesthetic matter, I don't believe the world has seen but a few times such a spectacle of magnificent, widespread union of men about a common interest as this strike business."[52]

His frustration boiled over at the attacks on the union in major newspapers and journals. Early in July he wrote his wife, "Hard to keep one's balance; the only wonder is that when the 'higher classes'—damn them—take such views there aren't more downright socialists." Despite the strike's defeat, he took heart that it had "sobered" the upper classes by showing them what the unions working together might accomplish and provided "the public mind an object lesson that it won't soon forget."[53]

For Dewey himself, the object lesson appears to have been somewhat different. During his early months in Chicago, he appears to have come under the rather formidable influence of Jane Addams and become a veritable "Hull House convert," as Jay Martin has observed. Dewey and Addams had a substantial conversation in the early fall of 1894, the touchstone of which was their assessment of the recent Pullman conflict. Antagonism, for Addams, was "not only useless and harmful, but entirely unnecessary." She believed that whatever "objective differences" might exist would "always grow into unity if left alone." Dewey did not easily give up the idea of the utility of certain antagonisms, such as between labor and capital. But in Addams's view, "historically only evil comes from antagonism." In ways that echoed the racially tainted views of other reformers, Addams cited the case of the Civil War: "We freed the slaves by war, but what benefit did this conflict bring? Now we have to free them all over individually and pay the costs of the war once more, even as we reckon with the added bitterness of the southerner besides."[54]

Observing the jeopardy in which some of his more outspoken colleagues placed themselves, Dewey scrupulously avoided public expression of sympathy with the strikers or antagonism toward the "higher classes." And later in his career, as Westbrook has noted, he rationalized a dispassionate approach to controversial subjects in language that suggested the lessons he had drawn from the stormy days of the Pullman boycott. Implicitly noting the fate of more outspoken academics, he argued that the scholar might choose different approaches:

> He might go at the problem in such an objective, historic, and constructive manner as not to excite the prejudices or inflame the passions even of those who thoroughly disagreed with him. On the other hand . . . the same can be stated in such a way as to rasp the feelings of everyone exercising the capitalistic function. What will stand or fall upon its own scientific merits, if presented as a case of objective social evolution, is mixed up with all sorts of extraneous and passion-inflaming factors when set forth as the outcome of the conscious and aggressive selfishness of a class.[55]

Like political economists Ely, Adams, and Carter, Dewey constructed out of his own engagement with the labor problem a professional identity and a reform philosophy that occupied a more neutral ground than his private pronouncements had implied. Bearing the imprint of the practical lessons learned at the feet of Jane Addams, he looked toward a resolution of class differences through a revived democratic polity.

EDWARD W. BEMIS

For another prominent academic, the Pullman strike became a major event in one of the most celebrated academic freedom cases of the era. Edward Bemis had been a rising star in the field of political economy when hired by President William Rainey Harper at the University of Chicago. Harper, with financial backing from John D. Rockefeller, had set about creating a new university and an impressive faculty of young scholars. Bemis, a student of Richard T. Ely, represented a cadre of young, socially committed economists who regarded state regulation and even public ownership of monopolies as a necessary response to economic concentration. They remained skeptical that market forces could sustain competition among the "natural monopolies." Bemis, like Ely, identified with the goals of the labor movement, but his particular area of expertise had come to be the municipal ownership of utilities.[56]

At the University of Chicago, he maintained close contact with the reform community. When the Chicago Civic Federation formed in the fall of 1893, he played a visible role in its initial organization. And the following year, the national Congress on Industrial Arbitration and Conciliation named him to its "National Commission."[57]

But controversy rapidly called into jeopardy Bemis's tenure at the University of Chicago. His participation in the political fight to limit street railway franchises and establish municipal control of the gas monopoly led to complaints and even threats of retaliation against the university. Bemis's department chair, a more conservative economist, J. Laurence Laughlin, consigned him to "extension" teaching. Even before the Pullman strike, President Harper began a quiet campaign to persuade Bemis to resign.[58]

As the strike unfolded, Bemis joined Jane Addams and others in the Civic Federation calling for arbitration. He testified before the U.S. Strike Commission in September 1894 about various models of voluntary arbitration that might resolve such disruptive labor conflicts. While cautiously suggesting that "the time is coming when experiments in government ownership of railroads will be tried," he also favored a licensing system for railroad employees as a guarantee of responsible behavior. "It seems to me," he wrote, "that the great third party, the public, has a right to be heard on this question, not with the idea of injuring the employee or employer, but to prevent our railroads from being tied up." His reflections on the meaning of the Pullman strike continued in an essay published the following year in the Paris journal *Revue d' Économie Politique* and summarized in the New York edition of the *Review of Reviews*. In what the latter journal called "a calm and unbiased review of the great strike," Bemis canvassed the causes of the strike and the roles played by the General Managers' Association and the American Railway Union. He concluded that "neither one can be trusted. Public control, in some way, of the relations of labor and capital in our enormous transportation lines has become a necessity." While warning of the lawlessness that such strikes bred and the flood of immigrant wage workers "largely ignorant of American institutions" they involved, Bemis nevertheless found cause for hope "in a wave of municipal reforms . . . that is rapidly spreading among our professional and middle classes." He further hoped that such developments might be "powerful enough to secure a peaceful and gradual introduction of moderate but greatly needed social reforms and to render less bitter the relations between capital and labor."[59]

In the aftermath of the Pullman strike, Bemis harbored little hope of retaining his position at the University of Chicago. Even as he solicited help from academic colleagues and his mentor Richard Ely in finding a new academic position, he vacillated between determination to make a public fight for his position at Chicago and simply resigning from "such a millionaire ridden institution as 'The University of Chicago, Founded by John D. Rockefeller.'" He also gently criticized Ely for his own survival tactics when tried for academic heresy by the board of regents of the University of Wisconsin: "That was a glorious victory for you. I was only sorry that you seemed to show a vigor of denial as to entertaining a walking delegate or counseling strikers as if either were wrong, instead of under certain circumstances a *duty*."[60]

Bemis left academic life in the wake of Pullman to pursue a very visible, if sometimes tenuous, role in urban reform as a proponent of municipal ownership. He served with the Bureau of Economic Research in New York, taught briefly at Kansas State Agricultural College when Populists gained control of the university's state board of regents, and in 1901 was appointed by newly elected mayor Tom Johnson to run Cleveland's municipal waterworks.[61] But despite his own personal misfortune, Bemis's advocacy of the public's interest in class reconciliation placed him well within the circle of the emerging Progressive movement.

RAY STANNARD BAKER

As a young reporter for the *Chicago Record*, Ray Stannard Baker found Chicago in the 1890s an infectiously exciting and challenging place to be. Through encounters with the likes of W. T. Stead, the English reformer and author of *If Christ Came to Chicago*, through his observations of the "grand and glorious Columbian World's Exposition," and through his descriptions of an increasingly desperate and impoverished immigrant community, Baker began to define for himself a journalistic style that fit the times. He bore the prejudices of his class along with the inquisitiveness of youth in early reports on growing poverty and unemployment. "Tramps, vagabonds, paupers, maimed and crippled beggars and sunken-eyed women with hungry children are flocking to Chicago in hundreds," he wrote in 1892. "Some of them are criminals by choice and some by dire necessity. . . . Like a deadly infectious disease, they creep silently, insidiously into our midst. Every daybreak sees them gnawing closer to the heart of public morals and personal safety."[62]

Baker reported sympathetically on Jacob Coxey's "army" of unemployed workers in the spring of 1894. He then returned to Chicago to cover the Pullman strike, witnessing in the boycott "one of the greatest industrial conflicts in the history of the country—perhaps the most important of all in its significances."[63] Responding to criticisms of the strikers leveled by his conservative father, Baker declared that the laboring classes would eventually "arrive at the proper degree of self control and calm foresight which will eventually make them winners against organized capital."[64] Deeply moved by the plight of the suffering strikers and by the humanity and compassion of Eugene V. Debs, he was nonetheless troubled by "the huge mobs running wild." Like other middle-class observers of the strike, he asked himself, "Could such anarchy be permitted in a civilized society? . . . Hasn't order somehow got to be restored?"[65]

Baker went on to be a prominent voice in the new reform journalism and, like others, a proponent of class reconciliation. Years later, in a memoir of his "youth," he concluded with an appeal that people should not "jump at conclusions, nor accept shibboleths and slogans, nor wind themselves up in organizations and parties trying to do wholesale what can only be done a little at a time." Like many reformers of his generation, touched by the social conflicts around them, Baker wished only to have been "a maker of understandings—those deep understandings which must underlie any social change that is effective and permanent."[66]

The ruminations of Jane Addams, John Dewey, Edward Bemis, and Ray Stannard Baker, precipitated by the events in Chicago and across the country in July 1894, reflected a renewed consciousness among reformers that classes must be reconciled and the problem of class conflict resolved if social progress was to be achieved. The experience of the Pullman strike cemented their conviction that they must become agents of a new order. Committed to the democratic ideals of a Lincolnesque republican tradition to which they saw themselves as heirs, devoted by their own class position to conciliation and amelioration of class differences, they sought to forge a more harmonious society from what Dewey called "the material for a new creation."

2

Constituting Progressivism

The happy harmony with which professors, business
men, ministers, workingmen, artists, men and women,
had got into the habit of working in the World's Fair enabled this task of remaking the city to be carried on with
marvelous efficiency and rapidity. The professors showed
that the municipal enterprises being undertaken in one
city or another, however unlike they seemed, had really a
common origin. They were manifestations of the rise among
the people of new capabilities of self-government, and of
working together. The professors pointed out, too, that
these movements had not only a common origin but a
common destiny—to prove that the city like the nation,
or the church, or any other society could be successful
only as far as it was a brotherhood.
—Henry Demarest Lloyd, "No Mean City," 1898

Henry Demarest Lloyd, like many American reformers, viewed the
World's Columbian Exposition of 1893 as a moment of great, if unrealized,
promise. For a brief summer, a planned "White City," the orderly architec-
ture and carefully orchestrated congresses of which suggested the possibility
of a new urban order, materialized on the shores of Lake Michigan. Staged,
ironically, in the first months of the century's deepest depression and on the
eve of its most bitter episode of labor conflict, the Chicago fair nonetheless
served as a beacon for many would-be reformers long after its gates closed. In
lectures to middle-class audiences during the remaining years of the century,
Lloyd would repeatedly conjure from the fair's legacy a still finer and more
promising vision of a utopian successor to the White City. His imagined "No
Mean City," an arcadian development on the urban fringe, would surround
and eventually consume the old city and become a flourishing reserve for the
untapped energies of the unemployed. Accompanying the social transformation of the city would be "the evolution of the human heart," which, accord-

ing to Lloyd, "carried its amelioration of temper into the relations between employer and employed, rich and poor, the classes and the masses. . . . It simply became hopelessly unfashionable, and then absolutely vulgar for any one to threaten or rage against another fellow-being."[1] His vision, both utopian and practical, looked backward and forward. Like the reformers among whom he moved in the 1890s, Lloyd valued above all things social amelioration.

What would come to be called progressive reform constituted itself as a movement on two related levels in the 1890s. Out of a republican tradition broadly conceived and recast in a crucible of class conflict, liberal intellectuals and social activists constructed a new language of reform with distinctive ideological underpinnings.[2] That language, emphasizing ideals of social harmony, the amelioration of class divisions, and a reaffirmation of national purpose, reconceived "the people" to include a broad cross-section of Americans irrespective of class. The reformers' construction of the people carried with it new social boundaries that excluded corrupting elements on both ends of the social spectrum. On the one hand stood corporate monopolists, franchise holders, and their political henchmen ("boodlers"), and on the other those social groups most susceptible to corruption, identified by some social reformers as a "submerged tenth" of shiftless laborers, new immigrants, and African Americans.[3] The new language of reform, deployed with increasing frequency in the crises of the 1890s, developed a powerful appeal that cut across seemingly diverse and contentious interests.[4] The idea of the people resonated powerfully with reformers. They focused on inclusion not exclusion, social amelioration not division, harmony not conflict.

On a second, more concrete level, a Progressive movement constituted itself out of the overlapping ties between segments of an emerging reform community, the connecting webs of which grew denser as the 1890s unfolded. In a host of new associations, conferences, and journals, through new organizational initiatives to address intractable social and economic problems, and in private correspondence and social interchange, a widening circle of reformers constructed a broad sense of common purpose. Sharp differences abounded and regularly disrupted coordinated action. But through a common language and moral vision, the reformers demonstrated a resilient capacity to repair and expand their organizational web.

Reconceiving "The People"

William T. Stead, the English journalist and Christian reformer, visited Chicago's White City in the summer of 1893 and stayed on to explore the city's other side in the months after the World's Columbian Exposition officially closed. As Jane Addams wrote years later, "I can vividly recall his visits to Hull-House, some of them between eleven and twelve o'clock at night, when he would come in wet and hungry from an investigation of the levee district . . . or his adventures with a crook, who mistook him for one of his own kind and offered him a place as an agent for a gambling house, which he promptly accepted."[5]

Deeply troubled by what he saw, Stead asked, "What evils are there in the city which we should be ashamed to point out to Christ if he really came on a tour of inspection?" He called a public meeting at Chicago's Central Music Hall to which representatives of all classes, or in Jane Addams's terms, "the diverse moral forces of the city," were invited to consider what evils stood in the path of reform. But his agenda went further. He hoped, out of the meeting, to constitute "an organization that would represent all the better elements in the town[,] . . . a spiritual counterpart to the City Council" that could see to it that "the whole moral affairs of the community were thrown in the way of good government and against the rogues."[6]

The meeting, which convened on November 12, turned into a tumultuous affair. Stead and several other speakers became lightning rods for the hostility of audience members who ridiculed their message of social harmony. The afternoon gathering finally broke up with a strident call from the gallery. As the *Chicago Tribune* reported, "High in the center of the upper gallery a loud voice shrieked for the attention of the Chairman. The speaker introduced himself as a man from Texas and Mexico. 'Let your churches alone; let your schools alone; but change your system of production and distribution of wealth if you would restore social harmony.'"[7] Here was an unreconstructed voice of working-class producerism "shrieking" his message in the face of a new vision of "social harmony" promoted by Stead and his liberal allies. In a crude but forceful manner, this dissonant voice symbolized a more radical, class-based agenda for reform that in various guises challenged the premise of those who promoted social harmony. Such voices continued to pose an alternative path of reform based on a fundamental redistribution of class power, even as the dominant wing of progressivism consolidated its social vision and its organizational base.[8]

Undeterred, the reformers reconvened that November evening and appointed, as Stead had hoped, a committee of "representative citizens" to further the organization of what he had already dubbed the "Civic Federation." The Civic Federation of Chicago articulated a reform vision that reconceived the social relations of the city. It proposed "to serve as a medium of sympathy and acquaintance between persons and societies who pursue various and differing vocations and objects . . . and who agree in the desire to promote the greater welfare of the people of this city."[9] The prospect of a cross-class coalition acting on behalf of the people to restore harmony to society galvanized the group.

The Civic Federation became for a time the organizational vehicle for a reform program that captured the imagination and support of a broad cross-section of Chicago activists. Antimonopolist Henry Demarest Lloyd applauded Stead's initiative and occupied a prominent position on the stage at the initial gathering. He enlisted in the Civic Federation's arbitration and conciliation efforts the following year. Jane Addams assumed a highly visible position as a member of the organizing committee and with Lloyd served on the industrial conciliation committee. Edward Bemis and Graham Taylor, a University of Chicago sociologist and cofounder of the Chicago Commons settlement, worked closely with the Civic Federation in its early years. Richard T. Ely was regularly consulted. He also served as a member of the diverse ensemble of reformers and trade union leaders that constituted the National Commission on Conciliation and Arbitration appointed by the Civic Federation just months after the conclusion of the Pullman boycott.[10]

Reformers articulated different social visions in the early 1890s. Their constituencies overlapped untidily, symbolizing the cross-class appeal many of them made. To a surprising degree, elite mugwump reformers of an older generation rubbed shoulders with Edward Bellamy's nationalists and apostles of Henry George's single tax. Social gospel ministers reconceived their religious mission in ways that brought them closer to trade unionists. And academic social investigators—political economists, sociologists, and philosophers—took postgraduate "training" under the tutelage of young settlement house women. To disentangle these strands of reform is to suggest the breadth, diversity, and internal tensions of the movement Progressives created in the 1890s.

Mugwumps and Good Government

Mugwump reformers hailed from an elite stratum of society. They yearned for "a harmonious community" and emphasized the individual, not a class, as the agent and the object of reform.[11] Appalled by post–Civil War political corruption and the rise of urban and state political machines, these "best men," operating most influentially in the municipal realm, constructed cross-class alliances for reform in one city after another. In New York, their campaigns in the early 1870s led directly, if briefly, to the downfall of the Tweed Ring's stranglehold on city government. In Chicago, elite reformers formed the Citizens' Association of Chicago in 1874 and for nearly two decades pursued the harmonization of interests with various representatives of Chicago's workers. Combining agitation for moral and political reform, some mugwumps, like Chicago bank president Lyman Gage, flirted on and off with more formal alliances that promised to bring conflicting class interests into greater harmony. The sudden rise of the Union Labor Party in 1886 provided one such occasion, the unsuccessful defense of the Haymarket martyrs another, and the planning for the World's Columbian Exposition a third.[12]

In Cincinnati, the spectacular rise of "Boss" George B. Cox, elected by a largely middle-class constituency residing outside the city's central immigrant wards, prompted a coalition of good government reformers in the 1890s to attack political corruption and seek limitations on government spending and social programs.[13] "Citizens'" tickets in 1894 and 1897 rallied opponents of the Cox machine under the banner of reducing the expenditures of city government "to the lowest level consistent with efficient and capable administration" and called for mobilizing voters "on the side of pure government, economically administered."[14] But some workers in 1897, reflecting an oppositional producerist strand of reform, asked of the Citizens, "Who are the People? Where do the Workingmen come in?" Noting the absence of workers on the ticket, they asserted that Gustav Tafel, the Citizens' mayoral candidate, must find a sounder basis "than a few ephemeral reformers, Mugwumps and disgruntled gangsters" if he expected working-class support.[15]

By the 1890s, mugwumps had engineered the enactment of federal civil service reform, which a number of states followed in due course. Their reform efforts promoted competition within both major parties that destabilized factional alliances and laid the groundwork for the emergence in each party of new reform factions committed to purifying the political process. Preaching a "good government" gospel, mugwumps found a surprisingly broad and diverse response to their demands. Direct legislation, nonpartisanism, and initiative and referendum gained support from trade unionists, farmers, and urban businessmen, each for their own reasons. Their calls for political and moral purification cut across class constituencies and knit together citizens' coalitions that promised to restore democracy.[16] Theodore Roosevelt cast an impressive shadow across many of these reform circles in New York, first as a good government legislator and subsequently as a mayoral candidate, U.S. Civil Service commissioner, New York police commissioner, partner with Jacob Riis in campaigns for tenement reform, and, finally, governor.[17] This cross-class, republican mission to reinvent American democracy became the touchstone for Progressives of varied political stripes.

The Social Gospel and Secular Reform

Developments within Protestant Christianity during the late nineteenth century stimulated a profound awakening to the social crisis among middle-class Americans. While millennial as well as conservative strains of Christian social thought exerted some influence within the working class, middle-class Americans were most profoundly influenced by the new "applied Christianity."[18] Without question many of the most visible and articulate reformers drew deeply on their religious upbringing and values to define their social reform vision. Yet as significant as these influences may have been on reformers such as Richard T. Ely, Jane Addams, Edward Bellamy, and Rev. W. D. P. Bliss, they crafted a language of reform that was profoundly secular. In "applying" their Christian values to the work of improving the world, they left aside, to a large degree, organized religion and the theological justification for reform.[19]

The social gospel movement called at once for Christian renewal and secular reform. Moving out of the sanctuary, protestant ministers such as Washington Gladden, R. Heber Newton, Walter Rauschenbusch, and George D. Herron encountered a secular world in crisis. The application of Christian ideals illuminated pathways of reform that seemed to offer social as well as personal redemption.[20] The industrial turmoil of the 1880s and 1890s stirred Gladden and many of his generation to believe that labor must be accorded recognition by employers and that an evolving form of profit sharing offered an attractive alternative to the "antisocial" competitive marketplace. In an 1886 statement calling for class reconciliation, Gladden asked, "Is it Peace or War?" Neither, he answered. "Permit me to say that I know something about this war. . . . I know that the wrong is not all on one side, and that the harsh judgments and the fierce talk of both sides are inexcusable."[21]

Like their kindred spirits among mugwump reformers, social gospel Christians placed the individual at the center of their reform efforts. They focused on character and personality formation. But unlike those who advocated the moral reform of individuals as the route to salvation, social gospelers, such as Walter Rauschenbusch, addressed the social context of individual salvation in ways that led them to advocate the reform of industrial society.[22] Rauschenbusch moved further than some of his fellow Christians by suggesting that reformers in their idealistic quest to avoid "class war" must take "a leaf from the book of socialism." But he also redefined social reform as extracting the ethical, or "humanizing," dimension of *religious* faith and applying it to society. "Christianizing the social order means bringing it into harmony with the ethical convictions which we identify with Christ," he wrote.[23] And with these sentiments, a large segment of the secular reform community found themselves in agreement.

Social gospel forces provided institutional support for the labor movement through organizations such as the Church Association for the Advancement of the Interests of Labor (CAIL) and the Christian Social Union (CSU). They exerted some influence within a few denominations, but to many in the trade union movement, their efforts seemed marginal compared to the overwhelmingly conservative influence of organized religion. Terence Powderly, the deeply religious leader of the Knights of Labor, and other overtly anticlerical labor leaders saw little but active hostility toward labor unions in the world of organized religion. And they returned those sentiments in kind.[24]

Workers and many of their leaders may have drawn on Christian traditions to shape and articulate their resistance to the dehumanizing influence of late-nineteenth-century capitalism, but organized Christianity generally provided a bulwark for the defense of capital. Even in the hands of sympathetic protestant reformers, Christianity served at best to mediate social tensions and impose limits on class conflict. Gladden, as minister to the business class in Gilded Age Columbus, Ohio, preached against class war, calling the industrial system a "social solecism." He pleaded with both sides, "Is it well, brother men, is it well to fight? Is it not better to be friends? . . . Your war is not only wholesale fratricide, it is social suicide."[25] Although his faith in cooperation rather than socialism persisted, Gladden gradually became an unqualified partisan of labor. In so doing, he left behind many reformers and fellow social gospelers. In Philadelphia, socially concerned clergymen lent qualified support to the trade unions' pursuit of trade agreements and recognition in return for a commitment to the peaceful resolution of labor disputes and the disavowal of socialist objectives.[26] Social gospel reformers hoped to transcend class polarization in late-nineteenth-century America through a strategy of amelioration and mediation. Their ideal society was "a vast fellowship of like-minded and mutually supportive citizens."[27]

The Utopians

The social crises of the late nineteenth century provided fertile ground for utopian theorists to imagine alternatives to the present social system. Some had a specifically religious cast; others, like Henry Demarest Lloyd's "No Mean City," were avowedly secular.[28] None enjoyed more profound influence than Edward Bellamy through his novel *Looking Backward*. Bellamy provided a whole generation of reformers with the most concrete account they could imagine of a society redeemed from disorder and the social chaos spawned by the destructive growth of capitalism. The novel captured their imagination. After reading it, temperance reformer Frances Willard asked the publisher "who, when and what this Edward Bellamy might be." He wrote back to say, "We do not know except that his letters are mailed from Chicopee Falls, Massachusetts."[29]

Obscure and retiring though Bellamy may have been, his portrait of an America freed from the throes of class conflict and reconstructed on the basis of an equitable and rational deployment of labor touched the sensibilities of diverse reformers. W. D. P. Bliss and Henry Demarest Lloyd assessed his influence on social beliefs to have been among the greatest of their generation. For Thorstein and Emily Veblen, as for socialists Julius Wayland and Eugene Debs, he made a cooperative future seem practicable.[30] Despite the excitement Bellamy's novel generated and the meteorlike influence he enjoyed, recent historians have viewed his contributions in a more critical light. Some see in Dr. Leete, one of the novel's central characters, the yearnings of a mugwump reformer not fully reconciled to the reality of industrialism.[31] Others note the antidemocratic and authoritarian strains of Bellamy's social vision, the "barracks socialism" that appealed to Progressive reformers suspicious of working-class democratic participation and enamored of bureaucratic and administrative reform.[32] Bellamy allowed little space for the agency of workers or their unions in his collectivist future. Indeed, he saw them as having little capacity to conceive an alternative to the system of "private capitalism." *Looking Backward* stood virtually silent on the process by which the new order had evolved from the old, noting only that the transition was peaceful and that an educated elite played a leading role. The central character, Julian West, asked how such a "stupendous change" was accomplished "without great bloodshed and terrible convulsions," and Dr. Leete replied simply that "public opinion had become fully ripe for it . . . [and] there was no more possibility of opposing it by force than by argument."[33]

Bellamy's writings stimulated a brief frenzy of organizational activity aimed at moving society toward his ideals. "Nationalism" became a movement without central direction. Although the novel appealed to a broad cross-section of Americans, its primary attraction lay with an urban middle class unsettled by the conditions Bellamy so powerfully described in his opening chapters. Indeed, nationalist clubs appealed primarily to such a constituency. A Bellamy contemporary wrote, "It was made an unwritten law that this new club should be composed as much as possible of men who had been successful in the present fierce competitive struggle. They were not the weak, crying for mercy; they were the strong, demanding justice. They were not the crank or uneducated foreigner, importing ideas declared to be 'exotics'; they were men of position, educated, conservative in speech and of the oldest New England stock."[34]

Bellamy's "doubled vision," at once practical and fanciful, proffered an alternative to the chaotic social conditions that nineteenth-century capitalism had bred. He conceived an army of "industrial" citizens, a classless mass led by a nationalist vanguard that forged peaceful, harmonious change. As Leete told Julian West, the "national organization of labor under one direction was the complete solution of what was, in your day and under your system, justly regarded as the insoluble labor problem."[35]

When the nationalist movement disintegrated, it left behind an agenda of specific, practical reforms. But without the integrative vision of Bellamy's collectivism, what distinguished the agenda was only its cross-class appeal and peaceful intents. Bellamy did not regard his heirs to be the socialists, "the followers of the red flag," whom Leete viewed as hindering real progress: "Their talk so disgusted people as to deprive the best considered projects for social reform of a hearing."[36] Bellamy and his followers, to the extent that they succeeded, helped constitute a broadly progressive reform impulse.

Like Bellamy, Henry George propounded a "Republic of the future" that captured for a time the imagination of American workers and their middle-class sympathizers. George's vision of an alternative future, achieved by the implementation of a single tax, may have been more limited than Bellamy's, but it posed in the mid-1880s a more immediate political challenge to existing property relations. In peculiar and ironic ways, George's critique of the land monopoly fired the imaginations of America's urban workers.[37] They adopted George and constructed from his ideas an oppositional ideology that briefly shook the two-party system.[38]

George's vision, set down most fully in *Progress and Poverty*, looked backward and forward. Society had not developed along the lines that eighteenth-century proponents of progress had envisioned. The idea of an egalitarian republic of property-owning producers had given way under the harsh conditions spawned by industrialization to a society sharply divided between misery and wealth. "The 'tramp' comes with the locomotive, and almshouses and prisons are as surely the marks of 'material progress' as are costly dwellings, rich warehouses, and magnificent churches," George wrote. "Upon streets lighted with gas and patrolled by uniformed policemen, beggars wait for the passer-by, and in the shadow of college, and library, and museum, are gathering the more hideous Huns and fiercer Vandals of whom Macaulay prophesied."[39]

George's diagnosis of these social ills left him in "an ideological no-man's land."[40] Subscribing neither to individualist solutions, like those of mugwumps and social Darwinists, nor to the collectivist alternatives of trade unionists, cooperationists, or socialists, George conceived a remarkably simple resolution, the single tax. That instrument invested government with expanded power of limited range. It provided a "simple yet sovereign remedy" that involved "the taking by the community, for the use of the community, of that value which is the creation of the community." In George's view, the social transformation would be dramatic: "The change I have proposed would destroy the conditions that distort impulses in themselves beneficent, and would transmute the forces which now tend to disintegrate society into forces which would tend to unite and purify it. Give labor a free field and its full earnings; take for the benefit of the whole community that fund which the growth of the community creates, and want and the fear of want would be gone."[41]

George rejected class conflict as a means of realizing his "republic of the future." He noted that "it is difficult for workingmen to get over the idea that there is a real antagonism between capital and labor."[42] He believed, as he told a correspondent, that "successful efforts can come from the class above, not below." Even during his New York mayoral campaign in the midst of the great upheaval of 1886, he sought to enlist "that great body of citizens, who, though not workingmen in the narrow sense of the term, feel the bitterness of the struggle for existence as much as does the manual laborer and are as deeply conscious of the corruptions of our politics and the wrong of our social system."[43]

The New York Central Labor Union, which had drafted him as its mayoral candidate in 1886, appropriated his single-tax ideology into its own program because George had come to symbolize popular resistance to monopoly and a broad republican critique of unjust accumulation. The Clarendon Platform, and George's defense of it during the campaign, functioned, according to historian David Scoby, as an ideological "open-site where the other elements of the alliance, especially middle-class reformers, could both find a common ground with working-class militants and contest it."[44] George deliberately fused the language of class with that of citizenship. Although his support came overwhelmingly from the working class, he resisted the notion that the mission of the United Labor Party could be defined in class terms. Addressing himself to his Democratic Party opponent, iron manufacturer Abram Hewitt, George said, "You have heard so much of the working class that you have evidently forgotten that 'the working class' is in reality not a class, but *the mass*, and that any political movement in which they are engaged is not that of one class against other classes, but as an English statesman has happily phrased it, a movement of 'the masses against the classes.' The men who earn their bread by manual toil are in this, as in every community, the vast majority. Their interests must be the interests of the community at large."[45]

In the 1886 mayoral election, which he is generally thought to have won, George made a respectable run but ultimately succumbed to defeat at the hands of the Tammany machine. After the campaign, the tenuous alliances George had forged fell apart, in no small measure as a result of his own actions. Seeking to broaden his appeal within the reform-minded middle class, he expelled socialists from the United Labor Party in the summer of 1887, ran an anemic campaign for secretary of state that year, and left the party in shambles the following year.

Although Henry George remained a celebrated reform figure through the late 1880s and 1890s, he never again achieved the influence among workers that he enjoyed during the heady months following Haymarket. Single-tax demands did appear from time to time in labor platforms and in the discourse of working-class leaders.[46] George's ideas found a more consistent audience within some circles of middle-class reform. Ignoring classes defined by the relations of production, George focused instead on exchange and the monopoly in land. He appealed for gradual change, what historian John Thomas has called "a maturing of social altruism," and stressed the socializing effects of education. He constructed a millennial language of reform that offered a simple, practical program of action consistent with republican values. According to historian Steven Ross, George "spoke of citizens, not classes; of nonproducers and speculators, not capitalists; of democracy, not socialism."[47]

George's influence among middle-class reformers grew as his classless version of producerism lost working-class adherents. Representative of that influence was the conversion of streetcar magnate and future Cleveland municipal reformer Tom L. Johnson. By his own account, Johnson stumbled on George's writings while traveling by train in the mid-1880s. A bookseller plying his wares pushed on him a copy of George's *Social Problems*. A conductor, who knew Johnson, urged him to read the book. Reading it through and finding its arguments persuasive but at odds with his own conceptions of political economy, Johnson read it a second time. He insisted that a business partner in the steel trade read it. "If this book is right then your business and mine are all wrong," he declaimed. Gathering the partner, his attorney, and another business associate, he spent an entire night in a hotel room dissecting and debating the book's arguments. By dawn the group concluded that despite their best critical attacks, "the book was sound. . . . We were converted to an unnamed philosophy, by an unknown prophet, an obscure man of whom we had never before heard." Johnson began a search for George, finding him eventually in Brooklyn, ensconced in his study.[48]

Thus began a fifteen-year association that deeply influenced the course of Johnson's considerable public career. Johnson, on the one hand, played a significant financial role in George's own public career from the mid-1880s on, and George, in turn, urged Johnson to bring the "land question" into politics. During his 1901 campaign for mayor of Cleveland, Johnson told an impressionable, young mugwump reformer, Frederic Howe, that he had been frustrated by his two terms in Congress. "There isn't much to be done there," he said. He found the municipal arena a more appropriate one for his single tax–based reform program. And in the single tax, he saw with an entrepreneur's eye a key to unlocking vast potential productivity:

> The place to begin is the city. If one city should adopt the single tax, other cities would have to follow suit. If we are the first to take taxes off houses, factories, and machinery, we will have a tremendous advantage. Factories will be attracted to Cleveland; it will be a cheap city to do business in, cheap to live in. Untaxing the things people use will cheapen them, it will encourage production. And if we tax the land heavily enough, we will discourage speculation. With cheap land on the one hand and cheap houses, factories, and goods on the other, Cleveland will be the most attractive city in America.[49]

While many reformers regarded the single tax more skeptically than Johnson and viewed its "philosopher" as a crank, others found that George's ideas fit a reform vision that subordinated class to citizenship, held the promise of controlling speculative wealth and its corrupting influences, and might unleash democratizing economic growth. Around these core principles that united mugwumps and social gospelers, nationalists and single-taxers, settlement folk and younger social scientists, reformers gathered in the 1890s to constitute themselves as a Progressive movement.

Gathering a Movement

The movement assembled in diverse venues. Settlement houses by all accounts functioned as "free spaces" in decaying and corrupt cities, entry points for neophytes to the world of reform and its associations. Social reform activists constructed those spaces in ways that permitted the intimate association of women with other women. They were spaces of refinement and social engagement, places where lofty ideals gave meaning to pedestrian tasks, and where newcomers, feeling their way into the community of reformers, might find something useful to do. Such was the experience of countless young, middle-class recruits, among them future documentary photographer Lewis Hine, New Deal labor secretary Frances Perkins, and Eleanor Roosevelt.[50] But some talented young immigrants from the neighborhood were drawn into the community of reform as well. Hilda Polacheck, a Jewish immigrant from Russia, recalled her early encounter with "Miss Addams" and what Hull-House came to mean for her: "I look back and realize how much of my leisure time was spent at Hull-House and how my life was molded by the influence of Jane Addams." Sewing cuffs in a garment factory during the day, she found the settlement to be "an oasis in a desert of disease and monotony." Evenings at Hull-House "made the day's work bearable."[51]

The settlements also functioned as hothouses for debate over reform ideas. Jane Addams described the 1890s as "a decade of economic discussion." The Working Peoples' Social Science Club, which met weekly for seven years at Hull-House, symbolized the settlement as "a place for enthusiasms, a spot to which those who have a passion for the equalization of human joys and opportunities are early attracted." Often frustrated by the dogmatism and abstractness of talks by would-be allies, among them socialists, Addams nevertheless appreciated the lively debate.[52] Numerous academics, like John Dewey, were drawn to the "applied social science" of the settlement community and saw in the settlements a test of relevance for their efforts to reconceive society and its evolution.[53] Vida Scudder, a budding socialist teaching at Wellesley College, found Denison House in Boston an intellectual and social refuge. Her encounters with labor leaders tested and reshaped her consciousness as a reformer. She joined an AFL federal labor union that met at Denison House and with Helena Dudley was appointed delegate to the Boston Central Labor Union. She learned of the "terrifying chasm that yawns between Employer and Employees—a chasm never to be filled by pleasant and platitudinous moral aspirations."[54]

Finally, the settlements played a crucial role in building and cementing reform coalitions. The research undertakings of Florence Kelley and Robert Hunter, for instance, connected them through proliferating networks to an expanding circle of reformers in the 1890s. Florence Kelley, fleeing an abusive marriage, arrived on the snowy doorstep of Hull-House in the last week of 1891 with three young children in tow. College educated and a committed socialist, she almost immediately became a central figure in the community of Hull-House women. Little more than a year after her arrival, she was asked by Carroll Wright, the U.S. commissioner of labor, to carry out the Chicago portion of a national study of slums. That investigation led directly to the publication *Hull-House Maps and Papers* and attracted the attention of local and national reformers. She had become a knowledgeable guide to the teeming neighborhood and its sweatshops. Through her friendship with Hull-House supporters Henry Demarest Lloyd and Jessie Bross Lloyd, Governor John Peter Altgeld appointed her to be the first factory inspector for Illinois in 1893. Then in 1897, after the departure of Altgeld from office, John Graham Brooks asked her to move to New York and head the National Consumers' League.[55] Always "sharp" in her criticism and deeply committed to the ideal of an evolving socialist society, Kelley also imbibed deeply the "class-bridging" spirit of Hull-House reform. In historian Kathryn Sklar's terms, she functioned as "an integrative force within a wide range of coalitions of women and men, both middle-class and working-class."[56]

Although male reformers functioned on the margins of the settlement world, their reform interests intersected those of women at many points. Henry Demarest Lloyd lacked the intimate community of reform enjoyed by Kelley, but he nonetheless figured prominently at the nexus of reform initiatives that developed over the course of the 1890s. Graham Taylor in Chicago, Robert Woods in Boston, and Paul Kellogg in New York were key coalition builders in their own domains. Robert Hunter, after graduating from Indiana University, worked for the Chicago Board of Charities and lived at several settlement houses. While at Hull-House in 1901, he completed a major study of Chicago's tenement houses, then moved to the University Settlement in New York, from which he agitated for municipal reform, child-labor legislation, and an end to poverty. Hunter, like Kelley, was an important bridge between the settlement movement and reform-minded socialists.[57]

The Muckrakers

Proliferating reform-oriented journals and newspapers paralleled and reinforced the growing network of reformers associated with the settlement houses. Changes in the publishing world revolutionized periodical publications in ways that reduced costs and stimulated the search for new audiences. *McClure's* and *Cosmopolitan* dropped their prices and enlivened their formats in the mid-1890s in a successful search for readers. Although neither could be classed a "muckraking" journal, they opened a field for journalistic experimentation that gave greater play to societal concerns. B. O. Flower's *Arena*, founded in 1889, was conceived from the outset as a journal engaged with current social conditions and an outlet for reform ideas. Notable for his new and aggressive style of journalism, Julius Wayland made the *Coming Nation* and later the *Appeal to Reason* influential within a growing field of labor and socialist publications.[58]

By the end of the 1890s, a more extensive array of popular journals existed within which reformers found outlets for their views. Ida Tarbell and Ray Stannard Baker, recruited to write for *McClure's* by Sam McClure, along with Lincoln Steffens, Frank Norris, and other young journalists, created a unique environment. "I have wondered," Baker later recalled, "if there could have been a more interesting editorial office than ours, one with more of the ozone of great ideas, touch-and-go experimentation, magic success. We were all young." Before these journalists turned to muckraking, they pioneered a new kind of writing: "It always seemed to me, after we began publishing the so-called exposure articles, that it was not the evils of politics and business, or the threat to our democratic system, that impressed [McClure] most, but the excitement and interest and sensation of uncovering a world of unrecognized evils—shocking people!"[59] When he was "called" to New York in 1897 by S. S. McClure, Baker knew the magazine represented "something new and different . . . not merely about people, aloof and critical objectivity, but the people seemed to be there in person, alive and talking." He remembered its first issues in 1893, which he had saved religiously, as "human documents" and "real conversations."[60]

Out of these beginnings, a new style of "exposure" journalism arose and briefly exerted enormous influence on public consciousness and political life. Its peak influence may well have been the notable January 1903 issue of *McClure's*, in which an installment of Ida Tarbell's continuing revelations of Standard Oil corruption appeared alongside Lincoln Steffen's exposé of political corruption, "The Shame of Minneapolis," and Ray Stannard Baker's indictment of the abuse of labor union power. In his editorial, S. S. McClure summed up the import of the findings by suggesting that such corruption represented a debt that the public, the people, must one day pay. "And in the end the sum total of the debt will be our liberty," he concluded.[61] By the time President Roosevelt affixed the unflattering name "muckrakers" to the practitioners of this variety of journalism, the tide of their influence had turned. Historian Richard L. McCormick has argued that "the discovery that business corrupts politics" formed an important component of an emerging progressive consciousness that both intensified and limited the reach of reform.[62]

Although exposure journalism of the type Tarbell, Steffens, and Baker pioneered may have become less influential, it did not disappear altogether. Other journals, including the *Survey, Outlook,* and the *Arena,* as well as *Cosmopolitan, Everybody's, American Magazine,* the *Independent,* and eventually the *New Republic,* focused more on "constructive" reform and combined reporting on corruption and social ills with prescriptive writing on the solutions reformers undertook.

Diverse influences produced muckraking journalism. Some were specific to the dynamic technical changes in publishing and photographic representation; others bore the marks of the antimonopoly sentiment that enjoyed considerable political license in the 1890s. While reflecting popular political currents, muckraking journalists also contributed to a new reform consciousness and the self-definition of a reform movement committed to restoring social harmony and purifying democratic institutions.[63]

Convening for Reform

Beyond the settlement outposts in cities and the new "exposure" journalism, Progressives constituted a movement most visibly in a series of national conferences over the course of the 1890s. These conferences were called for no single set of purposes. They created no central organization. And they represented diverse, even contending, reform ideas. But they contributed to shaping a movement and a language of reform that by the end of the century acquired a discernible identity. In a decade torn by depression, class conflict, and a sense of impending social crisis, these conferences gave voice and public visibility to meliorist reformers committed to constructing social stability and class harmony as an alternative to the producerist class program of populists, socialists, and militant industrial unionists.

WORLD'S LABOR CONGRESS

The World's Columbian Exposition provided one occasion for reformers to assemble and put forward to a wider public their prescriptions for social improvement. After years of contentious planning, it opened to great fanfare in Chicago in May 1893. Controversy swirled about the White City, which was, in the view of renowned architect Louis Sullivan "an appalling calamity . . . an imposition of the spurious." But others took a different view. Henry Demarest Lloyd saw an architectural creation that "revealed to the people possibilities of social beauty, utility, and harmony."[64] Henry Adams, unblinded as usual by any trace of utopianism, conceived the White City as the resolution of two contradictory tendencies, one "industrial" and one "capitalistic." The fair affirmed, in his view, the virtues of capitalist leadership. It would be the height of nonsense "to run so complex and so concentrated a machine by Southern and Western farmers in grotesque alliance with city day-laborers."[65]

The very structure of the fair, the contrast between the Midway Plaisance and the White City, conveyed a message of progress, national unity, and above all racial hierarchy that reflected the values of an emerging Progressive movement. As historian Robert Rydell has remarked, the Midway presented an evolutionary "spectrum of human 'types' . . . leading up to the White City." The Midway allowed Americans "regardless of class" to "study ethnography practically." It made equality a function of race, and among *white* Americans led to "blurring class lines."[66]

The World's Congress Auxiliary, as part of the exhibition, convened various gatherings around specific interests and social concerns.[67] The general chairman of the congress, Charles C. Bonney, had issued a call for presentations that would highlight "the intellectual and moral progress of the world." Complementing the vast assemblage of products from around the world, the congress aspired to bring all such "departments of human progress into harmonious relations with each other."[68] A specific World's Labor Congress took as its charge "some share in the solution of these problems that so disturb society and hinder prosperity." The Labor Congress addressed the problems of labor and capital, industrial advancement, and the need for labor legislation. It sought "a peaceable solution" to current crises, in order that "the suicidal war which threatens the industrial world shall culminate not in disaster."[69]

Key reformers took major roles in planning the congress. During the winter and spring of 1893, Henry Demarest Lloyd, as secretary of the Committee on Programme and Correspondence, issued invitations to speakers. Chicago attorney Clarence Darrow and Cardinal John Gibbons joined him on the general committee. Richard T. Ely and Rev. Washington Gladden represented the committee in Europe during visits there in the months before the fair.[70]

The Labor Congress convened at the end of August with the fair in full swing but in an atmosphere shaped by deepening economic depression and unemployment. The afternoon session of the first day adjourned for the speakers to go out to address a lakefront demonstration of the unemployed, whose numbers, the *Chicago Tribune* noted, had "swelled to a surging torrent of humanity that filled Michigan Avenue." None of the "loiterers" joined the evening meeting at the Art Institute, however. Instead, women and "the better paid class of toilers or men of moderate means and leisure" predominated. They heard labor reformer George McNeill defend the philosophy of the labor movement as the "brotherhood that Christ proclaimed." Illinois factory inspector and Hull-House activist Florence Kelley attacked the sweatshop system, as did a paper from English Fabian Beatrice Webb read by Jessie Bross Lloyd. Ethelbert Stewart from the U.S. Bureau of Labor Statistics discussed the condition of workingmen's homes, and Anna Briggs and Richard T. Ely both spoke briefly on farmers' unions. However, the most riveting moment came when Samuel Gompers, president of the American Federation of Labor, who was not scheduled to speak that evening, was called from his seat on the stage to offer some remarks. Gompers described the demonstrations outside the halls of the Congress as "a sad commentary upon our civilization." He lamented that all across the country, unemployed men and women were making preparations for similar demonstrations. He asked employers to reduce, not extend, the hours of labor and thereby increase employment and relieve distress. In language that evoked nineteenth-century producerism, he noted that some might condemn such demonstrations and "deprecate the spirit of force and incendiary language." But, he asked, "does not society bring the storm about its ears by allowing those who produce the wealth of the world at one time to be thrown upon the streets to starve at another."[71]

For the next few days, major figures in the reform community presented their remedies for current conditions to the Labor Congress. Ely again spoke on public ownership of natural monopolies, a view seconded by socialist Laurence Gronlund. Not surprisingly, Henry George promoted the single tax. Trade unionist J. W. Sullivan argued for direct democracy based on the Swiss system, and political economist Henry C. Adams asserted the right of workers to employment. English Fabian Sidney Webb concluded the evening session with a philosophical defense of the eight-hour system. At the next-to-last session on Sunday, September 3, Archbishop John Ireland of St. Paul, Minnesota, spoke at length on the church's duty to support labor. Reverends P. J. Coyle and W. D. P. Bliss offered remarks critical of the church's past failure to support labor's demand for shorter hours.

Samuel Gompers concluded the Labor Congress with a formal address. For his audience of reformers, Gompers totaled up the costs of this system.[72] Citing the failure of "the possessors of the tools and means of industry" to establish "order in their own ranks" by allowing the robbery of "wealth producers" by "parasitic" and "bogus" capitalists, he concluded that society had begun to see trade unions as the hope of civilization. Appealing to a cross-class audience, he asserted that trade unions, knowing capitalists as they do, desired no revenge. They were "conservative" in methods, "evolutionary" in outlook. He identified labor's highest aspirations as a share of "the earth and the fullness thereof" and cited a primary, concrete demand: reduce the hours of labor to eight, "fewer to-morrow." Labor wanted a livelihood, he argued, appropriate to a civilized society's standards. Then, in a peroration that linked labor's aspirations to a broader progressive reform program, he said,

> Save our children in their infancy from being forced into the maelstrom of wage slavery. See to it that they are not dwarfed in body and mind or brought to a premature death by early drudgery. Give them the sunshine of the school and playground instead of the factory, the mine and the workshop.
>
> We want more school houses and less jails; more books and less arsenals; more learning and less vice; more constant work and less crime; more leisure and less greed; more justice and less revenge; in fact, more of the opportunities to cultivate our better natures, to make manhood more noble, womanhood more beautiful and childhood more happy and bright.[73]

Gompers, in short, provided the outlines of a program around which moderate trade unionists and social reformers might gather to reconcile the interests of labor and employers.

The World's Labor Congress attracted a broad coalition of forward-looking, prominent members of society. Challenged by labor's spokesmen, businessmen such as Lyman Gage joined a cross-section of reformers that included socialite Mrs. Potter Palmer, academics Richard Ely and Graham Taylor, social gospel clerics John Ireland and Washington Gladden, and social reformers Henry Demarest Lloyd, Clarence Darrow, and Jane Addams to craft a language of social harmony that embraced the legitimate aspirations of a labor movement committed to social evolution by conservative means. If the Congress did not create a "world-wide fraternity" of moral and intellectual influence, as its organizers had hoped, it nonetheless laid the groundwork for an influential, loose-knit confederation of reformers committed to ameliorating class conflict.[74]

In the months immediately following the Labor Congress, Chicago reformers remained active in the vanguard of reform developments. William T. Stead's provocative invocation of Christ's imaginary visit to Chicago and his Central Music Hall gathering in November 1893 led directly to the formation of the Chicago Civic Federation. Despite the polarizing effects of the Pullman strike and the Populists' challenge to the established parties in fall 1894, the Civic Federation summoned a national conference on arbitration and conciliation that in many ways picked up where the Labor Congress had left off.

CONGRESS ON INDUSTRIAL CONCILIATION AND ARBITRATION

During the Pullman boycott, the Chicago Civic Federation organized a provisional board of conciliation representing diverse class interests. Frustrated in their efforts to settle the strike, the board called for a national conference that would draft a broadly conceived arbitration bill.[75]

The Congress on Industrial Conciliation and Arbitration drew a large attendance and notable array of speakers to its sessions in mid-November 1894. Lyman Gage, president of the Civic Federation, called the congress a step forward, beyond the "mutual suspicions and misunderstandings, growing out of apparently opposing interests," that "have led the way to bitterness, hostility, human suffering, and social disasters." Joseph Weeks, editor of the *American Manufacturer and Iron World,* challenged the business crowd to form "strong unions" of employers and employees to settle their disputes. Editors of the *Outlook* observed that "when representatives of the capitalists can speak in this way of the necessity of combinations among their employees, there seems less danger than before that the two classes of our citizens should drift hopelessly apart."[76] Edward Bemis, though in some jeopardy at the University of Chicago over his sympathy for strikers, spoke eloquently and with some poignancy about the disruptive influence of labor disputes. Such "class hatreds" made it difficult for "either teacher, preacher, or editor to preserve that temperament which is an absolute prerequisite for a wise social and industrial evolution."[77] Jane Addams argued even more forcefully against the "class distinctions" that divide the world into "capitalists and laboring men." In her view, the progress of human society made it "too late" for such distinctions. "We are all bound together in a solidarity . . . which shall enfranchise all of us and give all of us our place in the national existence." Arbitration of industrial disputes, she claimed, would "accelerate that liberation."[78]

Nearly all of the speakers supported the voluntary arbitration of industrial disputes and viewed the court of public opinion as the most powerful agency for producing such settlements. Carroll D. Wright, the U.S. commissioner of labor and just then chair of the commission charged with investigating the Pullman strike, voiced the consensus view that if the results of an arbitration commission were "set . . . before the public, public opinion will take care of the rest without the intervention of the sheriff." H. H. Garland, president of the once-powerful Amalgamated Association of Iron, Steel and Tin Workers, seconded Wright's faith in the "curative" power of public sentiment. But for others in the labor movement, notably Samuel Gompers and carpenters' union president P. J. McGuire, the first priority was thorough organization of labor. The mutual organization of labor and capital would permit them to "settle their own affairs." Gompers worried that the imposition of arbitration might harm the organization of labor.[79]

At the conclusion of the congress, the speakers and members of the Civic Federation's industrial committee called for a "national commission" to "give representation to all classes of society." The commission aided the promotion of Illinois legislation that mandated state and local boards of arbitration. It supported the incorporation of arbitration principles into proposed new legislation governing railroad labor disputes that eventually became the Erdman Act of 1898.[80] But more important, the congress and the commission fostered the expansion of a network of reformers and a language of conciliation that represented, in Jane Addams's words, a new social "solidarity" committed to transcending class divisions.

NATIONAL CONFERENCE ON SOCIAL AND POLITICAL REFORMS

Between mid-decade and the end of the nineteenth century, the reform community grew and diversified. The shattering of the Populist Party and fusion of some of its elements with Bryan Democrats in 1896 left the remaining agrarian radicals in search of allies. The return of prosperity and the proliferation of trusts in what historians have come to call "the great merger movement" stirred antimonopoly sentiments brewing since the 1870s.[81] Contention over the place of trusts in American life was displayed in a conference organized by the Civic Federation of Chicago in September 1899, followed five months later by the National Anti-Trust Conference organized by the antitrust faction of the prior Civic Federation Conference.[82]

As the American Federation of Labor, under Gompers's direction, surged in organizational strength, it jettisoned elements of the labor reform community that had supported socialist planks and general unionism. Remnants of the American Railway Union, refugees from Daniel DeLeon's Socialist Labor Party, and Fabian socialists searched the political landscape for a home and moved by various routes toward a new social democratic alternative.[83] Beachheads of municipal reform had been secured in a few cities, notably Detroit and Toledo. Inspired by Hazen Pingree and Samuel "Golden Rule" Jones, reformers in other cities embarked on their own versions of "civic revival." In this context, but preceding the Civic Federation's conference on trusts, a broad group of reformers called for a National Conference on Social and Political Reforms for June 28 to July 4, 1899, in Buffalo.

The call for the conference invited "progressive men and women of various political and social beliefs" to consider the present conditions for reform and to determine "what is the next thing to do." The signers of the call were a diverse lot, including current and former political officeholders, Governor Pingree, Senator Allen of Nebraska, Mayor Jones, and John Peter Altgeld; representatives of the academic community such as George D. Herron, formerly of Grinnell, Richard Ely, and Frank Parsons; and journalists and writers such as William D. Howells, Willis Abbott, and Eltweed Pomeroy, editor of the *Direct Legislation Record*.[84] Later additions to the general committee for the conference included Booker T. Washington and trade unionists Samuel Gompers and Joseph R. Buchanan. Although some advocated a "new party," the organizers regarded such an initiative as hopelessly divisive. They looked toward bringing "reformers of different parties, with different measures most at heart, into personal relations with one another" to achieve broad agreement on priorities and methods to be pursued.[85]

The *Arena* described the conference as "a reform 'sociable,' . . . or more properly, a school of method, a normal institute for teachers of political economy." Invited were men and women "who regard not creed or faction when facing the future."[86] Despite such optimism, serious divisions erupted among the conferees over the U.S. role in the Philippines and whether to organize themselves politically. Nonetheless, these differences did not preclude creation of the Social Reform Union and the development of a program of five planks around which broad agreement coalesced. The platform advocated direct legislation, public ownership of utilities, taxation on land values, government-issued legal tender, and antimilitarism. The Reverend W. D. P. Bliss, the well-established, peripatetic agitator for reform, was named president of the Social Reform Union. Reflecting the breadth of the reform community at the end of the nineteenth century, the officers included some forty-eight vice presidents and a national committee of representatives from thirty-five states.[87]

The organizational fate of the Social Reform Union is less important than the progressive vision it articulated. W. D. P. Bliss proved to be an idiosyncratic leader who alienated other reformers allied with his principles. Some key leaders found themselves drawn to the Debsian Social Democratic Party or returned to agitational work within the reform factions of the Democratic or Republican Parties. A number of liberal academics, including Ely, gravitated toward more conservative reform and professional organizations.[88] If the Buffalo conference did not realize its promise organizationally, it nevertheless inspired a spirit of nonpartisan reform and a commitment to a higher social unity that infused the Progressive movement of the following decade.[89]

For most who gathered in Buffalo, the central issue, "deeply felt among all classes of our citizens," was "the recent monstrous growth of corporation power." They believed the people, undivided by "sectionalism or class feeling," were ready to act.[90] More than a year after the conclusion of the Buffalo conference and the discouraging election of 1900, Bliss announced the inauguration of a new periodical, the *Social Unity*, devoted to the union's principles. In "An Open Letter on the Political Situation," he reflected on the shortcomings of Republicans, Democrats, and Social Democrats. He argued that reformers needed not a new party ("partizans can do that") but a nonpartisan organization that would embody "the unity of the people." He eschewed organization on a class basis. Although "social progress will inevitably spring mainly . . . from the workers, the lowly, the humble," he believed it a mistake to think that "a Republic of Brotherhood can be brought in by first declaring war, the belief that classes can be overthrown by means of class struggle. War begets war. Strife begets strife. Parties beget partizans."[91] Marginal though Bliss may have become in the evolving world of reform, he articulated a language of social harmony that a broad community of reformers had helped to craft over the course of the 1890s. That language of reform differentiated Progressives' vision from the class perspective of the producers' movement and left a deep imprint on their social imagination and the boundaries of the movement they sought to organize. Few would follow the specific organizational path defined by Bliss and the Social Reform Union, but the conception that they embraced of a broad, cross-class unity representing itself in the name of "the people" mobilized against "the interests" lay at the heart of the Progressive movement's future development, whether organized on a partisan or nonpartisan basis.

3

The Politics of Reform

[To face] the painful condition of endeavoring to minister
to genuine social needs, through the political machinery,
and at the same time to remodel that machinery so that it
shall be adequate to its new task, is to encounter the inevitable discomfort of a transition into a new type of democratic relation. . . . As the acceptance of democracy brings a
certain life-giving power, so it has its own sanctions and
comforts. Perhaps the most obvious one is the curious sense
which comes to us from time to time, that we belong to the
whole, that a certain basic well being can never be taken
away from us whatever the turn of fortune.

—Jane Addams, *Democracy and Social Ethics*, 1902

Jane Addams's battle with ward boss Johnny Powers gave her a healthy respect for the ability of "corrupt" politicians to insinuate themselves into the lives of their constituents. Local bosses addressed the individual needs of their constituents and cemented political loyalty through human friendliness. She called machine politics "this stalking survival of village kindness." By contrast, the cold and aloof approach of "good men" seeking to root out corruption so often failed because of their conviction that "the righteous do not need to be agreeable." Finding loyalty to the machine to be a natural product of the human environment encountered by the urban poor, Addams, like John Dewey, proposed to enlist those values on behalf of a higher standard, an "enlarged and socialized" civic loyalty that encompassed a shared public interest.[1]

Disturbed by the corruption that infected American politics at the end of the century, many reformers sought to uncouple their agenda from the excesses of partisanship. By reinventing civic virtue, freed from slavish party loyalty, they hoped to constitute a more potent political force—the people—whose citizenship transcended differences of class or neighborhood. To do that, they had to contend with the partisan grip that ruled American politics. If, as many reformers had come to believe, the state was a necessary agent for remedying the social ills spawned by industrialism, then a new democracy cleansed of political corruption constituted the precondition for effective state action.

Some budding reformers in the 1890s sought to turn partisan loyalty to their own purposes. As Democrats or Republicans, they seized the opportunity presented by their own deeply factionalized parties to create new political space for reform within the two-party system. Others, uncomfortable with the constraints of party loyalty on their reform efforts, explored varieties of *nonpartisan* political activity to achieve their reform agenda. Most hoped to enlist the state in the tasks of social reconstruction, but to do so they had to confront what many saw as a precondition: the elimination of political corruption. Even as reformers fought to purify democracy through electoral reform, they applauded the judiciary's tentative support for state economic regulation and the programmatic efforts of some leading Democratic and Republican politicians to strengthen the regulatory capacity of government at all levels. But beyond the reformers' campaigns to craft a new democratic state capable of guaranteeing social stability and a measure of economic fairness, other political forces grounded in the class politics of cities and some unions advanced a more aggressive program to claim public jurisdiction over capital and dramatically enlarge the public sphere on behalf of a politically mobilized working class. Such a project reflected the divided mind of progressivism and the continued, unsettling presence of class as basis for political mobilization.

Decay and Competition in the Party System

Partisan political loyalties lay in disarray by the end of the 1880s. Forged in the heat of the Civil War crisis, party identities fractured in the social and economic crises of the late nineteenth century. The Republicans as victors and saviors of the Union waved the "bloody shirt" in one campaign after another. But with an aging cadre, immersed in maintaining party machinery and wallowing in the substantial largesse of the newly colonized continent, their appeal diminished with each contest. The Democrats, self-proclaimed heirs to a once-vigorous Jacksonian Democratic legacy, suffered the burdens of defeat. Suspected of disloyalty, they seemed consigned to the perpetual status of an oppositional minority. They shepherded a heterogeneous and unstable collection of diverse interests, and lacking the rewards of power and office, they faced disintegration even as the Republicans' hegemony eroded.[2]

Historians have come to call this world of late-nineteenth-century politics the third party system, a peculiar brew of ethnocultural and class loyalties that by the early 1890s had produced a competitive balance between the two internally fractured major parties.[3] The Republicans, like their militant abolitionist forebears, drew on a constellation of pietistic values that emphasized moral free agency and the responsibility of individuals to cleanse society of the corrupting influences of alcohol and other forms of popular licentiousness that fostered dependency. At the same time, in the name of the "pursuit of happiness," they defended the untrammeled rights of property and the acquisitive spirit of the age. Their core of Protestant native-born supporters, in this new age of mass immigration, represented a diminishing segment of the population, especially in larger cities.

The Democrats, defenders of plebeian rights and pleasures, drew heavily from the ranks of naturalized immigrants. They attracted a broad cross-section of "ritualists" who resented the intrusions of meddlesome moral reformers and the new rich with whom the reformers so often seemed allied. While not a "class" party, the Democrats more consistently echoed the egalitarian, producerist critique of industrial development. And more than the Republicans, they attempted to corral supporters of third-party movements that attacked the spreading cancer of monopoly. When they failed to deliver on their antimonopoly promises, the Democrats suffered disproportionately in the exodus of those movements.[4] By the same token, the Republican Party during the 1880s appeared to its most militant partisans insufficiently zealous in the pursuit of moral purity and faced the perpetual secession of prohibitionists who sought a more single-minded party.[5]

Disarray infected the ranks of the major parties at all levels. Urban politics had grown more volatile as the temperature of social conflict rose. Greenback-Laborites mounted impressive contests for political control of smaller industrial cities, especially railroad towns, after the 1877 railroad strikes.[6] By the mid-1880s, the Knights of Labor had energized a new wave of working-class political activism that elected local officials on Union Labor Party or Knights of Labor tickets in more than 120 cities. Henry George's campaign in the New York mayoral election of 1886 garnered the most national attention, but the KOL loosened the grip of the major parties in cities as diverse as Dubuque, Iowa; Rutland, Vermont; Kansas City, Kansas; and Richmond, Virginia. Urban populists joined their rural brethren in the 1890s to further shatter the Republicans' and Democrats' complacency by mounting impressive local challenges in Milwaukee, Chicago, Butte, Montana, and a number of other cities, setting the stage for the further unraveling of urban party politics.[7] A deepening ideological commitment to independent politics persuaded some segments of the labor movement to consider a labor party. And in the Rocky Mountain West, politically mobilized workers entered the urban arena under a variety of party identities to pursue their interests in the eight-hour day, to limit the power of employers to break strikes, and to improve the daily lives of workers.[8]

By the late 1890s in a number of major cities, reform administrations had been elected with support of working-class populist voters and middle-class "good government" interests who voted with increasing independence from the major parties. Hazen Pingree in Detroit (1890), Carter Harrison in Chicago (1897), Samuel "Golden Rule" Jones in Toledo (1897), Lee Meriwether in St. Louis (1900), Eugene Schmitz in San Francisco (1901), and Tom Johnson in Cleveland (1901) represented a new breed of big city mayors who shattered existing partisan alignments, even as they maintained, in most cases, traditional party identifications.[9]

Faced with competition at all levels in the decaying party system, Republicans and Democrats strove mightily, but with diminishing success, to hold their supporters and recruit converts while not fundamentally altering their partisan appeal. High voter turnout masked a crisis of partisan loyalty that became inescapable with the turn toward politics by the Farmers' Alliance and the appearance of the Populist Party in 1892. The appeal of these politicized producers threatened both Republicans and Democrats and, in the words of political scientist Walter Dean Burnham, offered the prospect of a farmer-labor coalition comprised of those most harmed by "concentrated corporate powers." In 1913, Oliver Wendell Holmes recalled the panic that in the 1890s spilled over into judicial doctrine when "a vague terror went over the earth and the word socialism began to be heard."[10]

That the crisis of the 1890s passed without a major political upheaval is attributable to a variety of factors. Not the least was the ability of the major parties in crucial midwestern states to accommodate the demands of the insurgents. Reform factions in the state and local organizations of both Republicans and Democrats challenged party stalwarts and undercut the appeal of independent parties.[11] In their quest to purify the political process and limit the corrupting influence of corporate franchise-holders and the political bosses who fed off them, the party reformers also undermined popular participation in politics.[12]

Renewing Partisanship through Reform

The social and economic crises of the 1890s bred a new inventiveness in the world of partisan politics. Facing the prospect of massive political defections and the rise of a new partisan alignment based on class, both major parties proved responsive to the appeals of reformers in their ranks. At the national level, the Democrats fused with middle-of-the-road Populists around the candidacy of William Jennings Bryan, and Republicans, somewhat more reluctantly, acquiesced to their own reformers, whose challenges to state party machines grew more insistent.[13] Partisan reformers made their most indelible mark at local and state levels. A few cases illustrate the patterns of partisan political reform in states and localities.

NEW YORK'S REFORMING REPUBLICANS

New York, like many other states in the Northeast and Old Northwest, possessed a well-established Republican machine in the late nineteenth century. Party manager Thomas C. Platt was a worthy successor to such Republican luminaries as William H. Seward and Roscoe Conkling.[14] Although the party enjoyed seemingly unassailable control of the state's rural districts, its influence in the cities was more contested. The Democrats' resurgence in the 1880s, however, did not displace the effective control Republicans exercised over the state legislature.

The appearance in the 1890s of a group of "urban independents" whose party loyalty was less firm altered the character of Republican politics in the state, according to historian Richard L. McCormick. At the same time, popular disaffection grew over the party's failure to address pressing economic issues.[15] With nonpartisanism on the rise, especially in the cities after the reorganization of city elections in 1897, and with increasing demands for the regulation of corporations involved in everything from streetcars to life insurance, Boss Platt recognized that the urban independents had to be reenlisted in the party's cause and to do so would require the state party to adopt a reform posture. Theodore Roosevelt was precisely the candidate who could convey both party regularity and independence. One correspondent confided to Platt in 1899 that "many Democrats and Mugwumps, (Independents as they are more politely termed) have said to me that they would vote for him."[16]

In New York state, then, the Republican Party remade itself into an instrument of reform, captured key urban votes, and successfully challenged the Democrats for control of the cities. The "principle of independence" infected the party, and Roosevelt, Benjamin Odell, and Charles Evans Hughes brought new reform departures in public policy and administration to state government. In New York City, a traditional elite reform constituency fused with a coalition of ethnic and working-class urban populist voters to elect reform mayors Seth Low and William Purroy Mitchell in 1901 and 1913. Tammany Hall Democrats also felt the winds of reform through challenges mounted by William Randolph Hearst and his immigrant working-class supporters in 1905 and 1909.[17] The Republicans succeeded nationally in 1896, in part because of parallel developments underway in other parts of the East and Old Northwest.[18]

CLEVELAND DEMOCRATS' CITY ON A HILL

Following a different path, the Democrats in Cleveland reinvented themselves as a party responsive to the needs of the city's working-class and middle-class residents after a polarizing episode of class conflict in 1899. Cleveland's politics, like that of many cities in the 1890s, had become an arena in which evenly matched Republican and Democratic Parties brawled from one election to the next over the relatively meager spoils of office, given the limitations on "home rule" for cities in Ohio and many other states. But by the mid-1890s, each party was honeycombed with competing factions. The Democratic regulars faced challenges from a coalition of labor reformers and populists that weakened the party's base among the old immigrant stock, skilled workers. The Republican machine, controlled by Mark Hanna, whose political interests extended well beyond Cleveland, contended with an insurgent reformer, Robert McKisson, who garnered some support from the mugwumpish Municipal Association. Elected mayor in 1895 as a Republican, McKisson saw the Hanna machine turn against him and support his Democratic opponent in 1899. To further disorganize matters, the Democrat-inclined urban populists threw their support to Republican McKisson.[19]

Cleveland's streets erupted in a bitter transit strike during the first months of Democratic mayor Farley's term in July 1899. As the conflict worsened, the mayor called for the National Guard and promptly earned the enduring enmity of a large segment of Cleveland's working class. Samuel "Golden Rule" Jones, the reform mayor of Toledo, formerly a Republican but now a self-proclaimed "man without a party," brought his nonpartisan campaign for governor to Cleveland in the midst of the streetcar strike. His presence sent panic through the ranks of both parties, and with good reason. In the election that fall, Jones won 56 percent of the Cleveland vote, compared to 30 percent for the Republican and 11 percent for the Democratic candidate. In key working-class wards, among unskilled and skilled workers, both new immigrant and old, Jones amassed more than 70 percent of the vote. Although his support came mostly from the working class, Jones crafted an appeal that crossed class lines. Local party politicians predicted "further trouble" from these voters in the future.[20]

During the next eighteen months, the local Democratic Party came back to life through its own "born-again" reform wing, which proved capable of recapturing the votes of working people. Tom Johnson, a single-taxer and streetcar magnate, returned to the city in the spring of 1901 at the behest of the local Democratic machine and orchestrated a successful mayoral campaign around demands for home rule, lower streetcar fares, and the promise of municipal ownership. He reestablished a Democratic, cross-class constituency, augmented by reformers and independents drawn to his program. He rebuilt the Democratic Party as an instrument of municipal reform and attracted to it many streetcar strikers and their supporters, as well as old Populists and labor reformers. By 1905, muckraking journalist Lincoln Steffens would pronounce Johnson "the best mayor in the best-governed city in the United States."[21]

ROBERT M. LA FOLLETTE AND WISCONSIN'S REPUBLICAN STALWARTS

The near-legendary story of Robert M. La Follette and the transformation of the Republican Party in Wisconsin provides a third illustration of the impact of reform on partisan politics in the late nineteenth and early twentieth centuries. La Follette carefully crafted the story of his own role in the rise of Wisconsin progressivism. His autobiography, written in 1910, detailed the "turning point" in his political career, when the titular head of the Republican machine in Wisconsin, Philetus Sawyer, allegedly offered him a bribe to influence a federal judge who happened to be La Follette's brother-in-law. Read out of the party by its leadership after he publicized the incident, La Follette embarked on a journey of political self-discovery. He recalled that during his previous terms in Congress, he had "seen the evils singly—here and there a manifest wrong." But he experienced in the incident with Sawyer "a terrible shock that opened my eyes for the first time." He now interpreted the skirmishes of his congressional career in a new light. "Corporations and individuals allied with corporations were invited to come in and take what they would, if only the country might be developed." Thrown by circumstances against this "organized power," he determined to attack the corruption that had deeply infected government in Wisconsin.[22] The touchstone of La Follette's progressivism, like that of Addams and Dewey, became revitalization of democratic institutions and practices.

Historians attribute the birth of Wisconsin progressivism less to La Follette's personal conversion than to the convergence of his ambition and a constituency for reform created by the harsh circumstances of the 1890s depression.[23] Hardship and unrest spawned by the depression cut across class lines.

The birth of social progressivism and a new "classless civic consciousness" provided a political base for reform. This constituency, together with the pragmatic alliances forged by La Follette and others within the Republican Party but outside the control of the stalwart machine, made a new state politics possible after 1897. They created a concept of "the public interest," which bridged the yawning social chasm. The roots of their politics lay not in the producerist, class identifications that represented in some sense "the natural divisions of industrial society," but in a coalition of aroused consumers and taxpayers, citizens who shared a stake in the existing social order.[24]

By the time La Follette captured the governorship of Wisconsin, he had embraced key elements of a reform agenda crafted by social Progressives who had infiltrated both parties. Once Republican Party reformers achieved passage of a direct primary law, they turned their attention to utility-rate regulation and public ownership, elimination of railroad passes, limits on lobbying, the promulgation of municipal home rule, corporate tax reform, and state measures protecting the health and safety of workers. La Follette by his own account chose to do battle within the fold of the party. He could see no reason for separating himself from the party's rank and file, in whose integrity he still believed.[25]

The patterns evident in New York, Cleveland, and Wisconsin were replicated with variations across the political landscape at the turn of the century. Toledo, Detroit, St. Louis, Milwaukee, Chicago, Los Angeles, and San Francisco saw the appearance of a new reform politics shaped by workers' grievances. A species of civic reform, animated by demands for public ownership and often fueled by the competition from independent labor or socialist parties, entered the field. In Iowa and New Jersey, North Carolina and Georgia, Missouri and California, Progressive coalitions challenged entrenched state party organizations and crafted programs for political and economic change that in broad outline followed the trail blazed by Democrats in Cleveland or Republicans in New York and Wisconsin.[26]

The Shifting Politics of Nonpartisan Reform

While some reformers invested their political energies in existing parties, others looked to a purer politics of nonpartisan reform. This new politics threatened at times to unravel the very fabric of two-party competition. Reformers constructed a cross-class appeal that stressed administrative solutions to social problems, electoral reform, and an enhanced role for professionals in governance. Whether partisan or not, the Progressive movement's engagement with politics at local and state levels codified its vision of so-cial harmony and inscribed boundaries on the qualifications for citizenship that challenged urban machines and effectively disfranchised their new im-migrant constituents.

The line between partisan politics and nonpartisan rhetoric was not always clearly drawn. In some cities, a new strain of independent, reform politics, drained of class and partisan content, emerged. Toledo mayor Samuel Jones, the "man without a party," symbolized this new nonpartisan politics in the municipal realm. And Cleveland mayor Tom Johnson, although a partisan Democrat and a political product of local class conflict, nonetheless ham-mered together a cross-class constituency and appealed to the electorate in the language of nonpartisan reform. In Chicago, the "new liberal" adminis-tration of Carter Harrison II forged alliances with the Chicago Federation of Labor, the Municipal Voters League (MVL), and the Chicago Civic Feder-ation to promote a reform agenda for the city. This new liberalism operated through voluntary channels outside the realm of formal politics as well as through the administrations of reform Democratic mayors Harrison and Ed-ward F. Dunne. Historian Richard Schneirov has argued, "Many new liber-als in the Civic Federation, the MVL and the social settlement house move-ment . . . self-consciously relinquished and transcended their middle or upper class backgrounds in order to mediate and bridge the interests of all classes in the public interest."[27] Lacking the vote, women municipal activists in Chi-cago fought for municipal suffrage and conducted direct campaigns for re-form of schools, housing, sanitation, and recreation.[28]

Nonpartisan politics sprang from a long tradition of antipartyism em-bedded in American political culture. It appeared with particular virulence during the disintegration of the second party system in the early 1850s, when, as historian Michael Holt has demonstrated, "malignant distrust of politi-cians as self-centered and corrupt wirepullers out of touch with the people spread like an epidemic."[29] It resurfaced in mugwump reformers' post–Civil War attacks on the degrading influence of party and glorification of the spirit of independence in politics. Municipal reformers in the 1870s had seen the corrupting influence of party machines as the chief roadblock to civic improvement and modernization.[30] Civil service reformers in the 1880s con-ceived their mission as breaking the hold of party loyalty on public admin-istration.[31] And by the 1890s, the efforts of civic reformers to make govern-ment efficient, less costly, and free from the influence of urban vice fueled reform politics in a number of cities. Although such efforts occasionally allied the reformers with urban Populists, more often they opposed the Populists Party's class-based political program, which called for expansion of government, progressive taxation, and support for labor.[32]

Excluded from direct participation in partisan politics, women readily turned to the nonpartisan space of issue-oriented reform. Despite occasional defections from the nonpartisan gospel, most women reformers remained committed to its principles.[33] Indeed, together with mugwump reformers and a growing cadre of direct-democracy advocates, they served as its most vociferous champions. Nevertheless, eager to increase their influence over public policy, some nonpartisan reformers embraced what has been called "regulated partisanship." Continuing to oppose boss rule and corrupt political practices, they joined other reformers to promote change from within party ranks.[34]

The boundary between "regulated partisanship" and outright party affiliation was not always clear.[35] The work of the New York City Women's Municipal League illustrates not only women's nonpartisan political activity but also the irresistible claims that partisan politics might make on such reform efforts. According to historian Melanie Gustafson, "They engaged not the 'dirty' business of partisan politics but the 'clean arena of nonpartisan work on city problems.'"[36] But such reform work led them to petition City Hall and ultimately to a concern with who might occupy its offices. The Women's Municipal League together with other New York reform organizations threw its support to the insurgent Democratic candidate Seth Low in his campaign against the Tammany Hall machine.[37]

Other historians have stressed the persistent nonpartisan cast that women's political involvement retained.[38] Susan B. Anthony wanted the New York constitutional convention of 1894 to include female enfranchisement because women were "naturally nonpartisan" and therefore resistant to the power of party bosses, whereas men were deeply implicated in the world of partisan loyalties.[39] Through organizations such as the Woman's City Club of Chicago, women activists promoted general education for citizenship and organized to investigate and promote municipal reform without party affiliation.[40]

The formation of the Progressive Party in 1912 forged a coalition, "nonpartisan" in spirit but organized for immediate partisan objectives. Because, in Gustafson's view, the Progressive Party broke with established lines of partisan political loyalty, it embodied for many of its adherents a nonpartisan spirit. Although the party's leadership behaved in partisan ways, the candidacy of Theodore Roosevelt elevated the campaign beyond the realm of party politics. For many of his supporters, such as Jane Addams, the program, not the candidate or party, commanded their loyalty. Something less than fully articulated partisanship was at work. Disaffected Republicans joined staunch nonpartisans to campaign for the issues and principles that the new party claimed to represent. Even at the moment of Roosevelt's nomination, Addams articulated a nonpartisan rationale for supporting his candidacy. "I rise to second the nomination stirred by the splendid platform adopted by this convention," she declared. "Measures of industrial amelioration, demands for social justice, long discussed by small groups in charity conferences and economic associations, have here been considered in a great national convention and are at last thrust into the stern arena of political action."[41]

The tension between nonpartisan sentiments and partisan alignment also lay at the heart of the American Federation of Labor's shifting politics during the Progressive Era. Chastened by its own debate over independent labor politics in 1894 and its experience with the Populists, the AFL retreated in principle to a nonpartisan, or "voluntarist" position, as its leaders preferred to term it. Gompers's call to reward labor's friends and punish its enemies prescribed an antiparty posture that held sway through the first years of the new century. But labor's enemies, specifically the National Association of Manufacturers, emerged victorious repeatedly from the halls of Congress in battles over injunctions, the eight-hour day, and immigration restriction, largely through their influence with the stalwart Republican leadership. Forced to reconsider its position, the AFL, beginning in 1906 and with greater visibility and determination in 1908, threw its support nationally to Democratic candidates who promised legislative remedies for labor in its primary areas of concern. Even as the alliance with the Democratic Party deepened, AFL leaders remained wary of state regulation. Attacked for its promise to "deliver the labor vote," the AFL retreated after 1908 to a less visible but nonetheless partisan role in support of the Democratic Party in national politics.[42]

Local labor activists continued to practice a more pragmatic style of partisan politics. Workers supported Democrat Tom Johnson's municipal progressivism in Cleveland, William Randolph Hearst's Public Ownership Party in New York, the Socialist Party in Milwaukee and a host of other cities, a labor party in San Francisco and St. Louis, and on occasion Republican stalwarts or Democratic urban bosses. In the Rocky Mountain West, workers in many different cities chose one or another of these paths.[43] Like nonpartisans in the reform community, they secured piecemeal and uneven support for their program from partisan politicians in return for their allegiance, however contingent it might be.

Purifying Democracy

Within the reform community, partisans and nonpartisans alike made cleaning up the democratic process their political starting point. Echoing republican rhetoric of the previous century and asserting their faith in the "free agency" of the individual citizen, reformers attacked the methods by which political machines and corporations prostituted democracy for their own selfish purposes.[44] In their view, the project of restoring democracy entailed two primary tasks. First, reformers put forward an ideal of citizenship that defined fundamental conditions for participation in the political process. John Dewey's vision of "moral democracy" presupposed a reconstructed educational system that developed "democratic character" in would-be citizens.[45] While citizenship implied the right of access to the franchise, many reformers sought to draw boundaries that limited voter participation to those who might exercise that right in ways they deemed responsible. Political machines, they argued, thrived on an ignorant and corruptible populace. New immigrants, African Americans, and the laboring poor generally had not been adequately prepared to exercise the responsibilities of citizenship. Behind the banner of such rhetoric, reformers in the North and the South sought to codify access to the ballot in ways that might ensure a responsible and an incorruptible electorate.[46]

Women were a different case. Their "unfitness" for the ballot, in the eyes of suffrage opponents, derived from a strict application of the ideology of separate spheres. But within the ranks of the reform movement, women's claims to the full rights of citizenship were no longer seriously disputed. Indeed, many reformers applied a separate spheres ideology to justify women's suffrage. Women had become essential to the achievement of other reforms because they brought a higher moral disposition to politics. Their immersion in the concerns of family and neighborhood heightened their commitment to reform and in turn their claims to the franchise. And as Addams argued, somewhat facetiously, the absence of the franchise led women to "influence" the votes of men in ways that imperiled men's free exercise of the ballot.[47]

Democratic reformers faced a second task. They had to define specific electoral reforms by which enlightened citizens might actually purify democracy. In their minds, electoral reform served as a precondition for the realization of other reforms. Prescriptions abounded; among them were the direct primary, nonpartisan municipal elections, voter registration, the Australian (neutral) ballot, initiatives and referenda, direct election of senators, at-large municipal elections, city manager and commission government, civil service reform, and restrictions on lobbying.[48] These reforms, in different ways, would cleanse the political process, foster the creation of a public-spirited electorate, and make government responsive to the public's will.

That such democratic reforms attacked the very fiber of political partisanship and contributed to a general decline in popular politics neither surprised nor disturbed many reformers. Purging the system of constituencies most susceptible to corruption would enhance democracy. Americanized immigrants, responsible workers, and an educated segment of the African American community might be admitted to the electorate as they acquired the status of "sovereign individuals" and proved themselves immune to the appeals of political machines.[49]

The record of electoral demobilization is clear. Following the election of 1896, the proportion of eligible voters participating in elections fell steadily and dramatically. For the country as a whole, nearly 78 percent of eligible voters went to the polls in the presidential election of 1896. Only the Harrison-Cleveland contest of 1888, with a turnout of 81 percent, had been higher. But by 1912, in the hotly contested presidential race at the height of the progressive reform movement, only 56 percent of eligible voters went to the polls. By 1924, voter turnout in the presidential election reached a low point of 45 percent. Regional trends in voter participation fit the national pattern, but the South declined more sharply. Consistently fewer voters went to the polls in the South: 57 percent of voting aged males in 1896, 25 percent in 1912, and 18 percent in 1924. And these figures reflect the massive disfranchisement of African Americans and to a lesser degree poor whites in southern states between 1890 and 1908. In the North, a larger percentage of those who might have been eligible went to the polls, but their numbers also declined: 84 percent in 1896, 64 percent in 1912, and 52 percent in 1924.[50]

Dramatic declines in voter participation stemmed from two changes in Progressive Era politics. First, reformers, through their attacks on partisan techniques of political mobilization, succeeded in curtailing the effectiveness of parties. A number of "reforms" weakened party organization: the spread of direct primaries, the substitution of the Australian ballot for party-distributed ballots, and the use of antifusion laws to prohibit the cross-listing of candidates. By 1896, a vast majority of the states, with 92 percent of the total electorate, had adopted the Australian ballot. The direct primary came more slowly, but between 1903 and 1915 most states adopted it.[51]

In addition to attacking the partisan apparatus so central to voter mobilization, reformers also sought to restrict eligibility and make exercising the franchise more difficult. Recent studies suggest that urban reformers exaggerated the extent of political corruption in the late nineteenth century. Victims of their own recitation of anecdotal evidence, they joined forces with those whose instincts were more overtly antimajoritarian and who for explicitly racist or nativist reasons sought to restrict the voting of others.[52] Concern over political corruption often, but not always, consorted with sentiment opposed to universal suffrage.[53]

The North and South chose different means to redefine voter eligibility. But in both sections the results took a strikingly class-specific turn, the largest decreases coming among lower-class voters. In the South, these effects had a notable racial dimension. While turnout rates for whites declined dramatically as they did in the North, the participation of black voters in most parts of the South fell nearly to zero by the end of the first decade of the twentieth century. Measures to determine eligibility, construed as "legal" and constitutional, generally enjoyed the support of white Progressives. Southern reformers saw disfranchisement as a means of stemming political corruption, which they perceived to be the legacy of more widespread voting by blacks during Reconstruction. The imposition of poll taxes, "literacy tests," personal registration, and property requirements, regularly enforced by extralegal terror, effectively removed black voters from the rolls.[54] These changes came in two waves, 1888–93 and 1898–1902, but the particulars of each campaign varied considerably, as Michael Perman has shown, from one state to another. The new restrictive statutes had an immediate and dramatic effect on voter participation, especially among black voters. The campaign, usually driven by conservative Democrats from black belt areas in each state, wrapped itself in the banner of efficiency and good government. Reformers claimed that suffrage restriction would foster government by "the voter," who Governor John Gary Evans of South Carolina described as having "sufficient intelligence to understand what he is doing" and has "some interest in the government which will induce him to vote aright." Southern Progressives believed, furthermore, that legal disfranchisement promoted the legitimacy of the South's political institutions and made it possible for would-be reformers to dispense with extralegal measures of exclusion "which have debased and lowered our moral tone."[55]

In the North, measures not nearly so draconian nevertheless had unmistakable effects on lower-class and immigrant voting.[56] The curtailment of alien registration, the introduction of residency requirements, the use of personal registration, and, in some nonsouthern states as well, the use of a literacy test disproportionately excluded immigrant and working-class voters.[57]

If the "costs" of personal registration bore most heavily on the lower classes, they were consistent with "liberal-individualist" values that middle-class Progressives viewed as essential for the responsible exercise of the franchise.[58]

Estimates suggest that voting in the new immigrant districts of larger northern cities may have been depressed as much as 40–50 percent through changes in the electoral "rules of the game." As the population of Chicago and New York mushroomed with new immigrants between 1900 and 1912, the number of male voters in presidential elections hardly changed, suggesting, as political scientist Gwendolyn Mink has noted, that "the electoral system had effectively sealed itself off from the entry of any significant numbers of new voters." The waves of newly arriving immigrants simply increased the "party of non-voters."[59]

The insulation of "popular" democracy took a variety of forms. The growing influence of interest group organization, reliance on experts, and the restructuring of urban governance reinforced restrictive changes in voting rules and nonpartisan attacks on the corrupting influence of partisan politics. The promotion of municipal at-large elections, the "professionalizing" of city government through commission and city manager forms of administration, and the separation of city elections from general elections redefined the universe of urban politics. These changes had the effect of reducing levels of working-class participation in what had been the most accessible and unstable realm of popular politics.[60] The adoption of such measures was at times undertaken explicitly to undermine the participation of working-class constituencies. The Republican sponsor of an 1895 re-registration law in Michigan aimed at immigrant supporters of Detroit's mayor Hazen Pingree made his intentions quite explicit: "It will take off the books just about enough Pingree votes to prevent his ever becoming mayor again."[61]

Democratic reform in the North and the South effected an electoral redefinition of the people that narrowed the social boundaries of political participation by excluding substantial numbers of lower-class black and white voters, who were deemed by reformers unqualified to vote. Within this restricted electorate, social harmony might reign, conflict be resolved, and government given a new lease to operate on behalf of the public interest. A *qualified* people exercising that most basic democratic right—the vote—might herald a new day in which government pursued the public interest rather than parochial concerns based on class or race. If such a day should arrive, parties and partisanship would lose their meaning and corrupting influence in public life.

The State and Social Harmony

Progressives looked to a democratically controlled state as the best means to regulate the behavior of private interests, arbitrate social conflicts, and promote the general welfare. For reformers, this "neutral" state represented a significant advance over the late nineteenth century, when, in many respects, the state had functioned as a promotional arm of capital and defender of existing property interests.

The idea that the state might play a useful regulatory function actually had deep roots in American political life and governance. Although the experience of living in a "well-regulated society" was embodied in the laws that governed virtually every aspect of life in local communities, the extension of economic regulation to the national state was no uncontested matter. In fits and starts, and most notably in the crises of the Civil War and Reconstruction, the powers of the federal government had been significantly increased.[62] Urging public control of "natural monopolies," new political economists, social gospel reformers, and a host of popular movements joined the battle with proponents of laissez-faire in the last decades of the nineteenth century. A growing body of reformers looked to the state to heal the social fractures spawned by industrialization. Drawing on local tradition and proposed new powers, reformers pushed to enhance state capacities at all levels, evidencing "an utter disregard of the *laissez-faire* principle."[63]

Through legislation at both state and federal levels and through the articulation of judicial doctrines that challenged unrestricted property rights, Progressives claimed beachheads for state or national economic regulation between 1877 and 1892. Legislative acts clothed in the rhetoric of restoring competition had begun in the 1870s to address two major problems: the inequities growing out of the capacity of large railroad corporations to insulate themselves from market forces and the more general problem of "monopoly" and its "restraint of trade." Widespread public fear that monopoly threatened to undermine political democracy energized politics and legislative reform. Only a more intrusive government, it seemed, could preserve a marketplace open to competition and at the same time protect democracy.

The federal courts had begun with increasing frequency in the late 1870s to assume authority over insolvent railroad property. Although in theory such equity receiverships transferred significant power to the public sector, in fact, the courts executed such authority in ways that maintained the rights of existing owners, protecting them from both the claims of creditors and their own employees.[64] In the area of railroad rates, the U.S. Supreme Court in *Munn v. Illinois* (1877) affirmed the right of state governments to regulate railroad rates. And in 1887, responding to the continuing grievances of farmers and shippers over rate discrimination, Congress created the Interstate Commerce Commission to monitor railroads rates and prohibit the corrupting practice of railroads showering politicians with free passes. But extensions of federal jurisdiction over railroad rate making, including subsequent legislation such as the Elkins Act (1903), the Hepburn Act (1906), the Mann-Elkins Act (1910), and the Transportation Act of 1920, represented only limited enlargements of federal power in an economic sector peculiarly prone to concentration.[65]

While conservative proponents of laissez-faire resisted government regulation of the marketplace, late-nineteenth-century reformers rekindled legal arguments that favored the use of "positive" government to regulate private property.[66] As Chief Justice Morrison Waite had asserted in 1877 (*Munn v. Illinois*), "Property does become clothed with a public interest when used in a manner to make it of public consequence, and affect the community at large."[67] And in an 1892 speech titled "Abuses of Corporate Privilege," St. Louis judge Seymour D. Thompson put the case for regulation in simple terms: "I say again, that if human government has any just office to perform, it is to arbitrate between the man who has everything and the man who has nothing."[68]

Congress addressed the problem of monopoly on a broader scale in 1890 and affirmed the federal government's power under the commerce clause of the Constitution to regulate monopolistic behavior. The Sherman Anti-Trust Act prohibited "every contract, combination in the form of trust or otherwise, or conspiracy, in restraint of trade or commerce." Despite its broad reach, the law as interpreted by the courts during the next decade failed to extend federal jurisdiction over corporate consolidation to any significant degree.

Conservatives saw great peril in the extension of the state's police power. And by the early 1890s, a conservative judicial tide had begun to flow, emboldened by the atmosphere of social crisis. Justice David J. Brewer, who along with Justice Stephen J. Field would become the high court's most vociferous defender of property rights, put forward the conservative argument at the 1891 Yale Law School commencement: "The demands of absolute and eternal justice forbid that any private property, legally acquired and legally held, should be spoliated or destroyed in the interests of public health, morals or welfare without compensation."[69]

Indeed, the Supreme Court, in what historian Morton Keller has called an "unholy trinity" of decisions in the mid-1890s, sharply limited the federal government's power to regulate the economy. The decision in *United States v. E.C. Knight Co.* (1895) narrowed the scope of the Sherman Anti-Trust Act literally to "commerce" as opposed to manufacturing. In *Pollack v. Farmers' Loan and Trust Co.* (1895), the justices declared unconstitutional the 1894 federal income tax. And in *In re Debs,* the court used the Sherman Act to uphold a federal injunction severely restricting the activities of striking members of the American Railway Union.[70] To the dismay of many reformers, these decisions established the Supreme Court of the 1890s and the early Progressive Era as a defender of antiregulatory public policy, just as popular sentiment for using public authority to restrain corporate power was growing.[71]

Progressive reformers and their legal allies swam against this conservative judicial tide with diminishing success in the 1890s. Still, long-established traditions of local regulation guided the practice of governance in American communities. And gradually, despite conservative opposition, a judicially constructed "liberal state" was built on those traditions of local regulation. That process was marked by continuing contention between conservatives defending individual rights and Progressives claiming legitimate limitations on the untrammeled exercise of property rights.[72] For Progressives such as Charles McCarthy of Wisconsin, this meant passing laws that sought "to equalize the position of the strong and the weak by 'a powerful state intervention.'"[73] Even in the twentieth century, however, such initiatives continued to be challenged and limited by a conservative judiciary.

The producerist strand of reformers envisioned a vastly expanded role for the state. The Populists, in their Omaha Platform, had stated unequivocally, "We believe that the powers of government—in other words, of the people—should be expanded (as in the case of the postal service) as rapidly and as far as the good sense of an intelligent people and the teachings of experience shall justify, to the end that oppression, injustice, and poverty shall eventually cease in the land."[74] The platform's specific planks called for government ownership of railroads, telephones, and telegraphs, federal financing of farm debt, a national government currency, a federal tax on incomes and land, and the enforcement of the eight-hour day for government work. Socialists in the 1890s went further, suggesting that government become an instrument for redistributing wealth and empowering workers. Laurence Gronlund, a popularizer of socialist ideas, believed the state was synonymous with "organized society" and functioned as the peoples' instrument "to redress natural defects and inequalities."[75] The 1894 Political Programme of the American Federation of Labor specifically advocated government ownership of railroads and mines, telephones, telegraphs, and municipal utilities.[76]

If most liberal reformers and social scientists did not countenance such a "producers" state, they nonetheless continued to advocate state activity of a more limited variety on behalf of the public's interest. By the early twentieth century, numerous state legislatures and eventually Congress felt the rising political winds of progressive reform and adopted increasingly pro-interventionist positions. The primary arguments put forward by reformers and their corporate liberal allies revolved around an older notion of the state as the balance wheel of society, an instrument for constructing and maintaining social harmony. Such a conception of regulation, however, continued the formal subordination of public to private authority. Certain specific powers might be granted to the state for the purpose of restoring competition, for instance, but their scope would be strictly limited.[77] Nevertheless, reformers at all levels moved to craft new legislation and administrative machinery that might help ensure social peace and address the most serious social needs. In cities, they sought authority to regulate housing standards, protect public health (milk testing), tax commercial property at full value, modernize poor relief, and regulate streetcar fares. Some cities went so far as to municipalize the provision of essential services: gas, water, and light. At the level of state government, Progressives pushed for state factory inspection, worker's compensation, regulation of utility rates, consumer protection, conservation of natural resources, and regulation of the insurance industry. Under pressure from reformers, the federal government gradually imposed some regulation on the manufacture of food and drugs, extended federal oversight of railroad rate making, and taxed railroad property at full value. Legislation would eventually be adopted regulating child labor, instituting banking reform, creating the Federal Trade Commission to monitor business practices, and requiring the eight-hour day for railroad workers.[78]

For most Progressives, the enhanced administrative capacities of the state, embodied in executive departments, commissions, and regulatory boards, represented the ideal of a smoothly functioning public bureaucracy staffed by professionals acting in the public interest. The image of the disinterested public servant meshed nicely with the Progressives' commitment to fostering a polity composed of "intelligent" citizens asserting their will through nonpartisan political activity. The crises of the late nineteenth century had revealed how susceptible to social disorder a political democracy navigating the shoals of industrial change might be. Progressives, therefore, sought to enhance government as the agent of the public's interest and to improve its efficiency and responsiveness.[79] Only the promise of a purified political process made it possible for middle-class reformers to imagine enlisting the state in their campaign for social harmony. In historian Robert Wiebe's felicitous phrase, the "heart of progressivism" lay in "the ambition of the new middle class to fulfill its destiny through bureaucratic means."[80] And that ambition fused moral outrage over "the discovery that business corrupts politics" with a commitment to construct new state administrative mechanisms for regulating business behavior and insulating the political process from corruption.[81]

Herbert Croly codified this reform vision in ways that privileged federal over state regulation, and Theodore Roosevelt's "new nationalism" gave that vision new political life when he reentered the national political arena in 1910. Croly's book, *The Promise of American Life,* captivated the imagination of a broad cross-section of reformers. He portrayed state and local regulation as parochial and peculiarly vulnerable to corruption in a national industrial economy. Local regulation was, in his view, a product of "the maladaptation of the whole system of American state government to its place in a Federal system." But he also carefully drew boundaries around federal regulatory intrusion so as not to deprive capital of its capacity to manage its resources rationally. For Croly, a reasonable national economic policy must accept the beneficial results of corporate organization on a large scale. Government should acknowledge capital's accomplishments and thereby legitimize the property that gave it competitive advantages in the first place. With government protection, he believed, these monopolies would in due course impart their benefits to the whole community. The state would, thereby, convert them into economic agents acting in the public interest and gradually appropriate their "substantial economic advantages." While Croly favored "concentrated responsibility" and could imagine, in some circumstances, public ownership offering the most efficient alternative, he preferred the maintenance of socially responsible private ownership guided by a national interest that did not impair efficiency or injure individual interest.[82]

A protracted debate over the nature and extent of federal intervention in the economy centered on proposals for revision of the Sherman Anti-Trust Act that eventually produced the compromises embodied in the Clayton Anti-Trust Act and the Federal Trade Commission. Clayton and the FTC represented, according to Martin Sklar, a national political consensus by upholding a "corporate-administered market" orchestrated "by 'apolitical' experts and the judicial process, both of which were removed from the direct impact of electoral politics." This represented the perfect progressive solution to the trust problem that had bedeviled reformers for nearly a generation.[83] With new antitrust legislation in 1914, administrative solutions to the problem of business concentration and corruption preempted unreliable judicial review and other, more far-reaching reforms.[84] State regulation of business misbehavior provided in theory the necessary basis for harmonizing the interests of capital, the public, and labor.

Two developments frustrated this new administrative politics of social harmony. First, class conflict did not disappear but seemed to intensify in successive strike waves in 1901–4 and, even more dramatically, 1909–15. And second, bureaucratic reformers had to contend with a hydra-headed politics of class that manifested itself most vigorously in cities. While the challenges posed by such a local politics ebbed and flowed during the Progressive Era, the threat it posed to local elites subsided only with the post–World War I Red scare and the contraction of the labor movement in the 1920s.

Class Politics and Urban Reform

Political insurgency, rooted in the producerism of the nineteenth century, had gained strength even as the visibility and support for bureaucratic reform rose in the late nineteenth and early twentieth centuries. Its manifestations varied. Advocates of public ownership of "natural monopolies" built substantial political movements at times within the ranks of established parties and at others independent of them.[85] The Democrats' claim to leadership of national reform rested in large part on the legacy of Populist-Democrat fusion in 1896 and the leadership of William Jennings Bryan. But the Democrats' program also grew out of the success of reformers in state legislatures and city government, where their promotion of issues ranging from worker's compensation to municipal ownership enlisted working-class voters.[86] The socialist movement's record of local political successes improved steadily between 1898 and 1910 and then dramatically from 1910 through the early years of World War I in Europe.[87] In its various manifestations, this local politics of class stood apart from the mainstream of bureaucratic, nonpartisan reform. In the first place, it was resolutely partisan. Second, it saw political corruption as the product of corporate manipulation and elite reformers' efforts to limit popular participation in politics rather than the failings of working-class voters, immigrant or otherwise.[88] And finally, following the lead of nineteenth-century producers, proponents of local class politics sought to expand radically the powers of government beyond the regulatory functions that most Progressive reformers might countenance.

With a watchful eye on the success of the Labor Party in Britain and Social

Democrats in Germany, America's urban political radicals focused their energies on local labor-oriented politics in four discernible episodes.[89] The first occupied the middle years of the 1890s, when major constituent unions in the AFL voiced strong support for independent labor politics and local labor-populist parties in a number of eastern and western cities attracted substantial support. The second emerged between 1901 and 1908, when Democratic and third-party politics with a municipal ownership agenda again seemed viable. In the third instance, the Socialist Party succeeded in winning significant municipal campaigns between 1910 and 1914 only to find its momentum and its ability to organize undercut by growing war hysteria. And finally, at the end of World War I in the political vacuum left by a shattered socialist movement, proponents of a labor party mounted a new third-party effort to defend the "industrial democracy" workers had achieved during the war years.[90]

These episodes reflect the uneasy jockeying for political leadership by middle-class reformers, radical intellectuals, working-class activists, and pragmatic politicians. The public ownership campaigns of William Randolph Hearst in the new century's first decade and the preeminently successful effort of Milwaukee's Social Democrats to create "socialism in one city" are two benchmarks of the Progressive Era's urban politics that signified the persistent challenge to Progressives from the Left.

WILLIAM RANDOLPH HEARST AND THE FIGHT FOR PUBLIC OWNERSHIP

No independent political movement associated with the broad-based campaign for public ownership generated more public interest or seemed more threatening to the two-party status quo than that associated with publisher William Randolph Hearst. Hearst cut his political teeth in municipal campaigns against utility franchise-holders in New York during the 1890s and built a popular movement for public ownership that led him to challenge conservative Democrat Alton Parker for the party's presidential nomination in 1904 and then nearly catapulted him into the New York mayor's office in 1905 against the assembled legions of Tammany Hall. Using his formidable journalistic empire—a chain of newspapers in New York, Boston, Chicago, and other cities—Hearst galvanized a loyal working-class following while tapping into middle-class discontent over political corruption and franchise monopolies.[91]

Calling his campaign for mayor of New York "the Progressive movement," Hearst drew to his banner a distinctly working-class following. The *New York Herald* reported that interviews with over two thousand businessmen showed a mere 11 percent supporting Hearst, whereas interviews with 3,022 workers, largely factory and transit employees, revealed that 72 percent of them would vote for Hearst.[92] Supported by scores of labor unions and the New York Women's Trade Union League, Hearst nonetheless appealed beyond the labor movement and its skilled worker base. His attacks on the trusts, calls for municipal ownership, and use of class rhetoric generated support that one historian has called an "almost religious fanaticism." His volatile campaign culminated in a mass rally at Madison Square Garden just before the election. He expressed admiration for the "peoples' friends" and pride that he faced the opposition of the "peoples' enemies." He was excited that "the laborers and immigrants became involved—really involved" in the campaign and believed their support held the promise of future victories. His enemies, most notably the *New York Times,* saw in his campaign only "red flag foolishness" and predicted that his antics would win the support of "the vicious element," no doubt "the whole of it."[93]

Other "Progressives" contested Hearst for the leadership of this movement. While sympathizing with the grievances that drove people to support him, they urged self-restraint and broad-mindedness. They asked, as Charles Sprague Smith put it, for the acceptance of "that leadership which counsels slow procedure through experiment and gradual change from the old to the new, rather than that which urges revolutionary processes." And in the most familiar terms, these reformers pleaded that "there should be no division between masses and classes." The socialists, who would lose nearly half of their vote to Hearst, warned that despite his support of municipal socialism, he was "just another capitalist."[94]

Hearst lost the mayoral campaign by a slim 3,472 votes (.6 percent) to Democrat George McClellan in a contest virtually all observers believed Tammany Hall had stolen. Nominated by the Independence League (formerly the Municipal Ownership League) for governor in 1906, Hearst gained the grudging support of Tammany and the Democrats. President Theodore Roosevelt showed an obsessive concern with the growing strength of Hearstism. In early October, he wrote to Henry Cabot Lodge, warning that "the labor men are very ugly and no one can tell how far such discontent will spread. . . . There has been during the last six or eight years a great growth of socialistic and radical spirit among the workingmen."[95] But despite strong backing from ethnic working-class communities in upstate industrial cities as well as New York City and official support from the Democrats, Hearst lost again by a slight margin, the victim of Tammany instructions to cut Hearst from the ticket. He nevertheless ate deeply into the socialist vote. Hearst was the only statewide

Democratic candidate to lose. His Republican opponent, Charles Evans Hughes, had benefited from strenuous efforts on his behalf by President Theodore Roosevelt, who sought to portray the campaign as one between responsible reformers and demagogues who "appeal to . . . greed, envy and sullen hatred." Roosevelt's surrogate campaigner, Secretary of State Elihu Root, voiced their shared concern that the election of Hearst "would be an injury and a discredit alike to all honest labor and to honest capital." But even after the campaign, a New York Republican, Paul Branact, warned Roosevelt that Hearstism represented a continuing threat in one form or another: "The adjustment of the misunderstandings between the rich and the poor which have made Hearstism possible, will, it seems to me, be the important political work for the next few years."[96] However compelling or repulsive Hearst was as a political personality and public figure, his public ownership movement reflected deep currents of popular, political discontent that profoundly unsettled the mainstream of progressive reform. His political program and his constituency had a decidedly class character.

MUNICIPAL SOCIALISM, MILWAUKEE STYLE

The "misunderstanding" between rich and poor, as Paul Branact termed it, continued to infect municipal politics in cities across the country. No case caught the public's attention more forcefully than the triumph of Milwaukee's Social Democrats in 1910. Methodically over the previous two decades, socialists in Milwaukee under Victor Berger's leadership had built the strength of the party. They had first become a political force to be reckoned with in alliance with the city's Populists. Later, as Branch 1 of Debs's Social Democracy of America in 1897, and then as the Social Democratic Party of Milwaukee (SDM), they built year by year a formidable electoral machine. The SDM formed the core of the "constructivist" wing of the Socialist Party of America after its founding in 1901. Crucial to its success was the official endorsement of the AFL-affiliated Milwaukee Federated Trades Council in February 1900. By the spring election of 1902, socialists were claiming every sixth voter in the city, garnering eighty-four hundred votes in the municipal campaign. In 1904, they nearly doubled their vote and elected nine aldermen to the city council.[97] And in 1906, they added five additional aldermanic seats. Even as the Social Democrats expanded their base in Milwaukee, they faced criticism from the national party over their electoral strategy and a platform that provided for regulation of streetcar franchises but not outright public ownership. By 1908, the party had gained a third of the citywide vote, displacing the Republicans as the second party. But under new state-imposed at-large election rules for city council, their seats fell to nine, despite winning the vote in more wards. Anticipating the need to appeal to a broader segment of voters, the SDM refashioned its platform:

> The Social-Democracy combats not alone the conditions which exploit and oppress the wage working classes, but every kind of exploitation and oppression whether directed against a class, a party, a sex, or a race. All its measures benefit not only the wage working class but the whole people, and while the working people are the banner bearers in this fight, in the last analysis everybody—the merchant, the professional man and the small shopkeeper—will profit thereby. Therefore we invite every honest and well-meaning voter, without regard to occupation, race or creed to join in our undertaking for the emancipation of mankind.[98]

Masking their disappointment over the loss of council seats, the SDM renewed its commitment to a "constructivist" municipal socialism. The key to victory now appeared to be the Polish working-class vote on the city's South Side, which continued to support the Democratic candidates.

The socialist victory in 1910 may have been unprecedented, but it came in soil that was well prepared. As Cleveland reformer Frederic Howe noted on visiting the city shortly after the election, "The Socialists have been represented in the Council for eight years. Since 1908 they have had a vigorous group of ten Aldermen [*sic*] who have given a suggestion of the honesty of the party. . . . The public had grown accustomed to the name and the spectacle of Socialists in office." In Victor Berger's view, Milwaukee had become a "convinced Socialist city," its politics "saturated with Socialist doctrine": "We have been at this twenty-six years, this education of Milwaukee. . . . We did not depart from our line of attack. Year after year we distributed literature from house to house. . . . Printer's ink is far more convincing than meetings or public speaking. In this way we reach thousands of persons who never attend a political gathering."[99] The socialists succeeded through the indefatigable work of "Bundle Brigades," which got party literature within forty-eight hours "to almost every house in the city in the language best understood by its inhabitants." Through more concentrated work in the Polish community, spearheaded by the publication of a Polish language newspaper, *Naprzod,* the party made significant inroads on Milwaukee's South Side.[100]

To read the victory of the Milwaukee Social Democrats as simply an instance of cross-class coalition building and a variant of progressive reform is to miss important features of the socialists' triumph. The socialists' gains came chiefly among working-class, not middle-class, voters. "Our growth was not among the wards where independent voting is prevalent," Berger noted. "Our great gains were among the Poles. . . . And once they have voted the Socialist ticket, the workingmen never desert us." While some historians see the drift of Polish Catholic voters to the Social Democrats in 1910 as ephemeral, a product in part of nationality splits in the Roman Catholic Church, others note continued support from Fourteenth Ward Polish voters in 1916 and at somewhat reduced levels after World War I.[101]

Milwaukee's Social Democrats put the party on the national map by electing a mayor, twenty-one of thirty-six aldermen, and eleven of sixteen county supervisors. In the fall 1910, the party sent Victor Berger to Congress and thirteen socialists to the state legislature. If their program bespoke reform, it did so in the cadences of class-conscious immigrant workers. While working for urban home rule and immediate, tangible reforms, the socialists spoke in the producerist tradition of "the cooperative commonwealth as a guiding star" of their reform program.[102] Mayor-elect Emil Seidel belittled the wastefulness of capitalism and applauded by contrast the efficiencies of publicly operated services. "See how easily we get along when the idea of profit is absent," he stated. And the socialists, unlike many Progressive municipal administrations, sought the expansion of the public sector: municipal ownership of streetcars and other city services, a city-owned terminal station, municipal baths, markets and cold storage plants, a public garbage disposal plant, a municipal ice plant, public works employment for the unemployed, free medical dispensaries and hospitals, an expanded system of parks and swimming pools, free textbooks, and the opening of schools as community social centers.[103] Furthermore, in the area of political reform, the socialists parted company with many municipal reformers by opposing at-large elections, short ballots, and commission forms of government. Berger in 1911 argued that such reforms "confuse the minds of the workers regarding the fundamental issue of today—the class struggle between the workers and owners. It tends to make workmen look to 'good men' and to reformed methods of election for relief, instead of working for a change of economic conditions." In his view, such political reforms were "not good mechanical devices for a democracy, for they limit the power of the people and tend to the establishment of an oligarchy."[104]

The Milwaukee socialists' municipal government proved short-lived in the face of Democratic and Republican fusion in 1912. But by 1916, the Social Democratic Party had reinvented itself as intervention in the European war loomed and elected as mayor Daniel Hoan, who had served as city attorney in the first socialist administration. Victor Berger returned to Congress in 1918, only to be denied his seat because of opposition to the war. Despite their wartime travails, Social Democrats continued to play a major role in Milwaukee municipal politics over the next forty years.[105]

Reformers watched the ebb and flow of class politics warily. They could applaud constructive socialists' electoral successes on occasion, but they remained skeptical that a class-based movement could renew democracy and promote social harmony. Producerist politics in the cities challenged the ideological premise of meliorist reformers that the people's interest might transcend parochial class loyalties and invent new remedies for the inequities and disabilities imposed by industrialization. Speaking of her fellow reformers, Vida Scudder recalled that "socialism in those days hovered for most of us on the horizon of Utopia. . . . In spite of my growing awareness of the class struggle, I, like my masters the Fabians, envisaged a 'revolution by consent' in which brave and enlightened spirits of all classes led."[106] The reformers believed that enlightened political leadership, infused with a nonpartisan spirit and committed to class reconciliation, would grow naturally out of the networks of reform they created.

4

Communities of Reformers

> I still think that among social movements (how they mul-
> tiply! I myself, at last counting, belonged to fifty-nine dues-
> paying societies bent on reform), those are most vital and
> plow deepest which bring members of the alienated or
> separated classes into close personal fellowship.
> —Vida Scudder, *On Journey,* 1937

Like many of her contemporaries, Vida Scudder moved within a
densely organized world of social reform during the early years of the Progressive Era. The orbits of her activity centered around Boston's settlements
and Wellesley College, where she taught English literature. With her reform
colleagues she shared a commitment to harmonizing the interests of the "alienated classes." Although she read Marx, supported strikers, and eventually
joined the Socialist Party, Scudder's commitment to the search for social unity
and a harmony of interests persisted.[1] And in those respects, she remained
deeply connected to the Progressive movement.

The pioneering efforts of a handful of settlements, investigatory commissions and conferences, and muckraking journalists in the 1890s spawned a spirited and diverse community of reformers who fed off the sense of social crisis that pervaded those years. They launched a host of discrete but related
reform initiatives that came to embody the Progressive movement. Much as
Florence Kelley at the turn of the century moved from Hull-House and her
duties as Illinois state factory inspector to head the National Consumers'
League, so did others enter and move through various organized sectors of
an expanding world of reform. The nodal points of reform proliferated. Some
materialized around publications such as *Charities and the Commons,* later the
Survey, others through cooperative investigations such as the Pittsburgh Survey. Coalitions of reformers who established the National Child Labor Committee reflected seemingly conflicting interests that nevertheless assembled
around a specific concern, or, like the Women's Trade Union League, mobi-

lized the energies of women across classes to pursue reforms that targeted the needs of an especially vulnerable population, in this case working women.

Both at the time and retrospectively, reformers vividly described being part of a wider movement. For some, such as Herbert Croly, their participation transcended the sincere but "unintelligently planned, insufficiently informed, and inadequately organized" campaigns carried out in the 1890s by the Populists and other such groups. But even Croly acknowledged that these agitations had the unintended consequence of breaking down a sense of national self-satisfaction and promoting a new synthesis of reform initiatives. A wave of muckraking, in his view, "broke over the country . . . [providing] a common bond, which tied reformers together" and committed them to reform not simply "disconnected abuses" but also "a perverted system." These bonds led to growing political effectiveness. Differences between Progressives and conservatives transcended party. In sum, Croly concluded, political leaders "who have offended the progressives" increasingly faced retirement from public life.[2]

Jane Addams, after a second twenty years at Hull-House, recalled feeling in 1909 that "our intellectual interests, our convictions and activities were all becoming parts of a larger movement." The investigation of social conditions, pioneered by the settlements, was being taken up in universities and by philanthropic foundations. In the five years that followed, before the outbreak of the world war, she recalled that the reformers forged bonds with many other movements. Simon Patten tied this great advance to "the growth of social expression," when "social workers found words to convey to each other what they saw." Recalling how reformers coalesced to launch the Progressive Party in 1912, Addams recaptured their language of common purpose: "We were convinced that the nexus between citizens could be more scientific and durable and at the same time more understanding and heartfelt."[3]

The sense of common purpose within the community of reform was powerfully shaped by the search for means to transcend the polarizing politics of class. They attacked social evils spawned by industrialism that bred misery and threatened a renewal of class warfare. While playing an influential role in the formation of the Progressive Party in 1912, they also witnessed an ominously rising tide of mass strikes between 1909 and 1914 that threatened to derail their larger reform project.

Battling on Many Fronts

By 1905, reformers in a variety of campaigns saw their interests as allied. The particularity of their concerns masked the broader community of reform that took shape through overlapping activities and the mutual aid they afforded one another. A new measure of professionalism crept into their work by virtue of the specialized knowledge they acquired, the full-time educational and agitational work in which they engaged, and the alliances they forged with social scientists and other academicians. Not all reformers came through the settlement houses, but those outposts continued to function as staging areas for the deployment of fresh legions battling on different fronts.

Several organizations played key roles as nodes of contact and sources of reform initiative, their influence radiating outward. Among the earliest was the National Consumers League (NCL), formed in 1898 by local leagues that sought to give consumers power to control the conditions under which goods were produced and sold. Florence Kelley had lost her job as chief factory inspector for Illinois when the Republicans took back the statehouse from John Peter Altgeld and the Democrats in 1897. While seeking another opportunity to use her considerable talents for reform, Kelley continued to work with Hull-House on a variety of projects. Among them was a campaign of the Chicago Consumers' League in alliance with cigar workers against the system of tenement-house cigar making. Kelley developed the idea of a "consumers' label" that, like the union label, would guide enlightened consumers to purchase products of workers who were well treated. When the NCL adopted the label as a national program, the organization turned inevitably to Kelley. Named the league's first corresponding secretary, she left Hull-House in 1899 to assume her new duties.[4] From her New York base, Kelley became a central figure during the next two decades in campaigns for protective labor legislation, the abolition of child labor, and other reforms.

The National Conference of Charities and Corrections (NCCC) functioned through its annual conventions as another meeting ground for reformers of varied concerns. As early as the 1890s, settlement activists infiltrated meetings of the NCCC and on occasion disrupted the proceedings with polemics against traditional philanthropy.[5] By the twentieth century, the program of its annual meeting reflected the interests of a broad spectrum of reformers concerned with child labor, factory conditions, housing deterioration, and public health. Its journal, *Charities,* merged in 1906 with the *Commons,* after the Pittsburgh Survey took the name the *Survey.* Jane Addams's election as president of the NCCC in 1909 symbolized the extent to which the settlement house movement had successfully challenged an older philanthropic establishment.[6] The NCCC, the American Public Health Association (APHA), and the National Council for City Planning (NCCP) formed close working relationships. Charles Probst, president of the APHA, noted in 1911 the connections between reform movements in housing, work, and recreation and the concerns of public health activists. Parallel organizing in the Children's Bureau, the School-City Movement, the American Cooperative League, the Municipal Ownership League, the Playground and Recreation Association, and the Women's Trade Union League fed directly a growing sense of community among reformers who, after 1909, saw with increasing clarity the political implications of the movement they had constituted.[7]

The New Philanthropy

Cooperation between settlement house workers and the philanthropic community had developed gradually. Real differences in perspective and approach separated reformers and charity workers through the 1890s. While reformers schooled in the settlements emphasized the environmental roots of poverty and spoke from direct experience as neighbors living with the poor, charity workers stressed defects in character and the dependent habits of the poor that required correction.[8]

Three established leaders in the philanthropic community created openings to new influences. Edward T. Devine, who had been a student of Simon Patten, was named general secretary of the New York Charity Organization Society (COS) in 1896. Lawrence Veiller, appointed secretary of the COS Tenement House Committee in 1898 and the New York Tenement House Commission in 1900, became the most persistent national advocate of tenement-house reform. Robert W. de Forest, prominent New Yorker and president of the New York COS in the late 1890s, served as patron of these spirited young reformers and helped move the COS and *Charities* toward accommodation of the reform perspectives flowing out of the settlements. In response to these influences, the National Conference on Charities and Corrections gradually transformed itself into the primary meeting ground for an enlarged reform community.[9]

Elected president of the NCCC in 1906, Devine put forward a compelling and powerfully articulated perspective that bridged the worlds of charity and reform. He acknowledged that the NCCC had been preoccupied with institutions "giving actual support to the indigent or discipline to the delinquent" and that this daily work with the "unfortunates" had led many charity workers to believe that they bore no responsibility for broader social change. But this was a mistake, he argued, and he indicted his colleagues for not having "appreciated the importance of the environmental causes of distress," focusing instead on "personal weaknesses" and misfortune. "It has been natural when we have seen an indigent consumptive with his hollow cheeks, or a worthless beggar with no signs of manhood left, or a premature little old man of fourteen whose life is apparently done, the fires of his energy all burned out before his time, to ask ourselves what was the personal weakness of this poor fellow, or what was his peculiar misfortune that he has thus been beaten in his struggle with life," he wrote. But would not "modern philanthropy" be less interested in "his weakness" than in "who has exploited him for personal profit?" This "modern philanthropy" may have identified the sources of greed, but it also recognized a role for enlightened businessmen in its campaign for "equality of opportunity."[10] Behind this call to reconcile old and new charity reform lay a vision that emphasized the commitment of society to "fix the levels below which the exploitation of workers and consumers would not be tolerated." Having established these norms, reformers were prepared to give a free hand to competitive interests.[11] By guaranteeing minimum standards of health and safety, housing and employment, and by setting norms for a reasonable standard of living, reformers would assist individuals to become functioning and productive members of society. Such a program did not challenge the fundamental tenets of the economic order. At the same time, it professed little patience with the corruption that perpetuated degrading conditions and social inefficiency that squandered the nation's human resources.[12]

Like Devine, economist Simon Patten constructed a framework for transcending the "old philanthropy." He exerted tremendous influence in redirecting social reformers away from an emphasis on individual uplift and toward social legislation that produced a "better environment."[13] Patten's belief in the salutary influence of "abundance" contributed to his substantial influence within the reform community. He rejected the "service altruism" of older philanthropists for an "income altruism" that should guide contemporary efforts. He believed fundamentally that the opportunities available in a regenerated environment together with the promise of abundance would encourage the reformation of character. Patten saw in industrialism a liberating potential that destroyed both aristocracies and the "working poor" and produced a new "social cooperation." He viewed the growth of cities optimistically as a means of "renewing and intensifying in all classes the motives to cooperation." With personal success, the individual's character would naturally change. "As time passes," Patten declared, "the habits formed for purely selfish, economic needs become new motives in the improving type of man."[14]

Patten was critical of the "good neighbor" model of charity work rooted in an old tradition of "social control." He pointed to a different, classless model of good citizens sharing a true solidarity of common culture and united in the project of promoting their interests in an environment of expanding opportunity. Like other voices at the end of the first decade of the new century, Patten urged the movement to work at diminishing social differences by improving access to income and resources and to focus its energies on areas such as housing, public health, education, and labor conditions.[15]

This new philanthropy reflected the programmatic innovations of the settlements. The alliances between new schools of social work and the settlements oriented a generation of social activists toward acquiring specific expertise. Still, these developments were contested. Faced with resistance, Jane Addams, Mary Simkhovitch, and Graham Taylor continued to argue for a "holistic" approach that stressed the cultural value of neighborhood work, the settlements as "experiment stations," and the necessity to "domesticate social work theories," even as they advocated a pragmatic acceptance of professional training and efficient management of services.[16]

The Russell Sage Foundation, established in 1907, served as an institutional bulwark for the developing professionalism of the reform community. The foundation supported research and education that would "contribute to long-term social amelioration." Deeply influenced by Robert W. de Forest, its funding decisions reflected the new philanthropy, and its commitment to environmental social reform began with the Pittsburgh Survey and extended to the founding of the *Survey,* sponsorship of community surveys based on what would become the Pittsburgh model, and the funding of other pioneering studies by "perhaps the best group of empirical social researchers in the nation."[17]

Paul Kellogg and the Survey

As a vehicle for disseminating reform ideas, *Charities and the Commons,* later the *Survey* magazine, acquired a preeminent position. Its editor, Paul Kellogg, made the journal the leading voice of the social reform community. Like many other reformers, Kellogg stumbled into the hothouse world of reform through a fortuitous connection that propelled his talents in new directions. After the 1901–2 academic year at Columbia, where he encountered the likes of sociologist Franklin Giddings, economist E. R. A Seligman, and government professors Frank J. Goodnow and Felix Adler, Kellogg enrolled in the Summer School of Philanthropic Work sponsored by the New York Charity Organization Society. He was promptly invited to join the staff of *Charities,* the society's "practical" publication, as an assistant editor.[18]

Almost from the outset he found the "stodgy" charitable orientation of the magazine stifling. Although many charity workers had begun to redefine poverty as a social disease, a residual moralism still lingered in the journal's dedication to enabling "the individual to eradicate . . . his personal defects before they have brought ruin and disaster." Kellogg sought comfort in the company of reformers whose experience had been shaped by the settlement movement. He recalled it being "a life saver to go up to the sixth floor of the Charities building and get a whiff of [Florence Kelley's] insurgent democratic spirit."[19]

Within the next year, *Charities* showed the effects of such influences in the subjects it treated and the authors it enlisted. A widening circle of reformers contributed, including Kelley (on child labor), Lawrence Veiller (on housing reform), and Mary Simkhovitch (on the settlements). By the fall of 1905, a merger with Graham Taylor's *Commons* had been consummated; the new publication was joined six months later by *Jewish Charity*.[20] Edward T. Devine, who remained the magazine's general editor throughout these transitional years, described in a 1908 editorial the cross-class philosophy that animated the reform community associated with *Charities and the Commons*. In his view, the journal represented no particular interest or class. "We seek to observe each impartially and sympathetically. . . . Our special task is to discover and to report . . . what financier and trade unionist, philanthropist and social worker, scientist and merchant, and all others, are doing for the common good."[21]

Paul Kellogg took leave from *Charities and the Commons* to direct the Pittsburgh Survey, a pioneering effort in social investigation. He drew on the expanding network of social reformers to advise and staff the undertaking. Key investigators included Elizabeth B. Butler, secretary of the Consumers' League of New Jersey, and young social investigators Crystal Eastman, Margaret Byington, and John A. Fitch, each of whom would have a distinguished career in the reform movement. He sought the advice of Florence Kelley, John R. Commons, and Robert A. Woods, director of South End House in Boston.[22] The Pittsburgh Survey brought the social survey to its highest level in the United States, even if some academic social scientists viewed it as insufficiently rigorous.[23]

The Pittsburgh Survey began as the outgrowth of a modest, seemingly casual, request by Alice B. Montgomery, chief probation officer of the Allegheny Juvenile Court, for an investigation of social conditions in Pittsburgh. But in the end, the survey crystallized a systematic approach to reform that redefined "social work" as a species of social engineering. The task became remaking man-made environments by identifying problems in the "community machinery" and recommending specific solutions.[24] Kellogg and his colleagues identified structural interconnections between the problems they uncovered. As he recalled years later, "The long neglected hazard of work accidents was found at the first staff conferences ramifying in so many directions that practically every member was faced with one phase or another of it."[25] The social survey might contribute to establishing standards for meeting human needs, but its most important function lay in bringing public attention to what settlement worker Robert Woods termed "piled-up actualities."[26] That civic action and a revitalized democracy would inevitably follow such investigations remained an article of faith for the social reformers.

Deeply influenced by his direct encounter in Pittsburgh with the "human measure" of the industrial revolution, Kellogg was determined to move *Charities and the Commons* even more to the heart of the reform movement. He pushed for alternative funding to supplant the New York Charity Organization Society and initially found it in the Russell Sage Foundation. He succeeded in getting the name of the journal changed to the *Survey,* and he created a new governing body for the journal, the Survey Associates, which shared his agenda for the integrated, guiding influence he believed the reform community needed.[27]

Toward a Public Interest in Labor's Welfare

The American Association for Labor Legislation (AALL) functioned as another gathering point within the emerging community of reform. Founded in 1906 as a section of the International Association for Labor Legislation, the AALL at its outset appeared a modest undertaking, attracting a core of influential academics interested in social insurance. But its initial membership of 21 grew to 3,348 by 1913.[28] Its organizing committee included Richard T. Ely, Henry W. Farnam, and Clinton Rogers Woodruff, influential economists with a reform bent. By 1908, John R. Commons and his student John B. Andrews were serving as secretary and executive secretary respectively; Florence Kelley represented the American section at the International's meeting in Lucerne; and sociologist and first secretary of the National Child Labor Committee, Samuel McCune Lindsay, called for "cooperative action" with "Departments of Factory Inspection, Trade Unions, American Federation of Labor, Child Labor Committees, Consumer Leagues, Christian Social Unions, and Church Departments of Labor." Vice presidents included Jane Addams, Samuel Gompers, Robert W. de Forest, and Warren S. Stone, president of the

Brotherhood of Locomotive Engineers.[29] From the outset, the AALL connected with a broad community of reformers and reform organizations, including the *Survey,* the NCCC, and key members of the settlement house movement.

The AALL embarked on the task of building an alliance of experts and reformers committed to what Theda Skocpol has called "interventionist public policies" in social insurance and labor-management reconciliation. Suspicious of the "selfish tendency" among trade union leaders and the shortsightedness of businessmen in a highly competitive environment, the AALL, like the Progressive movement in general, fought for what it saw as the public good. Adna Weber, labor statistician and the AALL's first secretary, argued that a growing body of reform-minded citizens realized that labor laws were not class legislation. "On the contrary," he declared, "they are realizing that it is vastly in the public interest to enact laws that will not only safeguard the health and morals of the people massed in large factories or employed in small sweatshops but also protect them from extortion and coercion, and secure to them some leisure in which to prepare themselves for the discharge of the duties of citizenship."[30]

Positioned between contending, parochial class interests, AALL reformers saw themselves as spokespersons for the broader public. At the same time, they considered themselves state builders. A durable social peace, they believed, would require the creation of new state structures embodying the public's interest, staffed by middle-class experts and empowered to oversee the enforcement of enlightened labor laws. John R. Commons foresaw the creation of "omnibus industrial commissions" modeled on the experiences of New York and Wisconsin. Such commissions, in his view, had to reflect "the constructive investigation of the administrator" if they were to supersede the unpredictable functions of the courts and legislatures.[31]

Around the time the AALL was founded, Commons presented an address to the American Sociological Association that attempted to answer the question "Is Class Conflict in America Growing and Is It Inevitable?" His answer on both counts was no, and his views corresponded closely to those of the AALL's founders. Roughly estimating the size of the contending classes, he asserted that 24 million men and boys were engaged in "industry" (by which he seems to have meant any form of nonagricultural employment or self-employment). Female wage earners appear to have been absent from his field of vision. Only 6 million "wage-earners" and 1.5 million "employers and investors," however, were "in the field where classes are forming." The rest were farmers, tenants, farm laborers, petty capitalists, servants, professionals, agents, clerks, or people residing in small towns and villages where employers and employees generally had close personal relations. Consequently, he estimated that fully "two-thirds of the *voting* population are spectators. We call them the public." Their chief interest was in "fair play," he stated, and the outcome of class conflict "depends on the way they are brought in."

Despite the dangers posed by the contending classes, Commons believed that certain changes worked against widening conflict. Like some reformers who accepted the fact and even the utility of the role played by big corporations, he noted that where the consolidation of trusts and reorganization of production on a large scale had gone furthest, class conflict was least likely. Ultimately, he looked to the great "third class," the public, to dampen and diffuse class conflict and to "assert its right to hold the balance between two struggling classes." Through direct democracy measures, adjudication of disputes, an end to class legislation, and their common interest as "consumers," the public's "class" interest—by which he really meant the interest of the people—would be served.[32]

Like other nodes of reform activity, the AALL enlisted support from a broad, cross-class constituency. Financial backing came disproportionately from large industrialists, including John D. Rockefeller, Elbert Gary, V. Everit Macy, and Thomas Lamont, some of whom on occasion opposed particular AALL legislative initiatives, such as compulsory unemployment insurance and specific proposals for public health insurance.[33] On the other end of the spectrum, socialists, such as Isaac Rubinow, enlisted in the campaign for compulsory social insurance and later health insurance out of a commitment to "readjust the distribution of the national product more equitably" and socialize the insecurity the worker faced in a wage-based economy.[34] For the most part, the AALL allowed its sister reform organization, the National Consumers' League, to attend to the conditions of women wage earners. Nevertheless, the two organizations worked closely together and shared many members within the reform community.[35]

Organized labor and the AALL found themselves regularly in conflict over the character of legislation designed to protect workers. Samuel Gompers and the AFL were reluctant to consign the defense of labor's interests to "'disinterested' outsiders." They preferred instead to defend their own interests. Although members of the AALL supported the principle of trade unionism and defended the right of labor to organize, they resisted the implicit class consciousness that undergirded labor's own reform efforts. Gompers was an organizational pragmatist. He did not reject the idea of conflicting social classes, and in historian Irwin Yellowitz's view, he "found little favor among social Progressives, who preferred a classless concept of the public interest."[36]

Saving the Children

No crusade tapped the moral outrage of the reform community more deeply than the campaign to abolish child labor. Lewis Hine's stark photographs of working children captured and focused that outrage on the plight of individual children—stunted and prematurely aged by their labor—whom he identified with precision: "Leo, 48 inches high, 8 years old, picks up bobbins at 15 cents a day. Fayetteville, Tennessee, November, 1910" or "Neil Gallagher, Worked Two Years in Breaker. Leg Crushed Between Cars. Wilkes Barre, Pennsylvania, November, 1909." Hine and other reformers grew bitter over the slow progress of reform. A 1914 pamphlet dripped sarcastically with Hine's anger: "It is perfectly obvious that our children must be reared in an atmosphere of work if they are to become Captains of Industry, and so we outdo the Montessori System itself. . . . Did I say tasks? Not so—they are 'opportunities' for the child and the family to enlist in the service of industry and humanity."[37] While child labor reformers mobilized a constituency that crossed classes and embraced some forward-looking businessmen, other corporate leaders associated with the National Civic Federation worried that sensational literature on child labor purveyed by "socialistic writers has done a great injustice to many fair-minded and humane employers in the South."[38]

The national campaign against child labor developed along parallel but distinct paths in the South and North. The Knights of Labor had succeeded in pressuring some states—notably Alabama—during the 1880s to pass laws setting age limits and restricting hours of work for children in factories. Lacking any mechanism for enforcement, such laws by the 1890s had become a dead letter or been repealed. A new effort in Alabama, spearheaded initially by AFL organizers and then by Episcopalian minister Edgar Gardner Murphy, built a more formidable campaign. Attacking what he termed a "monstrous" system, Murphy marshaled reform forces under the banner of the Alabama Child Labor Committee and in 1903 succeeded in getting a compromise piece of legislation enacted. It banned children under twelve from working in factories and prescribed a maximum sixty-six-hour work week for children under sixteen. At the time, the Alabama law set the most advanced child labor standard in any southern state.[39] Parallel efforts in New York built on longstanding labor concern over child labor by pushing through amendments to existing state laws that required documentation of ages for child workers, increased the number of days of compulsory school attendance, reduced hours to nine, and extended application of the law to the "street trades." A network of social settlement workers led by Florence Kelley and Lillian Wald ignited the campaign in 1902 by prompting the investigation and publicity of the inadequate protection existing legislation provided child workers. Their efforts led directly to the formation of the New York Child Labor Committee. The investigation, carried out largely by labor activist Helen Marot, gave an enormous push to the passage of the child labor amendments.[40]

Like its southern counterpart, the New York Child Labor Committee drew on an impressive array of wealthy supporters to provide legitimacy and fund its initial activities. Corporate financiers and railroad executives studded the leadership of the committee. They joined prominent academics and the ever-present social workers in establishing offices for the New York group late in 1902 just a block from the Charities Building, which had already become the hub of reform activity in the city.[41]

A national child labor movement followed quickly on the heels of the successes in Alabama and New York. A few months after Edgar Gardner Murphy spoke on "Child Labor as a National Problem" at the 1903 annual convention of the NCCC, Florence Kelley, Felix Adler, and William H. Baldwin organized a provisional national committee and called for a founding convention in New York on April 15, 1904. Adler focused the attention of delegates squarely on what he termed "a holocaust of the children—a condition which is intolerable." In so doing, he also prescribed limits to the concerns that would guide the new National Child Labor Committee: "That for which the Committee stands should be the absolute minimum which the enlightened public sentiment of the community demands. It should be plainly said that whatever happens in the sacrifice of adult workers, the public conscience inexorably demands that the children under twelve years of age shall not be touched; that childhood shall be sacred; that industrialism and commercialism shall not be allowed beyond this point to degrade humanity."[42]

Building on the networks of support established by the state committees, the NCLC embedded itself in the reform community. It shared offices initially with the National Consumer League in the Charities Building. Its membership expanded to include prominent national reformers, like Jane Addams, Graham Taylor, and Ben Lindsay. A stellar group of corporate and public figures joined the committee. For its professional staff, the committee hired talented, public-spirited academic Samuel McCune Lindsay as general secretary and two assistants, Owen J. Lovejoy and Alexander J. McKel-way, to carry out investigations in the North and South respectively.[43]

Child labor reformers framed their arguments in moral and pragmatic terms, but they did so in ways that rationalized the existing social order. Jane Addams argued that the labor of children "robs the assets of the community . . . [and] uses up those resources which should have kept industry going on for many years."[44] Samuel McCune Lindsay described his fellow child labor reformers as occupying a middle ground in the reform movement:

> With the muckraker and the socialist who gloats over the indecencies revealed by child labor as evidences of the unalterable rottenness of our industrial society, and with the mere sentimentalist who sees none of the practical difficulties or underlying causes of the Child Labor problem, North or South, the National Child Labor Committee has no sympathy. . . . I think I may safely say that the National Committee are meliorists, one and all, that is persons who have a sincere faith in the power of a united effort to ameliorate the conditions brought about by any industrial development or situation, however bad, through the better guidance and application of laws of natural and economic evolution.[45]

But even understood as a discrete social problem, child labor had spread, not receded, with the maturation of the industrial order. By the turn of the century, children were a staggering 30 percent of the work force in southern textile mills, comprising, in Edwin Markham's powerful phrases, "a gaunt goblin army" of cheap laborers, "pygmy people sucked in from the hills."[46] The textile industry of New England and the Piedmont South were inextricably interconnected by ownership and investment, which fed a sense of common cause among the reformers witnessing the spreading plague of child labor.[47]

The economic threads that tied North and South encouraged reformers in both regions to make common cause in a national campaign against the scourge of child labor. In doing so, the movement imbibed racial views that may have been expressed with greater rawness in the South but nonetheless stirred little obvious discomfort among northerners. Southern reformers believed that the stunting effects of child labor among whites promoted "race suicide" and eroded white supremacy. But Senator Albert Beveridge of Indiana, a powerful voice on behalf of a federal amendment banning child labor, also made this point unequivocally on the floor of the Senate in 1906: "Whereas the children of the white working people of the South are going to the mill and to decay, the Negro children are going to school and improvement."[48] Speaking to the fourth annual meeting of the NCLC at Atlanta in 1908, E. W. Lord, the secretary for New England, warned the assembled reformers that "long-cherished American ideals are in danger" from the influx of racially distinct foreigners. Racial thinking and the conservation of American citizenship unified the reformers as no other claim could. Felix Adler spoke of the deeper foundation on which the campaign against child labor rested: "That founda-tion is, in a word, the inconsistency of child labor with Americanism, with the ideas by which American civilization is characterized."[49]

The campaign against child labor rallied a cross-section of reformers. Its forces, while united around the need for public education and the use of state power to effect change, were deeply divided over the need for federal regula-tion. A residual states' rights sentiment focused the energies of many re-formers on the state level despite the limited effectiveness of state laws. Re-formers succeeded, however, in a long campaign to create a federal Children's Bureau that would investigate and advocate on behalf of children's issues. With support of first Roosevelt and then Taft, the bureau came into being in April 1912. Meanwhile, the NCLC had grown from a modest organization of fifty members in 1904 to a membership of more than sixty-four hundred with a budget of sixty thousand dollars in 1912. Marshaled in the child labor pha-lanx were state and national organizations, unions, and a broad cross-section of the reform community. They pushed Roosevelt's Progressive Party in Au-gust 1912 to adopt a platform plank calling for federal prohibition of child labor. But the Keating-Owen Act embodying such a prohibition and signed into law by Woodrow Wilson in 1916 tested the constitutional limits of fed-eral regulation and was found wanting by the Supreme Court two years later.[50]

Reforming the NCCC

Just as the *Survey* had become a major clearinghouse for reformers' ideas and activities, so too did the National Conference of Charities and Corrections function as an annual marketplace where reformers exchanged ideas and strengthened their organizational ties. The clearest index of the changing character of the NCCC is the influence over the annual meeting program that Kellogg, Florence Kelley, Owen Lovejoy, and other key reformers came to ex-ercise. Jane Addams served as president of the conference in 1909; Kellogg, Kelley, and Lovejoy chaired the committee on occupational standards from 1910 to 1912.[51]

Founded in 1873, the NCCC had functioned for nearly two decades as a na-tional meeting place for philanthropic workers associated with traditional private charities. By the new century, the organization was feeling the influences of neighborhood-based settlement work, the development of social investigation, and the professionalization of philanthropy.[52] Settlement workers may have found their efforts to influence the program largely rebuffed in the 1890s, but by 1904 the NCCC was showing signs of change. A session on "Neighborhood Improvements" attracted leaders of a number of settlements.[53] In 1903 and 1906, Robert W. de Forest and Edward T. Devine, respectively, served as president, introducing the ideas of the new philanthropy that were finding their way into *Charities*, the New York COS, and social work training.[54]

By 1909, a sea-change was underway in the NCCC. Key reformers committed themselves to the organization as a primary venue for mobilizing the broader reform community. The 1909 Buffalo convention elected Jane Addams president but also authorized the formation of a new committee on "Occupational Standards" chaired by Paul Kellogg. Addams, in her opening report for the Committee on Immigrants, noted that "charity is continually going out into new fields. . . . We are continually mixed up in this human tangle, all engaged in weeding the same neglected garden."[55]

Symptomatic of changes afoot in the NCCC, Robert Woods, who chaired the reconstituted Committee on Families and Neighborhoods, described the change from a "strictly almshouse method of dealing with poverty" to seeing families within "the spontaneous drama of the neighborhood." Woods connected changes in charity work to the need for citizenship and new roles the state might be called upon to perform.[56] Florence Kelley presented a caustic indictment of the "fool's paradise" of contemporary industrial society by contrasting the ideal of the home and the reality of women's wages—wages that shattered the lives of young working girls in the larger cities.[57] New York settlement worker Lillian Wald presented a paper to the organization's Immigrants section, chaired by Addams; Lewis Hine spoke to the Press and Publicity section on social photography. Rabbi Stephen Wise opened the Buffalo conference with a ringing call to put justice above charity. Still, substantial sections of the program remained devoted to such traditional subjects as "defectives," "law breakers," and "delinquency."[58]

The 1910 convention of the NCCC, over which Addams presided, embraced the community of reform. In her presidential address, Addams sought to demonstrate the common ground that the "charitable" and the "Radical" had come to occupy. "It is as if the Charitable had been brought, through the care of the individual, to a contemplation of social causes, and as if the Radical had been forced to test his social doctrine by a sympathetic observation of actual people," she said. Even in the new arena of "occupational standards," where "the state assumes new forms almost daily," reformers depended on the data gathered in charitable institutions to make their case that the common laborer's status as an "efficient" citizen must be protected.[59]

As Addams sought to knit together the reform interests of the "charitables" and "radicals," so did others at the conference pursue a broader amalgamation of reform interests. Mary Richmond, director of the Charity Organization Department for the Russell Sage Foundation and chair of the NCCC section on Families and Neighborhoods, made the focus of her report "the inter-relation of social movements." Richmond noted the proliferation of national movements, the numbers of which had grown steadily since the 1870s. Their cumulative efforts had produced the current emphasis on social analysis and specialization of services. She stressed the intersections between such national movements as the Consumers' League, the National Child Labor Committee, the Playground Association of America, and the Immigration Restriction League on the one hand and individual and neighborhood efforts of case workers and settlement workers on the other.[60]

In his report from the Committee on Occupational Standards, Paul Kellogg echoed a similar theme. He linked the committee's mission to the traditional work of the conference. The program to promote minimum industrial standards lay at the heart of Kellogg's vision. He foresaw a "rational and practicable" set of standards for the length of the working day, occupational diseases, industrial accidents, workers' health, child labor, and wages.

Kellogg also connected the enforcement of minimum standards through a mobilized public opinion with the larger project of ensuring the survival of democratic institutions. Using the language of human engineering, laden with racial meaning, he argued for occupational standards as a tool of "industrial eugenics." By blocking "thousands of cases of incipient ill health and inefficiency," a reforming public would guarantee "the industrial and social fitness of the American worker." Failing to set such standards threatened democracy, as society would continue to produce "a work-engrossed citizenship, which must leave to the leeching and loafing elements in the community the responsibility for carrying on town and county and State."[61]

As they sought to harmonize the visions of charity workers and social reformers, Addams, Richmond, and Kellogg stressed environmental change and minimum standards—hallmarks of the "new philanthropy"—as keys to creating an efficient, competitive, and wholesome work force. Such a program, they believed, was both rational and humane. It established a basis for class harmony by setting new rules for the game by which individuals might "pursue happiness," but it envisioned no fundamental reordering of society while remaining wary of the "leeching and loafing" elements.

Standing at Armageddon

By 1912, these reform interests had pushed to the center of national political debate a far-reaching program of social reform, crafted in annual gatherings over several years at the NCCC. The reformers found in the Progressive Party and its standard-bearer, Theodore Roosevelt, a receptive audience for their platform of "industrial minimums."

Jane Addams recalled the sense of urgency reformers felt during "the five years before the outbreak of the world war." In spite of success in particular campaigns, she noted, "we began to have a sense of futility" and to see the need for "a great cause which should pull together the detached groups in the various states." Those reformers, like Addams, Kellogg, Kelley, and Lovejoy, who had thrown their energies into the NCCC and its committee on industrial standards, saw the need by 1912 "to place these questions before the entire country as a coherent political program." They hoped to enlist in such a campaign all who were convinced that "industry should be subjected to certain tests of social efficiency." It was, Addams recalled, as if "from various directions . . . people were drawing toward a new political party. . . . One heard in the distance the grave and measured tread of history," the pace of which "increased during the first half of 1912 and became absolutely breathless by midsummer."[62]

No simple confluence of social reformers produced the Progressive Party that summer or the nomination of Theodore Roosevelt as its standard-bearer. The party's roots lay in the factional wars between reformers and stalwarts within the Republican Party that reached back into the 1890s. The frustrations of insurgent congressional Republicans grew deeper during the presidency of William Howard Taft. The interests of a reform-oriented segment of the business community also provided a catalyst. Identified with the National Civic Federation, they were determined to create a more orderly and predictable federal apparatus to legitimate and police the role of large corporations in American economic life. Herbert Croly's book, *The Promise of American Life,* forcefully articulated the vision of a nationally regulated capitalism freed from the piecemeal, Swiftian restraints it faced in a decentralized antimonopoly culture of reform. But among these diverse interests, the reform community played no small role in bringing to life this new political instrument for achieving social efficiency and ameliorating class conflict.[63]

At the annual convention of the NCCC in Cleveland during June 1912, among the delegates were the reformers who for nearly three years had used the Committee on Standards of Living and Labor as their forum and who, according to Paul Kellogg, represented the major national organizations devoted to social and industrial reform. They had spent the previous twelve months drafting planks for "a platform of industrial minimums" that addressed a living wage, hours of work, safety and health, housing, and the "term of working life." When the NCCC passed no resolutions on these matters, the reformers "adjourned as a section meeting" and "reconvened as citizens" to adopt the platform.[64]

The gathering delegated several reformer/citizens—among them Kellogg, New York charity worker John Kingsbury, Samuel McCune Lindsay, and Homer Folks, an expert on child welfare—to present the platform to the Republican convention in late June. A woman's suffrage delegation from the National American Woman Suffrage Association led by Jane Addams and including social reformers Sophonisba Breckinridge, Lillian Wald, and Mary Simkhovitch also appeared at the convention. Despite hearings before the Republican Party platform committee, both delegations failed to get their proposals adopted. They found consolation only in the fact that Theodore Roosevelt, who also experienced rejection at the hands of the Taft-dominated convention, seemed interested in their proposals.[65]

Finding the Republican convention thoroughly under the control of Taft and the stalwarts, Roosevelt delegates bolted and convened a rump meeting of Progressives. Within two weeks, sixty-three leaders issued a call for a convention on August 5 to form a new Progressive Party. The call asserted, on behalf of the people, the need for a "national progressive movement" to reclaim control of government. In the name of "modern industrial evolution," the new party pledged support for legislation that would achieve a "better and more equitable diffusion of prosperity" and "avert industrial revolution."[66] Kingsbury, Kellogg, and New York civic activist Henry Moskowitz consulted directly with Roosevelt on their proposals for the platform during mid-July at Roosevelt's Oyster Bay home. Kellogg later wrote to Addams that their "report was all grist to T. R.'s mill. . . . I wrote some paragraphs which he more or less put into his keynote speech. . . . He took over the Cleveland program of standards of life and labor practically bodily."[67] Juvenile justice reformer Judge Ben Lindsey of Colorado had played an important role in getting the woman's suffrage delegation a hearing at the Republican convention. In early July, he assured Jane Addams that Roosevelt had shown "a change of heart" on the suffrage question. Addams herself came to regard Roosevelt as a "convinced" though not an "ardent" supporter. But such conviction nonetheless drew strong support for the new party from suffrage-oriented reformers.[68]

The warmth with which the new party received the program of "industrial minimums" stunned social reformers. The Progressive Party's platform committee and Roosevelt himself responded "ardently" to the idea that "the human waste which modern large-scale industry throws back upon the community"—the "social deficit" of a modern economy—should "come within the sphere of governmental supervision and control." The party, Kellogg noted, has been "the signal for a political outcropping of social workers" who found themselves at the center of more powerful interests equally committed to progress. Through this coalition, they saw the potential for "a new alignment in American public life which may ultimately lead to a temperamental cleavage between the conservative and progressive." A "new national team" joined together "political reformers, conservationists, and social workers" in support of a positive program.[69]

When the Progressive Party convention opened in Chicago on August 5, 1912, it reminded many observers of a revival. Hymn singing, Roosevelt's "Confession of Faith," and the earnest and uplifting countenance on delegates' faces all suggested a moral movement turned to politics. The convention embodied the ideals of what Jane Addams had termed an "efficient citizenship," which the reformers believed would be the basis for a new, more progressive age.[70] The social reform community organized a "Jane Addams chorus," distributed bright red bandanas that became the party's symbol, and cheered wildly the nominating speeches by Addams, Ben Lindsey, and Raymond Robins. Addams herself described the festivities as reminiscent in some ways of an annual convention of the American Sociological Association or the NCCC because of the presence of so many reform colleagues. Her prominence at the convention, serving on the national committee and seconding the nomination of Roosevelt, gave to those she represented a sense of their importance to the proceedings.[71]

Some issues, notably the planks on antitrust action, proved divisive in the drafting of the Progressive's platform, but the party united on the social reform and direct democracy planks. The reformers grumbled over the provisions calling for building a strong navy and found deeply distressing the maneuverings, led by Roosevelt, that excluded southern black delegates in the interest of competing more effectively with the Democratic Party for southern white votes. The support of the reformers for the party despite its color bar revealed their fundamental ambivalence on matters of race.[72]

Nevertheless, the platform adopted by the convention represented on the whole a triumph for social reform Progressives. The preamble called on "the people" to use their power "to establish and maintain equal opportunity and industrial justice." It asserted that in order to "best promote the general interest . . . it is time to set the public welfare in the first place." Following closely the "minimum standards" proposed to the NCCC earlier in the summer, the platform enumerated in detail a series of proposals to conserve "human resources," including the abolition of child labor and the establishment of health and safety standards, a minimum wage, the eight-hour day, and worker's compensation.[73]

For the "social workers," and for the numerous women delegates and observers, the high point of the convention came in the speech by Jane Addams seconding the nomination of Theodore Roosevelt. Addams, accompanied by a contingent of women suffragists and reformers, proceeded to the speakers' platform. The entourage embodied the movement whose support undergirded the new party. She began her remarks with a testimonial not to the candidate but to the platform. "Measures of industrial amelioration, demands for social justice, long discussed by small groups in charity conferences and economic associations . . . are at last thrust into the stern arena of political action," she declared. Noting the party's commitment to the protection of children, the aged, overworked girls, and overburdened men, she saw it as a natural venue for the "great reservoir" of women's "moral energy so long undesired and unutilized in practical politics." As for the nomination of Roosevelt, she lent her support "because he is one of the few men in our public life who has been responsive to the social appeal and who has caught the significance of the modern movement."[74] During the campaign, Addams was asked whether women were interested in Roosevelt. She answered that they were "interested in and working for the platform of the Progressive Party, because it stands for social and economic measures, but we are very glad to have a distinguished man at the head of it."[75]

Years later, she remembered the convention as "a curious moment of release from inhibitions," the "barn raising of a new party" in which the reformers' belief in their leader was secondary to the platform. "I was there," she wrote, "because the platform expressed the social hopes so long ignored by politicians." She had found that the "uplifting sense of comradeship with old friends and coworkers" transcended the isolation and inadequacy they felt working in small groups. They recognized that their "sentiments of compassion and desire for social justice were futile unless they could at last find expression as an integral part of corporate government."[76]

The party's platform pledged itself to the general interest and "the conservation of human resources." Addams would later also remember the ameliorative intents that represented an "inner consent" between party activists and the wider citizenry. As she and the new party's faithful sailed off into what proved to be an "educational" campaign, they truly believed, with Roosevelt, that "we stand at Armageddon, and we battle for the Lord."[77]

Even before the Bull Moose Party, as it was sometimes known, made its appearance, ties between interest groups had proliferated, a common agenda had been forged, and the community of reform had cast itself increasingly in political terms. The Progressive bloc in the Senate provided one important point of political reference. But interest-group mobilization did not constitute itself inevitably in partisan terms. A commitment to nonpartisanism remained deeply embedded in the consciousness of reformers. Their suspicions of the corrupting influence of subservience to party inhibited for many of them outright political affiliation.

The Progressive Party may have taken shape out of interest-group mobilization, but it also represented a decisive shift toward partisanship on the part of reforming women in particular. These Bull Moosers at least viewed the party as the final phase, perhaps the logical extension, of a longer-term political mobilization of reformers begun outside existing partisan attachments. Even as they joined the partisan contest in the fall of 1912, many reformers' commitment remained programmatic, contingent, and nonpartisan in spirit. As Henry Moskowitz wrote to Lillian Wald in early August, "I look upon the movement as more important than any personality be it Roosevelt or La Follette."[78]

The new party and its platform seemed to affirm the identity of a Progressive movement and the relevance of its reform agenda to the politics of the day. A broad cross-section of that reform community threw its energies into the 1912 campaign. Indeed, Ralph Easley of the National Civic Federation noted with satisfaction after the campaign that the Progressive Party "accomplished a great piece of work in forcing a clear line of demarcation between 'Social Reform' and 'Socialism.'"[79]

Partisan Progressives after 1912

Despite defeat in November, reformers moved quickly to establish themselves as an ongoing, organized presence within the party whose name they claimed as their own. Through the organization of the Progressive Service, the brainchild of former settlement worker and social investigator Frances Kellor, they constructed a political instrument that transcended mere politics. On December 19, 1912, the party's executive committee officially endorsed National Progressive Service as one of four working bureaus. It would sustain the party's focus on the social and economic problems of industrial society, draft model legislation for adoption at state and national levels, and carry out public campaigns on behalf of such legislation. Kellor, with the support of Jane Addams and other key leaders, reassembled an impressive array of talent drawn from the reform community, including Gifford Pinchot, John Dewey, Edith and Grace Abbott, Ben Lindsey, Lillian Wald, and Paul Kellogg, to direct and advise the work of the Progressive Service.[80]

Kellor's agenda bore with it an inherent distrust of party politics and a desire to apply social scientific expertise to the reconstruction of American society. In Kellor's view, political parties might become "'laboratories' of social research whose work would be 'defined by scientific laws' and . . . manned by experts." Although the Progressive Service enjoyed some modest success drafting bills for sponsorship by Progressive legislators in several states, it also made itself a target for practical politicians and the more conservative wing of the Progressive Party led by businessman George W. Perkins. A strain of independence from the national party had been evident all along. The Progressive Service sustained the nonpartisan spirit and the contingent support given to Roosevelt and the party by many reformers in 1912. Kellor, Kellogg, and Lindsey traveled to Washington in April 1913 to meet with Progressives irrespective of party about proposed legislation. Party supporter Richard Washburn Child of Massachusetts expressed to Roosevelt in May the concern of many mainstream members that "the Progressive party has become too academic. It would please me to see the organization snuggle up to practical politics a little more, and perhaps, when it appears in public, to appear a little more as a political party, and a little less as a cult."[81]

Political divisions among Progressive Party adherents had been evident from the outset. Although many of the early supporters of Robert La Follette's candidacy, such as Walter Weyl, joined the bandwagon for Roosevelt in August, others continued to harbor suspicions about Roosevelt's ideological baggage and the interests that lurked behind his candidacy. With his defeat in November, party unity began to fray.[82]

Two axes defined the lines of division in the party. One lay in a fundamental debate over public policy regarding the role of corporations in American life that had been present in the discussions of reformers for at least two decades. As early as the National Civic Federation's Conference on Trusts in 1899, the proponents of vigorous antitrust policies found themselves pitted against supporters of a policy that Herbert Croly defined as "recognition" and "regulation" of large corporations to promote "American economic efficiency" and the "better organization of industry and commerce."[83] While the debate between so-called New Nationalist and New Freedom visions of how to police trusts is usually associated with the campaign between Roosevelt and Wilson in 1912, the division was, in some respects, even more pronounced *within* the Progressive Party. George Perkins, chair of the party's executive committee, partner of J. P. Morgan, and an influential director of the National Civic Federation, represented more conservative forces within the party that favored a "rational" policy to protect the trusts. Perkins played a prominent role in revising the party's platform to favor "constructive regulation" in place of its original language supporting equal competition and strict enforcement of the Sherman Anti-Trust Act. In doing so, he served as a lightning rod for the attacks of those in the party who favored a more competitive capitalism.[84]

A split between reformers and "politicians" formed a second axis of conflict within the party and overlapped divisions on trust policy. One group of reformers—Roosevelt called them "ultra-progressives"—assembled around a more radical wing of the party. They included Amos Pinchot, George Record, Frederic Howe, and academics Charles Merriam and Charles Mc-Carthy. By early 1913, they were committed to a campaign, destined for failure, to counteract the influence of Perkins and promote a program of municipal ownership of utilities, an urban single tax, government ownership of railroads, home rule for cities, and an end to unnatural business combinations.[85] Once convinced that they could not wean Roosevelt away from Perkins, they began to gravitate toward support for Wilson's program and ultimately his reelection campaign of 1916. At the same time, Frances Kellor and the Progressive Service lost influence in the party, and in January 1915 Perkins began dismembering the bureau and reassigning its key functions to other party bureaus. With the "politicians" in ascendance, the social reformers, like the antitrusters, began drifting toward a Wilson administration that seemed more responsive to their views.[86]

Not surprisingly, reformers had difficulty reconstituting the sense of a coherent community they had forged during the election campaign of 1912. Their political drift between 1912 and 1914 occurred in the context of renewed class conflict stirred by uprisings of unskilled workers in a variety of industries, often led by the IWW. While supporting the party's program for "social and industrial justice," Amos Pinchot and George Record moved steadily toward "declaring war against private monopoly" in what Pinchot called "the one great issue of the time." Pinchot's letter to the members of the Progressive National Committee in May 1914 framed the issue posed by George Perkins's leadership as requiring the party to "take sides in the struggle between democracy and privilege." But by defining the conflict as one between the people and the interests, Pinchot, like so many in the reform community, failed to acknowledge the renewed class warfare, graphically symbolized in the Ludlow massacre on Easter morning 1914, that left little room for programs of industrial amelioration and class reconciliation. Pinchot in due course would join a more radical, producerist wing of reformers around Frank Walsh in support of labor's claims to greater social power.[87]

Other factors complicated the political landscape for Progressives. Within a newly competitive party system, reform Democrats now occupied the presidency and made their influence felt in Congress. The American Federation of Labor had tied its own political agenda to the Democrats. The Socialist Party under Debs's leadership demonstrated growing strength even as it purged William D. Haywood and the IWW influence from its ranks. And finally, many Progressive Party activists returned to the ranks of the Republican Party. These shifts in political alignment shattered the reformers' sense that they had achieved through the Progressive Party a coherent political identity capable of contesting for control of the public's business in their own name.

As the leadership roles of Jane Addams and Frances Kellor in the Progressive Party suggest, women gained a national voice and at a critical stage helped shape the reform vision of a national party. If they did not wholly abandon their attachments to nonpartisanism, they nonetheless entered into the partisan campaign of 1912 with an unequivocal commitment to the party's principles. They drew directly on the cross-class models of reform organization that had been fundamental to the germination of the Progressive movement and resonated with the world of female social reform that defined the party's activist core.

5

Class Bridging and the World of Female Reform

Woman's place is Home. . . . But Home is not contained within the four walls of an individual house. Home is the community. The city full of people is the Family. The public school is the real Nursery. And badly do the Home and Family need their mother.

—Rheta Childe Dorr,
What Eighty Million Women Want, 1910

When journalist Rheta Childe Dorr sought to justify women's active role in public life, she easily turned to a maternalist metaphor that was commonplace among women reformers in 1910.[1] That metaphor wove together the "natural" claims of women as moral protectors of home and family with the argument that the fulfillment of such responsibilities required governmental action and, above all, woman suffrage. This "domestication of politics," which grew directly out of the gendered world of nineteenth-century women's reform activism, profoundly influenced the ideological and programmatic direction of the Progressive movement.

Through a host of voluntary organizations, women confronted what Mary Beard called "the breeding places of disease, as well as of vice, crime, poverty, and misery."[2] The habit of mind by which women domesticated municipal reform also led many to downplay the significance of class differences. As historian Paula Baker has noted, "'Woman' was a universal category in the minds of organized women. . . . Because all women shared certain qualities, and many the experience of motherhood, what helped one group of women benefited all. 'Motherhood' and 'womanhood' were powerful integrating forces that allowed women to cross class, and perhaps even racial, lines."[3]

Women reformers conceived "the people" as a category that bridged class differences and acted on that conception. They successfully constructed a "female dominion" of reform, centered in the settlement houses, the influence of which reached into a host of national movements, most notably the Mother's Congresses, the National Consumer's League, and the Women's Trade Union League.[4] A cross-class maternalism functioned as the necessary and, in the eyes of many, natural basis for women's claims to a voice in public life.

The barriers to women's social and political activism had dictated that women organize on a gendered basis around "women's issues" such as prohibition, female suffrage, and protective legislation. Those barriers lay not only in the realm of politics, where the campaign for the vote faced formidable opposition, but also in the labor movement. Because the AFL resisted organizing women and fighting for social insurance and government regulation of working conditions, these battles also took a gendered turn.[5]

Maternalism functioned as a cross-class justification for women's public activity that many hoped would also provide an opening for broader reform. At the same time, cross-class social action and claims on behalf of women's public space were never simple or uncontested. Class-bridging efforts at times barely disguised the different agendas that separated the *class* interests of working-class women and their maternalist allies.[6]

Women's activism in the late nineteenth century revolved around three primary poles—suffrage, temperance, and settlement house reform. The failure of Republicans and Democrats to support suffrage promoted the construction of an autonomous political culture rooted in such women's organizations as the National American Women's Suffrage Association (NAWSA) and the Women's Christian Temperance Union (WCTU). Although some activists embraced the world of partisan politics, these organizations appealed directly to women, formed local units that were female in composition, and built a web of alliances with other women's organizations, including the expanding network of women's clubs, that were fundamentally nonpartisan.

Out of these domains of nineteenth-century female reform, women brought to the emerging Progressive movement a language and organizational experience that affirmed the vision of a classless social order of freely associating individuals. The gendered concerns of maternalist reformers led others to articulate a broader set of reform questions: Why not protection for all workers? Why not safe living and working conditions for all? Why not shorter hours and social insurance that would benefit whole families? Some years back, historian Anne Firor Scott noted the "historical invisibility" of women's voluntary associations in accounts of progressive reform. Although recent scholarship has largely remedied that shortcoming, the observations of some Progressive Era commentators remain poignant. A journalist in 1910 noted, "Right under the eyes of men, but for the most part quite unsuspected by them, women are making the world according to their ideas of what the world should be." And as Scott observed, "That part of the Progressive movement that focused on practical improvement of community life was, by and large, women's work." Women consistently demonstrated "civic capacities" that contributed significantly to shaping a broader reform program.[7]

During the first decade of the twentieth century, women activists wove their reform agendas into the cloth of the Progressive movement. The National Conference of Charities and Corrections, the National Consumers' League, and the National Child Labor Committee are cases in point: women reformers' cross-class perspectives became the natural and logical building blocks of those organizations. Powerful firsthand testimony to the efficacy of that approach came from settlement workers' experience in bridging class differences. But to understand the boundaries that nevertheless demarcated the Progressives' inclusive vision of a classless, democratic people, we must consider the trajectory of nineteenth-century women's reform.

Female Reform in the Nineteenth Century

Antebellum female reform evolved in the organizational embrace of the abolitionist movement. A critique of patriarchal dominance over women's lives and labor, and their rights in matters of property, divorce, and reproduction, found support within the Garrisonian movement and its radical insistence on individual conscience. The demand for suffrage became an instrument for challenging women's dependent status but also for empowering the broader reform movement, and suffrage opponents understood this dynamic all too well.[8]

The Civil War drew legions of middle-class women into the work of the home front—caring for the impoverished families of soldiers, organizing charity and moral guidance for hard-pressed wage-earning women, and coordinating the provision of supplies and nursing services for the battlefront through local branches of the U.S. Sanitary Commission. The influence of a new "scientific" philanthropy and a commitment to reform that made protection of the home its centerpiece is discernable in each of these undertakings.[9]

Postwar reconstruction, the dismantling of slavery, and the recodification of citizenship through the Fourteenth Amendment seemed to women's rights activists the fortuitous moment for universal extension of the franchise. Instead, the language of the Reconstruction amendment enshrined the vote as a male prerogative. Although the women's rights movement shattered over tactics, it now focused centrally on the fight for suffrage.[10]

Woman suffrage, and the broader woman's rights agenda for which it stood, became in the 1870s more exclusively a female domain. The bitter division among abolitionists over the extension of the franchise and a radical critique of patriarchy created the conditions for a woman's movement that spoke to the particular oppressions based on gender. Abandoned by former abolitionist allies in their quest for women's right to vote, the suffragists "had to look to women themselves not only to articulate the problem, but to provide the solution to women's oppression," as historian Ellen DuBois has argued.[11]

The radical separatism of the postwar suffrage movement fit the tendency of middle-class women to organize from within the domestic sphere. A wide range of social reform organizations emphasized women's cultural difference. Building on their wartime experience in the Sanitary Commission, but now hemmed in by their isolation from former equal rights allies, women pushed outward the boundaries of the domestic sphere and, in the name of protecting women and children, claimed a voice in issues of women's work, tenement conditions, and the destructive impact of alcohol. Claims once based on equality now emphasized women's difference.[12] Elizabeth Cady Stanton spoke in 1869 of female difference as the basis for woman suffrage, contrasting the nobility and abhorrence of violence that women would naturally bring to the political process with the consequences of their continued exclusion. But in so doing, she also revealed the class and race prejudice that infected the movement. Alluding to the bitter fruits of the Fourteenth Amendment, she noted ironically the respectful hearing women received at the hands of autocratic rulers in Europe: "Shall American statesmen, claiming to be liberal, so amend their constitutions as to make their wives and mothers the political inferiors of unlettered and unwashed ditch-diggers, boot-blacks, butchers, and barbers, fresh from the slave plantations of the South, and the effete civilizations of the Old World?"[13] Like the Progressive movement to which it contributed so substantially, nineteenth-century middle-class women's activism was deeply infected with race and class prejudice.

On Behalf of Working Women

The impulse among women to set the world right found expression after the Civil War in a variety of venues. Middle-class women, for instance, moved to address the needs of self-supporting working women, whose numbers had grown during wartime. Susan B. Anthony helped form a working women's association to improve the living and working conditions of female wage earners and enlist them in the fight for suffrage. The Women's Educational and Industrial Union in Boston sought to provide vocational opportunities for working women within the limited domains of employment open to them.[14] These organizations, together with the YWCA, aspired to bridge class differences that might divide women. Seeking to overcome the hardships and class polarities spawned by industrialization, they invoked a "universal sisterhood" rooted in the shared experience of women.[15]

Working women did not always welcome such class-bridging efforts. In New York, they rebelled against the efforts of elite women to control the governing board of the Working Women's Protective Union.[16] At the same time, in a number of trades, women gravitated toward *class* organizations with men, in so far as they were welcomed. Shoe factory operatives organized the Daughters of St. Crispin (DOSC) in tandem with their brother Knights (KOSC) in the shoe trade. Although both organizations succumbed to employer offensives in the depression-swollen labor market of the 1870s, the experience of cross-gender class organization in New England shoe towns carried over into the Knights of Labor.[17]

The Knights of Labor fashioned the most impressive nineteenth-century organization that linked working women and men in a campaign for common class goals. Women in the KOL organized separate local assemblies and a women's department, but some, such as Elizabeth Rogers of Chicago, participated in and even led predominantly male assemblies. Women served as delegates to the General Assembly, one became editor of the organization's national newspaper, the *Journal of United Labor,* and several assumed the responsibility of general lecturer/organizers. But like Leonora Barry, general investigator of women's work, they continued to face discrimination within the order when they challenged the invisible ideological boundaries prescribed by the male Knights' commitment to their own conception of "labor's true woman."[18]

As the KOL collapsed, women in several trades, including tailoring, shoemaking, and textiles, won limited acceptance in the world of male trade unionism. But with the ascendancy of the AFL in the 1890s, women workers found themselves pushed again to the margins of organized labor through male trade unionists' "social construction of skill."[19] In their local struggles to improve the conditions of labor, working women's most reliable allies came to be middle-class women dedicated to social reform.

In 1903, faced with male trade unionists' intransigence, a cross-class, gender-based coalition of reformers founded the Women's Trade Union League (WTUL). That support, constructed around the distinctive claims of women and children for protective legislation, came largely from the female dominion of reform. By their agitation on behalf of working women (even by joining strikers on picket lines), middle-class and elite women reinforced the idea that the claims of gender might transcend the claims of class.[20]

For a time in the late 1880s and early 1890s, the Illinois Woman's Alliance had embodied this class-bridging spirit. Women activists from the Chicago Trades and Labor Assembly, including Elizabeth Morgan and Mary Kenney, formed an alliance with middle-class settlement workers and members of the Chicago Woman's Club to conduct campaigns against sweatshops, child labor, and lax enforcement of compulsory school attendance laws. Divisions erupted, however, within the alliance between elite and trade union women over resolutions expressing support for striking shoe workers and condemning manufacturers for combining to nullify state factory inspection laws. Also revealing were debates that pitted settlement house reformers against some female trade unionists over cooperation with the state in the appointment of school and factory inspectors.[21] Trade unionists such as Elizabeth Morgan feared political appointments would create a class of office seekers, with which Chicago's trade union community had ample unfortunate experience. Settlement workers Mary Kenney and Florence Kelley, on the other hand, grew skeptical of the trade unionists' avoidance of political entanglements and aligned themselves squarely with the "class-bridging activism" of Chicago's reform-minded women in their pursuit of legislative remedies.[22]

Women's War on Alcohol

In no realm of reform did middle-class women more thoroughly mobilize than on behalf of temperance. And the battle against alcohol in the late nineteenth century provided an important staging ground for the mobilization of women who would play a critical role in other Progressive Era reform efforts. The campaign against alcohol consumption had won considerable support in the pre–Civil War period, as part of the broader moral reform crusade stimulated in part by the Second Great Awakening and by the confluence of antislavery and workers' rights agitation. Women brought to the movement an objection not simply to drink but also to the subordination and legalized coverture that readily turned them into victims of "drunken husbands." The temperance movement became the vehicle for women to challenge state-enforced dependence and to affirm alternative conceptions of home and family in which the rights and dignity of women were respected. In the immediate postwar period, its base expanded, and it attracted women in growing numbers to its ranks. In the depression winter of 1873–74, the crusade became what some called a "war," as women carried the campaign against drink into the streets and saloons of towns across the country. The following fall, the women's crusade turned to more formal organization and gave birth to the Women's Christian Temperance Union.[23]

Almost from its founding, the WCTU felt the powerful energizing influence of Frances Willard. As president of the Chicago chapter, and after 1879 as national president, Willard conceived and put forward the idea of a "home protection ballot." At the Women's Congress of 1876 in Philadelphia, she argued for woman suffrage as a tool for the temperance campaign. "We have carried ballots to men year after year, urging them to vote; but we have made up our minds that it is just as easy for us to vote ourselves," she said.[24]

Home protection domesticated woman suffrage and gave it seemingly unassailable appeal through linkage to temperance. As Willard's biographer has noted, home protection "implied careful nurturance, womanly virtue, and love of family." It stressed the particular claims of women to a public voice based on their essential calling to protect the sphere of the home and the needs of children. But as one historian has argued recently, home protection was rooted in a "sexual contract" by virtue of which women claimed the right to defend themselves against abusive men and enter the political arena with their own reform agenda. By aggressively distributing the temperance pledge among men in their neighborhoods and pursuing tougher state legislation to restrict the liquor trade, women politicized the movement from the outset. But Willard, like other middle-class Protestant reformers, also carried the baggage of nativism. Fears of the contaminating influence of the "infidel foreign population" laced home protection politics. A supporter enthusiastically reported Willard's first speech for woman suffrage, delivered at the Old Orchard Beach temperance camp meeting: "She had long hesitated, but now that the ballot has been prostituted to undermine the Sabbath, and rob our children of the influence of the Bible in our schools, she thought it time that Woman, who is truest to God and our country by instinct and education, should have a voice at the polls, where the Sabbath and the Bible are now attacked by the infidel foreign population of our country."[25]

Willard and the WCTU moved into a broader confluence of reformers during the 1880s. In what came to be called a "Do Everything" strategy, temperance advocates linked their cause to concerns for women's sexual exploitation and "white slavery," the reform of women's prisons, the kindergarten movement, municipal hygiene, and the conditions of women's work.[26] Willard steadily guided the WCTU toward outright endorsement of the Prohibition Party, close association with the Knights of Labor, and sympathy for the cause of populism. In each case, the temperance advocates pushed their agenda while expressing support for a broader program of reform, and in all three instances such alliances generated heated internal debate. Willard argued in the early 1880s for cooperation with associations of reformers, such as the American Social Science Association and the National Conference of Charities and Corrections, that increasingly advocated scientific reform.[27]

In Chicago, women spun a particularly elaborate web of reform. Willard called the city "a paradise of exceptional women."[28] Its Woman's Club grew from a nucleus of women who had been active in the Civil War Sanitary Commission. Willard and the WCTU forged ties with trade union women and activists in the Knights of Labor during the 1880s. The Chicago Woman's League, organized in 1888, brought together representatives of diverse women's organizations—fifty-six in number—including missionary societies, trade unions, suffragists, and philanthropic societies. Described as a "spontaneous growth" of "organized womanhood," the league was a local expression of the National Council of Women, which Willard served as president. And later in 1888, as we have noted, woman's club members and trade union women formed the Illinois Woman's Alliance to push for enforcement of Chicago's factory ordinance and compulsory education throughout the state.[29]

The flowering of "social feminism" in the late nineteenth century gave expression to a powerful, alternative women's political culture. A conception of women's difference nurtured claims for suffrage and a voice in public affairs. Like Frances Willard and Jane Addams, these "new bourgeois women" embraced the expanding opportunities for higher education, public leadership, and political influence in the post–Civil War era. Nevertheless, they constructed institutions within a profoundly gendered social space as they aspired to transcend class boundaries, and they deployed arguments for reform in the logic and language of home protection and municipal housekeeping. As Mary Beard explained, "Having learned that effectively to 'swat the fly' they must swat its nest, women have also learned that to swat disease they must swat poor housing, evil labor conditions, ignorance, and vicious interests."[30]

Settling the Urban Wilderness

Women active in a variety of reform efforts learned important lessons through the work of the hardy band of settlement house pioneers. We have already noted their activism in a variety of reform campaigns, from the new philanthropy to social investigation to child labor reform. Drawn to the idea that class divisions might be bridged in part by middle-class women taking up residence among the poorest segments of the immigrant working class, a cohort of young, educated women, joined by a handful of men, "settled" in the slums of Chicago, New York, Boston, and, eventually, a score of other cities.

The settlement house saga has acquired mythic status largely through the autobiographical chronicles of its pioneers. Its narrative has become so deeply imbedded in the story of progressive reform as to be virtually inseparable from it.[31] Nonetheless, the settlements, Hull-House in particular, created gendered spaces within which women reformers articulated and acted out their reform vision. They did not do so in quite the isolation that is often attributed to them, however. Addams and Ellen Gates Starr, for instance, turned to the Chicago Woman's Club as a recruiting ground for Hull-House on the eve of its opening. Florence Kelley, seeking refuge in 1891, appears to have first approached the WCTU. The organization's impressive array of alternative female institutions—nurseries, an industrial school, a shelter for destitute women, medical dispensary and low cost restaurant—and its national network gave it enormous visibility.[32] Jane Addams and Kelley turned routinely to a wider network of middle-class women's organizations for financial and political support. They persuaded the Home Department of the Chicago Woman's Club to support financially Kelley's counseling with working women. They "insisted," as Addams noted, "that well-known Chicago women should accompany this first little group of settlement folk who with trade-unionists moved upon the state capitol in behalf of factory legislation."[33]

Settlements functioned as outposts of democratic renewal in the new urban wilderness at the turn of the century. In ways analogous to Frederick Jackson Turner's conception of the function of the frontier in American life, settlement pioneers hoped to see class differences melt and become inconsequential in the face of the rough equality and democratic participation the settlements recreated. The "democratic radicalism" that John Dewey witnessed at work in Hull-House apparently persuaded him to turn his activism toward educational reform in the interests of democracy.[34] Jane Addams spoke directly to the central democratic purposes of the settlements in her famous address "The Subjective Necessity of Social Settlements" a year before Turner presented his "thesis" at the Chicago World's Fair. On behalf of a generation of "educated young people" who "long to give tangible expression to the democratic ideal," she described the hopes of these pioneers "longing to socialize their democracy." But she also found it "difficult to see how the notion of a higher civic life can be fostered save through common intercourse."[35]

The settlements served, on the whole, as women's space in the world of reform. They provided a nexus of female-controlled institutions through which women reformers moved into previously forbidden realms of politics and public policy. As "a community of women," the settlement workers sustained and directed their creative energies in ways that daily confirmed the legitimacy of their cross-class gender consciousness. From this world of "separate female institutions," as Estelle Freedman has termed them, "they drew upon networks of personal friends and professional allies" to launch the work of reforming society.[36] Of the 215 settlements surveyed in 1911, 53 had only women residents; 2 percent were for men alone. But even in the mixed-gender environment of settlements such as Hull-House, which in 1896 housed twenty women and five men, women's influence predominated. Beatrice Webb, who visited Hull-House in 1898, noted that "the residents consist in the main of strong-minded, energetic women bustling about their various enterprises and professions, interspersed with earnest-faced, self-subordinating and mild-mannered men who slide from room to room apologetically."[37]

If the settlements resulted in part from the "subjective necessity" of educated, middle-class women to find a meaningful way to serve society, they nevertheless fashioned a program of reform that powerfully influenced the character of the broader Progressive movement. The campaign for legislation that protected working women and children became central to that program. In Illinois, agitation for state legislation regulating the employment of women and children began under the auspices of the Illinois Woman's Alliance in 1888, led by Elizabeth Morgan and women trade unionists. Before arriving in Chicago, Florence Kelley had helped organize a successful campaign, spearheaded by the New York Working Women's Society, to appoint female factory inspectors in that state. After 1892, she reenergized the effort in Illinois by broadening the base of the campaign through Hull-House ties to the middle class. As Addams recalled, "Before the passage of the law could be secured, it was necessary to appeal to all elements of the community, and a little group of us addressed the open meetings of trades-unions and of benefit societies, church organizations, and social clubs literally every evening for three months."[38] Although the first campaign had been led primarily by working women, in the second, middle-class women assumed the lead.[39] Nonetheless, Kelley, the first state factory inspector appointed under the new law, named trade union activists Alzina Stevens, Mary Kenney, and Abraham Bisno her chief deputies. All were intimately connected through the Hull-House community. Bisno recalled the civility and freedom of discussion at Hull-House with great affection. As an immigrant, socialist garment worker, he "did not agree with their Anglo-Saxon estimate of the nature of the social movement," but he appreciated "the nobility of their characters" and "the integrity of their effort."[40]

Settlement house ties proliferated exponentially in the early twentieth century as residents and sojourners moved into a variety of related organizations. Kelley left for New York in 1899 to become executive secretary of the National Consumer's League and took up residence at Lillian Wald's Henry Street Settlement. Former settlement house residents founded the National Women's Trade Union League and played key roles in the General Federation of Women's Clubs (GFWC) and in constituting the Mothers' Congresses. And as we have seen, they became the driving force behind the formation of the National Child Labor Committee and influenced the redirection of the National Conference of Charities and Corrections.

Much of this activity continued to be justified by reformers' arguments based on women's difference. Middle-class women, historian Robyn Muncy observes, naturally gravitated toward being "mediators between classes as they voluntarily went into poorer districts to convert heathens, staff missions, and offer charity. No one, they argued, was better qualified to mediate between the working and middle classes in 1900 than America's women." Marginalized in the new professions and excluded from the higher reaches of academic social science, women played crucial roles in colonizing the public realm for reform.[41] But in doing so, they also claimed "cultural authority" for a civilizing mission that typically carried racial overtones.[42]

Mary van Kleeck and the Female World of Reform

The career of Mary van Kleeck is representative of a life course in reform shared by scores of young women of her generation. Born in 1883, a graduate of Smith College, and daughter of a prominent Dutch Episcopalian family from Flushing, New York, she moved in the fall of 1905 to the College Settlement in New York City. She held a fellowship that combined study of social work at Columbia with an introduction to the practical work of social investigation through a network of settlement-based reformers. A daily record of her activities kept intermittently over the course of her first few years in the city reveals a socially conscious young woman plunged into the heady world of women's reform activity. Although she dutifully recorded her enrollment for courses with Professors Giddings, Burgess, and Moore (noting that the former failed to keep his office hours) and the hours she spent in the Charity Organization Society Library reading works on labor legislation and reports of the New York Labor Commission, her diary chronicles in far more enthusiastic detail her encounters with reformers—Florence Kelley, Helen Marot, and Josephine Goldmark—and her own fledgling efforts at social investigation.

She tells of attending meetings of the Women's Trade Union League, the National Consumers' League, a settlement committee on the enforcement of the sixty-hour-a-week factory law, a social club for young immigrant working girls (the Lilies of the Valley), the Association of Neighborhood Workers, and the New York Conference of Charities and Corrections. Critics referred to the "interlocking directorates of reform" constructed through personal, overlapping ties between reformers, and, indeed, a friend of the reformers, seeing a familiar gathering in the New York Charities Building, asked, "What's this bunch call itself today?"[43] As a neophyte reformer in early October 1905, Van Kleeck was swept up in this world. She recalled trying to engage a young milliner in conversation at an open meeting of the WTUL, only to be rebuffed: "Was I trying to find out something and what trade did *I* belong to." Within the month, however, she found herself enlisted in a campaign to document the long working hours of young garment workers by surreptitiously visiting shops after 8:00 P.M. She noted, "Mrs. Kelly [*sic*] wants facts collected as to hours of labor . . . to be used in introducing a more explicit labor law."[44]

By November, Van Kleeck had deeply immersed herself in plans for a broad investigation of "women in industry." At the Rivington Street settlement, she met Margaret McDowell from Chicago, who outlined the proposed plan of investigation. In March, after months investigating long working hours, she served as chair of the citywide committee on the enforcement of the sixty-hour factory law for women. By early January 1907, just a year and a few months after her arrival in New York, her involvement had expanded into a highly visible campaign on many fronts to expose the conditions of women's and children's work. She delivered speeches at Vassar College on the hours of women's work and on child labor to the Women's Auxiliary of the Ethical Culture Society, and she spoke on the Prentice bill (calling for a federal investigation of these matters) to the Smith Club, the Manhattan Trade School, and the Hudson Guild Girls Club. She pursued factory investigations, consulted school truancy records, recruited settlement workers to help in the investigations, interviewed trade union leaders (Rose Schneiderman) and physicians, visited factories with Jane Addams and Josephine Goldmark, and attended board meetings of the Consumers' League and the WTUL.[45] In 1907, a newly formed department of industrial investigation under the Alliance Employment Bureau supported Van Kleeck's studies of women's and children's labor. In 1908, the Russell Sage Foundation granted support to these investigations, and in 1910 the foundation incorporated the Committee on Women's Work directly under its auspices. Van Kleeck, serving first as secretary and later as director of the foundation's Department for Industrial Work, had become a leading voice in the movement to win protective legislation for women and children.[46]

Her odyssey in the world of women's reform between 1905 and 1912 signified the intensifying engagement of growing numbers of women with the "maternalist" reform agenda. Yet Van Kleeck, like many female reformers, followed a path of professional development that left her personally removed from day-to-day maternal responsibilities in the domestic sphere. Forced to organize within a largely gendered sphere, around issues framed in maternalist terms, these middle-class reformers promoted cross-class alliances among women that energized and gave direction to the broader Progressive movement between 1908 and 1914. Although Van Kleeck remained focused largely on the conditions of women's work during her early years with Russell Sage, she moved in a milieu that related women's work to the general conditions of industrial labor.[47]

Public Mothers and the Fight for Protection

Women reformers such as Van Kleeck, although unmarried and dedicated to lives of social service, saw themselves as "public mothers" and accepted a maternalist characterization of their work. As historian Carroll Smith-Rosenberg has shown, these "new women" believed women were "uncorrupted by the world of politics and trade, sexually pure, experienced in the loving care of others" and therefore "better fitted than men to fight for social justice and to advance the well-being of womankind and mankind alike." Their exclusion from male-dominated institutions and their shared experience in a variety of reform fields reinforced a gendered perspective that joined women across classes.[48] Julia Lathrop, a Hull-House veteran, effectively used her position as head of the U.S. Children's Bureau to create a cadre of female staff and department heads who made the bureau a vehicle for child welfare policy at the national level. When her request for an increased appropriation was in jeopardy, she turned naturally to the "female dominion" of reform for assistance. Mobilizing support through networks of settlement house reformers, state committees of the National Child Labor Committee, woman's clubs, the Mothers' Congress, and the Russell Sage Foundation, Lathrop got Congress in April 1914 to reconsider and fund her full request.[49]

The National Consumers' League functioned as one of the primary spheres of female activism in the Progressive Era. The NCL, together with the General Federation of Women's Clubs and the Women's Trade Union League, assumed chief responsibility for putting protective legislation for female and child workers on the nation's legislative agenda. Florence Kelley drew directly on her experience in Illinois to promote campaigns for restricting working hours for women in states across the country. Gradually, the NCL shifted its focus from organizing boycotts against firms that were unfair to their employees to coordinating the fight for protective legislation. The league fostered local and state coalitions that led the fight for state legislation. Between 1900 and 1917, NCL-led coalitions won shorter hours legislation in sixteen states; only nine states lacked any regulation of the working day for women.[50]

Local chapters of the General Federation of Woman's Clubs and some state and local unions affiliated with the American Federation of Labor typically functioned as partners of the NCL in these coalitions. At biennial gatherings of the GFWC, settlement house activists and factory inspectors regularly appeared to educate club women about the importance of restricting overwork and did so invariably in the language of maternalism. Speaking at the biennial conference in 1910, Ella Haas, a factory inspector in Ohio, drew on her own experience to implore women: "Use your influence which God has given you for the protection and for the preservation of the womanhood of our country. . . . I am advocating an eight-hour day from my own experience. I know that . . . when I was working ten hours . . . I was not fit to go into any man's home and be the proper wife or mother of that home. Do you want your daughter to be robbed of that God-given privilege? Now think of the other Mother."[51]

The NCL helped create legal space for protective legislation. This was no mean feat in the aftermath of *Ritchie v. The People,* which overturned an Illinois law restricting working hours for women in 1895, and the suffocating effect of *Lochner v. New York* (1905), in which the U.S. Supreme Court threw out a law restricting the hours of labor for male bakers. The turning point came in 1908. The NCL believed that the appeal to the Supreme Court of an Oregon case, *Muller v. Oregon,* might be the opportunity to establish the legality of laws protecting vulnerable workers. A Portland laundry had required a female employee to work beyond the ten-hour limit for women stipulated in a 1903 Oregon law. The owner, Curt Muller, was fined ten dollars and appealed.[52] The Oregon Supreme Court upheld the fine, but with the support of the laundry owners association, Muller took the case to the U.S. Supreme Court. Florence Kelley and Josephine Goldmark approached Louis D. Brandeis of Boston to take the case. He agreed on the condition that the NCL, in a very short period of time, produce as much documentation as possible on the deleterious effects of overwork on women. In Brandeis's judgment, they had to call into question the principle, enunciated by the majority in the *Lochner* case, that "no reasonable foundation" existed for treating a shorter hours law "as a health law." The courts had affirmed that under some circumstances, for public health and welfare, the Fourteenth Amendment's protection against the state depriving a person of "life, liberty or property" could be abrogated. The arguments on behalf of sex-differentiated use of state police power to protect women workers had been well rehearsed before Muller. Indeed, *Ritchie* stands as the lone exception in the cases involving laws specifically restricting the hours of women's work. In this respect, it was not only the influence of the famous "Brandeis brief," written by Goldmark, but also the precedents established in state court decisions that disposed the Supreme Court unanimously to uphold the Oregon hours law.[53]

Nonetheless, Goldmark's Brandeis brief in *Muller* proved to be a powerful weapon focusing the Court's attention on the "type of worker to be protected."[54] The brief's ninety-six pages demonstrated that overwork did impair the health and well-being of women. Drawing on research, much of it from international sources assembled by Kelley and Goldmark, it documented the toll long working hours took on the health and safety of women workers, on the "inevitable neglect" of their children, and on the destruction of their "moral fibre." Using what Oliver Wendell Holmes Jr. called "experience" rather than the narrow logic of the law, Brandeis established, with support of the reform community, a new basis for justifying statist intervention in the marketplace. Justice Brewer, writing for the unanimous court, accepted the maternalist logic that underlay the case Brandeis (and Kelley and Goldmark) made. In the narrow legal space left by *Lochner,* restricting the working hours for women became "reasonable" under the law only by arguing that the "two sexes differ in structure of body, in the functions to be performed by each, in the amount of physical strength, in the capacity for long-continued labor, particularly when done standing, the influence of vigorous health upon the future well-being of the race."[55]

Over the next several years, the NCL called on Brandeis repeatedly to extend the arguments used in *Muller* to cases in other states and to cases involving a minimum wage for women. For Kelley, the most gratifying decision came when the Illinois court reversed the fifteen-year-old *Ritchie* decision that had effectively stifled her work as Illinois factory inspector. Kelley noted that "the thousands of women and girls in Illinois whose fatigue will at once be reduced" were not the only beneficiaries of this case. The *Ritchie* decision had stifled progress for fifteen years. "This mildewing influence is now at an end, and we can go forward with new hope and assurance . . . in every state, and to all industries in the census period 1910–1920."[56] Kelley's optimism reflected a view that organized women had made the case for the use of government police power to protect society's most vulnerable populations. "Governmental maternalism" had been validated by a judiciary still fundamentally committed to individual property rights.[57]

Taken together, these key court decisions—*Ritchie, Lochner,* and *Muller*—reflected the gradual triumph of protectionism and a gendered, cross-class reform vision that lay at the heart of the Progressive movement. Effective though the coalition was that Florence Kelley and her compatriots fashioned and sustained, it faced real limits. The campaign for minimum wage laws for women did not enjoy the same support and was enacted in only a handful of states. To Kelley's great disappointment, the trade union movement, fearing the imposition of state-enforced limits on male wages, withheld its support for general minimum wage legislation and at best declared itself "neutral" on minimum wages for women. Samuel Gompers would not concede even this point, declaring, somewhat cynically given the federation's history, "Working Women, *Organize!*"[58]

Yet many reformers saw protective legislation as an opening wedge precisely for what Gompers and the AFL most feared, government-sanctioned protection of all workers, male and female, young and old. Lillian Wald wrote the U.S. Commission on Industrial Relations in 1914 to assert the wider principle: "Miss Kelley and I both hope very much that your Industrial Relations Commission will find it wise to make your recommendations for industry itself, rather than for women and children as distinct from boys and men."[59] Within trades in which women workers were a significant factor, union support for protective legislation became a means for excluding women by making the cost of their labor less competitive. John R. Commons argued that competition from women and children weakened "the wage bargaining power of men," and therefore, "a law restricting the hours of women and children may also be looked upon as a law to protect men in their bargaining power." Jane Norman Smith of the National Women's Party paraphrased the argument more baldly. Despite all the professed humanitarian concern for the conditions of women's labor, she believed, male trade unionists saw shorter hours legislation for women as a way to "drive the women out of the trade as fast as possible."[60]

Although reformers and trade unionists alike supported the ideal of a "family wage," they sought protective legislation for different reasons. In the eyes of many reformers, such protection would ameliorate the conditions women workers faced and might lead to statist protection for workers in general. For male trade unionists, such legislation, if useful at all, might enhance the ability of working men to bargain for more favorable wages and hours. By raising the cost of employing single women, such laws might ultimately drive them from the workplace and restore the family wage ideal of the domestic sphere. Both argued their positions based on conceptions of women's difference, but whereas reformers looked to cross-class maternalism to protect women's status as workers, trade unionists submerged women's interests within a campaign for collectively bargained improvements that would enable male workers to support their dependents and keep them out of the workplace.[61]

The Woman's City Club and the WTUL

The cross-class vision of female reformers is evident not only in the efforts of settlement house workers and in the National Consumers' League's campaigns for protective legislation. It surfaced repeatedly in municipal campaigns for garbage collection, public education, and the limits on police power undertaken by groups like the Woman's City Club of Chicago. The civic consciousness of woman's club activists transcended the narrow class perspective of their counterparts in the male City Club.[62]

The City Club women viewed the whole city as a community and argued for solutions to problems that affected all city dwellers. This led them to support municipalization of waste disposal, mediation of strikes, restrictions on the use of police power, and vocational education as means to provide "general education for citizenship." They applied the model of their domestic role as middle-class women to the wider community. Settlement worker Mary McDowell viewed "the struggle within the city" as "a fight for the welfare of all the children of all the people." And president of the Woman's Club, Louise deKoven Bowen, asked members to imagine a different kind of city: "Suppose we had a system of municipal relief which is built upon the principle that the community is one great family and that each member of it is bound to help the other, the burden of support falling on all alike?"[63]

Ideal as such cross-class alliances may have seemed in the eyes of middle-class women reformers, sustaining them in practice was not always so easy, even within the sisterhood of activists. The experience of the Women's Trade Union League and its New York branch is especially revealing. A group of social reformers established the WTUL in 1903. As historian Nancy Schrom Dye has noted, early WTUL activists believed that women could "surmount social and ethnic differences and unite on the basis of their common femininity."[64] They looked beyond the settlement house for an institution that would promote the unionization of women workers and pressure the AFL to make good on its commitment to organize women as well as men. Gertrude Barnum left work with Hull-House to play a central role in founding both the Chicago and New York branches of the WTUL. In 1905, she recalled that the settlement did much "to make the lives of working people less grim and hard." It may have "introduced into their lives books and flowers and music," but although it served as a meeting place and a nursery, "it did not raise their wages or shorten their hours."[65]

Socialist William English Walling and Mary Kenney O'Sullivan, a former bookbinder and associate of Hull-House turned AFL organizer, initiated meetings of social reformers and trade unionists in Boston to form the WTUL. Conceived as a cross-class institution of working women and social reform "allies," the WTUL, through Walling's initiative, sought leaders initially among nationally prominent reformers. At the outset, this "small band of enthusiasts" had little success attracting working women to its ranks. Historian Sarah Deutsch has described two alternative narratives that have dominated the history of the WTUL in a variety of cities. One stresses the successful efforts of working women and middle-class supporters to find common ground; the other portrays a WTUL "riddled with class conflict and dysfunctional."[66]

The energetic participation of middle-class allies led to their domination of the WTUL in its early years. Their access to funds, organizational skills, and desire to "be of use" set the tone for the organization. Rheta Childe Dorr, an early but transitory member, expressed faith in the class-bridging ideals that women brought to such activity. "Women now form a new social group, separate and to a degree homogeneous," she noted. "Already they have evolved a group opinion and a group ideal."[67]

But as the organization attracted working women, such as Leonora O'Reilly and Rose Schneiderman, differences in class background became a source of tension. WTUL functions such as "interpretive dance recitals" and "teas" designed to "stir up enthusiasm among the girls" had the opposite effect. On occasion, working women mustered the courage to give voice to the discomfort they felt. Leonora O'Reilly, an Irish shirtmaker and a key figure in the league, found that "contact with the Lady does harm in the long run." Others simply stayed away. Mary van Kleeck, just beginning her investigations of women's work, recorded her puzzlement at the inconsistency with which the working girls she recruited to the Lilies of the Valley club actually attended its meetings.[68] As the "allies" struggled to overcome the gulf of class experience that separated them from working women, they asserted their determination not to be driven from the organization. When O'Reilly criticized Laura Elliot for her "condescending attempts to uplift working women," Elliot defended her efforts and by implication those of other social reformers involved in the league:

> You cannot push me out and you cannot make me afraid of my working girl sisters or render me self-conscious before them, I refuse to be afraid to take them to the Metropolitan Museum and *teach* them and *help* them. . . . I have no fear in putting my side of the proposition up to any working girl. I'm not afraid to tell her that I have something to bring her and I'm never afraid that she will misunderstand or resent what I say. She needs my present help just as the whole race needs her uprising.[69]

A gulf of experience and culture but also differences over the significance of their class backgrounds divided WTUL members. Vida Scudder, who along with other middle-class women believed she could escape the constraint of her class, asserted that "class will never become to our minds a permanent factor of social life."[70] AFL organizer Helen Marot, herself from a comfortable background, commented favorably on the demeanor of Carola Woerishoffer, a wealthy New York WTULer. "The entire naturalness of her attitude towards her fellow workers, her apparent unconsciousness of any differences between her and them, made it possible for her to fall at once into friendly relations," she declared. "She was one of them."[71] But the few working-class activists in the league leadership did not always see relations in the same way. Leonora O'Reilly periodically resigned in frustration over the attempts by middle-class reformers to control the organization. She attributed her resignation in January 1906 to "an overdose of allies."[72] Her letter to the executive board alluded to a decision taken in "the best interests of the labor movement" after attending a state federation meeting and seeing that "the trade unionists must work out and solve their own problems in their own way." She desired to be free to work with labor "whereso ever I see fit" without being classed an "interloper."[73]

The WTUL faced frustration when it attempted to put its ideals into practice. Constrained by the inexperience and cultural miscues of its elite leadership, the organization enjoyed little success expanding its base among working women. Rose Schneiderman, who was elected to the executive board of the New York WTUL in 1905 and vice president the following year, told the board that their lack of organizing success came from the fact that they approached the work "like scholars, not trade unionists." They collected data, established committees, and lectured working women instead of allowing them to lead.[74]

The New York WTUL grew frustrated with the limited return on its efforts to encourage unionization of the city's laundresses, paper-box makers, retail clerks, and waitresses. It shifted strategy to respond to "actual appeals for organization" from working women, as opposed to efforts directed at organizing the most degraded trades.[75] WTUL policy, however, directed women wanting its support to avoid militant tactics in favor of "practical, orderly methods" and to seek affiliation with the AFL, even when male-dominated unions gave them little support.[76] But working-class activists such as Pauline Newman, Fannia Cohn, and Rose Pesotta faced continuous frustration with the male-dominated International Ladies' Garment Workers' Union (ILGWU). During a cap makers' strike, men got strike benefits as "breadwinners" and striking women got none. Pauline Newman quit at one point during an organizing campaign in Cleveland, when the ILGWU wanted her to work for less than male organizers.[77]

Between 1909 and 1913, developments beyond the influence of the league intensified debates about its relationship to AFL craft unions. In November 1909, young shirtwaist makers in New York responded enthusiastically to Clara Lemlich's call for a general strike in the trade. For a two-month period, the "uprising of the 20,000" captured the imaginations of some league activists. But neither the leadership of the WTUL nor the male leaders of Local 25 of the ILGWU, the union nominally in charge of the strike, could control the direction the strike took. When the police used rough tactics to control working-class women on the picket lines, elite supporters from the WTUL joined the strikers. The presence of the "mink brigade" lessened the police harassment but also reinforced the sense of class difference working-class activists felt.[78] When the strikers rejected a proposed settlement that granted improvements in wages and hours but maintained the open shop, many elite supporters severed their relations with the strikers.[79]

Although only piecemeal gains resulted from the shirtwaist strikes, a general strike of cloak makers in early 1913 and an earlier brilliant success in the 1910 Hart, Schaffner, and Marx strike in Chicago made the role of the WTUL more prominent but also more divisive. Helen Marot was distrustful of the

ILGWU leadership, both because it was male and because it was socialist, and argued for the WTUL to support conservative leaders and businesslike methods and to advance women to leadership positions in their unions. The dominant voices in the WTUL had no faith in the general strike or the socialist leadership of the ILGWU.[80]

The 1910 strike against Hart, Schaffner, and Marx in Chicago took on national significance as one of the largest local general strikes in the garment trade. Beginning as a spontaneous outbreak on September 22, 1910, ignited by two young working girls who refused to accept a cut in the rate for seaming pants, the strike grew into a "war" that pitted forty thousand strikers against one of the largest clothing manufacturers in the country. The Chicago WTUL and other social reformers involved themselves directly in the strike, offering moral support, occasional picket line duty, and a conduit to influential businessmen and politicians.[81] But the league also framed the strike in terms of its own "political grammar," emphasizing "Christian fellowship, the sanctity of motherhood, and the home." A league pamphlet warned of the perils ahead for class relations and a democratic society if the needs of these immigrant workers were not addressed:

> Are those Bohemians, Poles, Italians, and Russian Jews to become loyal and law-abiding American citizens? Or shall we allow them, through neglect and misunderstanding to grow embittered and resentful to the prosperity in which they have no part? Despair is the surest road to Anarchy. Indifference to this struggle on the part of the well-to-do is criminally selfish and short-sighted. The political and social as well as the economic well-being of our City depends on the education in citizenship we give to our Foreign population.[82]

The paradox of WTUL's faithfulness to the AFL was most tellingly revealed in its position during the Lawrence textile strike in 1912. The strike of unskilled and largely unorganized immigrant female operatives drew AFL hostility from the outset. They struck against a wage reduction that accompanied a legislatively mandated reduction in women's hours of work. The fact that the Industrial Workers of the World stepped in to provide strike assistance further alienated the AFL. The strike had deep roots in the work lives and traditions of collective action of Lawrence's laboring women. Their direct action and control of community space set the terms for the IWW's participation and the posture of the AFL.[83] A small, male craft local of the United Textile Workers tried to declare the strike off after a short time, and the WTUL officially terminated its strike support, producing fierce debate within the organization. The president of the Boston League, Sue Ainslie Clark, put the matter squarely to her sisters: "Are we, the Women's Trade Union League, to ally our-selves with the 'standpatters' of the Labor Movement or are we to hold our-selves ready to aid the insurgents—those who are freely fighting the fight of the exploited, the oppressed, and the weak among the workers?"[84] Such frus-trations led some WTUL members to propose greater flexibility and alternate forms of women's trade unionism; others simply grew disillusioned with the labor movement. But as the period of general strikes ebbed, the dominant leadership faction in the WTUL remained committed to AFL principles.

Ethnic and racial tensions reinforced class tensions within the league. The general strikes in the garment trades gave priority to the organization of Jew-ish and Italian women. When the momentum from initial successes flagged, a native-born faction within the WTUL argued that such immigrant women were not organizable and supported a reallocation of resources to other ef-forts. In New York, Helen Marot and Melinda Scott on the one hand, and Rose Schneiderman and Pauline Newman on the other, reflected these divisions. Schneiderman and Newman had joined the garment workers organizing campaign during the 1909 shirtwaist strike. Schneiderman became the league's primary organizer on the Lower East Side throughout the years of general strikes.[85] Melinda Scott had organized the English-speaking, uptown shirtwaist and dress shops. Enjoying some success among American-born workers, Scott and Marot argued in 1911 that the league should cease sup-porting efforts to build and sustain organization among Jewish workers and concentrate instead on "American girls." Although the argument may have expressed the needs and prejudices of American women, it also reflected the biases of many middle-class allies. Marot told the executive board of the New York WTUL in 1911, "We have realized for several years that the Russian Jew had little sense of administration and we have been used to ascribing their failures to their depending solely on their emotions and not on constructive work." Henceforth, organizing of immigrant working girls would be, she an-nounced, on "a basis approved by American trade unionists."[86]

These tensions within the league intensified in 1914, when, after Mary Dreier's resignation, Scott and Schneiderman contested the presidency of the WTUL. Scott won by a slim four votes, but according to Pauline New-man, the voting divided sharply along lines of class and ethnicity. Writing to Schneiderman after the election, Newman noted,

> Your vote, with the exception of three or four was a real trade Union vote. On the other hand, the vote for Linda was purely a vote of the social workers. Peo-ple who have not been near the League for four or five years, came to vote.

Imagine Frances Kellor and Mrs. Simcovitch [*sic*] and Ida Rau [*sic*]. . . . They have not been near the League for ever so long, but they could not get the girls from the Unions to vote against you. . . . So you see, that nothing was left undone by them to line up a vote for Linda on the ground that you were a socialist, a jewes [*sic*] and one interested in suffrage.[87]

Schneiderman focused on the role played by Helen Marot and other "American" League activists. "Never you mind," she wrote Newman, "Helen's day will come. Some day she will stand with the mask torn from her face and then everybody shall know that all her radicalism is not worth a pinch of snuff. . . . There is more trade unionism in my little finger than there is in her whole make up."[88]

Although class and ethnic divisions may not in fact have been quite so indelibly drawn, divisions are nevertheless undeniable. If the "uprising of the laborers" between 1909 and 1914 renewed the prospects for class war, undermined the legitimacy of the AFL as the embodiment of the aspirations of American workers, and fundamentally challenged the cross-class project of the social reformers, it did not ultimately unseat more conservative, middle-class, native-born leaders of the WTUL. After 1914, the league shifted toward more direct support of suffrage and protective legislation within a wider coalition of women's organizations. However, unionists such as Newman and Schneiderman continued, after a brief hiatus, to play significant roles within the organization. Others drifted away disillusioned with the failure of the organization to support the aspirations of the unskilled.[89]

The class tensions within the world of female reform played themselves out in still another arena. The campaign for suffrage had acquired an elite cast in the late nineteenth century. Elizabeth Cady Stanton and others argued that enfranchised (elite) women would act as a brake on political corruption fostered by the unlimited franchise for men. Stanton and her allies believed that with suffrage, elite women would guide working-class women in their use of the vote.[90] Stanton's daughter, Harriot Stanton Blatch, however, broke with her mother's elite framework in the early twentieth century and focused on the common bond of women's work as the justification for suffrage. Through her activism in the WTUL, she pursued the ideal of a movement that joined working women's industrial concerns with a broadened campaign for suffrage. In 1907, she announced the formation of the Equality League of Self-Supporting Women and sought to make the interests of working women central to the campaign for suffrage.[91] But no sooner did the suffrage movement open its door to working women through the Equality League than elite women reasserted their control in ways that marginalized the class concerns of trade union activists while professing to enlist all classes of women in the suffrage campaign. A new group, the American Suffragettes, promoted militant tactics of the British Women's Social and Political Union, but its open air activities increasingly featured elite spokeswomen. Mrs. B. Borrman Wells spoke of the movement as "the union of women of all shades of political thought and of all ranks of society on the single issue of their political enfranchisement."[92] Vida Scudder mourned the "loss of a certain aroma" of voluntary effort and utopian spirit that had infused the movement "as the crusading spirit of the early years yielded to a well-organized competency." But like many reformers, she welcomed the invigorating cross-class influence of "another force which commanded my warm sympathy—the economic emancipation of women."[93]

By 1910, the movement was enjoying growing support from elite women. According to historian Carol Ellen DuBois, "By the time suffragette militance became a national movement, its working-class origins and trade union associations had been submerged, and it was in the hands of women of wealth." But in a very real sense, the problem lay with the movement's inability or unwillingness to acknowledge that class mattered. "Class," in a word, "was the contradiction at the suffrage movement's heart."[94] And by extension, that same contradiction lay at the heart of the Progressive movement in general. The reinvention of "the people" was a project around which a broad spectrum of Progressives could rally in the name of a cross-class democratizing agenda. But that project also redefined the meaning of class by emphasizing ethnic and racial boundaries of difference. Beyond the people lay a heterogeneous mass of new immigrants, African Americans, and the laboring poor, unprepared for citizenship or incapable of exercising the democratic responsibilities reformers saw as essential to progress. In emphasizing such racially defined boundaries, reformers codified new limits on the scope of their class-bridging project.

6

The Boundaries of Difference

Each class or section of the nation is becoming conscious of an opposition between its standards and the activities and tendencies of some less developed class. The South has its negro, the city has its slums, organized labor has its "scab" workman, and the temperance movement has its drunkard and saloon-keeper. The friends of American institutions fear the ignorant immigrant, and the workingman dislikes the Chinese. Every one is beginning to differentiate those with proper qualifications for citizenship from some class or classes which he wishes to restrain or to exclude from society.

—Simon Patten, *Theory of Social Forces*, 1896

So long, then, as humble black folk, voluble with thanks receive barrels of old clothes from lordly and generous whites, there is much mental and moral satisfaction. But when the black man begins to dispute the white man's title to certain alleged bequests of the Father's in wage and position, authority and training; and when his attitude toward charity is sullen anger rather than humble jollity; when he insists on his human right to swagger and swear and waste—then the spell is suddenly broken and the philanthropist is apt to be ready to believe that Negroes are impudent, that the South is right, and that Japan wants to fight us.

—W. E. B. Du Bois, "The Souls of White Folk," 1910

Progressive reformers believed that harmony between the classes would come only by building democratic community. But like Simon Patten, they worried that racial and ethnic differences would impede that progress.[1] Society's capacity to prepare racially distinct people for the responsibilities of citizenship and ultimately assimilate them remained a central problem with which the reformers wrestled. Some, such as labor economist John R. Commons and journalist Ray Stannard Baker, believed the process would be protracted; others, such as Jane Addams and Mary White Ovington, had confidence that it could be accomplished more quickly with the correct approach.

If Progressives conjured up an ideal of the people as a body of citizens untainted by parochial class loyalties, they also circumscribed that citizenry by drawing around it sharply defined racial and ethnic boundaries. Racial differences, etched in reformers' minds, seemed profound and enduring. African Americans and poor immigrants posed a fundamental challenge to the reformers' ideal of a democratic society. They believed that blacks' social background and lack of education, legacies of slavery, left them unprepared for the responsibilities of citizenship and justified their continued marginalization. Likewise, reformers doubted the civic capacity of the newest immigrants, unaccustomed as they were to life in a democratic society and wedded to Old World cultural ties.[2]

By the early twentieth century, reformers saw the primary threat to democratic community coming from an unassimilated, "submerged tenth," which became easy prey for ethnic political leaders interested in perpetuating their own power. These prototypical machine politicians threatened the fabric of democratic community. Fear of their corrupting influence produced among reformers sympathy for southern Progressives who argued that premature black enfranchisement had fostered political corruption in their region. Commons and other reformers accepted the reigning scholarly interpretation of William R. Dunning and Ulrich B. Phillips that Reconstruction had failed by instituting black suffrage and thereby corrupting democratic institutions. As Commons described it, "By the cataclysm of a war in which it took no part, this race, after many thousand years of savagery and two centuries of slavery, was suddenly let loose into the liberty of citizenship and electoral suffrage." He worried that without "intelligence, self-control, and capacity for cooperation," self-government might be unrealistic. Under such conditions, "the ballot only makes way for the 'boss,' the corruptionist, or the oligarchy."[3]

Most social reformers found it difficult to challenge existing racial norms or even imagine an alternative to them. Citizenship by definition entailed assimilation to "whiteness."[4] They saw in eugenics a "scientific" tool for improving "these people" in ways that might make universal citizenship eventually plausible.[5] The promise of a eugenically reengineered human race proved intriguing. Reformers consorted rather effortlessly with those who sought to restrict immigration, and they worried about the prospect of "race suicide" in the face of swelling numbers of new immigrants. At the 1910 conventions of the National Conference of Charities and Corrections, Mary Richmond quite naturally listed the Immigration Restriction League among significant national reform organizations, and Jane Addams, on behalf of the NCCC's Immigration Committee, welcomed Jeremiah Jenks, a restrictionist member of the U.S. Immigration Commission, to speak to the convention on "The Racial Problem in Immigration."[6]

Race and Nineteenth-Century Reform

In the Civil War's aftermath, northerners came to interpret that conflict as an epic campaign to renew democracy in the face of an expansive slave-power aristocracy. But by the end of the century, Progressive Era reformers regarded the collapse of Reconstruction, the scandals associated with postwar economic expansion, and the corrupting influence of urban political machines as problems rooted in the social politics of Reconstruction itself. They called for new campaigns to restore democracy and tracked postwar corruption to one specific cause: the manipulation of dependent peoples, whether black or immigrant, not yet schooled in the ways of democracy. Northerners weary of the burdens of reconstructing the South, like white southerners eager to claim their own "natural" right to rule, asserted the incapacity of former slaves for self-government. That explanation fit the racial views harbored by most white Americans.[7] In a similar vein, northerners observed that sharply rising levels of immigration after the war and increasing congestion in cities bred a politics they viewed as especially unsavory. They readily turned to the prewar stock of nativist ideas that emphasized the unfitness of most immigrants for citizenship and prescribed a long period of preparation.[8]

The cyclical traumas of the American economy in the late nineteenth century intensified mugwump reformers' preoccupation with the perils democracy faced. The prospect of a new civil war between classes after 1877 increased the gravity of those perils. Class interest seemed at moments of economic unrest potentially to fuse restless black and white workers in the South and native and foreign-born workers in the North into a new proletariat. But at other moments, ethnic and racial consciousness shattered any broader sense of class identity. When members of the Workingmen's Party of San Francisco or the Knights of Labor in Rock Springs, Wyoming, attacked Chinese laborers, or when white workers in Richmond, Virginia, rejected the official interracialism of the KOL to support the White Man's Party, they demonstrated the centrifugal pull of racial identity.[9]

Gilded Age social reformers, whether of the mugwump or antimonopoly variety, perceived the problem of democratic renewal in distinctly racial terms. The colonization of former slaves in Africa again seemed appealing as a solution to the social problems engendered by Reconstruction.[10] Although social gospeler Washington Gladden's racial views would moderate in the twentieth century, especially after encountering W. E. B. Du Bois's works, he, like many of his reform colleagues, earlier expressed skepticism about the readiness of southern blacks and poor whites for the franchise. "Universal suffrage in a population of this sort means universal pillage and universal war," he declared.[11] Southern Progressives believed that the tasks of reform could be accomplished only by subordinating the race issue. They witnessed in the 1890s a radical, southern brand of populism shattered by the renewal of race politics. For years, the political flotsam of that movement animated a demagogic politics of race, evident in the "strange careers" of white politicians such as Tom Watson, Ben Tillman, and Cole Blease.[12] In a pragmatic reading of the new landscape of southern race politics, Booker T. Washington advocated political and social accommodation by blacks that for all intents and purposes conceded their unreadiness for civic rights. Washington's views appealed to white social reformers because he did not challenge their idea that racial fitness determined readiness for democratic responsibilities.[13]

In the North, coalitions of charity reformers, disciples of Henry George, and a cadre of influential political economists argued for immigration restriction that addressed what one charity worker called immigrants' "hereditary character of pauperism and crime." Persistent agitation had led to the Immigration Act of 1882 that federalized supervision of immigration and imposed modest restrictions against the admittance of immigrant "convicts, lunatics, idiots, and persons likely to become a public charge." Trade unionists, inside and outside the Knights of Labor, successfully fought for legislation prohibiting contract labor, a form of foreign labor recruitment that one critic described as the shipment by monopolists of "so many cattle, large numbers of degraded, ignorant, brutal . . . foreign serfs." Enacted in 1885, the law prohibiting contract labor had only limited practical effect but great symbolic value to a hard-pressed labor movement.[14] Finally, 1882 also saw the passage of federal legislation excluding new Chinese immigrants, who had become the subject of unremitting and frequently violent agitation since the mid-1870s in California and other parts of the West. A cross-class coalition led by San Francisco socialist Dennis Kearney, the Workingmen's Party, and a host of Democratic politicians succeeded after repeated attempts in forcing Congress to prohibit new Chinese immigration after 1882.[15]

The tide of racial exclusion rose steadily in the South after the demise of

Reconstruction. Although substantial numbers of black voters in the region remained part of the electorate for at least a decade after the Compromise of 1877, and although the pattern of segregation of public facilities was uneven at best until the 1890s, the South moved unmistakably toward a Jim Crow society. Other states quickly followed the adoption by Mississippi in 1890 of a plan for a state-level constitutionally mandated poll tax, literacy test, and the granting of great latitude to local registrars in determining fitness to vote. The Supreme Court's decision in *Plessy v. Ferguson* (1895) confirmed the new Jim Crow order that had already taken shape in much of the South. A division of society along racial lines under the masquerade of "separate but equal" would henceforth be enforced. In an atmosphere of escalating violence and lynching, black Americans sought refuge in their own communities. Many Progressive reformers, South and North, viewed voting restrictions and social segregation as a necessary, if sometimes excessive, preparation if lower-class blacks were eventually to exercise democratic rights.[16]

Race Improvement

Racialist thinking came naturally to Progressive social theorists. As historian George Fredrickson has shown, Lester F. Ward, Thomas Cooley, E. A. Ross, and John R. Commons rejected the radical individualism of social Darwinists. They found appealing Lamarckian ideas about biological differences among races and the possibilities for race improvement. French biologist Jean-Baptiste Lamarck had held that characteristics acquired through adaptation to the environment could be inherited. Some social theorists in the later nineteenth century saw in the idea of the inheritance of acquired traits the possibility for "race improvement" through changes in the social environment. They argued that diffusion of education among "inferior" races could enhance their capacity for the responsibilities of democratic citizenship.[17]

Many members of the reform community were racial accommodationists. Unlike the "competitive" racists, they did not view racial competition and conflict as inevitable and irreconcilable, but they saw the world as racially ordered. Sociologist Franklin Giddings regarded "ethnical subordination" as endemic. Higher and lower races, he believed, were products of historical development and only gradually susceptible to "purposive association."[18]

For Progressives, the race problem, like every other problem, manifested itself fundamentally as a problem of democracy. John R. Commons worried that "other races and peoples, accustomed to despotism and even savagery, and wholly unused to self-government, have been thrust into the delicate fabric" of democracy. The consequence, he believed, was that we "despotize our institutions in order to control these dissident elements, though still optimistically holding that we retain the original democracy." For Commons and other Progressives, racial difference held the prospect of hardening into class difference that potentially undermined democracy. In his view, the immigration of peoples unprepared for the responsibilities of democratic citizenship increased the danger of a society in which class division might be reinforced.[19]

Pessimistic and optimistic strains of progressive thought on race intermingled. Commons might assert the relative immutability of race characteristics, which would change, if at all, only over a long time, yet he, like other Progressives, invested great hope in a gradual process of preparation for citizenship. "This time the work will begin at the bottom by educating the negro for the ballot," he stated, "instead of beginning at the top by giving him the ballot before he knows what it should do for him."[20] He also advocated legislation not simply to limit but improve immigration. Only those who fell below certain standards would be excluded.[21]

The optimistic Lamarckian perspective leavened reformers' underlying pessimism about the possibilities for race assimilation. Some asserted that environmental influences—education, for instance—could alter inherited traits and foster race improvement. Whether segregated circumstances or direct tutelage by more civilized people offered the best prospects for improvement depended on social and regional circumstances. Southern Progressives such as Edgar Gardner Murphy believed segregation fostered racial progress. Such views also led northern philanthropists to support Booker T. Washington's program of racial uplift. Although leading proponents of the social gospel such as Walter Rauschenbusch were largely preoccupied with the problems of an industrial society, they nevertheless asked whites to adopt a "missionary and pedagogical spirit" toward blacks. Writing in the *American Missionary,* Rauschenbusch urged fellow white Protestants to reach out to the black man: "Urge him along the road of steady and intelligent labor, of property rights, of family fidelity, of hope and self-confidence, and of pride and joy in his race achievements."[22]

Edgar Gardner Murphy saw the tasks of racial uplift complicating the perfection of democracy. The mingling of races, he believed, required a different understanding of democracy: "It is no easy problem,—this problem of the strong living with the weak . . . so living as to assure peace without afflicting desolation, as to preserve order without defeating justice, as to [upbuild] a state which will express the life of its higher group without enfeebling or destroying that waiting manhood of weaker peoples which itself craves and deserves expression."[23]

Progressive journalist Ray Stannard Baker felt drawn to "follow the color line" in the South and the North after a brutal race riot in Atlanta in late September 1906 left twelve dead and seventy injured. Baker's inquiry into the condition of the Negro and the state of race relations codified progressive views on the race question. He also demonstrated, as Du Bois's biographer David Levering Lewis has shown, white Progressives' ignorance in matters of race and their unwillingness to challenge the deeply ingrained racial attitudes of whites.[24] Classification of blacks into categories of "good" and "bad" served as a rationale for the perpetuation of social barriers to racial mixing.[25] Troubled by the gulf separating "the best elements of the two races," Baker nonetheless focused on the criminal influence of the "worthless Negro." W. E. B. Du Bois, after reading a draft portion of the study, urged Baker to emphasize the social and economic conditions Negroes faced rather than "the influence of crime on race relations," which would only reinforce whites' prejudices. Baker ignored the advice.[26] Like other Progressives, he accepted southern whites' view of Reconstruction as a tragedy that revealed the unfitness of freed slaves for citizenship. But unlike many southerners, he professed optimism that "time and patience" could improve African Americans' fitness. "The vast majority of Negroes (and many foreigners and 'poor whites') are still densely ignorant, and have little appreciation of the duties of citizenship," he wrote. "It seems right that they should be required to wait before being allowed to vote until they are prepared."[27] Drawn to the racial uplift message of Booker T. Washington more than to "men like Dr. DuBois who agitate for rights," Baker viewed Jim Crow laws of the South as "the inevitable scaffolding of progress." Such laws, he argued, had unintended benefits: "For the white man has thus driven the Negroes together, forced ability to find its outlet in racial leadership, and by his severity produced a spirit of self-reliance which would not otherwise have existed."

Baker came back to a faith in education and in the "dignity of service" as the salvation for democracy. The challenge, as he and other Progressives viewed it, was to forge the sympathy and understanding that could link the best of both races: "Whether we like it or not the whole nation (indeed, the whole world) is tied by unbreakable bonds to its Negroes, its Chinamen, its slum-dwellers, its thieves, its murderers, its prostitutes. We cannot elevate ourselves by driving them back either with hatred or violence or neglect; but only by bringing them forward: by service."[28]

Like Baker, Theodore Roosevelt experienced an inner ideological war between racial nationalist and civic nationalist values that drew a sharp line of inferiority between the races while leaving open the door to civic life for qualified individuals. Writing in 1906, Roosevelt claimed no interest in allowing "the average Negro" the right to vote or permitting "Negro domination." Rather, he advocated only that "these occasionally good, well-educated, intelligent and honest colored men and women be given the pitiful chance to have a little reward, a little respect, a little regard, if they can by earnest useful work succeed in winning it."[29]

Assimilationists and Pluralists

Nowhere was the project of assimilating the racially and ethnically different more actively undertaken than among the settlement folk. They believed the immigrant neighborhoods served by settlement houses contributed to the construction of a new national identity, an "international nationality" that transcended the "racial and religious hatreds . . . of a selfish nationalism at home," as Grace Abbott put it. John Dewey saw in this new nationality a potentially harmonious whole.[30] But it was among individuals, not sociocultural groups, that such amalgamation occurred. If immigrants brought "gifts," and Progressives certainly believed they did, they did so as individuals. Jane Addams recalled her own moment of discovery. Preoccupied at one point by her difficulties coming into "genuine relations with Italian women" who commonly lost touch with their Americanized children, she one day found herself hailed from a doorstep by an immigrant woman sitting in the sun holding a distaff of yarn. The woman brightly called out that when she had spun enough, she intended to make a pair of stockings for her daughter. From this cue, Addams developed the idea for a Labor Museum in which immigrant children might come to appreciate the lost crafts and talents of their elders. Such encounters might serve as the "beginning toward that education which Dr. Dewey defines as 'a continuing reconstruction of experience.'"[31]

Social scientists, like their activist colleagues in the settlements, viewed the survival of some traditional attributes as an inevitable aspect of the process of individual assimilation. But Simon Patten believed the weight of tradition also perpetuated "hereditary" differences in ways that stifled democracy. "[The man with the hoe] comes to us from yesterday's wrongs, and he generates beings who are carrying into to-morrow the birth-marks of to-day's evils," he wrote. "Men are molded into their classes by the pressure of social things accumulating generation after generation, which finally sum themselves into an acquired heredity binding men firmly to their places."[32]

The solvent of democracy, according to sociologist Robert Park, eventually promoted the formation of larger, more heterogeneous groups.[33]

In contrast to the dominant assimilationist strain in progressive social thought, immigrant intellectual Horace Kallen celebrated the perpetuation of diversity. But his views stood alone when he first articulated them. In an essay published in early 1915, "Democracy versus the Melting Pot: A Study of American Nationality," Kallen responded to the disquiet of Anglo-Americans reflected in E. A. Ross's recent book, *The Old World in the New.* Despite the proclamations of the Progressive Party for "human rights against property rights," the "Anglo-Saxon American," according to Kallen, was troubled less by economic than "ethnic disparity." Entrepreneurs produced ethnic diversity by seeking the cheapest labor; "greed has set the standard." Having created the problem, they grew anxious over "this perversion of our public life and social ideals."[34] In Kallen's view, the immigrants encountered Americanism as external and superficial while they experienced ethnic nationality as "intrinsic": "Men may change their clothes, their politics, their wives, their religions, their philosophies, to a greater or lesser extent: they cannot change their grandfathers." Immigrants expressed their "Natio" in language and in religion, which together worked against assimilation. The question then was, "What *shall* this cacophony become—a unison or a harmony?" He saw a process of "dissimilation" whereby life in the Republic fosters "the rise of the cultural consciousness and social autonomy of the immigrant." In sum, ironically, "Americanization has liberated nationality."[35]

What troubled Progressives such as Ross, according to Kallen, was not the growth of inequality but *"difference."* The program of "unison" implied forced Americanization, abolition of parochial education, enforced instruction in English, and its exclusive use in daily intercourse. A different version of democracy inspired Kallen's critique. He envisioned a "commonwealth of nationalities" in which immigrants enjoy "inalienable" liberty to maintain their "ancestrally determined" selfhood. As with the instruments of an orchestra, "so in society each ethnic group is the natural instrument, its spirit and culture are its theme and melody, and the harmony and dissonances and discords of them all make the symphony of civilization. . . . In the symphony of civilization the playing is the writing. . . . The range and variety of the harmonies may become wider and richer and more beautiful."[36] Dewey and other Progressives disagreed. The individual in the new sociocultural environment of America would change his orientation away from the traditional group. A new nationality, if not a new race, would emerge. But Kallen's "romantic racialism" did not logically lead to exclusion. Unlike racial exclusionists such as Madison Grant and Lothrop Stoddard, who also emphasized the permanent hereditary character of racial differences, Kallen believed diversity renewed and enriched democratic life.[37]

Kallen perceived that Progressive reformers conflated class and ethnic differences. Even as they hoped to solve the "class problem," they feared that new class divisions might develop and persist as a consequence of the persistent "peasantism" of hordes of new immigrants resistant to Americanism or the racial incapacity of African Americans to exercise the responsibilities of citizenship. The reformers then logically turned to immigration restriction, an active campaign of Americanization, and racial segregation as necessary components of democratic reform.

Many social commentators saw the domestic problem of racial assimilation as analogous to the task posed by the new imperial responsibilities America had acquired in the war with Spain. And here, too, racial thinking infected the visions of reformers as they examined the social needs of the new colonial possessions.

Progressives and the New Empire

The Spanish-American War, whether by design or accident, produced an insular empire for the United States and ignited a fierce debate over the meaning and advisability of this new departure. Although precedents and rationales abounded from the experience over three centuries of colonizing Indians within the American continental domain, the annexation of territories across the Pacific and in the Caribbean appeared to be novel. Progressives hardly stood on the sidelines of this debate. In many ways they became leading voices in *both* imperialist and anti-imperialist camps. Some saw in the colonizing enterprise the opportunity to test reform ideas in virgin territory without the corrupting influences of urban political machines and combative class interests. Whether pro or con, they shared to a very large extent a common racial discourse that led them either to embrace or disdain the enterprise.

Racial thinking infused the imperial enterprise with a legitimizing destiny born of nineteenth-century developments. A dozen years before the outbreak of the Spanish-American War, the Reverend Josiah Strong had marked Americans as "a race of unequaled energy" that would "impress its institutions upon mankind" and "spread itself across the earth." In so doing, it must inevitably "dispossess many weaker races, assimilate others, and mold the remainder, until, in a very true and important sense, it has Anglo-Saxonized mankind."[38]

In the throes of the controversy that swirled about the acquisition of dependent territories and peoples following the Treaty of Paris in 1899, proponents of expansion reiterated these sentiments. The editors of the *Outlook* in the summer of 1900 asked whether Americans should shrink from the policies of the immediately preceding years out of fear that such policies might mean imperialism, "or shall we rejoice in the opportunity which lies before us to extend over lands beyond the sea that sovereignty which has created in the wilderness the American Nation, in the faith that wherever our flag goes it will mean in the future, as it has in the past, justice and liberty?"[39]

For many advocates of imperial progressivism, the United States held a special responsibility to prepare benighted peoples for self-government. President William McKinley reported to a group of churchmen that he had sought divine guidance in reaching the conclusion that "there was nothing left for us to do but take them all, and to educate the Filipinos and uplift and Christianize them."[40] But numerous proponents of expansionism warned that the task of imparting democratic values was arduous. The capacity for self-government might come through "long centuries of training," as had been the case for Anglo-Saxons, or from "contiguity and companionship," as was the case for immigrants. But as the *Outlook* noted, to assume that such capacity "is possessed by a people without training, and to leave them to exercise it without supervision, counsel or control, would be a blunder only comparable to that of a father who should affirm that all children have a dormant capacity for self-support, and therefore the new-born babe may be left to take care of himself."[41]

Many Progressives, then, marched under the banner of an imperial experiment that sought to "save a harassed and distressed people from anarchy." The firm, guiding hand of reform would provide, through the exercise of "strong government," the infrastructure of stability and progress. In the Philippines, the Board of Commissioners appointed by President McKinley undertook to create that infrastructure: public revenues, an educational system, civil service, courts, and local government.[42] American military occupation and administration of Cuba between 1899 and 1902 provided what historian Howard Gillette has called a "workshop for American progressivism." With a decided bias toward urban development, Col. Leonard Wood, appointed military governor by fellow Rough Rider Theodore Roosevelt, set about reforming the legal and administrative fabric of Cuba. He instituted far-reaching legal reforms, a public-works program, model city charters, a railroad regulatory commission, and reforms in health, sanitation, and education. Administrative efficiency, what Wood called "a businesslike way of doing things," unencumbered by domestic politics may have been more easily instituted under military direction, but for a whole group of reformers the experiment held great lessons for the United States. Leo Rowe, a specialist in municipal reform, wrote extensively on American reform efforts in the former Spanish colonies. These efforts, he asserted, "will modify our political ideas . . . and react upon domestic politics, with the result of raising the level of public life."[43]

Amid the euphoric optimism about such opportunities for global uplift, cautionary voices even among those who supported the enterprise could be heard. William Howard Taft, president of the Philippine Commission and future president of the United States, warned that the Filipinos might "need the training of fifty or a hundred years before they shall ever realize what Anglo-Saxon liberty is." An observer of the "unruly" Puerto Rican elections in 1900 pronounced that "Liberty is a habit" that "tropical peoples" learn with some difficulty.[44]

Voices on both sides of the debate conjured up the object lessons of America's own recent tumultuous past to argue both for and against imperial expansion. The need for a strong interventionist state seemed to many readily apparent. The danger for America did not lay in the extension of its military and administrative power but from the opposite direction—decentralization, weak government, and by "paltering with the mob . . . incited sometimes by demagogues, sometimes by honest enthusiasts, into passion, and united for factional ends." Government must be strong enough to put down the mob. The editors of the *Outlook* in 1900 reminded their readers of the not-too-remote experience of domestic turmoil in which "successive mobs have attempted to take control of the railroads and determine what trains might run; to occupy Pittsburgh, Chicago, Brooklyn, Cleveland, and St. Louis and prevent free carriage in the public streets; to lay siege to the iron mills at Homestead and determine who might enter and who might not; and in countless cases to prevent by force free Americans from working for such wages and on such conditions as they were willing to accept." The real imperial danger, they argued, lay in the imperialism of the mob, whether in the Philippines or the United States. "We are anti-imperialists," they proclaimed, and "are therefore in favor of a strong government," both at home and abroad.[45]

Their opponents marched under a different "anti-imperial" banner, and while disputing virtually every argument in favor of expansion, they nonetheless shared the imperialists' dread of domestic disorder. The *Arena* provided a major outlet among reformers for anti-imperialist viewpoints. One correspondent argued in 1900 that deep social and political conflict in the

United States already threatened the Republic: "The conflicts between labor and capital, such as those that led to the riots at Pittsburgh and Chicago within the last few years . . . show that the Republic is liable at any time to experience convulsions arising from internal troubles which may tax her vital powers to overcome." To add "the constant anxieties and burdens" that would come with being "an empire-seeking Power" would allow "militarism to assert itself" in ways that threatened the Republic.[46]

But the anti-imperialists also wove unmistakable racial themes into their rhetoric of opposition. The *New York World* noted that the United States had a "black elephant" in the South. Did it "really need a white elephant in the Philippines, a leper elephant in Hawaii, a brown elephant in Porto Rico and perhaps a yellow elephant in Cuba?" As the campaign of 1900 focused increasingly on the issue of imperialism to the exclusion of other differences, Democrats worried about the effects of racial amalgamation on republican institutions. A writer to the *Arena* argued that to achieve "progress and prosperity," a people must be "sufficiently homogeneous" to be "placed on a perfect equality in respect to the rights of citizenship." If different groups "of widely different stages of civilization" must function under the same government, then "the least enlightened group" will "check the progress of the other, or, perhaps overwhelm it by force of numbers."[47]

William Jennings Bryan, again the Democratic presidential nominee in 1900, articulated the central linkage in anti-imperialist thinking. If colonized peoples were racially incapable of assuming the responsibilities of citizenship, did the Republic not contaminate its political ideals by making them dependent subjects?[48] With Bryan's defeat in 1900, the anti-imperialist tide would subside. But the common stock of racial thinking that those opposing and favoring expansion shared would continue to infect reformers' thinking as the U.S. role in Latin America and the Caribbean grew and as the tide of new immigrants swelled. The boundaries of difference and the fear of disorder precipitated by racial "others" remained deeply etched in the project of reform, whether abroad or at home.

Restricting and Protecting Immigrants

As American power and influence expanded abroad, so did the flow of immigrants to American shores grow. Restrictionists and antirestrictionists in the reform community divided over the extent of their confidence in the possibility of Americanizing the swelling numbers of "new" immigrants. They shared a belief, however, in the racial ordering of peoples and the unfitness of certain types of immigrants for life in a democratic society. In some respects, their debate echoed the racialized rhetoric of anti-imperialists and imperialists.

The appointment of a federal commission in 1907 to investigate immigration and its effects on American society resulted from frustration and compromise in the legislative arena. Unable to win agreement on restrictionist proposals for a literacy test, a House and Senate conference committee forwarded a bill establishing an investigatory commission, which would guide future legislation with its recommendations. In the bargain, the bill doubled the head tax on immigrants from two to four dollars, in part to fund the work of the commission. Three senators, three congressmen, and three citizens, the latter appointed by the president, comprised the Dillingham commission.[49] Reformers warmly greeted the commission and agreed with President Roosevelt that no problem greater than immigration faced the American people.

As immigration levels rose rapidly after the end of the depression of the 1890s, the public perceived that its character had changed. Increasing steadily from a late-nineteenth-century low of 225,000, the "new immigration," comprised chiefly of southern and eastern Europeans, peaked at 1.3 million in 1907 and, after a brief but sharp decline, rose again to 1 million in 1910 and 1.2 million in 1914.[50] The *Survey* reported that on the very day in late 1909 when the U.S. Immigration Commission made its first report to Congress, the steamer *President Grant* landed in New York with the largest number of steerage passengers, 3,001, ever delivered by a single ship. A large proportion of the predominantly Austrian-Galacians on board had responded to word of improving labor market conditions in the United States.[51]

Networks of organizations servicing the needs and promoting the Americanization of immigrants had been called into action.[52] Jane Addams spoke for many front-line settlement workers when she argued that "the average American is inhibited by something akin to contempt" from knowing the immigrants in their midst. "America thus fails to develop possibilities that would be of inestimable value to the cultural as well as to the industrial forces of the national life."[53]

Local organizations of many varieties took up the task of "protecting" immigrants. Hull-House workers organized the Immigrant Protective League in 1908 to attend to the problems immigrants faced adjusting to life in the United States.[54] A New York branch of the National Civic League for Immigrants, like many such organizations, combined labor recruitment with protecting immigrants "on the docks, in courts, in the banking of their savings," and with "education in civics."[55] Edward Steiner, immigrant of an earlier generation and professor at Grinnell College in Iowa, lent a sympathetic voice to the chorus of Americanizers. In *On the Trail of the Immigrant,* a book written in 1906, he expressed gratitude for his own immigration experience as a steerage passenger. The possibility of "a new gigantic race . . . being born between the Atlantic and the Pacific" fueled his optimism. "[I am] grateful that I could stand among those tangling threads out of which our national life is being woven, and see the woof and the warp, and know that the woof is good. I am conscious of the fact that it will take strong sound warp to hold it together, to fill out our pattern and complete our plan."[56]

For all of the optimism reformers invested in Americanization, they also harbored underlying concerns about the speed and efficiency with which it could be accomplished.[57] Some were openly skeptical about the prospects. Addressing Steiner's views directly, Joseph Lee, a national director of the Immigration Restriction League and critic of the antirestrictionist voices on the U.S. Immigration Commission, asked, "Can Jonah Swallow the Whale?" He answered that Americans must first develop "a red hot faith in the mission and destiny of America"; they must create "something to which people can be assimilated." Turning to a digestive metaphor, he asserted that "our gastric juice must be masterful in its attack if such large meals as are now being fed to us are to be digested." Jane Addams, he believed, had already given up on such a process of Americanization. For Lee and many restrictionists who advocated Americanization, the choice was stark: "Either we must greatly limit immigration, by laws that shall select upon the whole the better and more assimilable foreign elements, and try to remain fundamentally an American civilization; or else we must give up the idea of assimilation, leave our gates wide open, and await the process of the melting pot, which in the course of centuries may or may not work out a new and successful human variety and social type."[58]

American social reformers anticipated the report and recommendations of the Dillingham commission with some anxiety. Preliminary indications suggested that the commission's findings would support an optimistic assessment of the prospects for Americanization. William Bennett, a congressional opponent of restriction and member of the commission, reported that anthropologist Franz Boas's study of changes in the bodily form of descendants of immigrants showed significant improvements in stature and the shape of the head. A report in the *Survey* argued that "social conditions, climate, food—what not, are moulding a distinct American type, probably an approximate mean of the many races entering into our population." Freighted with Lamarckian notions of "race improvement," the preliminary report reinforced the idea of classifiably distinct racial types and the susceptibility of presumably hereditary characteristics to evolutionary change.[59]

When finally presented to Congress in December 1910, the summary and recommendations of the commission elicited diverse responses from the reform community. The commission found economic motives to be driving immigration, in particular the disparity in wages and opportunities for the unskilled in Europe and the United States. Temporary sojourners seeking an early return and resistant to American ways of life made up a large proportion of immigrants—some suggested as much as 40 percent. Mass immigration of unskilled laborers had, in the commission's view, held down wages while accelerating the growth of industry. Even if the American economy had not yet reached the "saturation point," the continuation of present high levels of immigration would produce conditions that, according to commission staff member Parker Willis, would be "of questionable value to the community as a whole." On the conditions faced by immigrants, the commissioners concluded that the newcomers required greater protection from exploitation, but the report also found "an immense mass of unassimilated material," a kind of "foreign body in the national social organism" that "might become actively poisonous at some future time, if not shortly broken up and reduced to a basis of uniformity with the surrounding population." The commission saw the need for a better distribution of immigrants and greater attention to education and enforcement of school laws, child labor regulations, and coordinated private and public philanthropy.[60]

Jett Lauck, who headed the industrial investigations for the commission, reported on the isolation of immigrants in cities: "A situation exists of alien colonies being established on American soil . . . living largely under their own systems of control and practically isolated from all direct contact with American life and institutions." Lauck and many other reformers worried about the prospect for American institutions stemming from the "possible political and social manipulation of the recent immigrant population by unscrupulous leaders." Fear of a new, racially defined class was barely veiled. He called for Americans to enter the field of social and religious work, which offered vast possibilities for meeting the challenges that confronted "a self-governing republic."[61]

The specific recommendations of the commission focused on ensuring a "quality and quantity" of immigration that guaranteed rapid assimilation. To that end, the commission proposed tighter restrictions on criminals, prostitutes, those receiving charity, Asians, and surplus unskilled laborers. A literacy test, the centerpiece of the commission's proposals, would accomplish the exclusion of the least desirable laborers, particularly when combined with an increased head tax and quotas applied to specific "races" and single men.[62] Some reformers saw in the commission's recommendations a realistic assessment of the dangers ahead should immigrant overcrowding persist. For Theodore Marburg, failure to curtail immigration might mean "throwing away the inheritance of our children" and declining to European living standards.[63]

Arthur Mayer and Grace Abbott, on the other hand, belittled the commission's analysis and its fears. Immigrant motives were not purely economic, the circumstances of return migration more complex, the notion of a vibrant industrial economy saturated with unskilled labor ludicrous, and the problems of "adjusting" the immigrant not nearly so formidable.[64] It fell to Paul Kellogg, editor of the *Survey*, to define a common ground. Choosing his words carefully, Kellogg argued that Americans had the right to claim their national heritage: "To some extent this heritage is one of race. Its creators gave it to us with their blood. It has been enriched by many crossings of races, but biologists tell us that mingling within limits is beneficial, beyond those limits productive only of a mongrel and degenerate breed."[65] He did not, however, want these sentiments to be read as expressing a "shred of bigotry or prejudice against any of the peoples of the world." A humane critique of the demand for cheap immigrant labor did not preclude "the maintenance of community and national standards." He sought to rally reformers around this national flag of standards by proposing a tax on immigrant labor that would force employers to pay no less than a $2.50 minimum daily wage to immigrants during their first five years in the country. What some saw as an ingenious opening wedge for minimum wage standards in general, others regarded as hopelessly utopian or as requiring police state apparatus to enforce. Kellogg envisioned the device as a way of both restricting and upgrading immigration while directly preventing exploitation.[66] Many reformers could applaud such a program that combined immigration restriction and race improvement, utopian though it might seem.

Progressives, then, generally supported immigration restriction as a remedy for declining living standards produced by unregulated immigration. In fact, Jenks and Lauck saw "a redistribution of wealth" as the probable consequence of restriction. But restriction must go hand in hand with "thoroughly organized . . . assimilative and distributive relief measures" if Americans were to protect their way of life.[67]

Progressives found immigration restriction and Americanization palatable because they offered means for protecting democracy from corrupting influences. With the disappearance of classes and class conflict, unassimilable races could become the source of social divisions that posed the greatest threat to democratic institutions. Racially inferior peoples might then constitute the basis for a new hierarchy of classes and new social tensions. Jenks and Lauck summed up this view in their account of the Immigration Commission's findings: "The coming in of people who will not be assimilated creates discord and makes separate classes or castes in a community. Usually this process does not tend toward an improvement of political institutions, but rather toward their deterioration, entirely aside from the question as to whether the immigrants were lower or higher in the scale of civilization."[68]

In the Laboratory of the Settlements

It fell to settlement houses to work out practical assimilation of racially different people. In the debates over immigration restriction that swirled about the work of the U.S. Immigration Commission, the settlement workers consistently directed more attention to the treatment and acceptance of immigrants than to restriction.[69] Nevertheless, their views of immigrants varied. One segment, represented by Robert A. Woods of Boston's South End House, saw restriction as the only means of preventing the perpetuation of unassimilable ethnic enclaves.[70] But "liberal Progressives" such as Jane Addams, her Hull-House colleagues, and the Chicago intellectuals who worked closely with her, saw the possibility of a more extended and less coercive assimilation process.[71] They confronted the problem directly. Settlement workers found a staggering diversity of ethnic groups in their immediate neighborhoods and observed firsthand the transiency, poverty, and dependency that made immigrants fodder for political manipulation.

Chicago sociologist W. I. Thomas gave theoretical form to the practical problem of reshaping immigrant identities. He defined the common memories that formed a basis for mutual understanding within immigrant groups as an "apperception mass." Although such "sentimental memories" shared by groups of immigrants could harmlessly remain "unmolested in the region of personal life," immigrant children, in the view of reformers Edith Abbott and Sophonisba Breckinridge, must also be trained into the "American apperception mass," that is, "a civic life that has grown out of American experience and Anglo-Saxon tradition."[72] For these reformers, toleration of diversity meant focusing on the individual, not the ethnic group. In Addams's view, each individual's "identification with the common lot . . . is the essential idea of Democracy."[73]

In practice, Hull-House instituted programs that would promote ethnic mixing and further the process of assimilation. Its workers remained suspicious of parochial and bilingual education, which reinforced immigrants' identification with their ethnic community. John Dewey viewed Hull-House as "a social clearing-house . . . bringing people together . . . doing away with barriers of caste, or class, or race, or type of experience that keep people from real communion with each other."[74]

Hull-House reformers, or the liberal Progressives for whom they spoke, occupied a seemingly contradictory space among Americanizers. On the one hand, they were suspicious of the ethnic employment agencies, immigrant banks, fraternal organizations, and what historian Rivka Lissak calls "political interest groups" tied to urban machines. At the same time, these reformers affirmed a "cosmopolitan" idea of American nationality that blended, not melted, the cultural contributions of *individual* immigrants. John Dewey described it as "a unity created by drawing out and composing into a harmonious whole the best, the most characteristic, which each contributing race and people has to offer. Our national motto 'One from Many,' cuts deep and extends far."[75]

Hull-House reformers in Chicago supported measures restricting ethnic influence in education, such as a requirement of English proficiency for children leaving school to work and state supervision of parochial education. Eventually they supported changes in public school curriculum—the introduction of "ethnic studies" and foreign language instruction—that would promote self-respect among immigrant children, an appreciation of their parents, and enable them "to have a sense of ease in America, a first consciousness of being at home."[76] This meant the introduction of a handful of western European languages, not the culture of most new immigrants, into high school curricula, to which few immigrant children had access in the first place. Although the settlement reformers might speak of their houses as "cathedrals of humanity," they appealed most effectively to assimilation-oriented immigrants drawn to the refined atmosphere and the opportunities for self-improvement the settlements offered. These individuals functioned in turn as "cultural brokers" for the settlements in the wider community.[77]

The Progressives retained the idea of a cultural ladder up which different groups ascended. Hull-House produced no real amalgamation of immigrant and American cultures. A genteel Anglo-Saxonism prevailed; Yiddish was disregarded, referred to in one Hull-House publication as "a demoralizing jargon." Only western European and native-born "cosmopolitan heroes" who served the "common lot" adorned the settlement theater's walls.[78]

Settlements and the Color Line

Although the social settlements opened their doors to an ethnically diverse population and crafted programs that promoted Americanization, they generally regarded the integration of African Americans in northern cities with greater skepticism. Social reformers, by and large, were prisoners of a racial ideology that defined blacks as other—so different from whites that social equality was inconceivable. Even "friends of the Negro" believed a "lack of inherited control" set blacks apart. Although Jane Addams did not advocate integration, she did oppose the complete segregation of blacks that placed them "outside the immediate action of that imperceptible but powerful social control which influences the rest of the population."[79] A cross-section of liberal reformers shared with Addams a view that blacks lacked the "self-restraint" that formed a necessary condition of social life, fixing blame for this condition on slavery, the historical failings of Reconstruction, and blacks themselves. As New York social investigator and Progressive Party activist Frances Kellor argued, the "Negro at present has neither the perceptions nor the solidity of character that would enable him to lead his race."[80] Although Addams and other reformers sympathetic to the plight of blacks in the North promoted the cause of legal equality, helped form the NAACP, and encouraged settlement activity in black neighborhoods, they adhered to a policy of strict separation. In practice, this meant that white settlements served white ethnic neighborhoods and black settlements, usually with white philanthropic support, served black neighborhoods.[81]

In Chicago, only one settlement house serving the black belt survived the first two decades of the twentieth century. Eight others, at one time or another, opened their doors only to see them close. Most had been started and supported financially by whites. At one extreme, white reformer Celia Parker Woolley founded the Frederick Douglass Center in 1905 located in a white neighborhood just across elevated tracks that marked the boundary of the black belt east of State Street. The Douglass Center, under Woolley's direction, served "the ever increasing number of colored people who have earned the right to be believed in and respected." She sought to create an atmosphere in which "amicable relations between the white and colored people" might be possible, in which "right living" as well as "industry, honesty and thrift" might be taught. At the same time, Woolley's principal black assistant assured supporters that although the center sought to reduce the separation of the races, it did so only "in their non-social relations."[82] Others, like the Emanual Settlement, directed and largely funded from within the black community, served a poor neighborhood in a "congested district of colored people." Mrs. Fannie Emanuel offered undiscriminating relief, manual training, a free dental clinic, and an employment bureau. But within five years of its founding in 1908, Emanual closed its doors for lack of funds.

The settlements' "practical philosophy along the color line" meant a separation of services on the basis of race and effective white control of institutions serving black communities. A 1918 report, for instance, described Flanner House in Indianapolis as having an "appropriate" arrangement with "a staff of white people cooperating with and working among the colored people." Whites sitting on a biracial board enjoyed more effective control "than would be the case if the money were turned over to a staff consisting exclusively of colored workers."[83]

The habit of white direction, which even the most liberal social reformers found natural, pervaded reform work as it did other spheres in which whites and blacks interacted. On the whole, a philosophy of accommodation, consonant with the pervasive racial climate of Progressive Era America and the influence of Booker T. Washington's ideas, reigned among social reformers. This did not prevent, however, a commitment to "Negro uplift" in the name of progress that enabled the individual to overcome "the shadow of an insistent race caste [that] has continually darkened his pathway of emancipation."[84]

In her account of Flanner House, historian Ruth Crocker captured the inherent dualism that lay at the heart of white reformers' work with blacks: "The two purposes, reform and control, coexisted in the agency from the beginning: in the black settlement house the goals of white philanthropy merged with the black elite's goal of racial uplift to carry out progressive reforms without disturbing the basic relations of class and race." For black elites, uplift meant, as historian Kevin Gaines has argued, that a "better class" of blacks "sought to rehabilitate the race's image by embodying respectability, enacted through an ethos of service to the masses." To pursue "race progress" in the Jim Crow era entailed the "defensive appropriation of dominant racial theories" in pursuit of a "positive black identity."[85]

Although the mainstream settlement movement was trapped by its own racial ideology and by social conventions that excluded race mixing, settlement work in black neighborhoods developed in ways that gave African American women greater voice and control. Urban reformers' bias against church sponsorship of settlement work left denominational initiatives in black communities with little outside support. But because black churches had deep roots in communities north and south, they often functioned under the control of the congregation and neighborhood simultaneously. Southern schools founded on the Hampton/Tuskegee model survived within the interstices of Jim Crow society and provided an "education for life" that transcended the narrow limitations of industrial education. Georgia Washington's People's Village School in Mt. Meigs, Alabama, for instance, trained teachers and at the same time promoted wider community improvement.[86]

Worlds of White and Black Reform

The racial gulf that separated the worlds of white and black reform reflected the dominant racial order of Progressive Era America. Few bridges crossed this racial divide. Ironically, as white reformers gained influence and widened the network of reform organizations in ways that heightened their expectation of success, they did so by further marginalizing the cause of interracialism.

White reformers had no natural immunity to the virus of racism. They generally viewed the world as racially ordered, and their disposition on matters of race led them to accept the logic of segregation, the fear of Negro criminality, and the conviction that premature enfranchisement of blacks only fostered corruption.

Frances Willard, president of the WCTU, had reflected these tendencies in her response to the epidemic of lynching that swept across the South in the 1890s. Horrified by the tide of violence, Willard pushed for an antilynching resolution at the 1893 WCTU convention. But her language betrayed her own race prejudice and her susceptibility to southerners' rationales for the continued segregation of the South. In her presidential address, she spoke of the responsibilities of northern reformers: "Our duty to the colored people have [sic] never impressed me so solemnly as this year when the antagonism between them and the white race have [sic] seemed to be more vivid than at any previous time, and lurid vengeance has devoured the devourers of women and children."[87] By giving legitimacy to the notion that black men were "devourers of women and children," Willard revealed a profound inability to understand race relations in the South. She believed the record of the WCTU in organizing blacks, albeit in segregated locals, and her own support of the interests of black people, spoke for themselves. When she was attacked by Ida B. Wells on the lynching issue, other reformers, among them Frederick Douglass, William Lloyd Garrison, and Julia Ward Howe, came to her defense.[88] But Willard, like other reformers, tried to reconcile the needs of black people, as she understood them, and the prejudices of southern whites. Such reconciliation in the New South could come only through legitimation of racial segregation.

Booker T. Washington provided a path by which northern philanthropists and social reformers, along with southern whites, could achieve reconciliation without foregoing their prejudices. In his historic "Atlanta Compromise" speech to the Cotton States and International Exposition in September 1895, he accepted the social order of the South, denied any intention to assert equal rights, and called on African Americans (and whites) to "cast down your buckets where you stand." Through self-help and industrial training and with the assistance of white philanthropists, blacks would gradually advance their position without challenging the existing social order. Here was a message that won instantaneous, broad appeal, not least among white social reformers.

Washington's message of progress through reconciliation was one to which northern whites, weary of class warfare, could also respond. He asserted that blacks would prove themselves a "patient, faithful, law-abiding, and unresentful people" if conceded industrial education and "the opportunity to earn a dollar in a factory." He urged a corollary principle that generated an ecstatic response among whites committed to the existing social order, namely, the abandonment of "the agitation of questions of social equality" as "the extremest folly." Using his own hand to convey the brilliant but well-rehearsed metaphor, he said, "In all things that are purely social we can be as separate as the fingers, yet one as the hand in all things essential to mutual progress."[89]

The speech catapulted Washington and his philosophy of accommodation to an unquestioned position of leadership. Most voices from the black community, even an enthusiastic young professor from Wilberforce University, W. E. B. Du Bois, applauded Washington's program for a settlement with whites. Northern philanthropists and sympathetic politicians found reassurance for their own ideals of social reconciliation and uplift.[90]

In time, other voices, including most prominently that of Du Bois, would rise to challenge the accommodationist path blazed by Washington and his supporters.[91] With the publication of Du Bois's *Souls of Black Folk* in 1903, any remaining cordiality and mutual respect between Washington's Tuskegee machine and his opponents disintegrated. Each camp jockeyed organizationally to upstage, if not displace, the other. In October 1904, Du Bois published a "credo" in the *Independent* that defined more explicitly the "rights" agenda he and other opponents of Washington would pursue. "I believe in Liberty for all men; the space to stretch their arms and souls; the right to breathe and the right to vote, the freedom to choose their friends, enjoy the sunshine and ride on the railroads, uncursed by color; thinking, dreaming, working as they will in a kingdom of God and love," he declared. That same month, as Du Bois biographer David Levering Lewis points out, Du Bois suggested to the American Missionary Association that the race problem "was but the sign of growing class privilege and caste distinction in America." Du Bois's perspective directly challenged Progressives who wished to believe class distinctions were subsiding and saw race divisions as simply an unwelcome intrusion from the margins of society, not a reaffirmation of class.[92]

A series of African American leadership gatherings of Du Bois's "talented tenth" set an organizational course that directly challenged Washington's accommodationism and contributed eventually to the founding of the National Association for the Advancement of Colored People in 1910.[93] Nevertheless, many charity workers and some members of the settlement community shared white philanthropists' loyalty to Washingtonian accommodation. Like most whites, they were deeply suspicious of "social equality."[94]

By 1905, a more diverse chorus of voices regarding the "condition of the Negro" had begun to emanate from the social reform community. *Charities and the Commons* displayed that diversity in a special issue on "The Negro in the Cities of the North." Numbers of authors focused on the peculiar environmental circumstances that blacks faced in northern cities and the segregation that dictated inferior opportunities in housing and employment. Fannie Williams of the Frederick Douglass Center in Chicago and Mary White Ovington, a future disciple of Du Bois, writing from the vantage point of Greenwich House in New York, examined in detail the consequences of segregation. Franz Boas debunked popular notions of racial inferiority.[95]

Many social reformers, however, still made a distinction between good and bad blacks. Writing in the aftermath of the Springfield, Illinois, race riot, Graham Taylor described conditions in the city that had "allowed that population to become in large part so depraved." Celia Woolley, from the Douglass Center, believed social reformers had a special obligation to "the educated colored people in our midst" but manifested little comparable empathy for the black masses. Oswald Garrison Villard, like Ray Stannard Baker, would later insist for the sake of balance that Du Bois regularly publish in the *Crisis* "a list of crimes" committed by blacks along with a list of lynchings.[96]

Organizational jockeying between partisans of Washington and a cluster of his opponents, who looked to Du Bois for leadership, produced two rival national forums. The first, the Committee of Twelve for the Advancement of the Interests of the Negro Race, which formed in 1903 with the blessings of Washington's white patrons, turned out to be simply another vehicle for Washington's machinelike control over the black leadership. Du Bois called into existence the second, the Niagara movement, as a forum for opponents of Washington to define a rights-oriented agenda and create an alternative national leadership.

Du Bois outlined demands that made concrete the break with the Washingtonians: "First, we would vote; with the right to vote goes everything." The address called for an end to discrimination in public accommodations, equal protection of the law, and the freedom of association and expression. Here was a claim of rights, not a strategy of separate development.[97]

Progressives and the NAACP

The crisis in American race relations deepened between 1905 and 1910, punctuated by a series of racial conflicts: the Brownsville Raid in Texas in 1905, the Atlanta race riot of 1906, and the Springfield, Illinois, race riot in 1908. The Niagara movement attempted to hold together its ranks in the face of intensifying racism.

Despite the political and intellectual isolation that beset Du Bois and the Niagaraites by late 1909, a new initiative laid the groundwork for the most important organizational development in Progressive Era race relations. By all accounts, the organizational spark came from an impassioned essay on the Springfield riot, "Race War in the North," penned by socialist William English Walling and published in the *Independent* on September 3, 1908. "Either the spirit of the abolitionists, of Lincoln and Lovejoy, must be revived and we must come to treat the Negro on a plane of absolute political and social equality," Walling wrote, "or Vardaman and Tillman will soon have transferred the race war to the North—Yet who realizes the seriousness of the situation, and what large and powerful body of citizens is ready to come to their aid?"[98]

In the months that followed, socialite reform activist Mary White Ovington, whose concern for the Negro had deepened with her own experience, pestered Walling to initiate a meeting to devise a plan for gathering the "large and powerful body of citizens" for which he had called. White reformers took the initiative. Walling, Ovington, and New York social reformer Henry Moskowitz met in early January 1909. Other meetings followed close on the heels of the first and drew in a widening circle of reformers. By Lincoln's birthday, a "Committee on the Status of the Negro," now joined by a handful of prominent African Americans, issued a call for a conference at the end of May 1909. The sixty signatories of the call, headed by Jane Addams (in strict alphabetical order) and Ray Stannard Baker, included a cross-section of the national reform community: John Dewey, Rabbi Stephen Wise, Florence Kelley, Charles Edward Russell, Lincoln Steffens, Helen Stokes, Lillian Wald, and Oswald Garrison Villard. A number of African Americans identified with the anti-Washington camp added their names, including Du Bois, Ida Wells-Barnett, Bishop Alexander Walters, Dr. William L. Bulkley, and Mary Church Terrell.[99]

The historic meeting of the National Negro Conference opened on the morning of May 31 in the auditorium of New York's Charity Organization Society. White reformers dominated the gathering but were joined by a sprinkling of African Americans. Nevertheless, as Du Bois noted, the "curiosity of the spectators was toward the darker and less known portion of the audience." The concerns and interests of the white reformers, at least initially, shaped the agenda. At the opening session, Columbia anthropologist Livingston Farrand and Cornell neurologist Burt Wilder asserted the mental and biological equality of blacks by disputing the "alleged prefrontal deficiency in the Negro brain." Du Bois would report enthusiastically (and with more than a touch of sarcasm) that "the two-day conclave had found the Negro to be fully human and the opposing argument to be 'utterly without scientific basis.'" John Dewey judged racism pragmatically as a tax on society's "social capital." And economist Edwin Seligman asserted that the economic environment, not Negro inferiority, had limited his progress. He also called on conference attenders to sympathize with the understandable social and political dilemmas that white southerners faced.[100]

Tensions between white and black participants surfaced subtly at first and then more openly. In his talk on "Politics and Industry" the first afternoon, Du Bois suggested that white reformers had mistaken "effects for causes" in their concern for the conditions blacks lived under and their morals. Blacks' lowly condition, he argued, stemmed not primarily from their economic and social condition but from the denial of their citizenship, which could be remedied only by the ballot.[101] Such an argument directly challenged white reformers' skepticism about blacks' readiness for the franchise.

The sense of a distinct African American agenda became palpable by the second day. As Du Bois later reported in the *Survey*, the "scientific calm" disappeared. "The black mass moved forward and stretched out their hands to take charge. It was their problem. They must name the condition." Ida Wells-Barnett and Monroe Trotter challenged a white participant who worried that there could be "too much racial agitation." Upon the suggestion that Booker T. Washington be asked to join the organizing committee, Wells-Barnett cried out, "They are betraying us again—these white friends of ours."[102] Despite painful wrangling over the composition of the Committee of Forty, which would be charged to carry forward the work of organization, Du Bois cast the meeting in a positive light, seeing in its composition and direction the best hope yet for putting the rights of black people on the American reform agenda and challenging the accommodationism of Washington. He wrote of a "vision of future cooperation, not simply as in the past, between giver and beggar—the older ideal of charity" but built on a "new alliance between experienced social workers and reformers" and "the great struggling mass of laborers of all kinds, whose conditions and needs know no color line." Du Bois signaled a reform alliance in which African Americans expected to claim equal, even senior, partnership.[103] In so doing, he challenged the reformers propensity to redefine class boundaries in racial terms.

From the outset, the leadership and direction of the NAACP became contested racial terrain. Manipulation of the membership on the Committee of Forty and the unilateral exclusion or addition of certain blacks bred distrust.[104] In the face of Walling's declining health, Oswald Garrison Villard assumed executive direction. Du Bois professed in his autobiography a certain respect for Villard but also noted that he "naturally expected" blacks "to be humble and thankful or certainly not assertive and aggressive." At the NAACP founding convention, Du Bois, despite the reservations of some, was chosen to be "Director of Publicity and Research," a salaried position he defined primarily through his editorship of the brash new publication the *Crisis*.[105] With its first issue in November 1910, the journal became an influential organ that articulated in unequivocal and uncompromising terms an African American perspective. It also became a dual center of power within the organization, regarded by Villard and white staff members with suspicion bordering at times on alarm. If Villard hoped not to burn all bridges to Washington and the Tuskegee machine, Du Bois harbored no such concerns. As the visibility of the *Crisis* grew, even eclipsing the more mundane work of organization building, Villard and the other white leaders grew impatient with Du Bois. He, on the other hand, saw a familiar expectation of racial deference at work within the organization, whereby "if the Negroes attempt to dominate and conduct the committee, the whites become dissatisfied." However, more than old habits of racial subordination and competing egos festered in the fledgling organization dedicated to battling for black civic and social rights. Political divisions and different conceptions of social equality between the races separated white and black reformers. Most white reformers, even those deeply dedicated to securing constitutionally guaranteed rights for black people, found what they termed "social equality" unacceptable. Du Bois used the term gingerly at times, suggesting that it implied simply "the right to be treated as a gentleman when one is among gentlemen and acts like a gentleman." But his advocacy, on occasion, of social interaction, and even intermarriage between the races, threatened to shatter relations with Villard, Addams, Kellogg, and even Florence Kelley.[106]

The Progressive Party and Race

The initial growth of the NAACP and the dramatically expanding circulation of the *Crisis* paralleled the rising influence of progressive reform. Although the social reform community centered around the *Survey* had reason to be encouraged by their access to Theodore Roosevelt and the newly forming Progressive Party, African American leaders of anti-Washington persuasion had their own less promising history with Roosevelt. They distrusted his patronage of Booker T. Washington, who had dined at the White House, and they criticized the erosion of his commitment to use federal appointments to further racial integration. Roosevelt's handling of the Brownsville Raid left a deep scar on the black community. Anti-Washington leaders, therefore, greeted his ascension as the putative standard-bearer of the Progressives with anything but enthusiasm. Their fears turned out to be well founded.

Roosevelt's belief that the "Negro problem" was "not as urgent, or as menacing, as other problems" enabled him to develop a southern strategy for achieving his "new nationalist" goals, which permitted southern supporters to build a "lily-white" Progressive Party in the South. The strategy demonstrated the degree to which Progressive reformers' views on race in the North and South paralleled mainstream white opinion. Roosevelt behaved in a politically expedient and ideologically consistent manner. So, for that matter, did Jane Addams.[107]

The race issue surfaced concretely at the Progressive Party convention in August 1912 because blacks in a number of southern states had sought to enlist in the party only to find themselves excluded. On the eve of the convention, three all-white delegations—from Alabama, Florida, and Mississippi—faced challenges before the Provisional National Progressive Committee.[108] During the previous weeks, Roosevelt had defined the policy the party would pursue. He was determined to create a truly national party that would overcome the sectional limitations the Republicans suffered. That meant detaching southern Progressives from their Democratic Party moorings. It also meant rejecting what remained of the Republican Party's "black and tan" tradition in the South. Because black delegates had overwhelmingly remained loyal to Taft at the Republican convention the previous month, Roosevelt and his allies found this maneuver more palatable.

But more was at stake than political revenge against the Republicans who had recently rejected Roosevelt's candidacy. Roosevelt, like many reform-minded and influential northern whites, supported Booker T. Washington. He believed blacks could progress but expected their achievement of "civilization" to be slow. He felt that Reconstruction had demonstrated "the perfectly flat failure of negro suffrage in the South." "That experiment," he told Jane Addams in October 1911, "showed that the effort to endow people with suffrage in order to enable them to improve themselves and maintain their rights may fail in the most complete and hopeless manner."[109] Blissfully ignoring the endemic brutality and discrimination blacks faced in the Jim Crow South, Roosevelt, like many Progressives, believed that their best hope lay with the "intelligent and benevolent" whites of the South. Hostile to a Republican Party he had come to view as corrupt, Roosevelt sought to avoid "exposing the whole movement to derision" by not "building up another futile vicious little black and tan organization in the ex-Confederate states." The real alternative, he flatly wrote a Massachusetts Unitarian minister, was "to try to make up our party in the South from among the men of real power, leadership and principle, and that means to try to organize it among the white people."[110]

Despite the pleadings of Progressives Joel Spingarn, Henry Moskowitz, and Jane Addams, party leaders and the convention ignored the race issue, included no plank in the platform that addressed Negro rights, and refused to seat blacks from southern states with contested delegations. Spingarn, Moskowitz, and Addams, representing the NAACP board, came to the convention armed with a resolution drafted by Du Bois that read in part, "The Progressive party recognizes that distinctions of race or class in political life have no place in a democracy. . . . The party, therefore, demands for the American of Negro descent the repeal of unfair discriminatory laws and the right to vote on the same terms on which other citizens vote." Spingarn and his colleagues redrafted the resolution in the hopes of getting Roosevelt's support, only to see it rejected by the platform committee. The redrafted resolution reveals the ways in which white Progressives understood the race issue. Like Du Bois's version, their redraft asserted that the "National" Progressive Party did not recognize distinctions of race "and" class as having a place in a democracy. But instead of "demanding" rights for the "American of Negro descent," it "assure[d] the American of African descent" that the party had a "deep interest in his welfare." It also affirmed the party's interest in the "gradual recognition by North and South" of the principle that "the colored man who has the same qualifications . . . [as] the white man" be entitled to the same political representation. White reformers, ostensible allies of Du Bois, were not prepared to give unqualified support to Du Bois's rights claims on behalf of African Americans. Etched in their minds, boundaries of difference based on race still divided those "qualified" for citizenship from those not yet prepared. Even as redrafted, the resolution still failed to win the support it needed from the committee—and even influential Progressives such as Charles McCarthy of Wisconsin.[111]

The reformers' moral and religious fervor stirred the Progressive Party convention deeply. The party cast Jane Addams in an especially prominent role. But on the special burdens of race, she, like the convention and its platform, was silent.[112] Indeed, the convention focused no attention on the condition of blacks in America, and the elected southern black delegates were shut out of the festivities. William Monroe Trotter had telegraphed Jane Addams an appeal to reconsider linking suffrage for women and blacks: "Women's suffrage will be stained with Negro blood unless women refuse alliance with Roosevelt," he declared.[113] Addams recalled years later the agony she had felt over platform planks supporting the building of battleships and the fortification of the Panama Canal: "I voted to adopt a platform, as a whole, which advocated the building of two battleships a year. . . . I confess that I found it very difficult to swallow those two battleships." She regarded it, as she recalled, "a serious matter even to appear to desert the cause and the comrades with which I had been for so many years identified." But the seating of lily-white southern delegations and the exclusion of southern blacks received no similar attention in her recollections.[114] Even the *New York Evening Post,* edited by her NAACP comrade Oswald Garrison Villard, commented on Roosevelt's cynicism and Addams's complicity. By "throwing out the Negro delegates from the South" and adopting "its platform without a single reference of any kind to the colored man," the Progressives ignored the manifold injustices done the Negro. "All of these things were forgotten because the apostle of justice himself hopes, with what Jane Addams herself called 'statesmanlike (!) policy,' to break up the solid South." A Du Bois editorial in the *Crisis* noted bitterly, "Lest there should be any misinterpretation of this silence," the party had effectively barred the representatives of eight million southern Negroes. "To seal this compact these Hosts at Armageddon stood and sang: 'Mine eyes have seen the glory of the coming of the Lord!'" To which Du Bois simply replied, "Selah!"[115] The reform-minded assistant attorney general of New Jersey listened from the convention gallery "to the strains of music of 'John

Brown's Body' and the 'Battle Hymn of the Republic'" while thinking of the black delegates excluded "on account of their race." "My heart sank. . . . I felt that human cant and hypocrisy could go no further; it had reached its fitting climax."[116] African Americans generally split their votes in the 1912 election, but Du Bois and other key black leaders associated with the NAACP broke with Republican tradition and threw their support not to the Progressives but to an untried but promising Democratic reformer from the South, Woodrow Wilson.

At a Hull-House meeting with "prominent negroes in Chicago" and in an article published in the November issue of the *Crisis,* Addams attempted to justify the actions of the Progressives.[117] She rehearsed her own support over the years, her role in founding the NAACP, and her advocacy of seating the black delegates at the convention. She also itemized the arguments made against seating. First, a number of black delegates were seated from northern states, setting a standard to which southern states might aspire when liberated from "the thraldom of war issues and old party alignments." She noted that "such are the limitations of local self-government that free political expression can only be secured to the colored man through the co-operative action of the patriotic and far-seeing citizens of the States in which he lives." Only when white and colored alike "engage upon common political problems will the colored man cease to be regarded as himself a problem." Her message to southern black Progressives seemed to be that they must shed whatever vestiges of Republican Party corruption clung to them and support the lily-white Progressives who had seized leadership of the new party in the South. Second, Addams reiterated the critique of Republican Party corruption, its complicity in disfranchisement, and its bankrupt representation of southern blacks, who in fact were largely voteless. Third, she noted that the introduction of "glittering phrases" on the race issue to the platform would have been "a very simple matter" but would have perpetuated "the old shams." Addams said she asked herself how her abolitionist father and spiritual forebears would have responded and determined to follow her own moral ideals, which started with her faith in democracy. "We all believe that a wide extension of political power is the only sound basis of self-government," she wrote. But she believed it was not opportunistic to seek to know how the voter has been influenced and his vote secured. If bribery was involved, then "the whole system of representative government has broken down." She believed it no more unpatriotic to question the influence of liquor interests than to question the "political status of the colored man." The "remarkable convention," as she termed it, "where we caught a hint of the action of 'the collective mind,' so often spoken of and so seldom apprehended," had "at least taken the color question away from sectionalism and put it in a national setting which might clear the way for a larger perspective."

She addressed the broader context only elliptically in the final paragraph of her essay, where she noted that the new party sought to avoid "the old Civil War cleavages." By taking the race issue out of discussion, she presumably saw the party able to focus on other, more important progressive issues: "The issues were those of political democracy and industrial justice—a merging of political insurgency in the West and country districts with the social insurgency of the cities. Imbedded in this new movement is a strong ethical motive." Once "crystallized" through a "body of people" with a "national foothold," this movement "is bound to lift this question of the races, as all other questions, out of the grip of the past and into a new era of solution."[118]

Addams, like so many white Progressives, even those associated with the NAACP, saw black problems as part of a larger set of reform issues with which the community must contend. Inclusion would come gradually, perhaps very gradually, for the lowest segments of the black population as strategies of uplift and race improvement did their work. By redefining the class problem as a "race" problem, she, like other Progressive reformers, looked to the favored project of democratic uplift as a solution, whereby the "colored" man would cease to become "a problem" through the benevolent efforts of "the patriotic and far-seeing [white] citizens of the States in which he lives."[119]

Addams's justification of the Progressive Party's action received no direct comment from Du Bois, except editorial reiteration of the *Crisis*'s support for Wilson. With the dawning of the new year, he published a sober "Philosophy for 1913," in which his sense that African Americans must chart their own course and remain faithful to their own ideals is palpable. The essay's opening line is unequivocal: "I am by birth and law a free black American citizen." The bitter lessons of the recent campaign echo through the subsequent lines: "Boldly and without flinching, I will face the hard fact that in this, my fatherland, I must expect insult and discrimination from persons who call themselves philanthropists and Christians and gentlemen." The course he charted would firmly demand certain basic rights: to vote, to frequent public places, and "to appear as a man among men." With a strong sense of independence from the reformers who had shown themselves fickle, he wrote, "Without bitterness (but also without lies), without useless recrimination (but also without cowardly acquiescence), without unnecessary heartache (but with no self-deception), I will walk my way, with uplifted head and level eyes, respecting myself too much to endure without protest studied disrespect from others."[120]

After the debacle of the Progressive Party, tensions within the NAACP between white reformers and Du Bois exploded into open warfare.[121] The central disputes revolved around NAACP control over the increasingly influential and independent *Crisis* and Du Bois's inclination to view himself as an equal of the organization's first chairman, Oswald Garrison Villard, and his successor, Joel Spingarn, each of whom clashed openly and acrimoniously with Du Bois. For Du Bois, as he wrote to an ally, the "old thing that we always fear is tending to happen in the Association. It is tending to become a white man's organization working for the colored people in which no colored people have any real power." Villard, and later Spingarn, found Du Bois increasingly contentious, independent, and, in their view, uncooperative. David Levering Lewis notes that well-meaning whites, including Florence Kelley, "time and again . . . would depart from the boardroom in a red-faced hurry, discommoded and furious." Among the white leaders, only Ovington saw what was at stake in such conflicts. She urged conciliation on Villard. "To me it means a confession to the world that we cannot work with colored people unless they are our subordinates," she declared. Du Bois, whose *Crisis* was an enormous success, maneuvered the organization toward a greater leadership role for blacks and autonomy from whites' control. Their resources nonetheless remained crucial to the movement's success.[122]

Beneath the surface, other divisions festered. Many white reformers remained uncomfortable with what they called "social equality." Du Bois believed Paul Kellogg rejected an essay he submitted to the *Survey* because of its frank discussion of "social rights" to intermarry and freely socialize. Florence Kelley nearly resigned from the NAACP board in 1920 because of a Du Bois editorial that called social equality "just as much a human right as political or economic equality."[123] Internal and external pressures moved the NAACP, despite some resistance from its white leadership, toward being an organization more firmly rooted in the black community and reflecting a race consciousness.[124]

The social and ideological boundaries defined by race deeply infected the Progressive movement. Reformers affirmed their objective to facilitate democratic community by increasing opportunity and diminishing the hardships faced by the most disadvantaged. They believed deeply in "race improvement" through environmental change and social uplift. Drawn first to Booker T. Washington's program of racial accommodation and self-help, they never wholly accepted the more assertive, rights-oriented position of Washington's opponents. Faced with a deepening racial crisis in 1908–9, they pioneered formation of the NAACP, in which African Americans initially played a subordinate role. Some but not all accepted the Progressive Party strategy of subordinating race concerns to a broader social reform agenda. They reacted with uneasiness when Du Bois contended that rights claims had first priority and with outright hostility when he asserted those rights claims within the NAACP itself. Concerned with healing a social order riven by endemic class conflict and rebuilding social harmony between classes through social and democratic reform, white Progressives showed less interest in the "rights" of racially subordinate and marginalized peoples, whether African Americans or new immigrants, whom they generally regarded as ill prepared for full citizenship.[125]

Du Bois and other anti-Washington leaders had found political coalition with Progressive reformers attractive during their own crisis of isolation in 1908–9. In that context, they helped form the NAACP. But embedded in the organization lay a contradiction between the rights or liberty orientation of its leading black members and white reformers' commitment to constructing and gradually enlarging political community through social amelioration. Du Bois and other black leaders entered the coalition with white reformers because they too recognized the need to expand democratic community and relieve the conditions black faced.

These coalitional politics broke apart in the summer of 1912, when the Progressive Party refused to accept southern black delegates. In the interest of party unity, Addams and the social reformers went along with the party's position on race. Du Bois and other black activists reaffirmed their commitment to rights over and above political community. Therein, they believed, lay the only assurance for blacks that the social harmony and democratic community to which white Progressives claimed to be committed would become a truly inclusive community and not just a rhetorical mirage. Ultimately, the white Progressives deferred the promise of a racially inclusive political democracy. And black activists pursued more exclusively race-based organization as the means to win their rights. The social boundary of race had become the new class problem, and Du Bois articulated a compelling new agenda with which Progressive reformers and their liberal heirs would eventually have to contend: "The problem of the twentieth century is the problem of the color line."[126]

But etched in the consciousness of white reformers were racialized boundaries of social difference. As they set about reinventing "the people" and renewing democratic community, they left to the margins African Americans and new immigrants, whose access to the full rights and duties of citizenship, the reformers believed, would be contingent on their gradual social progress.

7

Class Wars and
the Crisis of Progressivism

> [Walsh's] colleagues are bitter against him because
> of his pro-labor attitude, his socialistic propaganda, and
> his efforts to damage this case of the employer.
>
> —Harris Weinstock, employer representative,
> U.S. Commission on Industrial Relations, 1915

> The committee asserts that no alleged or actual
> altruism of more fortunately circumstanced classes will
> avail to remove existing injustices. . . . It shares labor's
> distrust of so-called welfare work where such work is not in
> the hands of men representing the interests of workers
> and directed to fitting the workers to exercise an ever-
> increasing measure of control over the industry
> in which they are engaged.
>
> —Frank Walsh, chairman,
> U.S. Commission on Industrial Relations, 1915

When Frank Walsh accepted the chairmanship of the U.S. Commission on Industrial Relations (USCIR) in the fall of 1913 and its charge to investigate "the causes of industrial unrest," he publicly expressed views on class conflict that seemed consistent with a tradition of class reconciliation deeply rooted in the mainstream of the Progressive movement. At the same time, he agreed privately with the sentiments of close political allies from Kansas City who argued that "our present industrial system should be placed on trial."[1]

During two years of hearings that crisscrossed the country and produced acrimonious encounters with corporate titans and meliorist reformers, Walsh came to represent a labor progressivism that challenged the reformers' ideal of social harmony.[2] Those reformers had fought to create such a commission and saw themselves as architects of its mission.[3] By the spring of 1915, deep into public hearings on the causes of industrial unrest, Walsh pleaded with Edward J. Ward, "For heaven's sake, don't accuse me publicly of being a 'constructive statesman.' Phrases and terms constantly take on new meanings. In the industrial field, at the present time, a constructive statesman might be defined as one who would substitute statutes for wages, with the chloroforming of public opinion as a byproduct." He belittled the "Wisconsin Idea," propounded by his fellow commissioner, John R. Commons, and commission staffer Charles McCarthy. He discounted their legalistic approach to investigation whereby "fundamentals remain largely untouched."[4]

The turmoil within the USCIR played out in public and behind the scenes. But despite the attention historians have lavished on the story, the implications of the commission's undertaking for the fate of the Progressive movement and for the nature and meaning of progressivism itself have not been adequately explored. Progressive reformers divided sharply over the work and substantive conclusions of the USCIR. Under Walsh's leadership, the commission asserted that reformers must reckon with class interests and class power if the "causes of industrial unrest" were to be addressed. In so doing, he became an iconic figure to the producerist and socialist wings of the labor movement and their reform allies.[5]

As class conflict intensified after 1909, an ideological division among Progressives grew deeper. A minority of reformers had advocated class-conscious support of labor's interest, but the more dominant wings of the movement pursued the ideal of class reconciliation through programs of social amelioration. Frank Walsh, the commission's vigorous chairman, came to view labor's interest as paramount and concluded that "no alleged or actual altruism of more fortunately circumstanced classes will avail to remove existing injustices." Instead, he came to argue that any constructive work must be "in the hands of men representing the interests of workers and directed to fitting the workers to exercise an ever-increasing measure of control over the industry in which they are engaged."[6]

The broad coalition of reformers that conceived the USCIR took a different view. Their movement had achieved unprecedented breadth and coherence in 1911–12, as we have seen. Its vital center lay in an extensive network of reform organizations and their intellectual allies. They pursued public policy initiatives designed to mitigate social crisis at local, state, and national levels. These reformers articulated a coherent vision of a society of self-directed individual citizens—the people—pursuing the public good in a democratic polity purged of corrupting influences. They saw themselves in resolutely modern terms, agents of an efficient and democratic order.

Shaken, like so many Americans, by the bitter class conflict of the late nineteenth century, they sought to invent social machinery for overcoming class polarization. Most Progressive reformers did not imagine a society that was literally without class differences but rather a society in which class differences were of diminishing importance and not a basis for political mobilization.

Two accomplishments in 1912–13 signified the reform movement's growing influence. First, by crafting a platform of "Industrial Minimums" at the June 1912 meeting of the National Conference of Charities and Corrections and publicizing the program through the *Survey,* reformers proved instrumental in shaping the platform of the Progressive Party on social and industrial issues.[7] Second, the reformers managed to persuade two administrations, one Republican and one Democrat, to undertake a major investigation of the "causes of industrial unrest" using the favored instrument of a public commission staffed by experts.

The resurgence of class conflict troubled the reform movement. After 1909, class warfare again disrupted industrial peace in ways that reformers could not ignore. Mass strikes and even pitched battles became not simply a "western" phenomenon but a symptom of renewed national crisis.

Labor conflict had, of course, not disappeared in the years since the great upheaval of the late nineteenth century. Anthracite coal miners, machinists, packinghouse workers, teamsters, and workers in other trades struck in the early, prosperous years of the twentieth century as unions affiliated with the AFL asserted a new sense of power and then fought back against employers' open-shop tactics. But in the years immediately following the strike of immigrant steel workers at McKees Rocks, Pennsylvania, in July 1909, a "revolt of the laborers" gathered steam and threatened to undermine the edifice of reform legislation and labor conciliation at the very moment reformers acquired the influence needed to reshape public policy and politics at the national level.[8] Class warfare, on a scale comparable to the crisis years of the late nineteenth century, gave their efforts to reconcile the interests of labor and capital new urgency. Ultimately, the "revolt of the laborers" consumed the commission it had spawned, pitting one segment of reformers against another and driving a deep wedge into the heart of the Progressive movement.

Laborers Revolt

Unprecedented circumstances converged in 1909 and the years immediately following to produce one of the most tumultuous periods of labor conflict in American history. After a sharp, year-long depression in 1907–8, the economy showed signs of recovery. But unskilled workers in the mass production industries, including many recent immigrants, confronted a new sense of the precariousness of their employment.[9] Faith in the potency of the craft unions had waned since the growth years of 1898–1903; overall membership had not kept pace with the growth of the economy, and with the ongoing technological revolution in basic industry, several prominent craft unions faced decline if not extinction.[10] Industrial unionism enjoyed a new lease on life. AFL affiliates, such as the Brewery Workers and the United Mine Workers, had kept the flame of industrial organization burning since the eclipse of the Knights of Labor. But the Industrial Workers of the World, having freed itself from the Socialist Labor Party albatross, demonstrated a strength in the West that promised expanded organizing. Strike data for the period are woefully inadequate, but some evidence suggests that in key sectors of the economy, labor relations had moved to a "war" footing.

Three strikes between mid-1909 and early 1910 heralded new patterns of labor conflict. The first, at McKees Rocks, Pennsylvania, pitted immigrant, largely unskilled steelworkers against the Pressed Steel Car Company, a U.S. Steel subsidiary. The strike erupted on July 15 with the walkout of five thousand workers, among them sixteen nationalities. Despite considerable brutality at the hands of the Pennsylvania constabulary and thirteen deaths during the course of the walkout, the strikers, assisted by a cadre of IWW organizers, declared victory on September 8. Observers found it remarkable that unskilled "new" immigrant workers, whom the AFL and most social reformers believed to be unorganizable, should have emerged victorious. That they did so with the assistance of key IWW organizers was especially troubling.[11] Late in November 1909, twenty thousand mostly immigrant, female shirtwaist makers walked off their jobs in New York's garment industry demanding a wage increase and union recognition.[12] And a few months later, in early 1910, ten thousand Philadelphia shirtwaist makers called their own strike. Although both clothing strikes ended in February without substantial gains, the gospel of unionism had spread among previously unorganized workers.[13] Even as the strike of Philadelphia garment workers drew to a conclusion, the city's streetcar workers struck the intransigent Philadelphia Transit Company. Following a pattern well established in metropolitan streetcar strikes, huge crowds involving tens of thousands of working-class Philadelphians attacked the cars. When the company refused arbitration, an estimated one hundred thousand workers on March 4 joined a citywide general strike in sympathy with the streetcar workers. The impressive general strike, lasting nearly three weeks, set the stage for a settlement of the transit strike that brought a partial victory for the union.[14]

During the next two years, increasingly violent conflict spread to new centers. On October 1, 1910, during a bitter strike of structural ironworkers, a powerful bomb exploded in the *Los Angeles Times* building, killing twenty people and setting the stage for a divisive and ultimately disastrous campaign to defend the accused McNamara brothers, officials of the union. In 1911, massive strikes on the Harriman-owned Illinois Central Railroad lines and among Chicago garment workers erupted, followed by the Lawrence textile strike in early 1912 and strikes of West Virginia coal miners, Paterson silk workers, iron miners in northern Michigan, and Colorado coal miners. Labor conflict attended by significant violence seemed to spread unchecked from one mass production center to another, taking root especially among unskilled, new immigrant workers.[15]

A sample of 1,434 strikes between 1908 and 1914 shows that some level of significant violence occurred in 267, or 19 percent, of them.[16] The characteristics of these violent strikes are particularly noteworthy. Strikes in mining, railroads, and other transportation sectors (especially street railways) followed an exceptionally violent course. Garment making and heavy manufacturing had a disproportionately large share of violent strikes. Strikes of industrial unions more than craft unions had violence associated with them, and they erupted more commonly in smaller industrial communities. Strikes over recognition turned violent more than those over wages and hours. Nine strikes, 3.4 percent of all "violent strikes," had extremely high levels of violence, involving multiple incidents in which fatalities, injuries, and "riots" occurred.[17] These strikes suggest a pattern of conflict between 1909 and 1914 that pushed the "class problem" and industrial unrest back to the center of public attention.

Social Reform and Class Conflict

The rising levels of class conflict particularly troubled an influential network of social reformers who formed the core of the Progressive movement. In the fall of 1911, more than a year after the fatal explosion at the *Los Angeles Times* building, the accused McNamara brothers confessed to the crime. Although the labor movement had largely come to their defense despite the mounting case against them, the social reformers viewed the bombing and the defense of the accused with alarm. The brothers' confession loosed an agonized torrent of sentiment favoring class reconciliation. The reformers called for an industrial commission to investigate the causes of unrest and recommend new "laws and methods for industrial adjustment." Paul Kellogg expressed in the *Survey* the consensus view of the twenty-nine reformers who participated in the magazine's forum on the "Larger Bearings of the McNamara Case." "The situation," he wrote, "is too much freighted with the public well-being to be left to contending forces to keep striking false balances." Speaking on behalf of "the whole people," he asserted that "we must give structure to fair play; reality to justice; and buttressed channels to those economic forces which, when they work at cross-purposes, jam up the currents of our national life." In a theme that would become central to the "industrial program" social reformers brought to the Progressive Party, Kellogg decried the waste of "our human strength" much as the natural environment had been desecrated.[18]

Differences in emphasis abounded among the reformers who were queried on the meaning of the McNamara case, but nearly all stressed the need for recognition of labor, for eliminating "predatory" organization among labor and capital, and for addressing the underlying conditions that produce violence. Florence Kelley stressed that such violence must include the catastrophic fiery deaths of the Triangle Shirtwaist workers and the "entombment of miners." With Henry Seager, many urged their reform colleagues to look beyond "the class struggle" to those elementary, democratic values shared by members of all classes.[19]

No strike of this era generated more sympathy for workers and more distress among social reformers than the Lawrence textile strike of early 1912. Even as Progressive reformers struggled to come to terms with the implications of the McNamaras' confession, they turned their attention to the sudden, unruly walkout of textile operatives in Lawrence, Massachusetts. Craft unionists viewed these new immigrants speaking myriad tongues with concern. To many reformers they seemed unassimilable. Shunned by a male-dominated labor movement that saw women factory operatives as interlopers in the labor market, the force of largely female operatives was called by one millowner "radicals of the worst sort." By their spontaneous as well as organized behavior in the strike, the female strikers, according to historian Ardis Cameron, defined themselves in the public mind as a riotous mob. The press characterized them as those "'unruly female elements' who hurled insults along with rocks, tore officers' coats, stuck hat pins in the horses of cavalry boys, and spread 'anarchy everywhere.'"[20]

Early reports by Progressive journalists covering the strike evidenced more sympathy for the strikers, especially over the issue of reduced wages, which employers had imposed along with legislated shorter hours. At the same time, progressive journals expressed concern over the intransigence IWW leaders brought to the strike. "What turn affairs would have taken without Ettor in the lead," the *Survey* wrote, "is a matter of speculation, but his speeches to the strikers on Saturday and Sunday certainly hastened the rioting on Monday."[21] At the root of the problem, according to the *Outlook,* lay "the evil practice of applying the methods of war instead of those of conciliation to labor problems." A senseless, "bitter conflict" resulted in "a great loss of money, great waste of time and labor . . . and deplorable violence." Nonetheless, many reformers applauded city and state authorities for their "sharp and stringent checking of violent demonstrations." As one correspondent noted in the *Outlook,* "When the Italian flag-bearer at the head of the mill-workers' procession shouted to the officer of the militia, 'The American flag can go anywhere,' that officer did the fit and right thing in first ordering his men to salute the flag, and then ordering them to fix bayonets to enforce his orders."[22]

Although the reform community deplored the failure of manufacturers to abandon their oligarchical practices, undercurrents of concern over the status and aspirations of new immigrant workers rose to the surface in many accounts of the strike.[23] Contrary to the myth that high tariffs protected the standards of American wage earners, veteran industrial investigator Jett Lauck reported that most mill workers were "pauper workmen" from assorted "races" of southern and eastern Europe and Asia. Tracing the growth of this largely foreign labor force, Lauck found it especially troubling that they showed little civic interest.[24] Boston settlement house worker Robert Woods worried that "the lowest scale of European and even Asiatic living [is] becoming inwrought into the very texture of the eastern Massachusetts community." To the argument that other immigrants began low and rose in the second generation to American levels, he replied that such social mobility has occurred "where the American leaven has had every chance to work; not where tens of thousands were fixing and crystallizing . . . in compact and congested immigrant masses, far away from anything like adequate recuperative forces."[25]

The strike seemed to hold troubling implications for the progress of reform, but some reformers saw the possibility for redemptive change. After the conclusion of the strike, Paul Kellogg warned of the dangers of anarchy on both sides. He even asserted that the abolition of slavery could have been accomplished peacefully without civil war had there been a willingness to make the necessary sacrifices. And by analogy, the abolition of poverty—the "squalor and misery on which social discontent thrives"—could be accomplished by the simple removal of "the seven wonders of the modern world—infectious disease, overwork, congestion, alcoholism, mental degeneracy, an inadequate educational system, and an obsolete penal system."[26] Others, such as Vida Scudder, affirmed the essential justice of the strikers' cause while urging them to avoid violence.[27]

Other voices identified more closely with the strikers' cause. They articulated a class partisanship that challenged the reformers' appeal for mediation and vision of interclass harmony. John Adams of Boston characterized "the striker" as a "brother," not Robert Woods's "clod." Faced with employer "anarchy," the strikers could hardly be expected to embrace citizenship in a country that seemed to make them serfs instead.[28] F. S. Boyd addressed the "would-be social reformers of Massachusetts" directly during the strike. "Their own ethical responsibility," he asserted, "stares them in the face":

> Because they promoted a law for shorter hours while failing to address the issue of wages, they were called upon to stand behind the strikers in their demand. I therefore put it straight up to the prosperous membership of the reform bodies of Massachusetts—of the consumers' leagues, the associations for labor legislation, and all other philanthropic persons who stand for a shortened working week—whether they are not bound to make their law really effective by giving generous financial support to this strike against a cut in wages.[29]

The strike wave that began with the "uprising of the 20,000" and the Pressed Steel Car strike in 1909 mobilized the reform community as never before. But Progressives did not all view the labor movement and class conflict through the same lens. Whereas Florence Kelley and Vida Scudder generally identified closely with labor, others, such as Paul Kellogg and Jane Addams, took a more distanced, neutral position, focusing on the conditions that fostered conflict and inefficiency and supporting mediation and class reconciliation.[30] And as the strikes continued unabated in 1912 and 1913, they anxiously searched for remedies.

Investigating the Causes of Industrial Unrest

During the last weeks of December 1911, before the outbreak of the Lawrence strike, a remarkable group of social reformers met repeatedly in the offices of the *Survey* and elsewhere in New York City to consider how the problem of industrial conflict might be solved. Jane Addams presided over the first meeting, which included Kellogg, Lillian Wald, Florence Kelley, Rabbi Stephen Wise,

Samuel McCune Lindsay, and John Haynes Holmes. They met with a sense of urgency. Successive meetings expanded the circle to include other settlement workers, the director of the Russell Sage Foundation, and the secretary of the National Child Labor Committee, among others.[31] In a petition to President Taft delivered on December 30, the group laid out its case for a commission to investigate industrial relations. This self-styled "industrial relations committee" drew on a favored remedy when it called for a commission to investigate "the grave problems" that faced the nation: "The American people as a whole must think these things through. . . . We need more light. . . . Today, as fifty years ago, a house divided against itself cannot stand. We have yet to solve the problems of democracy in its industrial relationships and to solve them along industrial lines."[32] The outbreak of the Lawrence strike in early January gave the petition even greater urgency.

During the succeeding months, the campaign for an industrial relations commission gathered steam. Legislation submitted by President Taft in response to the reformers' petition moved slowly through Congress, shepherded at every stage by this ad hoc committee and its network of supporters. When President Taft finally signed the law on August 23, 1912, the battle shifted to the composition of the commission.[33] Taft's selection of undistinguished public members and his failure to appoint either a woman or a respected social scientist troubled the reformers and persuaded them to support postponement of the panel's ratification until the new president, Woodrow Wilson, could name his own.[34]

The leadership of the American Federation of Labor resented the reformers' presumptuous and paternalistic effort to dictate the commission's composition. The workers, the *American Federationist* contended, were "not bugs to be examined under the lenses of a microscope by the 'intellectuals' on a sociological slumming tour." Workers did not object to a thorough examination "but will examine themselves and in turn reverse the lens and examine the examiners at the other end."[35]

Wilson's nominees proved more acceptable to the reformers, largely because he included John R. Commons from the University of Wisconsin, whom Kellogg cited as "the one man in America, who, as economist and investigator, has thought out industrial reforms, as statesman has drafted them into laws . . . and as administrator has practically enforced those laws." But the two other public members had not been among those the committee recommended. Mrs. J. Borden (Florence) Harriman, a wealthy New York City reformer, was regarded by Florence Kelley as "a comparative amateur." And Frank Walsh, a Kansas City attorney, named to chair the commission by Wilson, was a left-leaning reform Democrat and Wilson supporter. He stood well outside the New York and Chicago reform orbits and was comparatively unknown to them.[36]

Walsh brought to the work of the commission an unusual mix of western partisan politics and a rough-and-tumble commitment to reform, colored by his own experience with poverty and reform politics in Kansas City. As his friend and colleague Dante Barton noted, he was well prepared for the "technical part" of the commission's work but "is better fitted for the fight that lies ahead—for the human side of it." From a boyhood that taught him "what life is at its hard angles," Walsh had developed a deep hatred of poverty as "an unnecessary evil."[37] Having taught himself the law, he had been an attorney in Kansas City since 1889. His practice gradually became entwined in the webs of local social reform, as did his activity in the Democratic Party. By the early twentieth century, he was moving toward a career in public service that included membership on the city's Tenement Commission, the Board of Civil Service, and Kansas City's pioneering Board of Public Welfare, designed, as Barton noted, to make "private charities unnecessary." Walsh fought running battles with the state Democratic Party machine and helped elect reform governor Joseph Folk in 1904. He was recruited in 1912 by Woodrow Wilson's campaign to form a Bureau of Social Service that looked toward promoting a broad program of reform after the election.[38] Walsh brought to his chairmanship of the commission views on labor that were already well developed. As he told George Creel, "I feel very strongly that the commission should not be conceived as an arbitration board or a smelling committee. . . . It is *causes* that we are after, not *symptoms*."[39]

The press and members of the reform community greeted the appointment of the U.S. Commission on Industrial Relations with great fanfare. Yet the cautious maneuverings behind the scenes revealed potential divisions. Frank Walsh had a close-knit circle of Kansas City reformers and publicists whom he enlisted to project his vision of industrial reform. L. A. Halbert, superintendent of the Kansas City Board of Public Welfare, wrote to congratulate his former colleague on his nomination. Halbert expressed the conviction that Walsh would go to the "heart of the problem," directly contradicting the Progressives who had fashioned the commission. "I hope that the Commission will not give much time to health, safety and comfort in factories, or to industrial education, or anything of that sort but will go directly at the question as to how much voice the laborers should have in determining the conditions under which they will earn their living," he wrote. Walsh agreed with "the spirit of your kind expression," which gave him encouragement to take on the challenges that lay ahead.[40]

Walsh revealed his intentions most clearly to his close friend George Creel, who was preparing a major profile of him for *Collier's* magazine. "We are going into conditions more than specific troubles," Walsh told him, and "if our investigation results in placing our whole industrial system upon trial and endorsing or condemning it, than this Commission ought to do so in brave and definite terms." While expressing profound frustration that the Supreme Court majority "are our real rulers," he asked Creel to adopt a "judicious note" but not "conceal a real sentiment I have with regard to these questions of industrial relations." He lent support to Commons's practical idea to put the commission's ideas in the form of proposed legislation but emphasized the agitational value of such a strategy: "I believe that out of this we could get up a people's lobby that would be something worthwhile."

In early September, with the nominations of Walsh and the other commissioners moving toward ratification by the Senate, Boyd Fisher wrote to Walsh ("Dear Uncle Frank") asserting that Wilson failed to realize the importance of the industrial commission. "The country is on the verge of great changes of opinion and policy upon industrial matters," he declared. He predicted that by the end of Wilson's term, "an astonishing crystallization of labor demands and labor discontent will take place." The political implications were already evident. "The masses are silent only because aside from the Socialists no party has sufficiently sounded their deep discontent. Mr. Wilson's reaper isn't set close enough to the ground; the grain is below."[41]

Even as Walsh and his closest colleagues devised strategies for the forthcoming hearings, key reformers from the Industrial Relations Committee, who had been largely responsible for creating the commission, moved to embrace and guide Walsh's initial efforts. With Walsh's nomination certain, they sought to enlist his support for the objectives they had done so much to define.[42] Paul Kellogg reminded Walsh that "no member of the committee which agitated for the legislation was named on the commission." But "as a volunteer body it is in a good position to follow up the work and cooperate in exploring the field which in its conception, gave fire to the movement from the start." The *Survey*'s symposium on the work of the commission illustrated "the closeness with which the work of this new body will be followed."[43]

The commission began its work amid great anticipation. Almost immediately, a division of responsibilities developed between its two branches: investigation through hearings intended to shape public opinion and "scientific" inquiry meant to influence the drafting of legislation. Presumably, hearings would build public support for legislation. Commons recalled that this division of responsibilities in fact sprang from an early conversation he had with Walsh in Kansas City: "He had charge of the public hearings . . . with his own staff. I had charge of the staff of investigators appointed on my recommendation." He believed the hearings were "of much importance, although the witnesses merely stated their opinions and interpretations." Commons's experience with the National Civic Federation and the Wisconsin Industrial Commission had convinced him that he could work more effectively through private channels to reconcile conflicting interests and reach agreements. And such agreements could provide a basis for future congressional legislation.[44] Present at the outset, these differences in perspective regarding the commission's work would grow over the next two years, revealing a fundamental schism among reformers.

Progressives Divided

The Commission on Industrial Relations organized itself slowly and with some difficulty.[45] Investigators fanned out across the country against a backdrop of labor conflict that gave heightened urgency to their work. Even before the first hearings opened or the preliminary reports of investigators were filed, violence broke out in the coalfields of Colorado. By early spring that conflict, culminating in the massacre of seventeen strikers and family members encamped at Ludlow, Colorado, cast a deepening shadow of bitterness and class polarity across the path of the commission and brought home the enormous chasm that still divided labor and capital.[46]

Charles McCarthy, a leading proponent of the Wisconsin Idea, had testified at Commons's behest in late December about the "method" of investigation the commission should adopt. He drew directly on his experience in Wisconsin, where for the previous thirteen years he had directed the Legislative Reference Bureau and had under his charge all "constructive work, every piece of it." McCarthy had a specific conception of "constructive work." Surveying past experience with investigatory commissions, he argued that faulty methods had been adopted: "In the early days when an investigation was started like this they would bring in almost all kinds of testimony to get at the facts and then that testimony would result in a great many volumes. You would not have anything left afterwards." McCarthy proposed instead that the commission select certain lines of inquiry that promised results and assign investigators to them. Knowledgeable people should draw up new legislation using models from other states and countries. McCarthy outlined precisely the program favored by Commons and the reformers who had promoted the commission.[47] Specifically, he foresaw concerted investigation and new legislation focused on the areas of social insurance, industrial education, minimum wage, and immigration.[48]

In early May, McCarthy received word of Jett Lauck's resignation as director of research for the commission, after months of growing concern about his effectiveness.[49] McCarthy offered his services to Walsh in late May, though for months he had hinted at his availability. Drawn to this "great statesman-like program of social betterment" and aware of the "question of administration" before the commission, he boldly asserted, "I have come to the conclusion that the only thing that can be done with it is for me to take hold of it in some way."[50] Welcomed enthusiastically by Walsh, McCarthy moved quickly to assume responsibility for the research program.[51] Like Commons, he argued for better utilizing the commission's scarce resources by cutting down on hearings and providing more adequate funding for research.

McCarthy found himself perched uneasily between alternative conceptions of the commission's work. He soon found the ground beneath his feet eroding.[52] A serious financial crisis threatened the completion of the work. The struggle over the remaining funds—symptomatic of ideological divisions within the commission—would intensify during the remaining months of McCarthy's tenure.[53]

From August 1914 until the appearance of the final reports a year later, a series of intersecting dramas played out within the commission that highlighted the divisions among Progressives over the causes of the industrial unrest that had swept across America. Did the unrest stem from the psychology of workers, the failure of legal institutions, the absence of effective state regulation, or, as Walsh and his allies came to believe, the distribution of wealth and power? Differences over what constituted the "constructive work" needed to remedy those problems also beset the commission. What role would be played by careful, scientific investigation, the drafting of precise and enforceable legislation, or, alternatively, by mobilizing public outrage and opinion, and creating a new politics of labor? The split over the relative importance of investigatory work or public hearings polarized the staff and led to a severe organizational rupture. The reformers, who retained a proprietary interest in the work of the commission, grew increasingly vocal in their criticism. Controversy over the Rockefeller Foundation's own investigation and over the relationship between the commission and the philanthropists and their social work allies, what Walsh came to call the "Charity Trust," further alienated the reformers. These bitter divisions would be reflected in the commission's multiple final reports and color subsequent assessments of the fruits of its work.[54]

Rockefeller and the Charity Trust

An issue of great symbolic significance surfaced in early October and magnified other divisions in the commission's work. In September 1914, the Rockefeller Foundation announced an investigation of its own into the problems of industrial unrest. The foundation had recruited distinguished Canadian industrial relations expert Mackenzie King to head the investigation. Some USCIR staff immediately linked the prominence of Rockefeller interests in the Colorado Fuel and Iron strike to the proposed investigation.

Paul Kellogg responded by bringing the issue forcefully to the surface in a *Survey* editorial. Announcing the new Rockefeller investigation, Kellogg noted with approval both the high scientific standard of previous foundation investigations into social hygiene and disease and "social evil" and the expertise and independence of Mackenzie King, "who has stood preeminently for the disinterested public in a succession of labor controversies." Kellogg criticized the USCIR, which had "floundered badly, without clear-cut division of responsibility, and with great areas of the field before it practically untouched." McCarthy's ascension as director of research in June "for the first time gave promise of coherence enough in the work to allow disinterested observers to make sure of its trend."[55] The *Survey* targeted the commission's failure to make the Colorado strike "a great laboratory exhibiting in masterful detail that industrial unrest which was prime subject matter for study" and its inability to avert a garment strike in New York the previous winter. Kellogg devoted most of the editorial to the new Rockefeller undertaking. He found its limitations less obvious than a public inquiry: no distraction of divergent viewpoints, no patronage assaults, ample resources of time and money. He acknowledged that the Rockefeller inquiry "draws its funds from an interested source" but noted that the investigation had no connection to a particular strike and had hired a preeminent, disinterested expert. He justified the inquiry "upon the broad need felt by managers and men alike for a betterment of the complex industrial relations and reactions which both alike find unsatisfactory and wasteful."[56]

By the time the *Survey* editorial appeared, events had moved swiftly on several fronts. Before learning of the editorial, Walsh had directed McCarthy to begin preparations for hearings, which would be used to examine the proposed investigation of the Rockefeller Foundation. He cited public and expert criticism of previous Rockefeller inquiries. Given the foundation's refusal to cooperate with other government agencies, "added to the Colorado situation," he noted, "we may have the background to make a report to Congress recommending that the activities of this alleged Foundation be prohibited by law." McCarthy himself had suggested, more pragmatically, that the Rockefeller inquiry be used as a basis for requesting an additional congressional appropriation in order to ensure "some view from an unbiased public standpoint." With Walsh's concurrence, McCarthy used his own personal channels to the Rockefeller Foundation, inviting its representatives to appear before the commission to explain their purposes. He warned them that "a great many laboring men are greatly alarmed" and that their investigation might "boomerang" unless they adopted a more democratic organization. The money should be given outright to an organization in which capital and labor will have confidence and "which the public will have something to say about."[57]

Amid the flurry of communications regarding the prospect of Rockefeller hearings, McCarthy received a visit in Madison from social investigator John Fitch, just returning from the West, where he had shadowed the commission's hearings and written periodic reports for the *Survey.* Fitch read the preliminary report that McCarthy had drafted of the commission's investigatory work and the plans for its completion. McCarthy reported to Walsh that Fitch seemed "very anxious" and he "thot [*sic*] it all important that I should meet the group in New York," by which he meant the social reformers who had been instrumental in launching the USCIR and, like Kellogg, remained critical of the approach taken by Walsh. Fitch then launched into an agenda for research on labor organizations that undoubtedly reflected the assumptions of the *Survey* crowd. "He said," McCarthy continued, "that we ought to determine once for all whether the labor unions were good or not; whether they were good institutions or not; whether they were not more than little monopolies; whether they did not tend to level men down; whether the union was or was not an efficient machine; whether there was democracy in the rules of admission. He cited an instance where the evidence showed that it took $150 to get into one of these unions."[58] Such a perspective must have reinforced Walsh's view that some members of the reform community provided cover for the strident anti-unionism of employers such as Rockefeller.

The intransigence of Rockefeller and his associates over opening the foundation's inquiry to public scrutiny and the continued meddling of Kellogg and the New York–based reformers prompted Walsh to respond with brutal frankness to Kellogg's editorial: "The editorial is cunning and dishonest. Though I sincerely regret it, I am forced to the conclusion that you were compelled to publish the same, at this particular time, by your patrons and masters, and that you are ashamed of it."[59]

Walsh's attack on the independence of Kellogg and the *Survey* precipitated a firestorm in the reform community. Kellogg insisted on publishing Walsh's more detailed critique of the *Survey* editorial in parallel columns with the editorial itself and all related correspondence. Walsh attacked the presumed impartiality of Mackenzie King and the Rockefeller inquiry and responded to the criticisms of the commission's early months of investigation. He explained in detail how and why the commission had investigated the Colorado situation as it did. One of Walsh's associates, George P. West, who had been the principal investigator of the Colorado situation, also replied to Kellogg's laudatory comments about previous Rockefeller-funded inquiries. "The difference is obvious between an inquiry in the field of the exact natural sciences and an inquiry in a field where the truth lies with one or the other of two conflicting social philosophies," he stated.[60]

The work of the commission, in the meantime, moved forward at an accelerating pace. Over the objections of the governor of Colorado, Walsh began the long-awaited hearings in Denver on December 3. Those hearings produced ample evidence of involvement by Rockefeller in directing the company's response to the strike. At the same time, commission staffer Basil Manly reported to Walsh the preparations being made for what would now be more far-reaching hearings in New York on "the policies, methods and results of the privately endowed and privately supported foundations and organizations." The commission would examine not only the planned Rockefeller inquiry but also the work of other charitable foundations, including Russell Sage, Carnegie, the National Civic Federation, and the Charity Organization Society. Manly reported that they would look into "what part the sources of their income play in the determination of their policies and methods and finally whether such self-perpetuating organizations must not necessarily be a menace. I think it can be shown that they inevitably take part in politics."[61] Manly also indicated that the wide-ranging hearings would consider the "centralization of industrial control and the labor policies of Big Business."

The New York hearings opened on January 18, and for the next month Frank Walsh elicited testimony around the central themes that would find their way into the commission's Final Report (the Manly Report). Criticism and defense of foundations as extensions of the corporations that spawned them was interwoven with personal testimony of survivors of the Ludlow massacre and leaders of the United Mine Workers of America (UMWA) in Colorado. John D. Rockefeller Jr. held center stage for several days of cross-examination by Walsh. Corporate magnates Andrew Carnegie (once again defending his role in the Homestead strike twenty-two years earlier), J. P. Morgan, Henry Ford, and George W. Perkins all testified in turn.[62]

While this round of hearings was underway, Walsh spoke at an open forum in Public School No. 62 on the East Side of New York and explained the connection, as he saw it, between an inquiry into "a labor war" and the great philanthropic foundations. He traced the development of work from the small shop to the great enterprise under the control of "absentee capital." He cited the growing industrial control over government in closed company towns exemplified by the "benevolent despotism" New York directors of Colorado Fuel and Iron exercised in two Colorado counties where workers are "robbed of the rights of free men." Such denial of rights, he asserted, prostrates republican government from the county to the national level. In a phrase that echoed the philosophy of the Knights of Labor, he asserted that an "injury to the weakest person in industry or out of industry is the concern of every person in the United States." The source of industrial unrest, he argued, has to do "with men's relations to the natural wealth. . . . Men have a right . . . to wrest a livelihood from nature." Herein lay the connection to the great foundations generated from the income of corporations. Only labor produces wealth. "If property is so produced, under a democracy, who shall have the first say as to what becomes of it, but the man who produces it?" Walsh saw clearly the path to solving the problem of industrial unrest: "Industry must be democratized . . . and the man who toils is little better than the slave unless he has a voice in the conditions of labor."[63]

At the heart of Walsh's battles with Kellogg and the New York reformers, and his deepening disagreement over methods with Commons and McCarthy, lay a different analysis of the problems the commission had set out to address. For Walsh and those reformers closest to him, America remained a profoundly class-divided society in which the problems of democratic reform could only be addressed by a fundamental redistribution of power, "a voice in the conditions of labor." The Progressive reformers, for whom Commons, McCarthy, and Kellogg spoke, did not believe class divisions were endemic. They spoke for a "public" convinced that capital and labor could find common ground. This process of class reconciliation would be facilitated by scientific inquiry, remedial legislation, and the proper administrative machinery for settling disputes, without significantly altering the existing distribution of power and wealth.[64]

The New York hearings fueled the fires of conflict with Kellogg. George Creel published a series of articles in *Pearson's Magazine* on "How 'Tainted' Money Taints," followed in succeeding months by Julian Leavitt's articles, "The Menace of Benevolence" and "The Middlemen of Charity." When Creel called the *Survey* "the voice of 'Monopolized Altruism'" and ridiculed Kellogg as the tool of the Rockefeller interests, the *Survey*'s editorial columns once again erupted. Kellogg bitterly criticized Walsh and "the pal of Chairman Walsh," George Creel, for unfairly attacking the *Survey* and denying him the opportunity to rebut the charges in testimony before the commission. He reiterated his criticisms of the commission's work, reminded his readers of his and the social reformers' role in originating the whole public investigation in the first place, and their continuing "responsibility, as a piece of citizenship, to follow, interpret, and criticize that commission."[65]

Progressives and the Class Divide

The public drama of the New York hearings and the divisions between Walsh and Kellogg signified a deeper, climactic crisis within the commission itself—a crisis rooted in fundamentally different conceptions of the commission's work, the sources of industrial unrest, and the role of Progressives in constructing remedies. The commission's fiscal crisis intensified divergent perceptions of the value of hearings.

Frank Walsh secured an additional appropriation of one hundred thousand dollars from Congress, significantly less than he had originally hoped, to finish the work. He allocated nearly forty thousand dollars to complete the investigations and edit and produce the final reports but would not agree to the larger "minimum necessary" budget proposed by McCarthy. Frustrated by his inability to crack John D. Rockefeller Jr. at the New York hearings, Walsh turned on McCarthy's longstanding relationship with Rockefeller.[66] McCarthy insisted that his relations with Rockefeller during his tenure with the commission were entirely consistent with Walsh's instructions. "You wanted no rough stuff and wanted me to break the thing gently to them and be friendly," he said. Walsh, however, suspected McCarthy of double-dealing. He remained committed to protecting the commission's dwindling resources for additional hearings. Rockefeller's success in winning over the public during the New York hearings irritated him. This combination of circumstances led him to fire

McCarthy, virtually dismantle the research division, and undertake a more vigorous exposé of Rockefeller's complicity in the Colorado strike. In the process, he expected to reveal the sham behind Rockefeller's own "neutral" investigation of the causes of industrial unrest, so warmly embraced by the New York reform community.[67]

Speaking on behalf of Progressives who had seen in the commission an opportunity to craft the machinery for class reconciliation, McCarthy vented his frustration. "The aim of the Commission from the beginning has been to work out constructive programs," he declared. He outlined how he had expected the work to unfold: "We were to bring out some [research] bulletins which the Commission were to pass upon on all the great questions. Then, about April, we were to take all the data which we had, get a bill drafting department and draft up this material so that these bulletins and bills could go together." He had pursued this idea with the expectation of presenting "a great program" to the president "which all the progressives in America could get behind." He saw it as a "statesman-like, clear orderly program" that had the "strength of logic behind it." But this was something Walsh "has never understood." Walsh's pursuit of more hearings, he declared, will "leave us nothing for constructive work whatsoever." Fitch had also written a long review of the commission's field investigations that directly criticized Walsh's emphasis on hearings at the expense of investigation.[68]

For his part, Walsh had come to represent a brand of progressivism that was distinctly at odds with the vision of Kellogg, McCarthy, and their reform allies. Nevertheless, he muted his public criticism of McCarthy even as he fired him. It was only in a personal letter a few weeks later to his old ally and friend from St. Louis, William Marion Reedy, that he decided to "dump" the whole thing. Nowhere did he more clearly lay out his deep philosophical differences with the so-called constructive Progressives. He characterized Commons as a "fine, well-meaning man." Intimately connected "in the Wisconsin University," Commons and McCarthy were both "heavily charged with the 'Wisconsin Idea', which would seem, at least, in this work, to be not to do any investigating or make any recommendations, unless approved by so-called advisory committees of employers and workers." Walsh relentlessly ridiculed the scientific and professional pretensions of those subscribing to the "Idea." They favor creating "what they call 'large constructive programs,'" he wrote, which, as he saw it, "consist of interminable 'bill-drafting'; the proposed measures containing legal machinery which would provide for countless employees, experts, and the like, 'of thorough scientific training', the very thought of which should throw the legal profession into spasms of delight, and the proletariat into hopeless despair. While this is going on, fundamentals remain practically untouched."[69]

Walsh next turned to a plan of "cooperation" promoted by the "Idea" men that he believed fell "little short of espionage." Here he alluded, unmistakably, to McCarthy's ties to Rockefeller. Clearly Walsh had something different in mind. He noted that McCarthy and Commons were "well thought of by the philanthropic trust in New York, who have made more or less strenuous efforts to apply the methods of scientific philanthropy to the work" of the commission. He found it amusing that his resistance to their plans had produced in these gentlemen "a state of irritation which would seem impossible for such cool and scientific beings." Walsh looked instead toward a final report that would have "the proper punch" and that would give "the real conditions of labor in the country and the true cause of industrial unrest."

In the final months of the commission's life, Walsh held the most dramatic and, in many ways, defining hearings of the investigation. He called Rockefeller back to the stand during the May hearings in Washington. Armed now with correspondence uncovered by his investigators that showed Rockefeller's involvement in all phases of the Colorado strike and its conduct, Walsh set upon him with a vengeance not seen in previous testimony. He later said that he had "turned the young man inside out" to get at the truth and "left him without a single justification for anything that took place in Colorado."[70] Walsh's "rough" handling of Rockefeller generated a flood of publicity and, as he had hoped, focused attention on the responsibility of large corporations and their philanthropic arms for the industrial unrest that beset the country. Walsh had already become the chief target for criticism of the commission's meddling in industrial relations. Now a torrent of abuse poured forth from conservative and business critics. The *Iron Trade Review* called his method "Walshing," which meant "to bully, to rage against 'capital' and 'plutocracy'; having the characteristics of a devil dancer, dervishkearney, a Haywood or a flubdubber; used to rock a fellow on the 'money' boat."[71]

Final Reports

With the public hearings concluded, Basil Manly, who now headed the pared-down commission staff, turned to producing the final report. When the Manly Report became available to commission members in July, the employer members and the two other public members, Commons and Mrs. Harriman, roundly dissented from its findings and recommendations. Unable to reach consensus, in August the members finally issued a series of reports and commentaries on one another's reports that illustrated the deep splits within the commission. The fundamental divide lay between the official report written by Manly, reflecting Walsh's views and supported by the three labor members, and the Commons Report, signed by Mrs. Harriman and, with some additional dissents, the three employer representatives.[72]

The Manly and Commons final reports, and the reactions they precipitated within the reform community, further reveal the impact that deepening class conflict had produced within the commission and among Progressives. In the Manly report, according to the *New Republic*, Walsh "secured the kind of report which he wished." In his own supplemental statement, Walsh offered (in bold print) his central indictment:

> we find the basic cause of industrial dissatisfaction to be low wages; or, stated in another way, the fact that the workers of the nation, through compulsory and oppressive methods, legal and illegal, are denied the full product of their toil.[73]

The Manly Report made four fundamental points about the causes of industrial unrest and proposed recommendations for action regarding each. First, the report argued that an unjust distribution of wealth, rooted in the growth of huge corporations, created vast poverty and undermined the ability of workers to defend their rights. Second, chronic unemployment and the "denial of an opportunity to earn a living" directly affected workers' incomes and security in a labor market dominated by monopolies. Third, the report indicted a judicial system that systematically thwarted workers' rights and aided employers in preventing their effective organization. Fourth, the denial of labor's right to organize constituted the primary reason for unrest to which all others related. The report recommended a steep, graduated tax on inheritance and the use of those monies for education and public works to relieve unemployment, the recovery of public control of all land and mineral rights "secured by fraud," new statutes and constitutional amendments to protect laborers' rights and personal liberties, and new legislation that would guarantee the right of labor to organize and bargain collectively without interference by employers.[74] In his own personal statement appended to the report, Walsh fixed the "social responsibility for these unfortunate conditions" in ways that suggested more concretely how they might be remedied. He did not "blame" employers for low wages and poor conditions, nor for attempting to gain economic and political advantage, because they had "merely followed the natural bent of men involved in the struggle of competitive industry." Rather, he held workers themselves responsible for being "blind to their collective strength and oftentimes deaf to the cries of their fellows," and he criticized the "great mass of citizens" who have failed to see that their prosperity and their rights are bound up with the welfare of those who suffer. But only workers, ultimately, using "their collective power," could bring "genuine and lasting improvement."[75] The Manly/Walsh recommendations looked to the political mobilization of labor on its own behalf and to a fundamental realignment of class power. They did not regard the administrative intervention of neutral experts or commissions as the primary avenue of redress. They placed little stock in mediation and conciliation.

The Commons Report offered a vastly different perspective. Short on analysis of the causes of industrial unrest and long on proposed remedies, Commons summarized the views of the expert investigators, many of them his own students who would dominate the field of industrial relations in years to come. Drawing directly on his experience with the Wisconsin Industrial Commission, Commons proposed permanently instituted state and federal industrial commissions and advisory bodies for each, composed of management, labor, and public members. These commissions would set standards for wages, hours, and working conditions and mediate labor disputes on a voluntary basis. Government would not be given a legislative mandate to regulate collective bargaining between private parties. But industrial commissions might facilitate dispute resolution and administer "laws on child labor, hours of labor, safety and health, workmen's compensation, sickness insurance, and minimum wage." Only where industries failed to create orderly industrial relations through trade agreements might more direct state intervention be necessary.[76] Again and again Commons stressed the impartial and deliberative nature of commissions. Only if industrial commissions are "removed from the heat of political controversy" could they "have the confidence of employers and employees." Saturated with Progressives' suspicion of politics and their belief in class reconciliation, the Commons Report staked out the rationale that underlay his plan: "The points of antagonism are enlarged and exaggerated when one side or the other, through practical politicians controls the offices. The points of harmony can only be discovered by investigation, and investigations must be cooperative between employers and unions, else neither side will have confidence in the results."[77] These views reflected the core convictions of the coalition of Progressive reformers who had pushed for a commission to investigate industrial relations in the first place.

Reviewing the fruits of the commission's work, most progressive publications found them wanting. The *New Republic* spoke for many when it declared that the "great task" set before the commission had been "to prepare the ground and point the way by which the democracy could accumulate the experience and the power for humanizing the conditions under which it works." Although admiring Walsh's "honorable human passion" to not only "find the truth, but to spread it," the editors criticized the "almost mystical belief in the value of friction" that animated Walsh and his allies. "He was frankly on the side of the poor and the oppressed," they asserted. Noting his emphasis on hearings at the expense of "expert investigation," the *New Republic* judged him to be an agitator. The "Walsh Report" (deliberately renamed) sounds like "uncritical denunciation" because it offers only "a skeleton of evils instead of a tissue of realities." Failing to confront "haphazard opinion" with "scientific inquiry," Walsh could not "distinguish between what witnesses said and what investigators found." Even more detrimental to the fate of the commission, "he suggests no machinery for the future by which the clash of views in the industrial struggle can be fertilized by a steady stream of carefully ascertained facts."[78]

The *New Republic*, like many in the community of reform, believed the Commons Report to be "wise but unexciting . . . significant, even revolutionary, and yet humdrum." The editors found congenial Commons's emphasis on impartiality, expert investigation, and administrative rather than political solutions. In their view, his vision of industrial relations encouraged the "constant cooperation of employers and employees." Once the employer accepted dealing with "an impartial administrative body, representing no merely hostile interest . . . his former opposition oozes." This was then the quintessentially progressive solution to orchestrating class harmony and labor peace in an era of industrial unrest. "In short, the whole idea of labor legislation by means of administrative order, issued after thorough investigation by an impartial industrial commission, cooperating with representatives of all parties, rests upon the assumption that there is a certain basis of common interest between labor and capital."[79]

The labor movement, too, took a close look at the results of the commission's work but gave enthusiastic support to the report signed by Walsh and the labor commissioners. But Walsh, more than anyone else, captured workers' imagination. Regarded initially "as the one unprejudiced and unaligned man on the Commission," he proved to be "heart and soul with labor . . . the greatest acquisition and force which has come to labor in a generation," according to the Colorado Federation of Labor.[80] To the accusation by Colorado governor Carlson that Frank Walsh had spread "mendacious state-ments" regarding the situation in his state, UMWA columnist Mabel Larue Germer wrote, "From his standpoint—yes. From the workers' standpoint— NO." She offered a perspective on industrial unrest at odds with that of Com-mons and the Progressive reformers: "Some of our smooth-tongued em-ployers have fed us a soothing tonic all these years which they call 'Identity of Interests.' That mixture is now causing indigestion in the minds of wideawake workers, because we know the interest of the employer and that of the employe [sic] is not identical. If it were, why the industrial strife?"[81] To a representative of the labor press, Walsh denied being "doctrinaire." Nor, he noted (somewhat tongue in cheek), was he "a political economist." The inquiry studied "life itself." And, he argued, "you cannot card-index the hopes, aspirations, happiness, miseries, laughter and tears of the human fam-ily." The concentration of capital, the seizure of the resources of the coun-try by a few to the detriment of "the rest of us," had been made clear. Con-vinced by the experience of the previous two years, he believed that "the people have a growing sense of their power to overthrow this injustice over night if they but will do it so. When enough of us get the idea, it may be done between days."[82]

In all its final disarray, the USCIR revealed the profoundly disquieting fact that class division, the bane of progressive reform, remained central to Amer-ican life and not, at least for the time being, susceptible to administrative so-lution. Walsh had become either "a Jacobin" or "the heart and soul of labor," depending on one's vantage point.[83] The "causes of industrial unrest" had been identified in the public mind as never before and the complicity of cap-ital arraigned, but no armistice in the "class war" seemed in sight.

Walsh and his allies proceeded to form their own "Committee on Indus-trial Relations" and to agitate and organize on behalf of the agenda put for-ward in the Manly Report. The committee attracted to its executive board a group of reformers unquestionably loyal to labor, in addition to the three labor members of the commission, and Walsh and Manly. They included Cleveland reformer and immigration commissioner Frederic Howe; Amos Pinchot, who had fought to wrest control of the Progressive Party from its corporate patrons; John Fitzpatrick, president of the Chicago Federation of Labor; Agnes Nestor of the WTUL; Helen Marot of the AFL; and John White of the UMWA. Conspicuously absent were any of the reformers who had lob-bied for the USCIR. The committee received strong financial backing from the United Mine Workers and in its public introduction sharply differenti-ated its appeal from progressive interests who might seek impartial mediation of class conflict. The committee announced that it would provide "a medium for the cooperation of the forces of organized labor and those citizens, who, though outside the labor movement, recognize in that movement the hope of democracy and realize the justice of its aims."[84]

By the early months of 1916, the war in Europe and the reelection campaign of Woodrow Wilson dominated the headlines and the attention of the reform community. The labor movement found itself in a rapidly changing political environment that enhanced its bargaining position and welcomed its participation in Wilson's campaign to "make the world safe for democracy." But shortly after the commission's final reports had been submitted to Congress, Basil Manly suggested to Frank Walsh ways in which the new climate of war might affect labor's program. He urged Walsh to use his Labor Day speech to make two points: "the necessity for labor organization as a basis for efficient industrial operation during war" and "the democratization of war preparations" (or, more directly, "the rich should pay"). Weaving together the themes of class war and European war, Manly suggested that "every union local should be made a voluntary military company and every union hall an armory. Organized on a volunteer basis militarism would be impossible." He believed that "a little agitation" on behalf of a "'Trade Union army' would do more to stop war talk than all the platitudes in the world." Finally, he noted, but urged Walsh not to mention it in his speech, that "there would be no Colorados or West Virginias with such a democratic army in existence."[85]

As the war drew closer, new alliances and new fissures erupted in the ranks of Progressive reformers. The concept of "industrial democracy" took on contradictory meanings as the magnetic pull of nationalism exerted greater force in American life. But before the United States became a partisan in the European war, before the debates over preparedness and war profiteers, before the Council on National Defense and George Creel's Minutemen were called into action, the reform community had confronted the facts of a domestic war of classes, publicized by Frank Walsh through the hearings and reports of the U.S. Commission on Industrial Relations.[86] The effort to diagnose causes of industrial unrest and prescribe remedies confronted the Progressives with contradictions that called into question the guiding vision and the success of their movement. Its appeal had been premised largely on the faith that class conflict could be eliminated and social divisions healed by a program of "constructive work" on behalf of a broadly shared public interest.

Many Progressives, in the context of war, recast their faith in the healing powers of the public's interest around a nationalist program that pledged, among other things, to secure democracy abroad. Other reformers, with close ties to labor, pushed a program of industrial democracy that sought to use the exigencies of war to finally grant labor a significant measure of control and recognition in the workplace and thereby address the problem of "industrial unrest" as they had come to understand it.

CONCLUSION

War and the
Ragged Edges of Reform

The first item in the program of self government is to drag the whole population well above the misery line. . . . You can't build a modern nation out of Georgia crackers, poverty-stricken negroes, the homeless and helpless of the great cities. They make a governing class essential. They are used by the forces of reaction. . . . Before you can begin to have democracy you need a country in which everyone has some stake and some taste of its promise.

—Walter Lippmann, *Drift and Mastery,* 1914

The historical record of twentieth-century liberalism is both triumphant and tortured. The roots of this "new liberalism" lay in its critique and, ultimately, abandonment of classical liberalism, with its excessive deference to individual liberty and faith in the natural justice of the marketplace. By the end of the nineteenth century, many reformers believed such principles had proved bankrupt in the face of deepening social crises. A new theory and practice of liberalism, in the guise of what contemporaries called "progressivism," gradually took shape out of the shock and disorientation brought on by raging industrialization and the class warfare it precipitated.[1] In conferences and new reform journals, in the vestibules of settlement houses and the offices of organizations dedicated to investigating social conditions, in party caucuses of partisan reformers and staff meetings of newly elected reform mayors, a Progressive movement was born.

Progressivism departed in significant ways from its classical antecedents, as reformers sought to find a new social balance between contending and at times conflicting interests. What John Dewey later called a "renascent liberalism" required the application of "intelligence" to a rationalized social order still committed to traditional liberal ideals of individual enhancement.[2] Progressives placed great faith in the capacity of a democratic community, enlisting where necessary the state, to manage and shape a future in which social harmony might reign. Community, so celebrated in the writings of Dewey and Jane Addams, would provide a check on the rampant individualism of a laissez-faire social order. That sense of community found its embodiment for many Progressives in the settlement house, a refuge in the urban "jungle" where classes crossed paths, found common purpose, cultivated civic responsibility, and ultimately enabled the individual to pull himself out of the "the submerged tenth" and become a worthy citizen. Progressives found in the state, once cleansed of corruption and the excesses of partisanship, a useful if not always reliable ally for civic action and community improvement. Even as the state might embody the public's interest, it was no substitute for the nonpartisan civic activism that "the people" might continue to pursue through interest-based organizations, responsible trade unions engaged in orderly collective bargaining or arbitration, or the tempering influence of a host of commissions, boards, and regulatory bodies staffed by experts.

Progressive reformers envisioned a world in which class conflict might be ameliorated and class differences gradually dissolved into a new civic order. But like their nineteenth-century liberal antecedents, they held racial views that consigned African Americans and new immigrants to the social margins. However compassionate most reformers were, they believed these racial "others" to be poor candidates for the responsibilities of citizenship. Only the slow processes of social uplift and education might bring them to the point of being admitted to the circle of full citizenship.

By 1915, Progressives stood at a precarious point in their own history. Brimming with a certain confidence based on their access to national prominence and influence over party platforms, they also faced the sobering fact that class warfare seemed again to be polarizing society. Encouraged by the legislative initiatives of a new administration that seemed committed to improving the conditions of labor, curtailing the scourge of child labor, and harnessing the trusts, Progressives worried about the distractions of a war in Europe that threatened to draw the United States into the conflict and sidetrack the domestic reform agenda. Nevertheless, they believed themselves to be agents of a revived national mission to renew democracy and expressed confidence about forging unity of "the race" out of diverse ethnic material. Social engineering still held the promise of meeting human needs, improving the mechanisms for class reconciliation, cultivating a better educated citizenry, and perfecting democratic institutions.

But as many historians have noted, this moment of optimism also held the seeds of the Progressive movement's disintegration. While the narrative of the movement's decline is not nearly as simple as it once seemed, the question, What happened to the progressive movement? still resonates through the work of historians today as it did that of earlier generations.[3] The conventional narrative constructed by Progressive historians and their intellectual descendants answered this question quite simply: World War I came and spread disarray in Progressives' ranks.[4] Reformers lost their sense of direction, and the war intensified their divisions. With U.S. entry into the war, the progressive project of national reconstruction took on a jingoist and antiradical coloration. The racial and nativist undercurrents in progressive thought surfaced with a harder edge. The frenzy of national mobilization absorbed and transformed the movement's domestic reform agenda and empowered its conservative opponents.[5]

This study has suggested that contradictions inhered in the Progressive movement itself and in the remedies it offered for America's social ills in the industrial age. Even before the European war reared its head, the project of harmonizing class relations and extending democratic citizenship by reforming the worst consequences of capitalist industrialization had foundered on the shoals of renewed class warfare. Progressives divided over how to meet this challenge. Could American society permanently transcend the class warfare of the past? Could the ideal of a classless "people" be sustained in the face of the ongoing transformation of industrial society? Did the growth of a new immigrant laboring class, the reproduction of inequality, and the social divisions based on race and ethnicity threaten the integrity of civic community? The persistence of class conflict in America challenged the defining feature of the Progressive movement—its promise of social harmony through democratic renewal. As historian Alan Dawley has argued, "class polarization" in the years immediately following the war "pinned progressives on the horns of a dilemma." The *New Republic* poignantly articulated that dilemma and the reformers' impotence: "Between organized labor, on the one hand, and organized capital on the other, the large class which lives by rendering services to both stands an excellent chance of being crushed as between the upper and nether millstones."[6]

The contested legacy of progressive reform—its ragged edges—played itself out in diverse arenas. First, the war appeared to energize a cadre of reformers who embraced preparedness and the mobilization for war as an opportunity to forge national unity and enhance the power of the state in the service of social reconstruction. Their opponents, the antiwar Progressives, despaired over the consequences of a war that might undermine progressive ends through the massive loss of life, the coercive use of state power, and the triumph of conservative nationalism. To the war's progressive opponents, the vision of a truly democratic "people" seemed betrayed by all that war implied.

But the war produced sharp differences in a second arena of reform. Despite calls for national unity, the economic imperatives of war unleashed the most dramatic wave of strikes in American history. Labor activists in basic industry—electrical, munitions, meat packing, steel, mining—seized the opportunities offered by the war economy to challenge employers for higher wages, shorter hours, an end to job classification, and a "voice in industry." As they expanded organizing, they challenged old trade union structures and sought to transform them into new forms of industrial unionism. Reformers, pursuing various versions of "industrial democracy," hoped to use the war emergency and a new malleability in industrial relations to realign the relations between labor and capital. Some, like Frank Walsh and his allies, enlisted with the Wilson administration and its National War Labor Board (NWLB) in a campaign to empower and win recognition for labor. These labor Progressives also hoped to find in the government ownership of the railroads during wartime a model for expanded public ownership in the postwar period. Others saw industrial democracy as a tool for reconciling the interests of labor and capital. They believed that labor's participation in applying the principles of scientific management to the workplace would enhance industrial efficiency and labor productivity, thereby bringing about an era of labor peace and social harmony through rationalized labor-management relations.[7]

Progressives and War

Facing the prospect of direct U.S. participation in the European war, many Progressives found new rhetorical uses for "the people" as a way to embody national identity and the democratic culture into which class differences might be dissolved. The war reshaped the ways many reformers defined this mission. It gave their sense of democratic destiny new national relevance. In short, the war, at least initially, appeared to bestow on progressivism a new lease on life, even as it enmeshed reformers in a nationalist rhetoric and a political community that threatened to dilute or submerge their domestic reform agenda.

Embracing war did not come easily or painlessly for many reformers. Some segments of the movement responded initially with uneasiness, then opposition, and only gradually accommodation. When the war broke out,

Walter Lippmann, who was in England recruiting support for the prospective *New Republic,* voiced the fears of many reformers when he wrote to Felix Frankfurter that "democratic hope" seemed now "like a flower in the path of a plough." At the same time he recognized a new incentive "to be interested in national and military affairs, and to get away from the old liberalism which concentrates entirely on local problems."[8]

Lippmann's book *Drift and Mastery* captured the optimism of the Progressive movement that had survived the 1912 election.[9] A recent refugee from the socialist camp, he built on the "new nationalism" Herbert Croly had outlined in *The Promise of American Life* and attacked "the chaos of a new freedom." He challenged Progressives to "use the political state for interesting and important purposes."[10] Still wedded to Roosevelt as the embodiment of those politics, Lippmann blazed a trail that led, perhaps unwittingly at first, in the direction of the Wilsonian camp. Like other Progressives in the spring of 1914, his chief preoccupation lay with the "labor wars." He accepted Roosevelt's invitation to write a position paper on the labor problem, later incorporated as a chapter in *Drift and Mastery.* The threat of "a class structure imperiled by insurrection" led him to assert the need for a strong labor movement. Like many in the Progressive movement, he saw little hope that a class of the dispossessed could be transformed into enlightened citizens.[11] But he shared the reformers' faith in the power of science and efficient management to achieve public control by "sucking the life out of private property," not through the socialist dream of public ownership but through the agency of large corporations themselves.[12]

No American intellectual exerted greater influence within the Progressive movement by 1915 than John Dewey. His odyssey as a "war intellectual," to use Randolph Bourne's disparaging term, reveals the complex ideological and rhetorical adjustments Progressives made in the "compressed time" of the war.[13] Dewey, like many liberal intellectuals, envisioned a process of social reconstruction driven forward by voluntary association. Education would play a crucial, instrumental role in promoting individual "socialized responsibility." Only by such means would the development of class divisions and social hierarchies that threatened the democratic functioning of communities be arrested.[14]

Although always preferring decentralized initiatives that might enhance democracy, Dewey recognized the necessity and value of some measure of state or national direction. The coming of war only accentuated these tendencies in his thought. He told the National Education Association in 1916 that schools must teach "the supremacy of the community interest over the private interest" or "class and sectional ideas and feelings will become dominant, and our democracy will fall to pieces." He saw the "national idea" of democracy as a blending of diverse backgrounds, "the surrender into a common fund of wisdom and experience" what each group has to offer. But in language reminiscent of Frederick Jackson Turner, he feared that the common project of subduing nature and the "unoccupied continent" had ended, and they were "already starting to fight against one another, class against class, haves against have-nots." American schools held a special responsibility for fostering "equal opportunity" and democratic values. With somewhat more ambivalence than the editors of the *New Republic*, a journal to which he regularly contributed during the war, Dewey embraced at the war's end the accomplishments of "the economists and business men called to the industrial front." They demonstrated "the practicable possibilities of governmental regulation of private business" more so than "professional Socialists had effected in a generation." But he also worried about the continuing effects of a "new paternalism" bred in wartime that controlled and shaped public opinion.[15]

At the war's end, Dewey looked to the future and foresaw on the whole an accrual of benefits—enhanced technology, the "social mobilization of science," and the prospect of a world federation of nations. The exigencies of war "brought into existence agencies for executing the supremacy of the public and social interest over the private and possessive interest which might otherwise have taken a long time to construct." Even as Dewey celebrated the expansion of public power brought by the war, a residue of skepticism about the virtues of centralized state administration marked his public voice. Specifically in the realm of industrial relations, he advocated an alternative "federation of self-governing industries" in which the state might function "as adjuster and arbiter" instead of owning or managing them outright. Like many Progressives, he shrank back from any massive, permanent extension of state power.[16] Walter Lippmann, too, believed that "out of this horror" might come a deeper commitment to democracy: "We shall turn with fresh interest to our own tyrannies—to our Colorado mines, our autocratic steel industries, our sweatshops and our slums. We shall call that man un-American and no patriot who prates of liberty in Europe and resists it at home. A force is loose in America as well."[17] Such reformers saw in war preparedness and then in the war itself possibilities for forging a national unity and purpose that would become the engine for sustaining progressive reform and reengineering American society around an ideal of class harmony.[18]

The war liberals faced a vigorous challenge from a minority of reformers who saw war as a bankrupt instrument for progressive change. Immediately following Woodrow Wilson's call for military preparedness in early November 1915, a prominent group of social reform Progressives gathered at the Henry Street Settlement in New York to form what would come to be called the American Union against Militarism. Over the next year and a half, as the Wilson administration and American public opinion were drawn deeper into the conflict, the lines of opposition to war wavered and then broke. Still, a coalition of antiwar Progressives maintained faith in reform and their antiwar posture despite their marginalization as war opponents. Randolph Bourne spoke disparagingly of the "war intellectuals" who believed that "this was a war in which we had to be." Bourne rehearsed their rationale for supporting the war: "It is only on the craft, in the stream . . . that one has any chance of controlling the current forces for liberal purposes. . . . If we obstruct, we surrender all power for influence."[19] Frustrated by both renewed class warfare and the hijacking of a sense of national community, the antiwar Progressives projected their own democratic faith outward in ways that distinguished them from Wilson's mission to use the war to spread democracy. Advocating peace and reconciliation, opposing preparedness for war and war itself, and struggling to sustain the day-to-day work of social reform in communities and neighborhoods, they looked toward a postwar era in which an internationalized movement for democracy might find a new lease on life.

No one spoke more consistently or eloquently against the war than Jane Addams. Disappointed after a lengthy conference with Wilson in February 1917, Addams worked with the Food Administration to ensure the survival of a warravaged civilian population and to maintain a spirit of "unshakable tolerance" at Hull-House.[20] Despite sharp attacks, Addams and other antiwar settlement reformers carried forward a program of practical, domestic reform centered on the needs of women and children.[21] But in the memoir of her "second twenty years" as a social reformer, Addams, quoting another liberal reformer, recalled the bitter disappointment the war visited on the reform community:

> Within a year after the war began the old causes were gone, and we were steadily forced back from our advanced positions—public ownership and enfranchisement of labor, economic freedom, industrial cooperation, and political equality for the black man with the white man, for the alien with the citizen—these were all abandoned like war trenches on the Western Front, and we found ourselves fighting in the last ditch for the primary bases of democratic society, the civil liberties proclaimed in the Declaration of Independence and guaranteed in the Constitution.[22]

Randolph Bourne found the war intellectuals naïve and self-delusional at best and profoundly cynical at worst. The national community at war became a balm for the class divisions that had grown deeper in the months before the

European war erupted. In Bourne's view, America's "latent colonialism" worked in tandem with "our longing for American unity." The war made for strange bedfellows indeed. "Hearts that had felt only ugly contempt for democratic strivings at home beat in tune for the struggle for freedom abroad." In Bourne's view, war intellectuals such as Dewey had "their thinking thrown out of gear." The war disabled, perhaps irreversibly, a promising movement for reform. "The task of making our own country detailedly fit for peace was abandoned in favor of a feverish concern for the management of war." Bourne's attacks on the war intellectuals left deep scars on and disquieting doubts within Dewey and others who had found themselves drawn like "moths" to the light.[23]

Campaigning for Industrial Democracy

Many other reformers, closely associated with labor, saw in the war an opportunity of a different kind. Before them lay a more favorable field of battle on which to carry forward the campaign for industrial democracy. For many of them, industrial democracy implied the "socializing" of industry, the forging of new ties among laboring people based on shared class interest, and the reconstruction of American democracy to promote economic equality and direct worker governance in industry.[24] In war, as in peacetime, these views set apart this coalition of labor reformers, socialists, and militant trade unionists from the dominant currents of progressive reform that favored programs fostering class reconciliation and social harmony.

The Walsh/Manly Report of the U.S. Commission on Industrial Relations embodied these views, as did the program of the Industrial Relations Committee formed by Walsh and others to promote the recommendations of the USCIR. These labor Progressives maintained close ties to more militant wings of the labor movement. They saw in the war economy conditions that could further the democratization of industry. And following Walsh's leadership, they had offered conditional support to the reelection campaign of Wilson.

With the U.S. declaration of war, Walsh and many labor Progressives found themselves in a precarious political position. On the one hand, they felt drawn to the aggressive defense of labor rights and civil liberties as the climate of war placed both in greater jeopardy. Walsh and a number of labor Progressives formed the National Labor Defense Council and hired veteran syndicalist Anton Johannsen as general organizer.[25] At the same time, however, Walsh sensed the political ground shifting in ways that seemed to make support for the war imperative. At the behest of his political ally George Creel, who now directed the administration's war propaganda arm, the Committee on Public Information, Walsh worked behind the scenes in early September 1917 to help form a new organization, the American Alliance for Labor and Democracy. Creel had fed Walsh resolutions declaring the war to be a "war of self-defense" and pledging labor's support. Other "radical" resolutions were to be introduced on the convention's last day calling for "putting the burden of war on wealth" and for government ownership of railroad, mines, and munitions industries. Walsh later reported the inaugural convention to have been "a great success" and Gompers and prowar socialist John Spargo reliable allies.[26]

Even as he lent his considerable credibility to the campaign to sell the war to American workers, Walsh worked assiduously *behind the scenes* to defend radicals and IWW organizers persecuted for their opposition to the war. He corresponded during the last months of 1917 and early 1918 with Emma Goldman, Bill Haywood, E. L. Boyle (Colorado Federation of Labor), J. J. McNamara and Frank Ryan (union officials incarcerated for the *Los Angeles Times* bombing), and syndicalist William Z. Foster. At the same time, he parried any effort to enlist him in the *public* defense of labor radicals. Although corresponding regularly with Roger Baldwin, director of the National Civil Liberties Bureau, about attacks on labor radicals, he declined to lend his name to the bureau's efforts to mount public opposition. Radical economist Scott Nearing expressed bitter disappointment over Walsh's vacillation. "You know about Paterson and Ludlow," he declared. "You knew who was behind them. You know that those same forces are throttling democracy in America today—in the name of liberty in Europe—Bisbee, Mooney & Frank Little—you are lending them your name and influence. The plutocrats are using your power to rivet the chains. How can you do it?"[27]

By the spring of 1918, having worked actively to win an arbitration award favorable to workers in the packinghouse industry, Walsh was appointed by Woodrow Wilson to the War Labor Policies Board (WLPB) as a labor member. The WLPB would design the machinery and establish the principles for resolving labor disputes to be followed by the NWLB. Then, in April 1918, Wilson appointed Walsh and former president William Howard Taft as co-chairs of the board. In the previous months, Walsh may well have been tending his political fences in the interest of serving labor through such an appointment.

By all accounts Walsh served with distinction as co-chair of the War Labor Board and lent what support he could to the defense of Tom Mooney and other IWW victims of wartime persecution. Energized by the possibilities for constructive work that the NWLB opened up, Walsh wrote to one ally in July 1918 that "our nation is now crossing the bridge between mere politics and cooperative and industrial government." And that meant ultimately "a deeper and more vital democracy." In his own carefully chosen words and in his NWLB rulings, Walsh laid the groundwork for what he believed was a future of "industrial democracy" for American workers.[28]

The unprecedented crescendo of strikes that rose from 1916 to a peak in 1919, and the insistent claims put forward by workers themselves, energized the labor Progressives' vision.[29] Powerful though the rhetoric of "industrial democracy" may have been during the waning months of war in 1918, it also proved to be remarkably evanescent. Historian Joseph McCartin has demonstrated how different constituencies invested the phrase with different meanings. And as journalist Samuel Crowther noted, it was adopted by everyone "from 'the craziest and most violent radical yelling and waving a red flag' to the 'most staid . . . hidebound employer.'"[30]

The war's end saw a sharp decline in the authority granted to the NWLB. And although some Progressive reformers broached the idea of a "peace labor board" to continue the work of industrial conciliation, employers generally pushed for dismantling the board altogether.[31] With rising unemployment, deepening racial tension, the renewed outbreak of industrial conflict, and the continued persecution of labor radicals and socialists under wartime statutes, employers seized the initiative to substitute an "American plan" of employee representation for genuine industrial democracy.[32]

While the federal government maintained some wartime reform initiatives, Progressive reformers lost their connection to a distinctive domestic reform agenda. By the end of the war, they lacked the sense of being part of a wider reform movement. A new conservatism took hold, reflected in the failure at Versailles to construct a new international order, in the dismantling of wartime regulatory agencies governing industry and labor relations, and in the persistence into peacetime of vicious antiradical, anti-immigrant sentiments in the support of which some Progressives had been complicit. Disillusionment set in, and with it came a certain skepticism about democracy and the possibility of assimilating difference into a broader national community. The wave of postwar strikes, race riots, and antiradical persecution only reinforced those sentiments.[33]

The labor Progressives themselves splintered in the postwar period. One wing, apostles of efficiency and worker-management cooperation, staked out positions in a few industries, notably clothing and electrical manufacturing, from which they promoted new strategies for harmonizing class interests, including managerial freedom to pursue efficiency schemes in return for union recognition. As McCartin has shown, industrial relations experts privatized the notion of "industrial citizenship" to facilitate a variety of "little democracies" that ranged from company unions to collaborative schemes of worker-employer cooperation. These industrial democrats, including Sidney Hillman, would ally with enlightened businessmen such as Gerard Swope of General Electric to promote acceptance of the idea of collective bargaining with industrial unions in mass production industry in return for greater management freedom to reorganize production.[34]

Another, more radical wing of industrial democrats pursued a program of reforms that included nationalization of railroads and coal along with aggressive organizing campaigns for industrial unions in steel, meat packing, and among railroad shop workers.[35] These proponents of industrial democracy fell victim to postwar depression and antiradical hysteria, the American Plan, and a sharp rightward shift in national politics. The socialist Left splintered into competing factions, proponents of a labor party saw their support dramatically shrink, and the fledgling Communist Party retreated for the time being underground.[36] The political Left would reemerge in support of union organizing campaigns later in the 1920s and in the unemployed organizing of the early Depression years. They would also contribute significantly to the industrial organizing of the early 1930s that prefigured the Congress of Industrial Organizations (CIO).

The Legacies of Progressive Reform

The remnants of the reform community that had constituted the dynamic core of the Progressive movement from 1907 to 1914 felt the effects of the rightward shift in American politics during the 1920s. Their efforts to keep alive a domestic reform agenda, focused on women and children, fell victim to gendered attacks that deployed a timely rhetoric of antiradicalism.[37] But many currents of voluntary reform remained active during the 1920s.[38] International peace and disarmament continued to be a defining beacon for some. Nevertheless, reformers now drifted in greater isolation from the centers of public power than had those in the prewar reform movement. Still unwilling to frame issues in class terms, they shared little common ground with more radical "industrial democrats," who also found themselves consigned to the margins of American public life.[39]

The project of solving the "class problem" did not expire with the era of World War I. A remarkable coalition of reformers, trade unionists, Taylor Society adherents, and enlightened employers sought to invest "harmony of interests" with new meaning during the 1920s and in so doing established a framework for industrial relations that prefigured the CIO and government-regulated collective bargaining as the path to industrial peace. They kept alive an ideology that historian Steve Fraser has called "the Marxism of the professional middle class, wise to the class antinomies of industrial society" but convinced that such conflicts could be pacified by "science and abundance."[40] Indeed, John Dewey in 1935 offered precisely such an alternative to class conflict in a liberalism that saw a "socialized economy" as "the means of free individual development." In phrasing that echoed the technocratic utopianism of Edward Bellamy, Dewey believed that organized "intelligence" might settle conflicting interests, class-based or otherwise, "in the interest of the widest possible contribution to the interests of all—or at least the great majority." Speaking for a "renascent liberalism" that he acknowledged his radical critics might label "a colorless 'middle of the road' doctrine," he could imagine no way forward except by the "method of democracy."[41]

The New Deal persuaded hard-pressed and politically mobilized workers and farmers to look inexorably to Washington and Franklin Roosevelt's Democratic Party in their "quest for security." But the Depression was not without its disquieting moments when class war seemed again on the agenda.[42] Labor's achievement of the right to bargain collectively in a framework defined by the Wagner Act nevertheless seemed to promise the long-deferred resolution of the class problem. As Fraser has perceptively noted, the New Deal produced a "double transformation: the ascendance of labor and the eclipse of the 'labor question.'"[43]

New Deal liberalism, like its Progressive antecedents and its later twentieth-century incarnations, was hardly monolithic.[44] While rejecting the class perspective associated with nineteenth-century producerism and the class agenda of radical industrial democrats, New Deal liberals and their Great Society heirs adopted the Progressives' core values and their project of using the state, albeit in more expansive ways, to engineer a society inclusive of the people and less vulnerable to the social upheavals the dispossessed might provoke.[45] To the extent that they succeeded, liberal reformers persuaded Americans that, despite persistent evidence of class divisions, the unfinished project of reinventing the people, enlarging the domain of opportunity, and fostering social harmony might still keep at bay the ravages of class war. That prospect had seemed a real danger for the first generation of Progressive reformers, as it would again in the turbulent years of the Great Depression and the tumultuous 1960s.

If the class problem moved perceptibly to the margins during the later stages of the New Deal and more decidedly after World War II, liberal reformers re-focused their attention on racial and ethnic discrimination. This was not a wholly new concern, but the rise of Nazism gave new urgency to the mean-ing of racial and ethnic differences in a democratic society and to the cultural and political changes needed to foster toleration and accommodate difference. The historic legacy of racial discrimination also took on new geopolitical sig-nificance in a decolonizing world rife with Soviet-American competition for the loyalties of nonwhite people.[46] For many liberal reformers, what had been social facts of secondary interest moved to the center. This reconfiguring of liberalism reinforced the displacement of the class problem, tainted as it now was in the McCarthy era by its association with communism.

Driven forward by the activism of African American people, social change in its racial dimension would dominate the postwar liberal reform agenda, setting the stage for a new wave of social legislation in the 1960s that addressed primarily civic and social, not economic, rights.[47] Great Society programs nev-ertheless reflected to some degree the persistent dual class/race concerns within liberalism through a "war on poverty" (class) and a campaign to ex-tend civil rights (race). But with the assassination of Martin Luther King Jr. and the eclipse of the "poor peoples" campaign in 1968, an explicit vocabu-lary of class receded even deeper into the lexicon of liberal reform as the twen-tieth century wound down.

Late-twentieth-century liberals, in many ways, fulfilled the destiny that Progressive reformers had defined for them in the century's early years. If the class problem had not been solved, it had at least been redefined in ways that made it seem antiquated and irrelevant by the century's end. The prob-lems of racial assimilation and a politics of identity, augmented by a new "rights" consciousness, dominated liberal discourse and the quest for dem-ocratic community.

Clinton era liberals were deeply shocked, then, to be accused by their right-wing opponents of preaching "class war" when they discussed tax inequities or sought to craft ameliorative legislation that addressed the health-care needs of working-class Americans. Ironically, it was right-wing activists, not liberals, who reinjected class into the language of politics and put it to novel and polarizing purposes in the 1990s and beyond. Liberals stood about dazed and confused, uncertain whether they too must now abandon the idea of class reconciliation for a new politics of class.[48]

Having successfully disarmed labor Progressives early in the century and jettisoned the language of class from their rhetoric of reform, liberals late in the century stood accused of promoting the very class perspective against which they had so persistently fought. Although reinventing *class* as a vehicle for reform seemed beyond the imagination of many early-twenty-first-century liberals, others recognized in the deepening chasm that separates the poor and rich in the United States and around the world a new imperative for a politics of class that might reclaim the producerist legacy of the nineteenth century and challenge the entrenched power and greed of the rich and their political allies.

Notes

Introduction

1. Jane Addams testimony, in U.S. Strike Commission, *Report of the Chicago Strike, 1894* (Washington, D.C.: GPO, 1895), 646–47.

2. Jane Addams, *Twenty Years at Hull-House* (New York: Macmillan, 1910), 38–39. Michael McGerr, *A Fierce Discontent: The Rise and Fall of the Progressive Movement in America, 1870–1920* (New York: Free Press, 2003), 56–59, recounts Addams's dilemma but with a different emphasis—on her presumed abandonment of "individualism." For further discussion of Pullman, see chapter 1 of this book.

3. Jane Addams, "The Settlement as a Factor in the Labor Movement," in *Hull-House Maps and Papers*, by the Residents of Hull-House (New York: Thomas Y. Crowell, 1895), 203–4.

4. For a perceptive discussion of Richard Hofstadter's contribution to debates about the nature of progressivism, see Eric Foner, "The Education of Richard Hofstadter," in *Who Owns History? Rethinking the Past in a Changing World*, by Eric Foner (New York: Hill and Wang, 2002), 42–46.

5. The currents of Progressive Era historiography are many and treacherous. For a recent collection of essays, both new and old, that examine diverse interpretations, see Glenda E. Gilmore, ed., *Who Were the Progressives?* (New York: St. Martin's, 2002). For useful older surveys, see Richard L. McCormick and Arthur S. Link, *Progressivism* (Arlington Heights, Ill.: Harlan Davidson, 1983); and David Kennedy, "Overview: The Progressive Era," *Historian* 37 (May 1975): 453–68. See also Daniel T. Rodgers, "In Search of Progressivism," *Reviews in American History* (December 1982): 113–31; Peter G. Filene, "An Obituary for 'The Progressive Movement,'" *American Quarterly* 22 (1970): 20–34; John D. Buenker, "Sovereign Individuals and Organic Networks: Political Cultures in Conflict during the Progressive Era," *American Quarterly* 40 (June

1988): 187–204; and Martin J. Sklar, "Periodization and Historiography: Studying American Political Development in the Progressive Era, 1890s-1916," *Studies in American Political Development* 5, no. 2 (Fall 1991): 173–213.

6. The most provocative "obituary" for the Progressive movement was Filene, "Obituary for 'The Progressive Movement.'"

7. The idea that Progressive reformers indeed constituted a movement has once again begun to find a place in new studies of the period. See, for instance, McGerr, *Fierce Discontent,* and Alan Dawley, *Struggles for Justice: Social Responsibility and the Liberal State* (Cambridge, Mass.: Harvard University Press, 1991). Amply documenting the international currents that helped shape American progressivism is Daniel T. Rodgers, *Atlantic Crossings: Social Politics in a Progressive Age* (Cambridge, Mass.: Harvard University Press, 1998). Like other recent synthesizers, Alan Dawley continues to suggest that the Progressive movement had a "syncopated," somewhat contradictory quality: "It hopped back and forth across all sorts of boundaries, grabbing political ideas here and there, and connecting diverse peoples across lines of class and culture." Alan Dawley, *Changing the World: American Progressives in War and Revolution* (Princeton, N.J.: Princeton University Press, 2003), 42.

8. Jacob Riis was an important purveyor of the notion of society's debased "other half." His documentation had a profound effect on how middle-class leaders saw the poor and understood their problems. While stimulating tenement house reform efforts, Riis's documentation also represented the denizens of places like "Bandit's Row" as "other." See Jacob Riis, *How the Other Half Lived: Studies among the Tenements of New York* (1890; reprint, New York: Hill and Wang, 1957).

9. Daniel Rodgers, *Contested Truths: Keywords in American Politics since Independence* (New York: Basic Books, 1987), 179.

10. Robert Wiebe has continued to underestimate the class edge to the Populists' (and the Knights of Labor's) producerism, as does Michael Kazin. Populists and Knights appealed to a broad class of producers and vigorously opposed a contending class of nonproducers. Their rhetoric differed in fundamental ways from the cross-class appeal of the Progressives. See Robert Wiebe, *The Search for Order, 1877–1920* (New York: Hill and Wang, 1967), 50–75, and Robert Wiebe, *Self-Rule: A Cultural History of Democracy* (Chicago: University of Chicago Press, 1995), 122–24. See also Michael Kazin, *The Populist Persuasion: An American History* (New York: Basic Books, 1995), 30–42.

11. William Allen White, *The Autobiography of William Allen White* (1946), quoted in John A. Gable, *The Bull Moose Years: Theodore Roosevelt and the Progressive Party* (Port Washington, N.Y.: Kennikat Press, 1978), 76.

12. Two works on contemporary politics that explore Americans' myopia with respect to class are Benjamin DeMott, *The Imperial Middle: Why Americans Can't Think Straight About Class* (New York: Morrow, 1990), and Kevin Phillips, *The Politics of Rich and Poor: Wealth and the American Electorate in the Reagan Aftermath* (New York: Random House, 1990); see also Michael Zweig, *The Working Class Majority: America's Best*

Kept Secret (Ithaca, N.Y.: Cornell University Press, 2000), and Reeve Vanneman and Lynn Weber Cannon, *The American Perception of Class* (Philadelphia: Temple University Press, 1987). See the conclusion of this book for a discussion of twentieth-century liberals' inability to talk about class.

13. Wiebe, *Self-Rule,* examines the elaboration of "the people" as a nineteenth-century conception of the democracy of white males. His argument about the class structure of the Progressive Era is less persuasive.

14. Edmund S. Morgan, *Inventing the People: The Rise of Popular Sovereignty in England and America* (New York: Norton, 1988), 306; Arthur Mann, *The One and the Many: Reflections on the American Identity* (Urbana: University of Illinois Press, 1979), 56.

15. David Montgomery offers a useful examination of the relationship between political democracy and the capitalist marketplace as the industrial revolution of the nineteenth century unfolded in his *Citizen Worker: The Experience of Workers in the United States with Democracy and the Free Market during the Nineteenth Century* (New York: Cambridge University Press, 1993).

16. For a discussion of that producerist legacy, see Shelton Stromquist, "The Crisis of 1894 and the Legacies of Producerism," in *The Pullman Strike and the Crisis of the 1890s: Essays on Labor and Politics,* ed. Richard Schneirov, Shelton Stromquist, and Nick Salvatore (Urbana: University of Illinois Press, 1999), 194–97. And for a helpful accounting of the contested meanings of "industrial democracy," see Joseph A. Mc-Cartin, *Labor's Great War: The Struggle for Industrial Democracy and the Origins of Modern American Labor Relations, 1912–1921* (Chapel Hill: University of North Carolina Press, 1997).

17. A widely distributed poster of the National Child Labor Committee in the early twentieth century, profusely illustrated with Lewis Hine photographs, accused employers of child labor of producing "human junk."

18. See Simon Patten, *The Theory of Social Forces* (1896), and Walter Weyl, *The New Democracy* (1912), quoted in Charles Forcey, *The Crossroads of Liberalism: Croly, Weyl, Lippman and the Progressive Era, 1900–1925* (New York: Oxford University Press, 1961), 63. See also Dorothy Ross, *The Origins of American Social Science* (New York: Cambridge University Press, 1991), 195–200, and for a Pattenesque analysis that emphasizes consumption as central to the new progressive consciousness of the twentieth century, see James Livingston, *Pragmatism and the Political Economy of Cultural Revolution, 1850–1940* (Chapel Hill: University of North Carolina Press, 1994), 66–83. Nancy Cohen sees the "invention of a new liberalism" in the Gilded Age/Progressive Era that revolved around twin poles of state regulation of large corporations and enhanced consumption as an antidote to working-class discontent. Nancy Cohen, *The Reconstruction of American Liberalism, 1865–1914* (Chapel Hill: University of North Carolina Press, 2002), 217–26.

19. Edward T. Devine, "Social Forces," *Charities and the Commons* 21 (October 3, 1908): 2.

20. Graham Taylor, "Class and Mass in Labor," *Charities and the Commons* 21 (Oc-

tober 3, 1908): 67–68; John Graham Brooks, "Industrial Democracy: Trade Unions and Politics," *Outlook* 85 (January 5, 1907): 29.

21. Vida Scudder, *On Journey* (New York: E. P. Dutton, 1937), 160.

22. The work of some political historians and political scientists suggest other, darker motives for such reforms of the political process, specifically, restriction of the franchise in the interest of limiting the influence of working-class voters. See Walter Dean Burnham, "The System of 1896: An Analysis," in *The Evolution of American Electoral Systems,* ed. Paul Kleppner (Westport, Conn.: Greenwood Press, 1981), and Samuel P. Hays, "The Politics of Reform in Municipal Government in the Progressive Era," *Pacific Northwest Quarterly* 55 (October 1964): 157–69.

23. John Dewey, *Ethics* (1908), quoted in Robert Westbrook, *John Dewey and American Democracy* (Ithaca, N.Y.: Cornell University Press, 1991), 188. Westbrook places Dewey in what he terms the "radical wing of progressivism" as the most "thoroughly democratic" reformer. Although he may be right, Dewey also emphasized a socially homogeneous democratic community as his ideal. As Westbrook notes, "Although he assumed a functionally differentiated division of labor, he carefully distinguished functions from classes" (188–89). Kevin Mattson offers a paean to democratic participation as the heart and soul of progressive reform in his *Creating a Democratic Public: The Struggle for Urban Participatory Democracy during the Progressive Era* (State College: Pennsylvania State University Press, 1998).

24. Mary P. Ryan, *Civic Wars: Democracy and Public Life in the American City during the Nineteenth Century* (Berkeley: University of California Press, 1997), 3, 12. Glenn C. Altschuler and Stuart M. Blumin, *Rude Republic: Americans and Their Politics in the Nineteenth Century* (Princeton, N.J.: Princeton University Press, 2000), suggest that the level of political engagement by Americans in the nineteenth century has been overdrawn.

25. On reformers' efforts to limit the franchise, see Alexander Keyssar, *The Right to Vote: The Contested History of Democracy in the United States* (New York: Basic Books, 2000), 119–62. See also Cohen, *Reconstruction of American Liberalism,* 225–26.

26. David Montgomery, *Beyond Equality: Labor and the Radical Republicans, 1862–1872* (New York: Random House, 1967), 446.

27. Dorothy Ross argues that reform-oriented social scientists responded directly to the threat of insurgent politics and socialism in the late nineteenth and early twentieth centuries; see Ross, *Origins of American Social Science.* The growing strength of the Socialist Party of America in the first two decades of the twentieth century and the influence of the Industrial Workers of the World (IWW) defined one boundary of the Progressives' influence, despite the ties of sympathy and support some reformers on occasion forged with these movements. On the complex relationship between Socialists and Progressives, see chapter 3 of this book; and for a discussion of the problems renewed class conflict, spawned in part by the influence of the IWW, posed for reformers, see chapter 7.

28. Jane Addams, *The Second Twenty Years at Hull-House, September 1909 to Sep-*

tember 1929 (New York: Macmillan, 1930), 13, 28. For a discussion of these "constituting" moments in the development of a Progressive movement, see chapters 2 and 4 of this book.

29. Scudder, *On Journey,* 166.

30. Ibid., 170.

31. Rodgers, "In Search of Progressivism," 113–31.

32. Nancy Cohen argues persuasively that progressive reform played out liberal reform initiatives well established in Gilded Age America. See Cohen, *Reconstruction of American Liberalism,* esp. 226–33.

33. Filene, "Obituary for 'The Progressive Movement'"; John D. Buenker, "The Progressive Era: A Search for Synthesis," *Mid-America* 51 (1969): 175–93; Rodgers, "In Search of Progressivism"; Richard L. McCormick, "The Discovery that Business Corrupts: A Reappraisal of the Origins of Progressivism," *American Historical Review* 86 (April 1981), reprinted in Richard L. McCormick, *The Party Period and Public Policy: American Politics from the Age of Jackson to the Progressive Era* (New York: Oxford University Press, 1986); and most recently, Michael McGerr, *Fierce Discontent.*

34. On the role of what he calls the "radical" middle class of reformers, see Robert D. Johnston, *The Radical Middle Class: Populist Democracy and the Question of Capitalism in Progressive Era Portland, Oregon* (Princeton, N.J.: Princeton University Press, 2003), esp. 3–17, and on the class-bridging work of women, see Maureen A. Flanagan, *Seeing with Their Hearts: Chicago Women and the Vision of the Good City, 1871–1933* (Princeton, N.J.: Princeton University Press, 2002), and Sarah Deutsch, *Women and the City: Gender, Space and Power in Boston, 1870–1940* (New York: Oxford University Press, 2000).

35. See chapters 5 and 6 of this book for discussions of the gender and racial boundaries of progressivism.

36. See chapter 7 of this book for a discussion of the impact of renewed class conflict on the Progressive movement.

37. These issues are discussed in the conclusion of this book. See also David Montgomery, *The Fall of the House of Labor: The Workplace, the State, and American Labor Activism, 1865–1925* (New York: Cambridge University Press, 1987); James R. Barrett, *Work and Community in the Jungle: Chicago's Packinghouse Workers, 1894–1922* (Urbana: University of Illinois Press, 1987); and James Grossman, *Land of Hope: Chicago, Black Southerners, and the Great Migration* (Chicago: University of Chicago Press, 1989). On the meanings of industrial democracy, see McCartin, *Labor's Great War,* and David Montgomery, "Industrial Democracy or Democracy in Industry? The Theory and Practice of the Labor Movement, 1870–1925," in *Industrial Democracy in America: The Ambiguous Promise,* ed. Nelson Lichtenstein and Howell John Harris (New York: Cambridge University Press, 1993).

38. Otis Graham Jr., *An Encore for Reform: The Old Progressives and the New Deal* (New York: Oxford University Press, 1967), argues that the New Deal was not a continuation of older progressive reform traditions but a set of new responses to con-

ditions confronted in the 1930s. Alan Brinkley, *The End of Reform: New Deal Liberalism in Recession and War* (New York: Vintage, 1995), sees a mix of innovation and continuity in New Deal liberalism. Other historians see greater continuity; for instance, Eugene M. Tobin, *Organize or Perish: America's Independent Progressives, 1913–1933* (Westport, Conn.: Greenwood Press, 1986), and William E. Leuchtenberg, "The New Deal and the Analogue of War," in *Change and Continuity in Twentieth-Century America*, ed. John Braeman, Robert H. Bremner, and David Brody (Columbus: Ohio State University Press, 1964), 81–143.

39. Like Alan Brinkley, Gary Gerstle sees an evolving liberalism in the twentieth century. See Gary Gerstle, "The Protean Character of American Liberalism," *American Historical Review* 99, no. 4 (October 1994): 1043–73.

40. Few contemporary studies give class the attention it deserves in analyses of American society and politics in the late twentieth century. Exceptions are DeMott's *Imperial Middle*, one-time conservative political commentator Kevin Phillips's *Politics of Rich and Poor*, and economist Michael Zweig's *Working Class Majority*.

Chapter 1: The Labor Problem and the Crisis of the Old Order

1. George McNeill, "The Labor Movement of 1878 in Chicago," pp. 1–10, Box 1, Miscellaneous, Labor Papers, State Historical Society of Wisconsin, Madison.

2. David Montgomery, *Beyond Equality: Labor and the Radical Republicans, 1862–1872* (New York: Random House, 1967), profiles the character of this "new working class" of the Civil War era whose status as "hirelings" made them a potent force in the North during Reconstruction.

3. The enormous appeal that the writings of Edward Bellamy and Lawrence Gronlund, along with Henry George, enjoyed and the surge of utopian writing and social experimentation in the 1880s and 1890s is testimony to this alternative vision. See John L. Thomas, *Alternative America: Henry George, Edward Bellamy, Henry Demarest Lloyd and the Adversary Tradition* (Cambridge, Mass.: Belknap Press, 1983). Knights of Labor assemblies were hotbeds of social experimentation in the form of cooperative enterprises, cultural and leisure activities, and the creation of social space controlled by workers themselves. See especially Robert E. Weir, *Beyond Labor's Veil: The Culture of the Knights of Labor* (University Park: Pennsylvania State University Press, 1996); see also Kim Voss, *The Making of American Exceptionalism: The Knights of Labor and Class Formation in the Nineteenth Century* (Ithaca, N.Y.: Cornell University Press, 1993).

4. The best account of the Civil War's impact on state formation is Morton Keller, *Affairs of State: Public Life in Late Nineteenth-Century America* (Cambridge, Mass.: Harvard University Press, 1977); see also Stephen Skowronek, *Building a New American State: The Expansion of National Administrative Capacities, 1877–1920* (New York: Cambridge University Press, 1982), and on Reconstruction itself, see Eric Foner, *Reconstruction: America's Unfinished Revolution, 1863–1877* (New York: Harper and Row,

1988). Charles Bright stresses the penetration and use of the nineteenth-century federal state by political parties in his essay "The State in the United States during the Nineteenth Century," in *Statemaking and Social Movements: Essays in History and Theory,* ed. Charles Bright and Susan Harding (Ann Arbor: University of Michigan Press, 1984), 121–58.

5. The term "movement culture" was coined by Lawrence Goodwyn to capture the cultural as well as political influence of the Farmers' Alliance. See his important book, *Democratic Promise: The Populist Moment in America* (New York: Oxford University Press, 1976). The literature on the Knights of Labor is substantial. See especially Norman Ware, *The Labor Movement in the United States, 1860–1895: A Study in Democracy* (New York: Appleton, 1929), and Gregory Kealey and Bryan Palmer, *Dreaming of What Might Be: The Knights of Labor in Ontario, 1880–1900* (New York: Cambridge University Press, 1982); Weir, *Beyond Labor's Veil;* and Richard Oestreicher, *Solidarity and Fragmentation: Working People and Class Consciousness in Detroit, 1875–1900* (Urbana: University of Illinois Press, 1986). The Knights and the Populists powerfully influenced a whole generation of labor and social reform leaders. The Knights found their way into popular fiction; see, for instance, Mary C. Grimes, *The Knights in Fiction: Two Labor Novels of the 1880s* (Urbana: University of Illinois Press, 1986). See also autobiographies by James Maurer (a socialist trade union leader from Reading, Pennsylvania), *It Can Be Done* (New York: Rand School Press, 1938), and Abraham Bisno (a Chicago garment cutter and union leader), *Abraham Bisno: Union Pioneer* (Madison: University of Wisconsin Press, 1967). Both cut their teeth in the Knights of Labor.

6. Robert Wiebe, *Self-Rule: A Cultural History of American Democracy* (Chicago: University of Chicago Press, 1995), 86–111, has a particularly nice account of how nineteenth-century conceptions of democracy and "the people" effectively excluded nonwhites and women.

7. See, for instance, Peter Rachleff, *Black Labor in Richmond, 1865–1890* (Urbana: University of Illinois Press, 1988); Eric Arnesen, *Waterfront Workers of New Orleans: Race, Class, and Politics, 1863–1923* (New York: Oxford University Press, 1991); Goodwyn, *Democratic Promise;* Herbert Gutman, "The Negro and the United Mine Workers of America: The Career and Letters of Richard L. Davis and Something of Their Meaning: 1890–1900," in *Work, Culture and Society in Industrializing America* (New York: Vintage, 1977), 121–208. For criticism of Gutman's essay, see Herbert Hill, "Mythmaking as Labor History: Herbert Gutman and the United Mine Workers of America," and a response by Steven Brier, "In Defense of Gutman: The Union's Case," both in *Politics, Culture, and Society* 2, no. 2 (Winter 1988): 132–200, 382–95; see also Mary Blewett, *Men, Women and Work: Class, Gender and Protest in the New England Shoe Industry, 1780–1910* (Urbana: University of Illinois Press, 1988); Susan Levine, *Labor's True Woman: Carpet Weavers, Industrialization, and Labor Reform in the Gilded Age* (Philadelphia: Temple University Press, 1984); and Ilene DeVault, *United Apart: Gender and the Rise of Craft Unionism* (Ithaca, N.Y.: Cornell University Press, 2004).

8. David Roediger, *The Wages of Whiteness: Race and the Making of the American Working Class* (London: Verso Press, 1991). See also Alexander Saxton, *The Indispensible Enemy: Labor and the Anti-Chinese Movement in California* (Berkeley: University of California Press, 1971), and Alexander Saxton, *The Rise and Fall of the White Republic: Class Politics and Mass Culture in Nineteenth-Century America* (London: Verso, 1990).

9. Important studies of middle-class formation in the nineteenth century include Stuart Blumin, *The Emergence of the Middle Class: Social Experience in the American City, 1760–1900* (New York: Cambridge University Press, 1989); Mary P. Ryan, *The Cradle of the Middle Class* (New York: Cambridge University Press, 1981); Nancy Cott, *The Bonds of Womanhood: "Woman's Sphere" in New England, 1780–1835* (New Haven, Conn.: Yale University Press, 1977); Kenneth Cmiel, *Democratic Eloquence: The Fight over Popular Speech in Nineteenth-Century America* (New York: William Morrow, 1990); Lawrence Levine, *Highbrow/LowBrow: The Emergence of Cultural Hierarchy in America* (Cambridge, Mass.: Harvard University Press, 1988); and David M. Scobey, "Anatomy of the Promenade: The Politics of Bourgeois Sociability in Nineteenth-Century New York," *Social History* 17 (May 1992): 203–27. See also Olivier Zunz, *Making America Corporate, 1870–1920* (Chicago: University of Chicago Press, 1990); on the development of common schools, see Carl Kaestle and Maris Vinovskis, *Education and Social Change in Nineteenth-Century Massachusetts* (New York: Cambridge University Press, 1980).

10. See chapter 2, "Constituting Progressivism," for a discussion of the Gilded Age roots of progressive reform; on the limits of mugwump reform, see Seymour Mandelbaum, *Boss Tweed's New York* (New York: J. Wiley, 1965), and John G. Sproat, *The Best Men: Liberal Reformers in the Gilded Age* (New York: Oxford University Press, 1968). On the limits of the social gospel movement, see Weir, *Beyond Labor's Veil;* Henry May, *The Protestant Churches and Industrial America* (New York: Harper and Row, 1967); and Kenneth Fones-Wolf, *Trade Union Gospel: Christianity and Labor in Industrial Philadelphia, 1865–1915* (Philadelphia: Temple University Press, 1989). The origins of the movement for railroad regulation among small businessmen of the Mississippi Valley are explored in George Miller, *Railroads and the Granger Laws* (Madison: University of Wisconsin Press, 1971); on the role of farmers, see Jeffrey Ostler, *Prairie Populism: The Fate of Agrarian Radicalism in Kansas, Nebraska, and Iowa, 1880–1892* (Lawrence: University of Kansas Press, 1993); women's role in the temperance crusade is explored in Ruth Bordin, *Woman and Temperance: The Quest for Power and Liberty, 1873–1900* (Philadelphia: Temple University Press, 1981).

11. A recent contribution that seeks to rehabilitate the middle class as an agent of democratic reform is Robert D. Johnston, *Populist Democracy and the Question of Capitalism in Progressive Era Portland, Oregon* (Princeton, N.J.: Princeton University Press, 2003).

12. Richard T. Ely to Joseph Labadie, August 14, 1885, quoted in Dorothy Ross, *The Origins of American Social Science* (New York: Cambridge University Press, 1991), 105.

13. Richard T. Ely uses the phrase "young rebels" to refer to the group of young political economists, all trained in Germany, who created the American Economic Association in 1885 as a vehicle for promoting their iconoclastic notion that economics was "foremost a science of human relationships." Richard T. Ely, *Ground Under Our Feet: An Autobiography* (New York: Macmillan, 1938), 121; see also Ross, *Origins of American Social Science*.

14. Ross, *Origins of American Social Science*, 107 (Ely, "American Labor Organizations"). See also Richard T. Ely, "Notebook on the Labor Movement, 1885," Box 29, File 8, Richard T. Ely Papers, State Historical Society of Wisconsin, Madison (hereafter cited as Ely Papers).

15. The 1870s, in particular the social consequences of the depression, continue to be overlooked as an important subject of study. Still very useful are Herbert G. Gutman, "Social and Economic Structure and Depression: American Labor in 1873 and 1874" (Ph.D. diss., University of Wisconsin, 1959), and a number of specific case studies published in his *Work, Culture and Society*. See also Alex Keyssar, *Out of Work: The First Century of Unemployment in Massachusetts* (Cambridge, U.K.: Cambridge University Press, 1986), and Dorsey Phelps, "Idled Outside, Overworked Inside: The Political Economy of Prison Labor during Depressions in Chicago, 1871–1897" (Ph.D. diss., University of Iowa, 1992).

16. On the 1877 railroad strikes and their impact, see Philip Foner, *The Great Labor Uprising of 1877* (New York: Monad Press, 1977); Nick Salvatore, *Eugene V. Debs: Citizen and Socialist* (Urbana: University of Illinois Press, 1982); Shelton Stromquist, *A Generation of Boomers: The Pattern of Railroad Labor Conflict in Nineteenth-Century America* (Urbana: University of Illinois Press, 1987); David O. Stowell, *Streets, Railroads, and the Great Strike of 1877* (Chicago: University of Chicago Press, 1999); and David O. Stowell, *The Great Strikes of 1877* (forthcoming).

17. For these alternative views expressed under pseudonyms by Burlington managers, see "Care for Railroad Employees," *Nation*, February 19, 1880, 134–35, and "Railroad Companies and Their Employees," *Nation*, March 18, 1880, 211–12; see also Richard C. Overton, *The Burlington Route: A History of the Burlington Lines* (New York: Knopf, 1965).

18. For the strike data itself, see U.S. Commissioner of Labor, "Strikes and Lockouts," *Third Annual Report* (Washington, D.C.: GPO, 1887), and U.S. Commissioner of Labor, *Tenth Annual Report* (Washington, D.C.: GPO, 1895). For analysis of strike patterns, see David Montgomery, "Workers Control of Machine Production in the Nineteenth Century," *Labor History* 17 (Fall 1976): 485–509; David Montgomery, "Strikes in Nineteenth-Century America," *Social Science History* 4 (February 1980); P. K. Edwards, *Strikes in the United States, 1881–1974* (New York: St. Martin's, 1981); Stromquist, *Generation of Boomers*; Stephen Brier and Jon Amsden, "Coal Miners on Strike: The Transformation of Strike Demands and the Formation of a National Union," *Journal of Interdisciplinary History* 7 (1977): 583–616; and Fred S. Hall, *Sympathetic Strikes and Sympathetic Lockouts* (1898; reprint, New York: AMS Press, 1968). A recent study that emphasizes

the importance of large, wage-related strikes in coal mining is Jörg Rössel, "Industrial Structure, Union Strategy, and Strike Activity in American Bituminous Coal Mining, 1881–1894," *Social Science History* 26, no. 1 (Spring 2002): 1–32.

19. For a general analysis of the pattern of strike activity that emphasizes the growing importance of "control issues," see David Montgomery, *Workers Control in America: Studies in the History of Work, Technology, and Labor Struggles* (New York: Cambridge University Press, 1979); Montgomery, "Strikes in Nineteenth-Century America"; Rössel, "Industrial Structure"; Stromquist, *Generation of Boomers*, 30–38, 40–42; and Edwards, *Strikes in the United States*. For a comparison of strikes among railroad workers and other industrial workers, see Stromquist, *Generation of Boomers*, 26–29, 276.

20. Montgomery, "Strikes in Nineteenth-Century America," 92–93; Stromquist, *Generation of Boomers*, 30–38, 277–78. See also Teresa Ann Case, "Free Labor on the Southwestern Railroads: The 1885–1886 Gould System Strikes" (Ph.D. diss., University of Texas, 2002).

21. Montgomery, *Workers Control in America*; Stromquist, *Generation of Boomers*, 36–47. Paul Krause, *The Battle for Homestead, 1880–1892: Politics, Culture, and Steel* (Pittsburgh: University of Pittsburgh Press, 1992), does a fine job in capturing for the steel industry this sense of an impending crisis of large proportions that culminated in the Homestead strike of 1892.

22. The literature on the structure and competitiveness of the nineteenth-century economy is large. The starting point remains Alfred D. Chandler Jr., *The Visible Hand: The Managerial Revolution in American Business* (Cambridge, Mass.: Harvard University Press, 1977); see also Edward Kirkland, *Industry Comes of Age: Business, Labor and Public Policy, 1860–1897* (New York: Henry Holt, 1961). Particularly insightful is James Livingston, "The Social Analysis of Economic History and Theory: Conjectures on Late Nineteenth-Century American Development," *American Historical Review* 92, no. 1 (February 1987): 69–95. See also Charles Sabel and Jonathan Zeitlin, "Historical Alternatives to Mass Production: Politics, Markets and Technology in Nineteenth-Century Industrialization," *Past & Present* 108 (1985): 133–76.

23. See Alfred Chandler, *Railroads: The Nation's First Big Business: Sources and Readings* (New York: Harcourt Brace, 1965); Walter Licht, *Working on the Railroad: The Organization of Work in the Nineteenth Century* (Princeton, N.J.: Princeton University Press, 1983); and Julius Grodinsky, *Transcontinental Railway Strategy, 1869–1893: A Study of Businessmen* (Philadelphia: University of Pennsylvania Press, 1962).

24. David Brody offers a fine, brief account of the competitive triumph of Carnegie Steel in *Steelworkers in America: The Nonunion Era* (New York: Harper and Row, 1969); on the wider scope and rhythms of consolidation, see Naomi Lamoreaux, *The Great Merger Movement in American Business, 1895–1904* (New York: Cambridge University Press, 1985).

25. On the halting development of "corporate collectivism" among railroad managers, see Paul V. Black, "The Development of Management Personnel Policies on the Burlington Railroad, 1860–1890" (Ph.D. diss., University of Wisconsin, 1972), and

Donald L. McMurry, "Labor Policies of the General Manager's Association of Chicago, 1886–1894," *Journal of Economic History* 13, no. 2 (Spring 1953): 160–79; see also Stromquist, *Generation of Boomers,* 248–57.

26. Clarence Bonnett, *Employer Associations in the United States: A Study of Typical Associations* (New York: Macmillan, 1922); Sidney Fine, *"Without Blare of Trumpets": Walter Drew, the National Erectors' Association, and the Open Shop Movement, 1903–57* (Ann Arbor: University of Michigan Press, 1995). See also Montgomery, *Workers Control in America;* James R. Barrett, *Work and Community in the Jungle: Chicago's Packinghouse Workers, 1894–1922* (Urbana: University of Illinois Press, 1987); and, for a different perspective on the NCF, James Weinstein, *The Corporate Ideal of the Liberal State, 1900–1918* (Boston: Beacon Press, 1968). For an account of the ways in which employer attacks on labor were played out on the legislative front and through the judiciary, see Julie Greene, *Pure and Simple Politics: The American Federation of Labor and Political Activism, 1881–1917* (New York: Cambridge University Press, 1998).

27. Terence V. Powderly repeatedly voiced his frustration at workers' propensity to strike at the drop of a hat during his leadership of the KOL and in *The Path I Trod: The Autobiography of Terence V. Powderly* (New York: Columbia University Press, 1940), 170–71.

28. On the culture of opposition the Knights created, see Oestreicher, *Solidarity and Fragmentation,* and Kealey and Palmer, *Dreaming of What Might Be.* Weir, *Beyond Labor's Veil,* offers the most comprehensive treatment of the Knights' culture, but see also Leon Fink, *Workingmen's Democracy: The Knights of Labor and American Politics* (Urbana: University of Illinois Press, 1983), and Robert E. Weir, *Knights Unhorsed: Internal Conflict in a Gilded Age Social Movement* (Detroit: Wayne State University Press, 2000). David Montgomery has captured the mutualistic ethos of the Knights in "Labor and the Republic in Industrial America, 1860–1920," *Mouvement Sociale* 111 (1980): 201–15; on the efforts to make the Knights an interracial union, see Rachleff, *Black Labor in Richmond,* and on Knights' organization among women workers, see Levine, *Labor's True Woman.* The influence of the Knights on a generation of young workers is captured in several autobiographical accounts; see especially, Maurer, *It Can Be Done.*

29. On the Knights' membership figures, see Richard Oestreicher, "A Note on Knights of Labor Membership Statistics," *Labor History* 25, no. 1 (1984): 102–8.

30. The formation of a class culture, associated with the growing influence of the Knights, is best documented in Weir, *Beyond Labor's Veil;* Fink, *Workingmen's Democracy;* and Oestreicher, *Solidarity and Fragmentation.* For specific communities, see Roy Rosenzweig, *Eight Hours for What We Will: Workers and Leisure in an Industrial City, 1870–1920* (New York: Cambridge University Press, 1983); Francis Couvares, *The Remaking of Pittsburgh: Class and Culture in an Industrializing City, 1877–1919* (Albany: State University of New York Press, 1984); Krause, *Battle for Homestead;* and Ralph Scharnau, "The Knights of Labor in Iowa," *Annals of Iowa* 50 (Spring 1991): 861–91. Jonathan Baxter Harrison's *Certain Dangerous Tendencies in American Life*

(1880) is quoted in Alan Trachtenberg, *The Incorporation of America: Culture and Society in the Gilded Age* (New York: Hill and Wang, 1982), 148–49.

31. On the language and ideology of "labor republicanism," see Leon Fink, "The New Labor History and the Powers of Historical Pessimism," *Journal of American History* 75 (June 1988): 115–36, and Shelton Stromquist, "The Pullman Strike and the Legacies of Producerism," in *The Pullman Strike and the Crisis of the 1890s: Essays on Labor and Politics*, ed. Richard Schneirov, Shelton Stromquist, and Nick Salvatore (Urbana: University of Illinois Press, 1999). For a different view of producerism, see Victoria Hattam, *Labor Visions and State Power: The Origins of Business Unionism in the United States* (Princeton, N.J.: Princeton University Press, 1993).See also William Forbath, "The Ambiguities of the Free Labor Ideology: Labor and the Law in the Gilded Age," *Wisconsin Law Review* (1985): n. 4, 767–817.

32. This account of Lloyd's and Medill's conflicting views on the 1877 railroad strikes is based on Chester M. Destler, *Henry Demarest Lloyd and the Empire of Reform* (Philadelphia: University of Pennsylvania Press, 1963), 104–6. For an astute discussion of the ways in which conflicting pressures toward political democracy and competitive capitalism played out in state policy of the late nineteenth century, see David Montgomery, *Citizen Worker: The Experience of Workers in the United States with Democracy and the Free Market during the Nineteenth Century* (New York: Cambridge University Press, 1993).

33. For a discussion of Henry Demarest Lloyd's continuing commitment to class reconciliation, see chapter 2 in this book and Richard Schneirov, "Labor and the New Liberalism in the Wake of the Pullman Strike," in Schneirov, Stromquist, and Salvatore, *Pullman Strike and the Crisis of the 1890s*, 216–17.

34. See Bruno Cartosio, "Strikes and Economics: Working-Class Insurgency and the Birth of Labor Historiography in the 1880s," in *American Labor and Immigration History, 1870–1920*, ed. Dirk Hoerder (Urbana: University of Illinois Press, 1983), and Herbert G. Gutman's introduction to *State Labor Reports: From the End of the Civil War to the Start of the Twentieth Century*, ed. Herbert G. Gutman (Westport, Conn.: Greenwood Press, 1970).

35. Cartosio, "Strikes and Economics," 21–22.

36. John Garraty, ed., *Labor and Capital in the Gilded Age: Testimony Taken upon the Relations between Labor and Capital, 1883* (Boston: Little Brown, 1968), 151.

37. For an overview of the role of investigatory commissions in labor relations, see Clarence Wunderlin, *Visions of a New Industrial Order: Social Science and Labor Theory in America's Progressive Era* (New York: Columbia University Press, 1992); see also Mary O. Furner, *Advocacy and Objectivity: A Crisis in the Professionalization of American Social Science, 1865–1905* (Lexington: University Press of Kentucky, 1975). The most thoroughly studied investigation is that of the U.S. Commission on Industrial Relations, chaired by Kansas City attorney Frank Walsh. See chapter 7 of this book. John R. Commons acted in the capacity of staff expert in the first investigation and commission member in the second; see his autobiographical account, *Myself* (New York: Macmillan, 1934).

38. Montgomery, *Citizen Worker*, discusses this ambiguous role of the state in re-

lation to the market economy. See Skowronek, *Building a New American State,* and Keller, *Affairs of State,* on the limits of state action. Victoria Hattam, *Labor Visions and State Power,* discusses the liberal use of judicial activism to restrain and redirect the labor movement in the late nineteenth century. On the changing views among some government officials and corporate leaders, see the discussion of Richard Olney's role in drafting of the Erdman Act in the 1890s in Gerald Eggert, *Richard Olney: Evolution of a Statesman* (University Park: Pennsylvania State University Press, 1974), 155–69; see also Stromquist, *Generation of Boomers,* 257–63.

39. Henry C. Adams et al., *Science Economic Discussion* (1886), quoted in Ross, *Origins of American Social Science,* 115–16.

40. For a superb account of these shifts in position by Ely, Adams, and Clark, see ibid., 115–17. See also Furner, *Advocacy and Objectivity,* 89–106, 125–62.

41. Ross, *Origins of American Social Science,* 120. See also Livingston, "Social Analysis of Economic History and Theory," 87–94.

42. Ross, *Origins of American Social Science,* 139–40.

43. Destler, *Henry Demarest Lloyd,* 214–16. On the internationalist orientation of these reformers, see Daniel T. Rodgers, *Transatlantic Crossings: Social Politics in a Progressive Age* (Cambridge, Mass.: Harvard University Press, 1998), 62–68.

44. Henry Demarest Lloyd, "The Safety of the Future Lies in Organized Labour," in *Men, the Workers,* by Henry Demarest Lloyd (New York: Doubleday, 1909), 87–88.

45. Henry D. Lloyd to Samuel Gompers, July 30, 1894, H. D. Lloyd Papers, State Historical Society of Wisconsin, Madison; Henry D. Lloyd to Samuel Gompers, August 14, 1894, in *Samuel Gompers Papers,* ed. Stuart B. Kaufman and Peter J. Albert (Urbana: University of Illinois Press, 1989), 3:561–62. For a discussion of the impact of the Pullman strike on public opinion, see Nancy Cohen, *The Reconstruction of American Liberalism, 1865–1914* (Chapel Hill: University of North Carolina, 2002), 192–202.

46. For accounts of the Pullman boycott, see Almont Lindsey, *The Pullman Strike: The Story of a Unique Experiment and of a Great Labor Upheaval* (Chicago: University of Chicago Press, 1942); Stromquist, *Generation of Boomers,* 79–97, 251–63; Gerald Eggert, *Railroad Labor Disputes: The Beginnings of Federal Strike Policy* (Ann Arbor: University of Michigan Press, 1967), 157–91; and United States Strike Commission, *Report on the Chicago Strike of June–July, 1894,* 53d Cong., 3d sess., Senate Executive Document No. 7 (Washington, D.C.: GPO, 1895). See also Ray Ginger, *The Bending Cross: A Biography of Eugene Victor Debs* (New Brunswick, N.J.: Rutgers University Press, 1949), and Salvatore, *Eugene V. Debs.* For a variety of perspectives on the significance of Pullman in the 1890s, see Schneirov, Stromquist, and Salvatore, *Pullman Strike and the Crisis of the 1890s.*

47. Jane Addams, *Twenty Years at Hull-House* (New York: Macmillan, 1910), 158–61. For an account that discusses the general efforts of middle-class Chicago women to mediate the strike, see Maureen A. Flanagan, *Seeing with Their Hearts: Chicago Women and the Vision of the Good City, 1871–1933* (Princeton, N.J.: Princeton University Press, 2002), 58.

48. Jane Addams testimony, U.S. Strike Commission, *Report on the Chicago Strike,* 646–47.

49. Albert Shaw to Jane Addams, January 18, 1896, and John Dewey to Jane Addams, January 19, 1896; also, for more extended critiques, Henry D. Lloyd to Jane Addams, February 23, 1896, and Horace Elisha Scudder to Mary Hawes Wilmarth, April 18, 1896, all in the Swarthmore Peace Collection of the Jane Addams Papers, Swarthmore College, Swarthmore, Pennsylvania, in the general microform collection "The Jane Addams Papers," 3-27, 3-29, 3-64, and 3-104. A number of historians have discussed Addams's efforts to publish "A Modern Lear," including Victoria Brown, "Advocate for Democracy: Jane Addams and the Pullman Strike," and Janice L. Reiff, "A Modern Lear and His Daughters: Gender in the Model Town of Pullman," both in Schneirov, Stromquist, and Salvatore, *Pullman Strike and the Crisis of the 1890s,* 130–58, 65–86; Victoria Bissell Brown, *The Education of Jane Addams* (Philadelphia: University of Pennsylvania Press, 2004), 288–93; Carl Smith, *Urban Disorder and the Shape of Belief: The Great Chicago Fire, the Haymarket Bomb, and the Model Town of Pullman* (Chicago: University of Chicago Press, 1995), 255–58; Michael McGerr, *A Fierce Discontent: The Rise and Fall of the Progressive Movement* (New York: Free Press, 2003), 57–59; and Jean Bethke Elshtain, *Jane Addams and the Dream of American Democracy* (New York: Basic Books, 2002), 111–13. For a discussion that focuses on Dewey and Addams, see Louis Menand, *The Metaphysical Club: A Story of Ideas in America* (New York: Farrar, Strauss, and Giroux, 2001), 312–16.

50. Jane Addams, "A Modern Lear," *Survey* 29 (November 2, 1912): 131–37.

51. Jane Addams, "The Settlement as a Factor in the Labor Movement," in *Hull-House Maps and Papers,* by the Residents of Hull-House (New York: Thomas Y. Crowell, 1895), 194–95, 202–4, 200–201.

52. John Dewey to Alice Dewey, July 2, 1894, cited in Robert Westbrook, *John Dewey and American Democracy* (Ithaca, N.Y.: Cornell University Press, 1991), 86–87. The label "radical democrat" is Westbrook's.

53. Ibid., 87–88.

54. The conversation between Dewey and Addams on October 9, 1894, is reconstructed from Dewey's correspondence with his wife in Jay Martin, *The Education of John Dewey: A Biography* (New York: Columbia University Press, 2002), 164–68.

55. John Dewey, "Academic Freedom" (1902), quoted in Westbrook, *John Dewey and American Democracy,* 92. Menand, *Metaphysical Club,* 295–305, emphasizes Dewey's privately expressed moral support for the strikers but fails to engage his public distancing from the conflict.

56. The most detailed account of the "Bemis controversy" is in Furner, *Advocacy and Objectivity,* 163–98; See also Ross, *Origins of American Social Science,* 133.

57. *Chicago Tribune,* November 14, 1893; Civic Federation of Chicago, *1st Annual Report of the Central Council* (Chicago: Civic Federation of Chicago, 1895), 76–78.

58. Furner, *Advocacy and Objectivity,* 170–71.

59. Testimony of Edward W. Bemis, U.S. Strike Commission, *Report on the Chicago Strike,* 644; "The Chicago Strike of 1894" (Edward W. Bemis), *Review of Reviews* 12 (October 1895): 466.

60. Edward W. Bemis to Richard T. Ely, October 4, 1894, Box 8, File 12, Ely Papers.

61. Furner, *Advocacy and Objectivity,* 197–98; Chicago Conference on Trusts, *Speeches, Debates, Resolutions, List of Delegates, Committees, etc.* (Chicago: Civic Federation of Chicago, 1900); "Social Science College Plan," July 12, 1899, Edward W. Bemis Papers, State Historical Society of Wisconsin, Madison; Tom Johnson, *My Story* (1911; reprint, New York: AMS Press, 1970).

62. John E. Semonche, *Ray Stannard Baker: A Quest for Democracy in Modern America, 1870–1918* (Chapel Hill: University of North Carolina Press, 1969), 57–62, quotation from 58 (*Chicago Record,* November 30, 1892).

63. Ray Stannard Baker [David Grayson], *American Chronicle: The Autobiography of Ray Stannard Baker* (New York: Scribner's, 1945), 36.

64. Robert C. Bannister, *Ray Stannard Baker: The Mind and Thought of a Progressive* (New Haven, Conn.: Yale University Press, 1966), 51.

65. Baker, *American Chronicle,* 38–39.

66. Ray Stannard Baker [David Grayson], *Native American: The Book of My Youth* (New York: Charles Scribner's Sons, 1941), 334–35.

Chapter 2: Constituting Progressivism

1. Henry Demarest Lloyd, "No Mean City," in *Mazzini and Other Essays,* by Henry Demarest Lloyd (New York: G. P. Putnam, 1910), 213. For a discussion of the significance of Lloyd's vision, see Robert Westbrook, *John Dewey and American Democracy* (Ithaca, N.Y.: Cornell University Press, 1991), 84–85, and Chester M. Destler, *Henry Demarest Lloyd and the Empire of Reform* (Philadelphia: University of Pennsylvania Press, 1963). On the context of the World's Columbian Exposition, see Alan Trachtenberg, "White City," in *The Incorporation of America,* by Alan Trachtenberg (New York: Hill and Wang, 1982), 208–34.

2. See Dorothy Ross, *The Origins of American Social Science* (New York: Cambridge University Press, 1991) for a brilliant account of social scientific progressivism that stresses its mission to revitalize "American exceptionalism."

3. This language of social harmony and reform is to be found in abundance in the autobiographies of settlement house "folk" and other urban reformers. For the paradigmatic statement, see Jane Addams, *Twenty Years at Hull-House* (New York: Macmillan, 1910).

4. Robert H. Wiebe, *Self-Rule: A Cultural History of American Democracy* (Chicago: University of Chicago Press, 1995), 180, 161, speaks of new class divisions that "fixed" older hierarchies based on race and gender.

5. Addams, *Twenty Years at Hull-House,* 122.

6. *Chicago Tribune,* November 11, 1893, p. 1. Brief accounts of Stead's activities are

also available in Ray Ginger, *Altgeld's America: The Lincoln Ideal versus Changing Re-alities* (1958; reprint, New York: New Viewpoints, 1973), 98, 235, 248–49; Frederic Whyte, *The Life of W. T. Stead* (New York: Houghton Mifflin, 1925), 2:42–49; and Graham Taylor, *Pioneering on Social Frontiers* (Chicago: University of Chicago Press, 1930), 28–34.

7. *Chicago Tribune*, November 13, 1893.

8. This alternative strand of radical reform—the direct heir of producerism—is discussed in more detail in chapters 3, 5, 6, and 7.

9. Civic Federation of Chicago, *1st Annual Report of the Central Council* (Chicago: Civic Federation of Chicago, 1895), 7.

10. Ibid., 76–78.

11. David Thelen, *The New Citizenship: Origins of Progressivism in Wisconsin, 1885–1900* (Columbia: University of Missouri Press, 1972), 10–11. See also John G. Sproat, *The Best Men: Liberal Reformers in the Gilded Age* (New York: Oxford University Press, 1968).

12. Seymour Mandelbaum, *Boss Tweed's New York* (New York: J. Wiley, 1965) re-mains the best account of the rise of the Tweed Ring and its mugwump opposition. See also Amy Bridges, *A City in the Republic: Antebellum New York and the Origins of Machine Politics* (New York: Cambridge University Press, 1984), and Martin Shefter, "Trade Unions and Political Machines: The Organization and Disorganization of the American Working Class in the Late Nineteenth Century," in *Class Formation*, ed. Ira Katznelson and Aristide Zolberg (Princeton, N.J.: Princeton University Press, 1986), 197–276. See also Richard Schneirov, "Rethinking the Relation of Labor to the Politics of Urban Social Reform in Late Nineteenth-Century America: The Case of Chicago," *International Labor and Working-Class History* 46 (1994): 93–108; for the most com-prehensive treatment of class and reform politics in Chicago, see Richard Schneirov, *Labor and Urban Politics: Class Conflict and the Origins of Modern Liberalism in Chi-cago, 1864–1897* (Urbana: University of Illinois Press, 1998).

13. See Zane L. Miller, *Boss Cox's Cincinnati: Urban Politics in the Progressive Era* (New York: Oxford University Press, 1968), and the *Cincinnati Enquirer*, March 18 and March 26, 1897, and *Cincinnati Chronicle*, March 1894.

14. *Cincinnati Enquirer*, February 25, 1894, March 18, 1897.

15. *Cincinnati Chronicle*, March 26, 1897.

16. Thelen, *New Citizenship*, 27–32; Paul Boyer, *Urban Masses and Moral Order in America, 1820–1920* (Cambridge, Mass.: Harvard University Press, 1978); see the Omaha Platform and AFL Political Programme of 1894 for Populist and labor sup-port for political reform. For an insightful account of the mugwump origins of a mu-nicipal reformer, see Frederic Howe, *Confessions of a Reformer* (New York: Scribner's, 1925). On the preeminent nonpartisan municipal reformer, Samuel "Golden Rule" Jones, see Marnie Jones, *Holy Toledo: Religion and Politics in the Life of "Golden Rule" Jones* (Lexington: University Press of Kentucky, 1998), and Hoyt L. Warner, *Progres-sivism in Ohio, 1897–1917* (Columbus: Ohio State University Press, 1964). On direct

democracy, see Robert D. Johnston, *The Radical Middle Class: Populist Democracy and the Question of Capitalism in Progressive Era Portland, Oregon* (Princeton, N.J.: Princeton University Press, 2003), esp. 115–37.

17. Roosevelt's influence is nicely captured in Jacob Riis's memoir, *The Making of an American* (New York: Macmillan, 1920), 224, 233, 254–60, 325–50, 381–82.

18. See Herbert Gutman, "Protestantism and the American Labor Movement: The Christian Spirit in the Gilded Age," *American Historical Review* 72, no. 1 (1966): 74–101. Henry May, *Protestant Churches and Industrial America* (New York: Harper Brothers, 1949) remains the starting point for consideration of the transformation of Protestantism in the late nineteenth century. For a skeptical assessment of the strength of social gospel reform in mainstream Protestantism, see Robert E. Weir, *Beyond Labor's Veil: The Culture of the Knights of Labor* (University Park: Pennsylvania State University Press, 1996), 67–101.

19. Historians of progressivism disagree to some degree on the centrality of religion to reform. I do not underestimate the contribution made by a whole range of reform-minded ministers, priests, and rabbis, let alone deeply religious laity, but I would argue that they participated largely in a movement that defined its identity in secular, moral terms. On this debate, see Richard Wightman Fox, "The Culture of Liberal Protestant Progressivism, 1875–1925," *Journal of Interdisciplinary History* 23, no. 3 (Winter 1993): 645–46.

20. See May, *Protestant Churches and Industrial America*, 170–77, and Robert Crunden, *Ministers of Reform: The Progressives' Achievement in American Civilization, 1889–1920* (New York: Basic Books, 1982), 40–51. See also Susan Curtis, *A Consuming Faith: The Social Gospel and Modern American Culture* (Baltimore: Johns Hopkins University Press, 1991), 1–15, emphasizes the cultural modernism of the movement.

21. May, *Protestant Churches and Industrial America*, 173–74. See also Gary J. Dorrien, *The Making of American Liberal Theology: Imagining Progressive Religion, 1805–1900* (Louisville, Ky.: Westminster John Knox Press, 2001), 304–11.

22. Fox, "Culture of Liberal Protestant Progressivism," 655, 658.

23. Walter Rauschenbusch, *Christianizing the Social Order* (1912), quoted in Gary J. Dorrien, *The Making of American Liberal Theology: Idealism, Realism and Modernity, 1900– 1950* (Louisville, Ky.: Westminster John Knox Press, 2003), 116, 110.

24. May, *Protestant Churches and Industrial America*, 217–23; Weir, *Beyond Labor's Veil*, 67–68, 76–78.

25. Quoted in Dorrien, *Making of American Liberal Theology: Imagining Progressive Religion*, 307. On Gladden, Rauschenbusch, and George D. Herron, see Curtis, *Consuming Faith*, 36–48, 101–14, 195–206; see also Peter J. Frederick, *Knights of the Golden Rule: The Intellectual as Christian Social Reformer in the 1890s* (Lexington: University Press of Kentucky, 1976), 141–84.

26. Ken Fones-Wolf, *Trade Union Gospel: Christianity and Labor in Industrial Philadelphia, 1865–1915* (Philadelphia: Temple University Press, 1989), xx, 113–21.

27. Fox, "Culture of Liberal Protestant Progressivism," 658.

28. One of the most influential utopian novels was William Dean Howells, *A Traveller from Altruria* (New York: Harper Brothers, 1895); see Neil Harris, "Utopian Fiction and Its Discontents," in *Uprooted Americans: Essays in Honor of Oscar Handlin,* ed. Richard L. Bushman, Neil Harris, David Rothman, Barbara Miller Solomon, and Stephen Thernstrom (Boston: Little Brown, 1979).

29. Frances E. Willard, "An Interview with Edward Bellamy" (1889), quoted in Howard Quint, *The Forging of American Socialism: Origins of the Modern Movement* (New York: Bobbs-Merrill, 1953), 73–74.

30. Quint, *Forging of American Socialism,* 72–73.

31. Milton Cantor, "The Backward Look of Bellamy's Socialism," in *Looking Backward, 1988–1888: Essays on Edward Bellamy,* ed. Daphne Patai (Amherst: University of Massachusetts Press, 1988), 28–29.

32. Arthur Lipow, *Authoritarian Socialism in America: Edward Bellamy and the Nationalist Movement* (Berkeley: University of California Press, 1982), 9–11.

33. Edward Bellamy, *Looking Backward, 2000–1887* (1888; reprint, New York: Penguin, 1982), 66.

34. Cyrus Field Willard, "A Retrospect" (1889), quoted in Lipow, *Authoritarian Socialism in America,* 127.

35. Bellamy, *Looking Backward,* 69. The phrase "double vision" is used by Daphne Patai in *Looking Backward,* 10.

36. Cantor, "Backward Look of Bellamy's Socialism," 33.

37. George's appeal among American workers may have been strongest among Irish immigrants and American supporters of the Irish Land League, among whom the centrality of land reform had particular resonance. See Eric Foner, "Class, Ethnicity, and Radicalism in the Gilded Age: The Land League and Irish-America," in *Politics and Ideology in the Age of the Civil War,* by Eric Foner (New York: Oxford University Press, 1980), 184–86, 197–99.

38. Two essays capture the intense and destabilizing commitment of workers to George's ideas between 1886 and 1888: David M. Scobey, "Boycotting the Politics Factory: Labor Radicalism and the New York Mayoral Election of 1884 [*sic*]," *Radical History Review* 28–30 (1984): 280–325, and Steven J. Ross, "The Culture of Political Economy: Henry George and the American Working Class," *Southern California Quarterly* 65, no. 2 (Summer 1983): 145–66.

39. Henry George, *Progress and Poverty,* as quoted in John L. Thomas, *Alternative America: Henry George, Edward Bellamy, Henry Demarest Lloyd and the Adversary Tradition* (Cambridge, Mass.: Harvard University Press, 1983), 105.

40. Ibid., 115.

41. Ibid., 115–21; Henry George, *Progress and Poverty: An Inquiry into the Cause of Industrial Depressions and of Increase of Want with Increase of Wealth. The Remedy* (New York: Robert Schalkenbach Foundation, 1962), 421, 461.

42. George, *Progress and Poverty,* 407.

43. Thomas, *Alternative America,* 174, 223, quoting from George to Charles Nordhoff (1880), and from George's first campaign speech.

44. Scobey, "Boycotting the Politics Factory," 306. On the limited scope of the Clarendon Platform, see Thomas, *Alternative America*, 224.

45. *John Swinton's Paper*, October 24, 1886, quoted in Ross, "Culture of Political Economy," 158.

46. See, for example, the Political Programme of the American Federation of Labor, December 1894. When the annual convention could not agree on the collectivist plank 10, a substitute was adopted that directly embodied George's principles; for example, "The abolition of the monopoly system of land holding and the substituting therefor of a title of occupancy and use only," in *A Verbatum [sic] Report of the Discussion on the Political Programme at the December Convention of the American Federation of Labor, December 14, 15, 1894,* 62. See also Nellie Kremenak, "Urban Workers in the Agricultural West, 1856–1893, with a Case Study of Fort Dodge and Webster, County, Iowa" (Ph.D. diss., University of Iowa, 1995), 240–74.

47. Thomas, *Alternative America*, 116; Ross, "Culture of Political Economy," 155.

48. Accounts of Johnson's conversion to the single tax may be found in his autobiography, Tom Johnson, *My Story* (1911; reprint, New York: AMS Press, 1970), 48–52, 66–67, and in Howe, *Confessions of a Reformer*, 95–98.

49. Howe, *Confessions of a Reformer*, 97–98.

50. See Linda K. Kerber, "Separate Spheres, Female Worlds, Woman's Place: The Rhetoric of Women's History," *Journal of American History* 75 (June 1988): 9–39; and Katherine Kish Sklar, "Hull House in the 1890s: A Community of Women Reformers," *Signs* 10, no. 4 (1985): 658–77. Judith Mara Gutman, *Lewis W. Hine and the American Social Conscience* (New York: Walker, 1967); Allen F. Davis, *Spearheads for Reform: The Social Settlements and the Progressive Movement, 1890–1914* (New York: Oxford University Press, 1967), 244; Joseph Lash, *Eleanor and Franklin: The Story of their Relationship, based on Eleanor Roosevelt's Private Papers* (New York: Norton, 1971).

51. Hilda Satt Polacheck, *I Came a Stranger: The Story of a Hull-House Girl* (Urbana: University of Illinois Press, 1989), 68, 73–75.

52. Addams, *Twenty Years at Hull-House*, 137, 143; Mina Carson, *Settlement Folk: Social Thought and the American Settlement Movement, 1885–1930* (Chicago: University of Chicago Press, 1990), 76. Anton Johansson, a Chicago trade unionist with anarchist leanings, appreciated Addams's ability to foster lively political discussion; Hutchins Hapgood, *The Spirit of Labor* (1907; reprint, Urbana: University of Illinois Press, 2004), 213–14.

53. Westbrook, *John Dewey and American Democracy*, 85.

54. Vida Scudder, *On Journey* (New York: E. P. Dutton, 1937), 155–56. On Scudder's fictional construction of Boston's gendered space, see Sarah Deutsch, *Women and the City: Gender, Space and Power in Boston, 1870–1940* (New York: Oxford University Press, 2000), 8–14, 23–24. Carson, *Settlement Folk*, 82–83. See the excellent account of Scudder's journey to social activism in Frederick, *Knights of the Golden Rule*, esp. 122–27.

55. Florence Kelley, *The Autobiography of Florence Kelley: Notes on Sixty Years,* ed. Kathryn Kish Sklar (Chicago: University of Chicago Press, 1986), 77–85; Carson, *Settlement Folk,* 90–91. Kathryn Kish Sklar, *Florence Kelley and the Nation's Work: The*

Rise of Women's Political Culture, 1830–1900 (New Haven, Conn.: Yale University Press, 1995), 171–72, 235–36.

56. Sklar, *Florence Kelley and the Nation's Work*, 215–16.

57. Carson, *Settlement Folk*, 97–98. On Hunter, see Peter d'A. Jones's introduction to Robert Hunter, *Poverty: Social Conscience in the Progressive Era* (New York: Macmillan, 1904). See also Ira Kipnis, *The American Socialist Movement, 1897–1912* (New York: Columbia University Press, 1952) on the alliance of reformers with socialists, 171–75, 199–217.

58. Louis Filler, *The Muckrakers* (University Park: Pennsylvania State University Press, 1968), 29–42. See also Arthur Weinberg and Lila Weinberg, eds., *The Muckrakers: The Era in Journalism that Moved America to Reform* (New York: Capricorn, 1964), xiii–xix. For a useful discussion of B. O. Flower and the *Arena*, see Frederick, *Knights of the Golden Rule*, 101–4. On the influence of Wayland and the *Appeal to Reason*, see Elliott Shore, *Talkin' Socialism: J. A. Wayland and the Role of the Press in American Radicalism, 1890–1912* (Lawrence: University of Kansas Press, 1988).

59. Ray Stannard Baker [David Grayson], *American Chronicle: The Autobiography of Ray Stannard Baker* (New York: Scribner's, 1945), 99, 96.

60. Ibid., 77.

61. S. S. McClure, "Editorial: Concerning Three Articles in this Number of McClure's, and a Coincidence that May Set Us Thinking," *McClure's,* January 1903, reprinted in Ellen F. Fitzpatrick, *Muckraking: Three Landmark Articles* (Boston: Bedford Books, 1994), 101–2. Fitzpatrick provides an excellent introduction to the articles by Tarbell, Steffens, and Baker, 1–39, and republishes their full text.

62. Richard L. McCormick, "The Discovery that Business Corrupts Politics: A Reappraisal of the Origins of Progressivism," in *The Party Period and Public Policy: American Politics from the Age of Jackson to the Progressive Era,* by Richard L. McCormick (New York: Oxford University Press, 1986), 315, 350–51.

63. For a historiographical assessment of the muckrakers, see Fitzpatrick, *Muckraking,* 103–16. And for an insightful discussion of the changing impact of photographic technology and journalistic representations of labor and capital, see Larry Peterson, "The Changing Image of Labor Conflict in the 1890s: Corporate, Labor, Government, and Media Attempts to Mold Public Perceptions of the Pullman Strike," in *The Pullman Strike and the Crisis of the 1890s: Essays on Labor and Politics,* ed. Richard Schneirov, Shelton Stromquist, and Nick Salvatore (Urbana: University of Illinois Press, 1999), 87–129.

64. Sullivan and Lloyd quoted in Alan Trachtenberg, *The Incorporation of America* (New York: Hill and Wang, 1982), 225, 218. Lloyd's essay "No Mean City" provides one glimpse of the possibilities for social reconstruction he saw embodied in the fair.

65. Ibid., 219–20.

66. Robert W. Rydell, *All the World's a Fair: Visions of Empire at American International Expositions, 1876–1916* (Chicago: University of Chicago Press, 1984), 38–71, esp. 52, 67–68.

67. Trachtenberg, *Incorporation of America*, 214.

68. The World's Congress Auxiliary of the World's Columbian Exposition, "Objects," preliminary publication, n.d., Box 6, File 12, Ely Papers.

69. Walter Thomas Mills, "Preliminary Address of the General Committee on Labor Congresses, including all Germane Industrial and Economic Problems," 1893, Box 6, File 12, Ely Papers.

70. Ibid., and H. D. Lloyd to Richard T. Ely, February 4, 1893, Box 6, File 2, Ely Papers.

71. *Chicago Tribune*, August 31, 1893, p. 9, and George McNeill, "The Philosophy of the Labor Movement," paper read before the International Labor Congress, Chicago, September 1893, Chicago Historical Society. Gompers's early tutelage in Marxism in the cigar shops of New York City continued to give a class edge to his rhetoric in the 1890s. Even as he steered the AFL in a more conservative direction, he spoke repeatedly of labor's "final emancipation."

72. Samuel Gompers, "What Does Labor Want?" paper read before the International Labor Congress, Chicago, September 1893, 4–5, Chicago Historical Society.

73. Gompers, "What Does Labor Want?" 7–8.

74. World's Congress Auxiliary, "Objects."

75. "Report of the Industrial Committee of the Civic Federation of Chicago," Congress on Industrial Conciliation and Arbitration (Chicago, 1894), 94, Chicago Historical Society.

76. *Chicago Tribune*, November 14, 1894, p. 5; *Outlook* 50, no. 22 (December 1, 1894): 896.

77. *Chicago Tribune*, November 14, 1894, p. 5.

78. "Report of the Industrial Committee," 48–49.

79. *Chicago Tribune*, November 15, 1894, p. 2; Samuel Gompers, "An Address before the Congress on Industrial Conciliation and Arbitration, Chicago, November 14, 1894," in *Samuel Gompers Papers*, ed. Stuart Kaufman and Peter J. Albert (Urbana: University of Illinois Press, 1989), 3:601; "Report of the Industrial Committee," 90.

80. Civic Federation of Chicago, *1st Annual Report*, 77–81. Joining the major speakers from the Congress on the National Commission were industrialists C. O. Pillsbury, Charles Francis Adams, and M. E. Ingalls; labor leaders P. M. Arthur of the Locomotive Engineers and Terence V. Powderly, former grand master workman of the Knights of Labor; and public representatives and reformers N. O. Nelson, Washington Gladden, L. S. Coffin, and Albion Small.

81. See Naomi Lamoreaux, *The Greater Merger Movement in American Business, 1895–1904* (New York: Cambridge University Press, 1985).

82. Reformers were split on the trust question. The *Chicago Tribune* noted three tendencies: a faction associated with the "Texas idea" that opposed all trusts and included western and southern delegates, as well as many trade unionists and farmers; a "New Jersey idea" faction from eastern and midwestern states that thought trusts were to be encouraged; and an "academic idea" faction that believed trusts were a natural out-

growth but in need of legal regulation. *Chicago Tribune,* September 14, 1899, p. 1. For general discussions of the conference on trusts, see Martin J. Sklar, *The Corporate Reconstruction of American Capitalism, 1890–1916* (New York: Cambridge University Press, 1988), 207–8; Mary O. Furner, *Advocacy and Objectivity: A Crisis in the Professionalization of American Social Science, 1865–1905* (Lexington: University Press of Kentucky, 1975), 268; and Destler, *Henry Demarest Lloyd,* 351– 52. On the formation of the National Civic Federation and the place of trusts in American public life, see James Weinstein, *The Corporate Ideal of the Liberal State, 1900–1918* (Boston: Beacon Press, 1968), and Marguerite Green, *The National Civic Federation and the American Labor Movement, 1900–1925* (Washington, D.C.: Catholic University of America Press, 1956), 6–7, 9–10, 198, 200–201.

83. Gompers lost the presidency of the AFL for one year in 1895 amid the fight over independent political action and a collectivist political program. See J. F. Finn, "AF of L Leaders and the Question of Politics in the Early 1890s," *American Studies* 7, no. 3 (1973): 243–65; "The Debate over the Political Programme of 1894," in *Samuel Gompers Papers,* ed. Stuart B. Kaufman and Peter J. Albert (Urbana: University of Illinois Press, 1989), vol. 3; and Shelton Stromquist, "The Crisis of 1894 and the Legacies of Producerism," in *Pullman Strike and the Crisis of the 1890s: Essays on Labor and Politics,* ed. Richard Schneirov, Shelton Stromquist, and Nick Salvatore (Urbana: University of Illinois Press, 1999), 192–93. For accounts of the reconstitution of a Social Democratic alternative, see Nick Salvatore, *Eugene V. Debs: Citizen and Socialist* (Urbana: University of Illinois Press, 1982), and Quint, *Forging of American Socialism.*

84. *Independent,* July 6, 1899, 1789, and *Arena* 21, no. 3 (March 1899): 395. See also Crunden, *Ministers of Reform,* 46–47, and Robert Bremner, "The Civic Revival in Ohio," *American Journal of Economics and Sociology,* October 1948–January 1951.

85. *Outlook* 62, no. 1 (May 6, 1899): 4.

86. *Arena* 22, no. 1 (July 1899): 71. The editors described those invited as "Democrats and republicans; all kinds of populists, socialists, and prohibitionists; Hebrews, Catholics, and Protestants, together with advocates of organized labor, direct legislation, good roads, the single tax, the Y.M.C.A., the Salvation Army, civil service, cooperation, municipal ownership and colonization."

87. On Bliss and the Buffalo conference, see Frederick, *Knights of the Golden Rule,* 93–98.

88. Furner, *Advocacy and Objectivity,* 267–68.

89. Quint, *Forging of American Socialism,* 109–41, 260–69, has the most complete assessment of W. D. P. Bliss and the Social Reform Union.

90. *Arena* 22, no. 1 (July 1899): 129–30.

91. W. D. P. Bliss, "An Open Letter on the Political Situation with a Definite Proposal," *Social Unity* 1, no. 1 (January 1, 1901): 6–7.

Chapter 3: The Politics of Reform

1. Jane Addams, *Democracy and Social Ethics* (New York: Macmillan, 1907), 240, 270–71, 268–69. See also Jean Bethke Elshtain, *Jane Addams and the Dream of Amer-*

ican Democracy: A Life (New York: Basic Books, 2002), 168–73, 184–87, for an extended discussion of Addams battles with Johnny Powers's machine.

2. Standard accounts of Gilded Age party politics begin with James Bryce, *American Commonwealth*, 2 vols. (New York: Macmillan, 1888). For a fascinating account of the political culture of northern Democrats, see Jean Baker, *Affairs of Party: The Political Culture of Northern Democrats in the Mid-Nineteenth Century* (Ithaca, N.Y.: Cornell University Press, 1983). The triumphs and spoils of the Republicans as the party of "free labor" and northern enterprise are chronicled in Eric Foner, *Reconstruction: America's Unfinished Revolution, 1863–1877* (New York: Harper and Row, 1988), and David Montgomery, *Beyond Equality: Labor and the Radical Republicans, 1862–1872* (New York: Random House, 1967). On the behavior of party activists, see Glenn Altschuler and Stuart Blumin, *Rude Republic: Americans and Their Politics in the Nineteenth Century* (Princeton, N.J.: Princeton University Press, 2000).

3. For historians' treatment of the third-party system, see Paul Kleppner, "Partisanship and Ethnoreligious Conflict: The Third Electoral System, 1853–1892," in *The Evolution of American Electoral Systems*, by Paul Kleppner (Westport, Conn.: Greenwood Press, 1981), 112–46; see also Paul Kleppner, *The Third Electoral System, 1853–1892: Parties, Voters and Political Cultures* (Chapel Hill: University of North Carolina Press, 1979); Richard Jensen, *The Winning of the Midwest: Social and Political Conflict, 1888–1896* (Chicago: University of Chicago, 1971); and, for critiques of ethnocultural analysis, Richard L. McCormick, *The Party Period and Public Policy: American Politics from the Age of Jackson to the Progressive Era* (New York: Oxford University Press, 1986), and Richard Oestreicher, "Urban Working-Class Political Behavior and Theories of American Electoral Politics, 1870–1940," *Journal of American History* 74 (March 1988): 1257–86.

4. For a study that is particularly sensitive to the intraparty dynamics of reform in the 1880s and 1890s, see Jeffrey Ostler, *Prairie Populism: The Fate of Agrarian Radicalism in Kansas, Nebraska, and Iowa, 1880–1892* (Lawrence: University of Kansas Press, 1993). Also, at the level of municipal politics, see Shelton Stromquist, "The Crucible of Class: Cleveland Politics and the Origins of Municipal Reform in the Progressive Era," *Journal of Urban History* 3, no. 2 (January 1997): 192–220.

5. The secession of prohibitionists from the Republicans and farmer/labor militants from the Democrats was a real threat to each in the 1880s and early 1890s. See Paul Kleppner, *The Cross of Culture: A Social Analysis of Midwestern Politics, 1850–1900* (New York: Free Press, 1970), and Ostler, *Prairie Populism.*

6. See Gretchen Ritter, *Goldbugs and Greenbacks: The Antimonopoly Tradition and the Politics of Finance in America* (New York: Cambridge University Press, 1997); Elizabeth Sanders, *Roots of Reform: Farmers, Workers, and the American State, 1877–1917* (Chicago: University of Chicago Press, 1999); and John D. French, "Reaping the Whirlwind: The Origins of the Allegheny County Greenback Labor Party in 1877," *Western Pennsylvania Historical Magazine* 64, no. 2 (April 1981): 97–119.

7. Leon Fink, *Workingmen's Democracy: The Knights of Labor and American Politics*

(Urbana: University of Illinois Press, 1983), and Richard Oestreicher, *Solidarity and Fragmentation; Working People and Class Consciousness in Detroit, 1875–1900* (Urbana: University of Illinois Press, 1986), are the two best studies of Knights of Labor politics. See also David M. Scobey, "Boycotting the Politics Factory: Labor Radicalism and the New York City Mayoral Election of 1884 [*sic*]," *Radical History Review* (1984): xxviii–xxx, and Ralph Scharnau, "Workers and Politics: The Knights of Labor in Iowa," *Annals of Iowa* 48 (1989): 353–77. On urban populism, see Chester M. Destler, *American Radicalism, 1865–1901: Essays and Documents* (New London: Connecticut College Press, 1946); see Richard Schneirov, *Labor and Urban Politics: Class Conflict and the Origins of Modern Liberalism in Chicago, 1864–1897* (Urbana: University of Illinois Press, 1998) on Chicago; and on Butte, see David Emmons, *The Butte Irish: Class and Ethnicity in an American Mining Town, 1875–1925* (Urbana: University of Illinois Press, 1989).

8. See the excellent study of western working-class politics by John P. Enyeart, "'By Laws of Their Own Making': Political Culture and the Everyday Politics of the Mountain West Working Class, 1870–1917" (Ph.D. diss., University of Colorado, 2002).

9. Melvin G. Holli, *Reform in Detroit: Hazen S. Pingree and Urban Politics* (New York: Oxford University Press, 1969); and Stromquist, "Crucible of Class," 195–96.

10. Walter Dean Burnham, "The System of 1896: An Analysis," in Kleppner, *Evolution of American Electoral Systems*, 160; Oliver Wendell Holmes, "Law and the Court," quoted in Burnham, "System of 1896," 162. On the conservative judicial response to the social crisis of the 1890s, see Arnold M. Paul, *Conservative Crisis and the Rule of Law: Attitudes of Bar and Bench, 1887–1895* (Ithaca, N.Y.: Cornell University Press, 1960), esp. 61–81. See discussion below.

11. Ostler, *Prairie Populism,* offers the clearest and most persuasive analysis of the state parties' competitive adaptiveness when threatened by political insurgency. For specific treatment of the Iowa and Wisconsin cases, see also Mark Carlile, "The Trials of Progressivism: Iowa Voting Behavior in the Progressive Era, 1901–1916" (Ph.D. diss., University of Iowa, 1995), and Roger Wyman, "Voting Behavior in the Progressive Era: Wisconsin a Case Study" (Ph.D. diss., University of Wisconsin, 1970). For an instructive discussion of some aspects of the reform politics in three major cities—New York, Cleveland, and Chicago—see Kenneth Finegold, *Experts and Politicians: Reform Challenges to Machine Politics in New York, Cleveland, and Chicago* (Princeton, N.J.: Princeton University Press, 1995).

12. The decline in what Michael McGerr has called "popular politics" is a complicated story that is addressed more fully later in this chapter. However, nearly all historians see the reduced influence of "party" as the central causal factor. The enhancement of state administrative capacities and the new opportunities for influence that such an administrative state offered organized interest groups at the expense of party organizations is also a significant explanatory factor. See Michael McGerr, *The Decline of Popular Politics: The American North, 1865–1928* (New York: Oxford University Press, 1986); Stephen Skowronek, *Building a New American State: The Expansion of National Administrative Capacities, 1877–1920* (New York: Cam-

bridge University Press, 1982); and Morton Keller, *Affairs of State: Public Life in Late Nineteenth-Century America* (Cambridge, Mass.: Harvard University Press, 1977). Altschuler and Blumin, *Rude Republic*, 252–73, argue that the extent of popular participation in nineteenth-century politics has been overdrawn and the extent of decline after 1896 therefore overstated.

13. For a helpful discussion of the reformers' continuing influence in the Democratic Party of the early twentieth century, see David Sarasohn, *The Party of Reform: Democrats in the Progressive Era* (Jackson: University of Mississippi Press, 1989). The Republicans' reabsorption of "radical" reform is nicely illustrated by the return of Populist direct democracy reformer William U'Ren to the Republican fold in Oregon. See the recent study by Robert D. Johnston, *The Radical Middle Class: Populist Democracy and the Question of Capitalism in Progressive Era Portland, Oregon* (Princeton, N.J.: Princeton University Press, 2003), 129–33.

14. The story of the origins of Progressive politics in New York state is most clearly told in Richard L. McCormick, "Prelude to Progressivism: The Transformation of New York State Politics, 1890–1910," in McCormick, *Party Period and Public Policy,* 289–310, and in greater depth in McCormick, *From Realignment to Reform: Political Change in New York State, 1893–1910* (Ithaca, N.Y.: Cornell University Press, 1981). See also David C. Hammack, *Power and Society: Greater New York at the Turn of the Century* (New York: Russell Sage Foundation, 1982), 180–81.

15. McCormick, "Prelude to Progressivism," 297–99.

16. Leroy H. Van Kirk to Platt, September 17, 1898, quoted in ibid., 300. Martin Shefter, "Political Incorporation and Containment: Regime Transformation in New York City," in *Power, Culture and Place: Essays on New York City,* ed. John H. Mollenkopf (New York: Russell Sage Foundation, 1988) describes the emergence of an "anti-machine 'fusion' movement" for reform that crossed party lines.

17. Augustus Cerillo Jr., "The Impact of Reform Ideology: Early Twentieth Century Municipal Government in New York City," in *The Age of Urban Reform: New Perspectives on the Progressive Era,* ed. Michael H. Ebner and Eugene M. Tobin (Port Washington, N.Y.: Kennikat Press, 1977), especially 76–85. Finegold, *Experts and Politicians,* 33–68, discusses the shifting constituency for reform in New York City with an emphasis on the incorporation of expertise into the reform programs of different city administrations. See the discussion of William Randolph Hearst's insurgency later in this chapter.

18. The debate over the character of the Republican realignment of 1896 revolves around the question of whether the Republicans actually wooed would-be Democratic voters from that party's ranks or whether their success was more attributable to drawing new voters, largely immigrants, into the political universe. Useful arguments are offered by Allan Lichtman, "Political Realignment and 'Ethnocultural' Voting in Late Nineteenth-Century America," *Journal of Social History* 16 (1983): 55–83; Richard L. McCormick, "The Realignment Synthesis in American History," in McCormick, *Party Period and Public Policy,* 64–88; and Burnham, "System of 1896."

19. For a fuller discussion of the reconstruction of urban politics and the origins of Cleveland progressivism, see Stromquist, "Crucible of Class." See also Finegold, *Experts and Politicians,* 69–117, for a study of Cleveland reform politics that emphasizes the role of experts in shaping reform policies. Robert Bionaz, "Streetcar City: Popular Politics and the Shaping of Urban Progressivism in Cleveland, 1880–1910" (Ph.D. diss., University of Iowa, 2002), explores the working-class roots of Cleveland's progressivism and the fate of Johnson's brand of urban reform in unprecedented detail.

20. See Stromquist, "Crucible of Class," 200–207; the events of the strike, the Jones campaign, and the election results were reported extensively in the *Cleveland Plain Dealer* and the *Cleveland Citizen* (the organ of the Cleveland Central Labor Union).

21. See Frederic C. Howe, *Confessions of a Reformer* (New York: Scribner's, 1925), 85–145; *Cleveland Plain Dealer,* November 8, 1899; Tom Johnson, *My Story* (1911; reprint, New York: AMS Press, 1970), 108–31. Johnson's program is outlined in the *Cleveland Plain Dealer,* February 7, 1901. For a standard account of Johnson's election, see Hoyt L. Warner, *Progressivism in Ohio, 1897–1917* (Columbus: Ohio State University Press, 1964), 54–86. None of the standard accounts gives adequate attention to the ways in which class conflict reshaped local party identities and constituencies. Lincoln Steffens's views on Johnson and Cleveland appeared in "Ohio: A Tale of Two Cities," *McClure's* 25 (July 1905): 301–2.

22. Robert M. La Follette, *La Follette's Autobiography: A Personal Narrative of Political Experiences* (Madison, Wisc.: Robert M. La Follette, 1913), 146–47, 163–64.

23. David Thelen, *The New Citizenship: The Origins of Progressivism in Wisconsin, 1885–1900* (Columbia: University of Missouri Press, 1972), 290–308.

24. Ibid., 311, 308, 312, and on the origins of social progressivism in Wisconsin, see 55–85. A study that similarly emphasizes the consumerist base of progressivism in another state is Steven L. Piott, *The Anti-Monopoly Persuasion: Popular Resistance to the Rise of Big Business in the Midwest* (Westport, Conn.: Greenwood Press, 1985). See also Lawrence Glickman, *A Living Wage: American Workers and the Making of Consumer Society* (Ithaca, N.Y.: Cornell University Press, 1997).

25. La Follette, *La Follette's Autobiography,* 171–72. He would, of course, take on the mantel of an independent Progressive Party in the presidential contest of 1924.

26. Johnston, *Radical Middle Class,* especially 3–28, vehemently argues that reform was animated by a broad coalition led by the "radical" middle class. What he fails to acknowledge is the extent to which the political interests and loyalties of workers and the middle class at times diverged in this period.

27. Richard Schneirov, "Labor and Post-Pullman Strike Politics in Chicago, 1894–1899: Populism or Progressivism," in *The Pullman Strike and the Crisis of the 1890s: Essays on Labor, Politics and the State,* ed. Richard Schneirov, Shelton Stromquist, and Nick Salvatore (Urbana: University of Illinois Press, 1999). See also Schneirov, *Labor and Urban Politics.*

28. Maureen A. Flanagan, *Seeing with Their Hearts: Chicago Women and the Vision of the Good City, 1871–1933* (Princeton, N.J.: Princeton University Press, 2002), 81–109.

29. Michael F. Holt, *The Political Crisis of the 1850s* (New York: John Wiley, 1978), 4, 130–38, as well as his more recent book, *The Rise and Fall of the American Whig Party: Jacksonian Politics and the Onset of the Civil War* (New York: Oxford University Press, 1999); see also Eric Foner, *Free Soil, Free Labor, Free Men: The Ideology of the Republican Party before the Civil War* (New York: Oxford University Press, 1970). See also Altschuler and Blumin, *Rude Republic.*

30. John G. Sproat, *"The Best Men": Liberal Reformers in the Gilded Age* (New York: Oxford University Press, 1968), 9, 69, 276. See also Seymour J. Mandelbaum, *Boss Tweed's New York* (New York: J. Wiley, 1965).

31. On the Pendleton Act, see Ari Hoogenboom, *Outlawing the Spoils* (Urbana: University of Illinois Press, 1961), and Ari Hoogenboom, *Spoilsmen and Reformers* (New York: Rand McNally, 1964).

32. Thelen, *New Citizenship,* 202–4; in Cincinnati and Cleveland, good government reformers mounted independent, nonpartisan campaigns for local government modernization, at times joined by urban populists and at other times not. See Howe, *Confessions of a Reformer,* and reports on "Citizens" ticket campaigns in 1894 and 1897 in *Cincinnati Enquirer,* February 25, 1894, and March 9, 11, 19, 1897. For a general account of Boss Cox's rule over Cincinnati and periodic attempts by reformers to unseat him, see Zane L. Miller, *Boss Cox's Cincinnati: Urban Politics in the Progressive Era* (New York: Oxford University Press, 1968). On the campaigns of urban populists, see Destler, *American Radicalism;* Schneirov, *Labor and Urban Politics;* and Fink, *Workingmen's Democracy.*

33. Melanie S. Gustafson, "Partisan and Nonpartisan: The Political Career of Judith Ellen Foster, 1881–1910," in *We Have Come to Stay: American Women and Political Parties, 1880–1960,* ed. Melanie S. Gustafson, Kristie Miller, and Elisabeth I. Perry (Albuquerque: University of New Mexico Press, 1999), 1–12; see also Melanie S. Gustafson, "Partisan Women: Gender, Politics, and the Progressive Party of 1912" (Ph.D. diss., New York University, 1993), 70–82, and Rebecca Edwards, *Angels in the Machinery: Gender in American Party Politics from the Civil War to the Progressive Era* (New York: Oxford University Press, 1997); Ruth Bordin, *Frances Willard: A Biography* (Chapel Hill: University of North Carolina Press, 1986); and Katherine Jellison, on the faithfulness of eastern Iowa WCTU members to Ellen Foster in spite of her partisan political break with Frances Willard, "Rural Women and the WCTU: The Case for Eastern Iowa, 1880–1900," *Nebraska Humanist* 9 (1986): 46–55. On the class-bridging reform work of women Progressives, see chapter 5 of this book.

34. The term "regulated partisanship" is Thelen's in *New Citizenship,* 211–18. See also Carlile, "Trials of Progressivism." On direct democracy, see Johnston, *Radical Middle Class,* especially 119–26.

35. Gustafson, "Partisan Women," 108; see also Melanie S. Gustafson, "Partisan Women in the Progressive Era: The Struggle for Inclusion in American Political Parties," *Journal of Women's History* 9, no. 2 (Summer 1997): 8–30.

36. Gustafson, "Partisan Women," 118–19. See also various accounts of the polit-

ical action that settlement women undertook: Jane Addams, *Twenty Years at Hull-House* (New York: Macmillan, 1910), 222–38; Kathryn Kish Sklar, *Florence Kelley and the Nation's Work: The Rise of Women's Political Culture, 1830–1900* (New Haven, Conn.: Yale University Press, 1995), 300–303; Mina Carson, *Settlement Folk: Social Thought and the American Settlement Movement, 1885–1930* (Chicago: University of Chicago, 1990); and Vida Scudder, *On Journey* (New York: E. P. Dutton, 1937).

37. Sara Monoson, "The Lady and the Tiger: Women's Electoral Activism in New York City before Suffrage," *Journal of Women's History* 2 (Fall 1990): 126. See also Finegold, *Experts and Politicians.*

38. Paula Baker, "The Domestication of Politics: Women and American Political Society, 1780–1920," *American Historical Review* 89 (June 1984): 620–47; Suzanne Lebsock, "Women and American Politics, 1880–1920," in *Women, Politics and Change,* ed. Louise A. Tilly and Patricia Gurin (New York: Russell Sage Foundation, 1990), 55–59.

39. Ellen Carol DuBois, "Working Women, Class Relations, and Suffrage Militance: Harriot Stanton Blatch and the New York Woman Suffrage Movement, 1894–1909," *Journal of American History* 74 (June 1987): 37.

40. Maureen A. Flanagan, "Gender and Urban Political Reform: The City Club and the Woman's City Club of Chicago in the Progressive Era," *American Historical Review* 95, no. 4 (October 1990): 1041, 1047–48. Flanagan shrewdly discusses activist women's ambivalence regarding *partisan* politics in *Seeing with Their Hearts,* 129–32.

41. Gustafson, "Partisan Women," 225. On this point, I interpret the evidence differently from Melanie S. Gustafson, who sees the commitment of Addams and others to the Progressive Party as an act of partisanship. I argue, rather, that they invested the campaign with their own nonpartisanism, refraining from a long-term commitment to the Progressive Party as a party. See discussion of Progressive Service in chapter 4 of this book.

42. For the best account of this shifting posture of the AFL toward political partisanship, see Julie Greene, *Pure and Simple Politics: The American Federation of Labor and Political Activism, 1881–1917* (New York: Cambridge University Press, 1998), esp. chaps. 3–5; see also Michael Rogin, "Voluntarism: The Political Functions of an Antipolitical Doctrine," *Industrial and Labor Relations Review* 15, no. 4 (July 1962): 521–35.

43. See Stromquist, "Crucible of Class"; on Hearst, see David Nasaw, *The Chief: The Life of William Randolph Hearst* (New York: Houghton Mifflin, 2000); Finegold, *Experts and Politicians;* and Roy Everett Littlefield III, *William Randolph Hearst: His Role in American Progressivism* (Boston: University Press of America, 1980). On other cases, see, for instance, Richard W. Judd, *Socialist Cities: Municipal Politics and the Grass Roots of American Socialism* (Albany: State University of New York Press, 1989); Michael Kazin, *The Barons of Labor: The San Francisco Building Trades and Union Power in the Progressive Era* (Urbana: University of Illinois Press, 1987); and Robert Emery Bionaz, "Streetcars and the Politics of Class: Voters, the Union Labor Party, and Municipal Ownership in San Francisco, 1901–1913" (master's thesis, San Francisco State University, 1997). On Chicago, see Georg Leidenberger, "'The Public Is the Labor

Union': Working-Class Progressivism in Turn-of-the-Century Chicago," *Labor History* 36, no. 2 (1995): 187–210; and for the Rocky Mountain West, see Enyeart, "'By Laws of Their Own Making,'" and Elizabeth Jameson, *All that Glitters: Class Conflict and Community in Cripple Creek* (Urbana: University of Illinois Press, 1998).

44. For a comprehensive study of the evolution of voting rights and efforts to restrict them, see Alexander Keyssar, *The Right to Vote: The Contested History of Democracy in the United States* (New York: Basic Books, 2000), esp. 117–59. Moral "free agency" was a staple of nineteenth-century reform, whether the object was the abolition of slavery or the prohibition of alcohol. See, for instance, Foner, *Free Soil*, and Kleppner, "Partisanship and Ethnoreligious Conflict," 113–46. John D. Buenker has pointed out the importance of the "sovereign individual" in the rhetoric of progressive reform; see "Sovereign Individuals and Organic Networks: Political Cultures in Conflict during the Progressive Era," *American Quarterly* 40, no. 2 (1988): 187–204.

45. Robert Westbrook, *John Dewey and American Democracy* (Ithaca, N.Y.: Cornell University Press, 1991), 104–11, 192.

46. For a discussion of the varieties of reform designed to purify democracy, see Walter Dean Burnham, *Critical Elections and the Mainsprings of American Politics* (New York: Norton, 1970), and Samuel P. Hays, "The Politics of Reform in Municipal Government in the Progressive Era," *Pacific Northwest Quarterly* 55 (October 1964): 157–69. Reformers' use of race to define boundaries of citizenship is also discussed at some length in chapter 6 of this book.

47. Addams, "Why Women Should Vote" (1910), in *The Social Thought of Jane Addams*, ed. Christopher Lasch (New York: Irvington, 1982), 149–50.

48. See Burnham, *Critical Elections*, and Hays, "Politics of Reform in Municipal Government." Robert D. Johnston offers a more sympathetic assessment of the Oregon System of direct democracy while conceding that Portland business men saw in the initiative and referendum what William U'Ren called "ample insurance against any revolutionary laws." Johnston, *Radical Middle Class*, 124.

49. McGerr, *Decline of Popular Politics*, 62–68, 184–90, 205–10. For a discussion of the Progressive Party and African Americans, see chapter 6 of this book. See also Gustafson, "Partisan Women," 198–240.

50. Burnham, "System of 1896," 190–93. See also J. Morgan Kousser, *The Shaping of Southern Politics: Suffrage Restriction and the Establishment of the One-Party South, 1880–1910* (New Haven, Conn.: Yale University Press, 1974), 145, 163.

51. On the "new electoral universe," North and South, in the early twentieth century, see Keyssar, *Right to Vote*, esp. 111–16, 168–71. See also Paul Kleppner, *Continuity and Change in Electoral Politics, 1893–1928* (Westport, Conn.: Greenwood Press, 1987), 164–65; Paul Kleppner, *Who Voted? The Dynamics of Electoral Turnout, 1870–1980* (New York: Praeger, 1982), 58–59; and Burnham, "System of 1896," 189. On antifusion laws and the impact of the Australian ballot, see Peter Argersinger, *The Limits of Agrarian Radicalism: Western Populism and American Politics* (Lawrence: University of Kansas Press, 1995), 136–75.

52. See Kleppner, *Who Voted?* 59–60, for discussion of the exaggerated construction of "corruption" by reformers; see also Kleppner, *Continuity and Change,* 163–64, 167–70. The claim that corruption was widespread appeared in periodicals as well as academic journals. Evidence to the contrary is found in Howard W. Allen and Kay Warren Allen, "Vote Fraud and Data Validity," in *Analyzing Electoral History: A Guide to the Study of American Voter Behavior,* ed. Jerome M. Clubb, William H. Flanigan, and Nancy H. Zingale (Beverly Hills, Calif.: Sage, 1981), 153–93, and Loomis Mayfield, "Voting Fraud in Early Twentieth-Century Pittsburgh," *Journal of Interdisciplinary History* 24, no. 1 (Summer 1993): 59–84.

53. Kleppner, *Continuity and Change,* 169.

54. The most recent and most impressive treatment of black disfranchisement in the South is Michael Perman, *Struggle for Mastery: Disfranchisement in the South, 1888–1908* (Chapel Hill: University of North Carolina Press, 2001). See also C. Vann Woodward, *The Origins of the New South, 1877–1913* (Baton Rouge: Louisiana State University Press, 1951), and Kousser, *Shaping of Southern Politics.* A perceptive case study of the political consequences of black disfranchisement is Lawrence Goodwyn, "Populist Dreams and Negro Rights: East Texas as a Case Study," *American Historical Review* 76 (1971). See also Jack Temple Kirby, *Darkness at the Dawning: Race and Reform in the Progressive South* (Philadelphia: Lippincott, 1972), and William A. Link, *The Paradox of Southern Progressivism, 1880–1930* (Chapel Hill: University of North Carolina Press, 1992).

55. Kousser, *Shaping of Southern Politics,* 238–46, 250–57, 263–64; quotations on 255, 263. Perman, *Struggle for Mastery,* esp. 313–28. See also Richard Franklin Bensel, *Sectionalism and American Political Development, 1880–1980* (Madison: University of Wisconsin Press, 1984), 81–83, on the decline in Mississippi voting.

56. Keyssar offers a very thoughtful survey and assessment of the restrictive measures adopted in a number of states in his *Right to Vote,* 127–71.

57. Kleppner, *Continuity and Change,* 165–70; Kleppner, *Who Voted?* 60–70.

58. Burnham, "System of 1896," 191.

59. Keyssar, *Right to Vote,* 136–41, on restriction bearing on new immigrants; Gwendolyn Mink, *Old Labor and New Immigrants in American Political Development: Union, Party, and State, 1875–1920* (Ithaca, N.Y.: Cornell University Press, 1986), 153–54.

60. The now classic study of this reconstruction of city politics is Hays, "Politics of Reform in Municipal Government," 157–69. See also Martin Schiesl, *The Politics of Efficiency: Municipal Administration and Reform in America, 1880–1920* (Berkeley: University of California Press, 1977). Bitter contests between sharply divided class interests were fought over the implementation of commission government. See Robert E. Bionaz, "Trickle-Down Democracy: The Commission Government Contest in Des Moines, 1905–1908," *Annals of Iowa* 58 (Summer 1999): 241–71. In Cleveland, reformers in the 1890s moved city elections to the spring; under Tom Johnson's brand of partisan progressivism, city elections were returned to the fall in 1905.

61. Keyssar, *Right to Vote,* 157.

62. William L. Novak, *The People's Welfare: Law and Regulation in Nineteenth-Century America* (Chapel Hill: University of North Carolina Press, 1996), 1, 3–9, 237–41. See also Keller, *Affairs of State,* and Foner, *Reconstruction.*

63. Sidney Fine's discussion of the rising tide of social welfare assaults on laissez-faire is the starting point for this discussion. See *Laissez-Faire and the General Welfare State: A Study of Conflict in American Thought, 1865–1901* (Ann Arbor: University of Michigan Press, 1964), 167–68, 198–251, 352–69 (quotation on 353). See also Dorothy Ross, *The Origins of American Social Science* (New York: Cambridge University Press, 1991), and David W. Noble, *The Paradox of Progressive Thought* (Minneapolis: University of Minnesota Press, 1958).

64. Keller, *Affairs of State,* 425–27, and Albro Martin, "Railroads and Equity Receiverships: An Essay on Institutional Change," *Journal of Economic History* 34 (September 1974): 686.

65. Keller, *Affairs of State,* 430. Colin J. Davis, *Power at Odds: The 1922 National Railroad Shopmen's Strike* (University of Illinois Press, 1997), 36–37, 49, discusses the exceptional period of direct government operation of the railroads during World War I.

66. Paul, *Conservative Crisis,* has a particularly useful discussion of contending judicial doctrines bearing on the regulatory powers of the state in the period of late-nineteenth-century social and economic crisis. For local regulatory traditions, see Novak, *People's Welfare.*

67. Chief Justice Morrison R. Waite, majority opinion, *Munn v. Illinois,* quoted in Paul, *Conservative Crisis,* 9.

68. Seymour D. Thompson, "Abuses of Corporate Privilege" (1892), quoted in ibid., 58.

69. Ibid., 71.

70. Keller, *Affairs of State,* 308–9, 366–67; see also Martin J. Sklar, *The Corporate Reconstruction of American Capitalism, 1890–1916* (New York: Cambridge University Press, 1988), 117–27.

71. Paul, *Conservative Crisis,* offers the most complete account of the impact of these decisions, 104–220.

72. Novak makes an important point at the conclusion of his study about the ascendance of national over local forms of regulation: "By the early decades of the twentieth century, a society legally and politically oriented around the relationship of individual subjects to a central nation-state had substantially replaced the well-regulated society's preference for articulating the roles of associative citizens in a confederated republic. Power and liberty, formerly interwoven in the notion of self-regulating, common law communities, were now necessary antipodes kept in balance only through the magnetic genius of an ascendant American constitutionalism." Novak, *People's Welfare,* 240–41.

73. Fine, *Laissez-Faire and the General Welfare State,* 384.

74. "The Omaha Platform" (1892), in Norman Pollack, ed., *The Populist Mind* (Indianapolis: Bobbs-Merrill, 1967), 62.

75. Laurence Gronlund, *The Cooperative Commonwealth*, excerpts reprinted in *Socialism in America: From the Shakers to the Third International: A Documentary History*, ed. Albert Fried (New York: Columbia University Press, 1970), 278–80.

76. American Federation of Labor, *A Verbatum [sic] Report of the Discussion on the Political Programme*, 1.

77. See Martin J. Sklar, "Periodization and Historiography: Studying American Political Development in the Progressive Era, 1890s-1916," *Studies in American Political Development* 5 (Fall 1991): 210–11; see also James Weinstein, *The Corporate Ideal of the Liberal State, 1900–1918* (Boston: Beacon Press, 1968).

78. For representative works on urban reform programs, see Finegold, *Experts and Politicians*, and John D. Buenker, *Urban Liberalism and Progressive Reform* (New York: Scribner's, 1973). For state and federal regulatory initiatives, see Patrick J. Maney, *Young Bob: A Biography of Robert M. La Follette* (Madison: State Historical Society of Wisconsin, 2003); Lewis L. Gould, *The Presidency of Theodore Roosevelt* (Lawrence: University of Kansas Press, 1991), 147–72; and older works, George E. Mowry, *The Era of Theodore Roosevelt and the Birth of Modern America, 1900–1912* (New York: Harper, 1958), and Arthur S. Link, *Woodrow Wilson and the Progressive Era, 1910–1917* (New York: Harper, 1954).

79. On the enhancement of state capacities in the late nineteenth century, see Skowronek, *Building a New American State*, and Charles C. Bright, "The State in the United States during the Nineteenth Century," in *Statemaking and Social Movements: Essays in History and Theory*, ed. Charles Bright and Susan Harding (Ann Arbor: University of Michigan Press, 1984), 151–53.

80. Robert Wiebe, *The Search for Order* (New York: Hill and Wang, 1967), 166.

81. Richard L. McCormick, "The Discovery that Business Corrupts Politics: A Reappraisal of the Origins of Progressivism," in McCormick, *Party Period and Public Policy*, 309–56; see also David Nord, "The Experts versus the Experts: Conflicting Philosophies of Municipal Regulation in the Progressive Era," *Wisconsin Magazine of History* 58 (1975): 219–36.

82. Herbert Croly, *The Promise of American Life* (1909; reprint, Boston: Northeastern University Press, 1989), 322, 369, 372, 362, 366, 379. See Edward A. Stettner, *Shaping Modern Liberalism: Herbert Croly and Progressive Thought* (Lawrence: University of Kansas Press, 1993), 57–76, and Donald W. Levy, *Herbert Croly of the New Republic: The Life and Thought of an American Progressive* (Princeton, N.J.: Princeton University Press, 1985), 96–131, for sympathetic assessments of Croly's contribution to progressive ideas. Sklar, *Corporate Reconstruction of American Capitalism*, 203–332, offers a different view of "new nationalism" as a significant expansion of *statist* intervention. See also Weinstein, *Corporate Ideal of the Liberal State*, on the Wilsonian version of corporatist state activity. On the new but somewhat ambiguous meanings that Progressives brought to the idea of federalism, see Martha Derthick and John J. Dinan,

"Progressivism and Federalism," in *Progressivism and the New Democracy,* ed. Sidney M. Milkis and Jerome M. Mileur (Amherst: University of Massachusetts Press, 1999), 81–98.

83. Sklar, *Corporate Reconstruction of American Capitalism,* 228–33, 331–32.

84. McCormick, "Discovery that Business Corrupts Politics," 350–51. Weinstein, *Corporate Ideal of the Liberal State,* 62–91.

85. On the politics of municipal ownership, see Finegold, *Experts and Politicians,* 18–22; Michael P. McCarthy, "'Suburban Power': A Footnote on Cleveland in the Tom Johnson Years," *Northwest Ohio Quarterly* 45, no. 1 (Winter 1972–73): 21–27; Stromquist, "Crucible of Class," 192–220; Holli, *Reform in Detroit;* and Marnie Jones, *Holy Toledo: Religion and Politics in the Life of "Golden Rule" Jones* (Lexington: University Press of Kentucky, 1998).

86. The foundational work on the subject of Democrats' reform program in local and state political arenas is J. Joseph Huthmacher, "Urban Liberalism and the Age of Reform," *Mississippi Valley Historical Review* 49 (September 1962): 231–41, and his *Robert F. Wagner and the Rise of Urban Liberalism* (New York: Atheneum, 1968); see also Buenker, *Urban Liberalism and Progressive Reform.* The case for the influence of Democrats' reform program at the national level is made effectively by Sarasohn, *Party of Reform,* esp. vii–xvii, 59–86.

87. The Socialist Party's growth is competently documented by Ira Kipnis, *The American Socialist Movement, 1897–1912* (New York: Columbia University Press, 1952); David Shannon, *The Socialist Party of America: A History* (Chicago: Quadrangle, 1967); James Weinstein, *The Decline of Socialism in America, 1912–1925* (New York: Monthly Review Press, 1967); Nick Salvatore, *Eugene V. Debs: Citizen and Socialist* (Urbana: University of Illinois Press, 1982); and Judd, *Socialist Cities.*

88. See Keyssar, *Right to Vote,* 127–71. For a local case study of structural reform in city government that limited working-class power, see Bionaz, "Trickle-down Democracy," 241–71.

89. Daniel T. Rodgers, *Atlantic Crossings: Social Politics in a Progressive Age* (Cambridge, Mass.: Harvard University Press, 1998), 126–59, provides an excellent introduction to the transatlantic municipal reform movement.

90. On urban populism of the mid-1890s, the best study remains Destler, *American Radicalism.* The battles over municipal ownership are documented in a number of case studies and memoirs of urban Progressives; see, for instance, Howe, *Confessions of a Reformer;* Johnson, *My Story;* Irwin Yellowitz, *Labor and the Progressive Movement in New York State, 1897–1916* (Ithaca, N.Y.: Cornell University Press, 1965); and Nasaw, *Chief.* On St. Louis, see Piott, *Anti-Monopoly Persuasion,* and for San Francisco, see Kazin, *Barons of Labor.* The case for the Socialist Party's ascending success during the years 1910–1916 is made most persuasively by Weinstein, *Decline of Socialism in America;* on postwar labor politics in the municipal arena, see Andrew Strouthous, *U.S. Labor and Political Action, 1918–24: A Comparison of Independent Political Action in New York, Chicago and Seattle* (New York: St. Martin's, 2000), and

David Montgomery, *The Fall of the House of Labor: The Workplace, the State, and American Labor Activism, 1865–1925* (New York: Cambridge University Press, 1987).

91. See Littlefield, *William Randolph Hearst*, 147–204; Nasaw, *Chief*, 168–226; and Finegold, *Experts and Politicians*, 45–49. For other treatments of Hearst's political career, see Ferdinand Lundberg, *Imperial Hearst: A Social Biography* (New York: Equinox Cooperative Press, 1936), 95–138, and W. A. Swanberg, *Citizen Hearst: A Biography of William Randolph Hearst* (New York: Scribner's, 1961), 195–271.

92. *New York Herald*, November 5, 1905, quoted in McCormick, *From Realignment to Reform*, 207; see also Yellowitz, *Labor and the Progressive Movement in New York State*.

93. Littlefield, *William Randolph Hearst*, 182, 185–86; and *New York Evening Journal*, November 6, 1905, W. R. Hearst to Arthur Brisbane, December 1, 1905, and *New York Times*, November 3, 1905, all quoted in Littlefield, *William Randolph Hearst*, 185, 197, 186.

94. Charles Sprague Smith to Charles Evans Hughes, October 3, 1906, quoted in Littlefield, *William Randolph Hearst*, 213–14; on Hearst's impact on the socialist vote, see Nasaw, *Chief*, 196, and Kipnis, *American Socialist Movement*, 375.

95. Theodore Roosevelt letter to Lodge quoted in Nasaw, *Chief*, 207.

96. Littlefield, *William Randolph Hearst*, 187, 205–6, 208–10, 222, 219, 225; McCormick, "Discovery that Business Corrupts Politics," 222–27.

97. On the Milwaukee socialists' alliance with the Populists, see Fink, *Workingmen's Democracy*, 204–11; Frederick I. Olson, "The Milwaukee Socialists, 1897–1941" (Ph.D. diss., Harvard University, 1952), 28–38, and on the formation of the Social Democratic Party, 39–53; Marvin Wachman, *History of the Social Democratic Party of Milwaukee, 1897–1910* (Urbana: University of Illinois Press, 1945), 13–29; and Sally Miller, *Victor Berger and the Promise of Constructive Socialism, 1910–1920* (Westport, Conn.: Greenwood Press, 1973).

98. *Social Democratic Herald*, March 7, 1908, quoted in Wachman, *History of the Social Democratic Party*, 64. For discussion of 1906 and 1908 campaigns, see Wachman, *History of the Social Democratic Party*, 58–65; Olson, "Milwaukee Socialists," 155–60; and Joseph A. Gasperetti, "The 1910 Social Democratic Mayoral Campaign in Milwaukee" (master's thesis, University of Wisconsin, Milwaukee, 1970), 44–53.

99. Frederic C. Howe, "Milwaukee, a Socialist City," *Outlook* 95 (June 25, 1910): 414, 416–17.

100. The Milwaukee socialists' campaign tactics are covered in Wachman, *History of the Social Democratic Party*, 62; A. W. Mance, *History of the Milwaukee Social-Democratic Victories* (Milwaukee: Milwaukee Social-Democratic Publishing, 1911), 15–18; and Robert Lewis Mikkelsen, "Immigrants in Politics: Poles, Germans, and the Social Democratic Party of Milwaukee," in *Labor Migration in the Atlantic Economies*, ed. Dirk Hoerder (Westport, Conn.: Greenwood Press, 1985), 289–90; see also Robert Mikkelsen, *The Social Democratic Party of Milwaukee, Wisconsin: A Study of Ethnic Composition and Political Development* (Oslo: Mars, 1976).

101. Mikkelsen, "Immigrants in Politics," 289–92.

102. Wachman, *History of the Social Democratic Party,* 70–73.

103. Howe, "Milwaukee, a Socialist City," 416, 420–21.

104. Olson, "Milwaukee Socialists," 115. See also Sally M. Miller, "Milwaukee: Of Ethnicity and Labor," in *Socialism and the Cities,* ed. Bruce M. Stave (Port Washington, N.Y.: Kennikat, 1975), esp. 51–54.

105. For a case study that emphasizes the resiliency of Milwaukee's Social Democratic politics in a very different era, see Eric Fure-Slocum, "The Challenge of the Working-Class City: Recasting Growth Politics and Liberalism in Milwaukee, 1937–1952" (Ph.D. diss., University of Iowa, 2001).

106. Scudder, *On Journey,* 163–64.

Chapter 4: Communities of Reformers

1. For an insightful treatment of Scudder, see Peter J. Frederick, *Knights of the Golden Rule: The Intellectual as Christian Social Reformer in the 1890s* (Lexington: University Press of Kentucky, 1976), 113–40, esp. 124–36.

2. Herbert Croly, *Progressive Democracy* (New York: Macmillan, 1914), 6, 8, 2.

3. Jane Addams, *The Second Twenty Years at Hull-House, September 1909 to September 1929* (New York: Macmillan, 1930), 10, 13, 26–27, 29.

4. Kathryn Kish Sklar, *Florence Kelley and the Nation's Work: The Rise of Women's Political Culture, 1830–1900* (New Haven, Conn.: Yale University Press, 1995), 306–15.

5. See, for instance, Florence Kelley's "searing criticism" of philanthropists' complicity with child labor in a talk titled "The Working Child," presented at the 1896 NCCC convention. Sklar, *Florence Kelley and the Nation's Work,* 291.

6. Louise C. Wade, *Graham Taylor: Pioneer for Social Justice, 1851–1938* (Chicago: University of Chicago Press, 1964), 155–56; Don S. Kirschner, *The Paradox of Professionalism: Reform and Public Service in Urban America, 1900–1940* (Westport, Conn.: Greenwood Press, 1986), 2–3.

7. On the political implications of this movement, see Elisabeth Perry, *Belle Moskowitz: Feminine Politics and the Exercise of Power in the Age of Alfred E. Smith* (New York: Oxford University Press, 1987), 58–114. Jane Addams provides a useful account of the development of the movement from 1909 to 1912 in *Second Twenty Years,* 10–34.

8. On the heritage of moral reform and scientific philanthropy, see Paul Boyer, *Urban Masses and Moral Order in America, 1820–1920* (Cambridge, Mass.: Harvard University Press, 1978), 144–47.

9. This convergence is nicely summarized in Mina Carson, *Settlement Folk: Social Thought and the American Settlement Movement, 1885–1930* (Chicago: University of Chicago Press, 1990), 122–26. See also Robert Bremner, *From the Depths: The Discovery of Poverty in the United States* (New York: New York University Press, 1956), 123–39, on the new view of poverty the settlements promoted.

10. Edward T. Devine, presidential address, "The Dominant Note of the Modern

Philanthropy," in *Proceedings of the National Conference of Charities and Correction* (hereafter cited as *Proceedings of the NCCC*), 33d annual session, Philadelphia, May 9–16, 1906, 1, 2, 5, 6, 8–10. See also Carson, *Settlement Folk*, 125.

11. Edward T. Devine, *When Social Work Was Young* (1939), quoted in Roy Lubove, *The Progressives and the Slums: Tenement House Reform in New York City, 1890–1917* (Pittsburgh: University of Pittsburgh Press, 1962), 186–87.

12. Edward T. Devine, *Misery and Its Causes* (New York: Macmillan, 1909), codifies these conditions. He discusses failed charitable institutions, chronic ill health, unemployment, occupational injury, and broken families. For his general argument, see 11–14.

13. For a thorough discussion of the influence of Patten's ideas on social workers, see Daniel M. Fox, *The Discovery of Abundance: Simon N. Patten and the Transformation of Social Theory* (Ithaca, N.Y.: Cornell University Press, 1967), 95–130, esp. 97–104.

14. Carson, *Settlement Folk*, 126–28; Carson notes that Patten's book was excerpted in *Charities and the Commons* between 1907 and 1909 and many "responsive editorials, reviews, and letters" were published. See also David W. Noble, *The Paradox of Progressive Thought* (Minneapolis: University of Minnesota Press, 1958), 174–98 (quotation from 191), and James Livingston, *Pragmatism and the Political Economy of Cultural Revolution, 1850–1940* (Chapel Hill: University of North Carolina Press, 1994), 66–69.

15. Simon N. Patten, "Who Is the Good Neighbor?" (1908), quoted in Carson, *Settlement Folk*, 128. Carson notes that the *Charities and the Commons* started to report regularly the proceedings of the ASA, AEA, APSA, and the AHA (240 n. 41).

16. Carson's account of the interaction of advocates of professionalizing social work and partisans of settlement work is particularly insightful; see *Settlement Folk*, 130–38. See also Ruth Crocker, *Social Work and Social Order: The Settlement Movement in Two Industrial Cities, 1889–1930* (Urbana: University of Illinois Press, 1992) for the perspective of more provincial settlement houses. Kirschner discusses the ways in which specialized reformers "discovered one another prowling about the same slum neighborhoods in a common quest for social reform" and "searched out a basis for cooperation across the lines of specialization." Kirschner, *Paradox of Professionalism*, 6.

17. Carson, *Settlement Folk*, 125; Bremner, *From the Depths*, 156–57; Clarke A. Chambers, *Paul Kellogg and the Survey: Voices for Social Welfare and Social Justice* (Minneapolis: University of Minnesota Press, 1971), 42–43; John M. Glenn, Lilian Brandt, and F. Emerson Andrews, *Russell Sage Foundation, 1907–1946*, 2 vols. (New York: Russell Sage Foundation, 1947), 1:67–68, 177–96, 210–13; Robert W. de Forest, "The Initial Activities of the Russell Sage Foundation," *Survey* 22 (1909): 71. Martin Bulmer, Kevin Bales, and Kathryn Kish Sklar, "The Social Survey in Historical Perspective," in *The Social Survey in Historical Perspective*, ed. Martin Bulmer, Kevin Bales, and Kathryn Kish Sklar (New York: Cambridge University Press, 1991), 30–31; David C. Hammack, "A Center of Intelligence for the Charity Organization Movement: The Foundation's Early Years," in *Social Science in the Making: Essays on the*

Russell Sage Foundation, 1907–1972, ed. David C. Hammack and Stanton Wheeler (New York: Russell Sage Foundation, 1994), 1–33, final quote on 26.

18. The essential study of Paul Kellogg and the *Survey* is Chambers, *Paul Kellogg and the Survey*, 18–19.

19. *Charities* (1901), quoted in ibid., 10–11, 19.

20. Ibid., 19–24.

21. *Charities and the Commons* 19 (January 4, 1908): 1305a.

22. Chambers, *Paul Kellogg and the Survey*, 34–36.

23. Roy Lubove, *Twentieth Century Pittsburgh: Government, Business and Environmental Change* (New York: Wiley, 1969). See also Steven R. Cohen, "The Pittsburgh Survey and the Social Survey Movement: A Sociological Road Not Taken," in *The Social Survey in Historical Perspective, 1880–1940*, ed. Martin Bulmer, Kevin Bales, and Kathryn Kish Sklar (New York: Cambridge University Press, 1991), esp. 259–65. On the Russell Sage Foundation role, see Hammack, "Center of Intelligence," 15–16.

24. Margo Anderson and Maurine Greenwald, "Introduction: The Pittsburgh Survey in Historical Perspective," 7, and Stephen Turner, "The Pittsburgh Survey and the Survey Movement: An Episode in the History of Expertise," 37, both in *Pittsburgh Surveyed: Social Science and Social Reform in the Early Twentieth Century*, ed. Maurine Greenwald and Margo Anderson (Pittsburgh: University of Pittsburgh Press, 1996).

25. Paul Kellogg and Neva R. Deardorff, "Social Research as Applied to Community Progress" (1928), quoted in Turner, "Pittsburgh Survey," 38.

26. Turner, "Pittsburgh Survey," 42–43.

27. Chambers, *Paul Kellogg and the Survey*, 44–45. See also Hammack, "Center of Intelligence," 15, 27.

28. Roy Lubove, *The Struggle for Social Security, 1900–1935* (Cambridge, Mass.: Harvard University Press, 1968), 29–30; Theda Skocpol, *Protecting Soldiers and Mothers: The Political Origins of Social Policy in the United States* (Cambridge, Mass.: Harvard University Press, 1992), 176–77.

29. *Proceedings of the Second Annual Meeting of the American Association for Labor Legislation*, December 29–30, 1908, 5, 10, 12–13.

30. Adna F. Weber, "Labor Legislation, National and International" (1907), quoted in Skocpol, *Protecting Soldiers and Mothers*, 186, 187.

31. Skocpol, *Protecting Soldiers and Mothers*, 187–89; John R. Commons, "Constructive Investigation and the Industrial Commission of Wisconsin," *Survey* 29 (January 4, 1913): 440–48. On Commons's role, see also Mary O. Furner, "The Republican Tradition and the New Liberalism: Social Investigation, State Building, and Social Learning in the Gilded Age," in *The State and Social Investigation in Britain and the United States*, ed. Michael J. Lacey and Mary O. Furner (Cambridge, Mass.: Cambridge University Press, 1993), 192–94.

32. John R. Commons, "Is Class Conflict in America Growing and Is It Inevitable?" *American Journal of Sociology* 13, no. 6 (1906): 756–66, esp. 756–57, 761–62, 764–65.

33. Skocpol makes the argument that despite corporate backing, the AALL enjoyed considerable autonomy because of the conflicting interests of its supporters. Skocpol, *Protecting Soldiers and Mothers*, 183–84.

34. I. M. Rubinow, *Social Insurance: with Special Reference to American Conditions* (1913), quoted in Lubove, *Struggle for Social Security*, 34–38. For a useful recent study that examines, among other things, the role the AALL played in the early struggles for national health insurance, see Colin Gordon, *Dead on Arrival: The Politics of Health Care in Twentieth-Century America* (Princeton, N.J.: Princeton University Press, 2003).

35. Skocpol, *Protecting Soldiers and Mothers*, 604–5. On the NCL and its work on behalf of women workers, see chapter 5 of this book.

36. Henry R. Seager, *Labor and Other Economic Essays* (1931), quoted in Irwin Yellowitz, *Labor and the Progressive Movement in New York State, 1897–1916* (Ithaca, N.Y.: Cornell University Press, 1965), 56–57; see also Yellowitz, *Labor and the Progressive Movement*, 56–58, and on the differences between labor and the AALL in the fight for state workmen's compensation legislation, see 107–20.

37. Judith Mara Gutman, *Lewis W. Hine and the American Social Conscience* (New York: Walker, 1967), 22–23, 79, 95; National Child Labor Committee, "Little Comrades Who Toil" (1914), quoted in Gutman, *Lewis W. Hine*, 22–23.

38. Ralph Easley to Nelson Aldrich, July 20, 1906, quoted in James Weinstein, *The Corporate Ideal of the Liberal State, 1900–1918* (Boston: Beacon Press, 1968), 28.

39. Walter I. Trattner, *Crusade for the Children: A History of the National Child Labor Committee and Child Labor Reform in America* (Chicago: Quadrangle Books, 1970), 50, 53, 55; Bremner, *From the Depths*, 217–18. See also Hugh Cunningham and Shelton Stromquist, "Child Labor and Children's Rights: Historical Patterns of Decline and Persistence," in *Child Labor and Human Rights: Making Children Matter*, ed. Burns H. Weston (Boulder, Colo.: Lynne Rienner, 2005).

40. Jeremy P. Felt, *Hostages of Fortune: Child Labor Reform in New York State* (Syracuse, N.Y.: Syracuse University Press, 1965), 42–47; Yellowitz, *Labor and the Progressive Movement*, 89–93; Walter I. Trattner, *Crusade for the Children*, 56–57.

41. Felt, *Hostages of Fortune*, 46–47. Corporate leaders included V. Everit Macy of Title Guarantee and Trust Company, Paul M. Warburg and Jacob Schiff of Kuhn and Loeb Investment Banking Company, and William H. Baldwin, president of the Long Island Railroad.

42. Minutes, first general meeting of the National Child Labor Committee (1904), quoted in Trattner, *Crusade for the Children*, 58–59.

43. Trattner, *Crusade for the Children*, 64–65; Bremner, *From the Depths*, 219. Other prominent figures on the NCLC national committee were Alexander J. Cassatt, president of the Pennsylvania Railroad; Stanley McCormick, International Harvester Corporation; Adolph S. Ochs, publisher of the *New York Times;* former president Grover Cleveland; Gifford Pinchot, an influential member of Theodore Roosevelt's administration; and Charles W. Eliot, president of Harvard.

44. Jane Addams, "Child Labor and Pauperism" (1903), quoted in Bremner, *From the Depths*, 216.

45. Samuel McCune Lindsay, "The Work, Policy, and Plans of the National Child Labor Committee" (1907), quoted in Trattner, *Crusade for the Children*, 66–67.

46. Bremner, *From the Depths*, 216–17; Edwin Markham, "The Hoe-man in the Making" (1906), quoted in Bremner, *From the Depths*, 217.

47. Bremner, *From the Depths*, 217; Trattner, *Crusade for the Children*, 54–55, 50.

48. Bremner, *From the Depths*, 223–24.

49. E. W. Lord, "Child Labor in New England," and Felix Adler, "The Basis of the Anti-Child Labor Movement in the Idea of American Civilization," *Proceedings of the Fourth Annual Meeting*, National Child Labor Committee, Atlanta, April 2–5, 1908, 38–39, 1.

50. For a detailed discussion of the campaign for a Children's Bureau and the debate over federal as opposed to state regulation of child labor, see Trattner, *Crusade for the Children*, 95–131; Bremner, *From the Depths*, 220–29; and Robyn Muncy, *Creating a Female Dominion in American Reform, 1890–1935* (New York: Oxford University Press, 1991), 38–60.

51. Chambers, *Paul Kellogg and the Survey*, 47–48; see also Allen F. Davis, *Spearheads for Reform: The Social Settlements and the Progressive Movement, 1890–1914* (New York: Oxford University Press, 1967), and annual reports of the NCCC.

52. On the development of social investigation, see Bulmer, Bales, and Sklar, "Social Survey in Historical Perspective," 1–48.

53. Sklar, *Florence Kelley and the Nation's Work*, 291; Davis, *Spearheads for Reform*, 21.

54. Carson, *Settlement Folk*, 122–23; Chambers, *Paul Kellogg and the Survey*, 6–7.

55. *Proceedings of the NCCC*, 36th annual session, Buffalo, 1909 (Fort Wayne, Ind.: Fort Wayne Printing, 1909), 215.

56. Robert A. Woods, "The Neighborhood and the Nation," *Proceedings of the NCCC*, 1909, 104–5.

57. Florence Kelley, "The Family and the Woman's Wage," *Proceedings of the NCCC*, 1909, 118–20.

58. "Minutes of the Meetings," *Proceedings of the NCCC*, 1909, 543. Addams felt called upon to reassure traditionalists that she, as the first woman president, would lead with caution and discretion.

59. Jane Addams, "Charity and Social Justice," *Proceedings of the NCCC*, St. Louis, Missouri, 1910, 1, 5, 15–16.

60. Mary E. Richmond, "The Inter-relation of Social Movements," Report of the Committee on Families and Neighborhoods, *Proceedings of the NCCC*, 1910 (Ft. Wayne, Ind.: Archer Printing, 1910), 212–14.

61. Paul U. Kellogg, "Occupational Standards," *Proceedings of the NCCC*, 1910, 373–76, 379, 383, 386, 388, 390.

62. Addams, *Second Twenty Years*, 13–28.

63. The story of the formation of the Progressive Party has been recounted in a variety of versions. See John A. Gable, *Bull Moose Years: Theodore Roosevelt and the Progressive Party* (Port Washington, N.Y.: Kennikat Press, 1978); John M. Cooper Jr., *The Warrior and the Priest: Woodrow Wilson and Theodore Roosevelt* (Cambridge,

Mass.: Harvard University Press, 1983); David Sarasohn, *The Party of Reform: Democrats in the Progressive Era* (Jackson: University of Mississippi Press, 1989), esp. 143–54; Amos E. Pinchot, *History of the Progressive Party, 1912–1916* (New York: New York University Press, 1958); and Crunden, *Ministers of Reform*, 200–224. For an interpretation that emphasizes the role of George Perkins and the NCF, see Weinstein, *Corporate Ideal of the Liberal State*. For a variant that stresses the ideas of Croly and Roosevelt, see Martin J. Sklar, *The Corporate Reconstruction of American Capitalism, 1890–1916* (New York: Cambridge University Press, 1988). An account of the role of "the social workers" is found in Davis, *Spearheads for Reform*, and in a slightly different version, Allen F. Davis, "The Social Workers and the Progressive Party, 1912–1916," *American Historical Review* 69, no. 3 (April 1964): 671–88.

64. "A Platform of Industrial Minimums," *Survey* 28, no. 14 (July 6, 1912): 517–18.

65. Davis, *Spearheads for Reform*, 196–97; Melanie S. Gustafson, "Partisan Women: Gender, Politics, and the Progressive Party of 1912" (Ph.D. diss., New York University, 1993), 157–58.

66. See Gable, *Bull Moose Years*, 17–19. *Outlook* 101 (July 1912), quoted in Gustafson, "Partisan Women," 160–61.

67. Addams, *Second Twenty Years*, 27.

68. Perry, *Belle Moskowitz*, 74–78. Ben Lindsay to Jane Addams, July 6, 1912, quoted in Gustafson, "Partisan Women," 173–74. Jean Bethke Elshtain, *Jane Addams and the Dream of American Democracy* (New York: Basic Books, 2002), 189–94, has a somewhat different account of Addams's relation to the formation of the Progressive Party.

69. Paul Kellogg, "The Industrial Platform of the New Party," *Survey* 28, no. 21 (August 24, 1912): 668–70.

70. Addams, "Charity and Social Justice," 16.

71. Davis, "Social Workers and the Progressive Party," 675–76. See also Addams, "My Experiences as a Progressive Delegate," *McClure's*, November 1912, also reprinted in Christopher Lasch, ed., *The Social Thought of Jane Addams* (New York: Irvington, 1965), 162–68.

72. For a more detailed discussion of race and the Progressive Party, see chapter 6. John Gable has the most complete account of the maneuverings within the platform committee between the Perkins and Pinchot forces over language pertaining to the regulation of trusts and the place of competition. Gable, *Bull Moose Years*, esp. 98–106. On the exclusion of blacks, see also Gustafson, "Partisan Women," 211–22.

73. Kirk H. Porter and Donald Bruce Johnson, comps., *National Party Platforms, 1840–1964* (Urbana: University of Illinois Press, 1966), 175–78.

74. Kellogg, "Industrial Platform of the New Party," 670; see also Gustafson, "Partisan Women," 224–25.

75. *New York Times*, September 27, 1912, quoted in Gustafson, "Partisan Women," 268.

76. Addams, *Second Twenty Years*, 28–33. Addams's terminology, "corporate gov-

ernment," is particularly interesting in light of the cross-class interests the Progressive Party embraced.

77. Ibid., 29–30. Ironically, Theodore Roosevelt's speeches to the Republican convention and the Progressive Party convention ended with the same reference to Armageddon. Gable, *Bull Moose Years*, 85.

78. This argument about the partisan commitment of women reformers in particular is indebted to Gustafson, "Partisan Women," 100–146. Henry Moskowitz to Lillian Wald, August 2, 1912, quoted in Davis, "Social Workers and the Progressive Party," 678.

79. Ralph Easley to Anne Morgan, November 18, 1912, quoted in Weinstein, *Corporate Ideal of the Liberal State*, 170.

80. For the most insightful account of Progressive Service, see Ellen Fitzpatrick, *Endless Crusade: Women Social Scientists and Progressive Reform* (New York: Oxford University Press, 1990), 149–57; see also Davis, "Social Workers and the Progressive Party," 684–86.

81. Fitzpatrick, *Endless Crusade*, 152, 153, quote on 155–56; Davis, "Social Workers and the Progressive Party," 686; Gable, *Bull Moose Years*, 186.

82. Charles Forcey, *The Crossroads of Liberalism: Croly, Weyl, Lippmann, and the Progressive Era, 1900–1925* (New York: Oxford University Press,1961), 147–52; Eugene M. Tobin, *Organize or Perish: America's Independent Progressives, 1913–1933* (Westport, Conn.: Greenwood Press, 1986), 15–19.

83. On the split over trust policy among the Progressives, see Weinstein, *Corporate Ideal of the Liberal State*, 139–71; see also Sklar, *Corporate Reconstruction of American Capitalism*, 333–430, and Herbert Croly, *The Promise of American Life* (1909; reprint, Boston: Northeastern University Press, 1989), 358–59. See also newspaper reports on NCF Conference on Trusts, *Chicago Tribune*, September 14, 15, 16, 17, 18, and 20, 1899, and *Outlook*, September 23, 1899.

84. On the influential role of Perkins, see Weinstein, *Corporate Ideal of the Liberal State*, 152–54, and Tobin, *Organize or Perish*, 15–18. For the planks of the Progressive Party platform pertaining to "Business," see Porter and Johnson, *National Party Platforms*, 178.

85. Tobin, *Organize or Perish*, 19–37.

86. Fitzpatrick, *Endless Crusade*, 154–57; Davis, "Social Workers and the Progressive Party," 686–88.

87. Tobin, *Organize or Perish*, 26, on Amos Pinchot's letter. See chapter 7 for a discussion of Pinchot's gravitation toward the position of Frank Walsh and his Committee on Industrial Relations.

Chapter 5: Class Bridging and the World of Female Reform

1. Rheta Childe Dorr, *What Eighty Million Women Want* (1910), quoted in Paula Baker, "The Domestication of Politics: Women and American Political Society,

1780–1920," *American Historical Review* 89 (June 1984): 620–47, quote from 631–32. The term "domestication of politics" is Paula Baker's.

2. Mary Beard, *Woman's Work in Municipalities* (1915), quoted in Baker, "Domestication of Politics," 640–41.

3. Baker, "Domestication of Politics," 633.

4. Robyn Muncy, *Creating a Female Dominion in American Reform, 1890–1935* (New York: Oxford University Press, 1991); Kathryn Kish Sklar, *Florence Kelley and the Nation's Work: The Rise of Women's Political Culture, 1830–1900* (New Haven, Conn.: Yale University Press, 1995); and Theda Skocpol, *Protecting Soldiers and Mothers: The Political Origins of Social Policy in the United States* (Cambridge, Mass.: Harvard University Press, 1992).

5. This argument is made with particular force by Theda Skocpol in her *Protecting Soldiers and Mothers: The Political Origins of Social Policy in the United States* (Cambridge, Mass.: Harvard University Press, 1992). For criticism of her use of the concept of maternalism and her lack of interest in social/structural explanations (e.g., class and gender), see Linda Gordon, "Gender, State and Society: A Debate with Theda Skocpol," *Contention* 2, no. 3 (Spring 1993): 139–56, and Skocpol's rejoinder, 157–83.

6. Sarah Deutsch offers a compelling portrait of these competing claims and contending interests in Boston in *Women and the City: Gender, Space, and Power in Boston, 1870–1940* (New York: Oxford University Press, 2000), 4–5, 136–40.

7. Anne Firor Scott, "On Seeing and Not Seeing: A Case of Historical Invisibility," *Journal of American History* 71, no. 1 (June 1984): 17, 15. For a parallel point, see Skocpol, *Protecting Soldiers and Mothers*, 354. A number of excellent recent studies contribute to this expanded view of women's political activism: Deutsch, *Women and the City;* Maureen A. Flanagan, *Seeing with Their Hearts: Chicago Women and the Vision of the Good City, 1871–1933* (Princeton, N.J.: Princeton University Press, 2002); Elizabeth York Enstam, *Women and the Creation of Urban Life, Dallas, Texas, 1843–1920* (College Station: Texas A&M Press, 1998); and Melanie S. Gustafson, *Women and the Republican Party, 1854–1924* (Urbana: University of Illinois Press, 2001).

8. Ellen DuBois, *Feminism and Suffrage: The Emergence of an Independent Women's Movement in America, 1848–1869* (Ithaca, N.Y.: Cornell University Press, 1978), 21–52. Steven M. Buechler, *Women's Movements in the United States: Woman Suffrage, Equal Rights, and Beyond* (New Brunswick, N.J.: Rutgers University Press, 1990), 46–47, 91–94.

9. On the charitable efforts directed at families of soldiers in a northern city and the campaign to strengthen soldiers' ties to their families at home, see Russell Johnson, *Warriors into Workers: The Civil War and the Formation of Urban-Industrial Society in a Northern City* (New York: Fordham University Press, 2003), 238–73. Alice Kessler-Harris, *Out to Work: A History of Wage-earning Women in the United States* (New York: Oxford University Press, 1982), 75–97, describes the tensions between working women's self-help and middle-class women's benevolent activities during

and immediately after the war. On the work of the Sanitary Commission, see Baker, "Domestication of Politics," 635–36; George M. Fredrickson, *The Inner Civil War: Northern Intellectuals and the Crisis of the Union* (New York: Harper and Row, 1965); and J. Matthew Gallman, *Mastering Wartime: A Social History of Philadelphia during the Civil War* (New York: Cambridge University Press, 1990).

10. See DuBois, *Feminism and Suffrage,* esp. 53–78; Eleanor Flexner, *Century of Struggle: The Woman's Rights Movement in the United States* (Cambridge, Mass.: Harvard University Press, 1959), 142–55; and Buechler, *Women's Movements in the United States,* 96–97.

11. DuBois, *Feminism and Suffrage,* 201. Anne Firor Scott and Andrew MacKay Scott, *One Half the People: The Fight for Woman Suffrage* (Urbana: University of Illinois Press, 1982), 16–19. On women's partisan politics in the Gilded Age, see Rebecca Edwards, *Angels in the Machinery: Gender in American Party Politics from the Civil War to the Progressive Era* (New York: Oxford University Press, 1997), 39–90; also on the expanding public sphere claimed by women, see Mary Ryan, *Women in Public: Between Banners and Ballots* (Baltimore: Johns Hopkins University Press, 1990).

12. DuBois, *Feminism and Suffrage,* 162–201, provides the most nuanced account of these developments. See also Buechler, *Women's Movements in the United States,* 96.

13. Susan B. Anthony et al., *History of Woman Suffrage* (1869), in Scott and Scott, ed., *One Half the People,* 64, 66.

14. Deutsch, *Women and the City,* 54–77, and Kessler-Harris, *Out to Work,* 92–97.

15. Mari Jo Buhle, *Women and American Socialism* (Urbana: University of Illinois Press, 1981), 53–60.

16. Kessler-Harris, *Out to Work,* esp. 91–94.

17. Mary Blewett, *Men, Women, and Work: Class, Gender, and Protest in the New England Shoe Industry, 1780–1910* (Urbana: University of Illinois Press, 1988), 142–266, and Mary Blewett, *We Will Rise in our Might: Working Women's Voices from Nineteenth-Century New England* (Ithaca, N.Y.: Cornell University Press, 1991), 106–21, 156–200.

18. On women and the Knights of Labor, see Susan Levine, "Labor's True Woman: Domesticity and Equal Rights in the Knights of Labor," *Journal of American History* 70 (September 1983): 323–39, and Susan Levine, *Labor's True Woman: Carpet Weavers, Industrialization and Labor Reform in the Gilded Age* (Philadelphia: Temple University Press, 1984); see also the important discussion of gender tensions within the KOL in Robert E. Weir, *Beyond Labor's Veil: The Culture of the Knights of Labor* (University Park: Pennsylvania State University Press, 1996), 180–90. A key document, subject to varied interpretations, is Leonora Barry, "Report of the General Instructor and Director of Women's Work," 1889, in Blewett, *We Will Rise in our Might,* 175–76.

19. See Ilene DeVault, "'To Sit among Men': Skill, Gender, and Craft Unionism in the Early American Federation of Labor," in *Labor Histories: Class, Politics, and the Working-Class Experience,* ed. Eric Arnesen, Julie Greene, and Bruce Laurie (Urbana: University of Illinois Press, 1998), 259–83, esp. 278; and Ilene DeVault, *United Apart: Gender and the Rise of Craft Unionism* (Ithaca, N.Y.: Cornell University Press,

2004). See also Meredith Tax, *The Rising of the Women: Feminist Solidarity and Class Conflict, 1880–1917* (New York: Monthly Review Press, 1980), 54–89.

20. On the WTUL, see especially Nancy Schrom Dye, *As Equals and Sisters: Feminism, the Labor Movement, and the Women's Trade Union League of New York* (Columbia: University of Missouri Press, 1980); Robin Miller Jacoby, "The Women's Trade Union League and American Feminism," in *Class, Sex and the Woman Worker,* ed. Bruce Laurie and Milton Cantor (Westport, Conn.: Greenwood Press, 1977), 203–24; Deutsch, *Women and the City,* 161–218; DeVault, *United Apart,* 215–17; and a number of other sources (see below).

21. For a detailed account of the origin and development of the Illinois Woman's Alliance, see Tax, *Rising of the Women,* 65–89; see also Ralph Scharnau, "Elisabeth Morgan: Crusader for Labor Reform," *Labor History* 14, no. 3 (1973): 340–51. On the broader context of middle-class efforts to ameliorate class conflict in Chicago, see Richard Schneirov, "Labor and the New Liberalism in the Wake of the Pullman Strike," in *The Pullman Strike and the Crisis of the 1890s: Essays on Labor and Politics,* ed. Richard Schneirov, Shelton Stromquist, and Nick Salvatore (Urbana: University of Illinois Press, 1999), esp. 206–12.

22. Sklar, *Florence Kelley and the Nation's Work,* 212–16. For a different view of the IWA that stresses the primacy of its class-bridging activities and its links to the development of Chicago women's municipal activism in general, see Flanagan, *Seeing with Their Hearts,* 37–40.

23. Jed Dannenbaum, "The Origins of Temperance Activism and Militancy among American Women," *Journal of Social History* 15 (Winter 1981): 235–53; Ruth Bordin, *Frances Willard: A Biography* (Chapel Hill: University of North Carolina Press, 1986), 65–67. See especially Rachel Bohlmann, "Drunken Husbands, Drunken State: The WCTU's Remaking of American Families and Public Communities in Chicago, 1874–1933" (Ph.D. diss., University of Iowa, 2001), 21, 28, 31–64, for a discussion of the grass-roots initiatives taken by women on behalf of the movement in Chicago and the political/legal context of their campaigns.

24. Bordin, *Frances Willard,* 100; see also Edwards, *Angels in the Machinery,* for a discussion of the partisan attachments of women in the late nineteenth century, especially 39–58.

25. Bohlmann, "Drunken Husbands, Drunken State," 71–93. Bordin, *Frances Willard,* 100, 98.

26. Richard Leeman, *"Do Everything" Reform: The Oratory of Frances E. Willard* (Westport, Conn.: Greenwood Press, 1992), 10–20.

27. Frances Willard, presidential address, WCTU Convention (1882), cited in Bordin, *Frances Willard,* 130. See also 129–44, 175–89.

28. On women's institution building in Chicago, see Rachel Bohlmann, "'Our House Beautiful': The Woman's Temple and the WCTU Effort to Establish Place and Identity in Downtown Chicago, 1887–1898," *Journal of Women's History* 11, no. 2 (Summer 1999): 110–34.

29. Bordin, *Frances Willard*, 150–53. On the Chicago Woman's Club and the founding of the Women's League, see Flanagan, *Seeing with Their Hearts*, 31–33, 36–37.

30. On the debate over social feminism, see William O'Neill, *Everyone Was Brave: A History of American Feminism* (Chicago: Quadrangle Books, 1971), 77–106; Nancy Cott, "What's in a Name: The Limits of 'Social Feminism'; or, Expanding the Vocabulary of Women's History," *Journal of American History* 76, no. 3 (1989): 809–29; and Buechler, *Women's Movements in the United States*, 52–53, 92–94. For a discussion of the "new bourgeois woman," see Carroll Smith Rosenberg, *Disorderly Conduct: Visions of Gender in Victorian America* (New York: Knopf, 1985); Mary Beard, *Women's Work in Municipalities*, quoted in Baker, "Domestication of Politics," 640–41.

31. The literature on settlement house reform is enormous. Useful starting points, largely within progressive discourse, are Allen F. Davis, *Spearheads for Reform: The Social Settlements and the Progressive Movement, 1890–1914* (New York: Oxford University Press, 1967), and more recently, Sklar, *Florence Kelley and the Nation's Work;* Mina Carson, *Settlement Folk: Social Thought and the American Settlement Movement, 1885–1930* (Chicago: University of Chicago Press, 1990); and Victoria Bissell Brown, *The Education of Jane Addams* (Philadelphia: University of Pennsylvania Press, 2004), 210–26. See also Muncy, *Creating a Female Dominion*. Important autobiographies include Jane Addams, *Twenty Years at Hull-House* (New York: Macmillan, 1910); Lillian Wald, *The House on Henry Street;* Florence Kelley, *Notes of Sixty Years: The Autobiography of Florence Kelley* (Chicago: C. H. Kerr, 1986); and Vida Scudder, *On Journey* (New York: E. P. Dutton, 1937). Critical examination of the settlement house mythology is offered by Rivka Lissak, *Pluralism and Progressives: Hull House and the New Immigrants, 1890–1919* (Chicago: University of Chicago Press, 1989), and Ruth Crocker, "Unsettling Perspectives: The Settlement Movement, the Rhetoric of Social History, and the Search for Synthesis," in *Contesting the Master Narrative: Essays in Social History,* ed. Jeffrey Cox and Shelton Stromquist (Iowa City: University of Iowa Press, 1998), 175–209.

32. Katherine Kish Sklar, "Hull House in the 1890s: A Community of Women," *Signs* 10, no. 4 (1985): 667; see also Ruth Bordin, *Woman and Temperance: The Quest for Power and Liberty, 1873–1900* (Philadelphia: Temple University Press, 1981), 14, and Bohlmann, "Our 'House Beautiful.'" On the gendered space of the settlements, see Linda K. Kerber, "Separate Spheres, Female Worlds, Woman's Place: The Rhetoric of Women's History," *Journal of American History* 75 (1988): 26–28, 33–37.

33. Sklar, "Hull House in the 1890s," 668.

34. Robert Westbrook, *John Dewey and American Democracy* (Ithaca, N.Y.: Cornell University Press, 1991), 85.

35. Addams, *Twenty Years at Hull-House*, 92.

36. Sklar, "Hull House in the 1890s," 659–60; Estelle Freedman, "Separatism as Strategy: Female Institution Building and American Feminism," *Feminist Studies* 5, no. 3 (Autumn 1979): 519. See also Kerber, "Separate Spheres," 32–36.

37. Muncy, *Creating a Female Dominion*, 9–10, 14. Quotation from Beatrice Webb, *Beatrice Webb's American Diary* (1898), 10.

38. Addams, *Twenty Years at Hull-House,* quoted in Sklar, "Hull House in the 1890s," 668.

39. Sklar, "Hull House in the 1890s," 669, makes this point explicitly.

40. Abraham Bisno, *Abraham Bisno: Union Pioneer* (Madison: University of Wisconsin Press, 1967), 115–24 (quote from 119). See also Sklar, "Hull House in the 1890s," 671.

41. Muncy, *Creating a Female Dominion,* 36–37; see Barbara Laslett, "Gender and the Rhetoric of Social Science: William Fielding Ogburn and Early Twentieth-Century Sociology in the United States," in *Contesting the Master Narrative: Essays in Social History,* ed. Jeffrey Cox and Shelton Stromquist (Iowa City: University of Iowa Press, 1998), 19–49, on exclusion of women reformers from the new "scientific" discipline of sociology.

42. Louise Michele Newman, *White Women's Rights: The Racial Origins of Feminism in the United States* (New York: Oxford University Press, 1999), 7–8, 14.

43. Quoted in Vivien Hart, *Bound by Our Constitution: Women, Workers, and the Minimum Wage* (Princeton, N.J.: Princeton University Press, 1994), 76–77.

44. Mary van Kleeck, "Daily Record," September 27, October 12, 1905, Mary van Kleeck Papers, Sophia Smith Collection, Smith College, Northampton, Massachusetts (hereafter cited as Van Kleeck Papers).

45. Mary van Kleeck, "Daily Record," November 22, 1905, January 1–June 1, 1907, Van Kleeck Papers.

46. Russell Sage Foundation, "Report of the Department of Industrial Studies, 1910–1917 (revised)," Van Kleeck Papers. See also Eleanor Midman Lewis, "Mary Van Kleeck," in *Notable American Women: The Modern Period,* eds. Barbara Sicherman and Carol Hurd Green (Cambridge, Mass.: Harvard University Press, 1980), 707–9, and John M. Glenn, Lilian Brandt, and F. Emerson Andrews, *Russell Sage Foundation, 1907–1946,* 2 vols. (New York: Russell Sage Foundation, 1947), 1:61, 152–53. David C. Hammack, "A Center of Intelligence for the Charity Organization Movement: The Foundation's Early Years," in *Social Science in the Making: Essays on the Russell Sage Foundation, 1907–1972,* ed. David C. Hammack and Stanton Wheeler (New York: Russell Sage Foundation, 1994), 24, briefly discusses Van Kleeck's role but without a clear sense of the experiential quality of her development as a social investigator.

47. Russell Sage Foundation, "Report of the Department of Industrial Studies, 1910–1917," vol. 1, Van Kleeck Papers.

48. Rosenberg, *Disorderly Conduct,* 263–65; this same point is made by Skocpol, *Protecting Soldiers and Mothers,* 353–54.

49. Muncy, *Creating a Female Dominion,* 63–65.

50. Skocpol, *Protecting Soldiers and Mothers,* 382–93. See also Kessler-Harris, *Out to Work,* 187–88, and Jane Jenson, "Representations of Gender: Policies to 'Protect' Women Workers and Infants in France and the United States before 1914," in *Women, the State and Welfare,* ed. Linda Gordon (Madison: University of Wisconsin Press, 1990), 152–77.

51. *Official Report of the Tenth Biennial Convention of the General Federation of Women's Clubs* (1910), quoted in Skocpol, *Protecting Soldiers and Mothers,* 399.

52. For an interpretation that suggests that Muller (or at least his attorneys) made an argument for women's equality that prefigured feminist critiques of protective legislation, see Robert D. Johnston, *The Radical Middle Class: Populist Democracy and the Question of Capitalism in Progressive Era Oregon* (Princeton, N.J.: Princeton University Press, 2003), 21–23. On Lochner, see Paul Kens, *Lochner v. New York: Economic Regulation on Trial* (Lawrence: University of Kansas Press, 1998).

53. Nancy S. Erickson, "*Muller v. Oregon* Reconsidered: The Origins of a Sex-based Doctrine of Liberty of Contract," *Labor History* 30, no. 2 (Spring 1989): 229–30, 246–50. For a different view of the development of the Court's police power and *Muller,* see Hart, *Bound by Our Constitution,* 88–92, 102–4, and Leonard Baker, *Brandeis and Frankfurter: A Dual Biography* (New York: Harper and Row, 1984), 8–17. See also Skocpol, *Protecting Soldiers and Mothers,* 393–96.

54. Erickson, "*Muller v. Oregon* Reconsidered," 247.

55. The Brandeis brief was unequivocal about women's difference, noting that "women are fundamentally weaker than men in all that makes for endurance: in muscular strength, in nervous energy, in the powers of persistent attention and application." Quoted in Kessler-Harris, *Out to Work,* 187.

56. *The Work of the National Consumers' League During the Year Ending March 1, 1910,* supplement to the *Annals of the American Academy of Political and Social Science* (1910), quoted in Skocpol, *Protecting Soldiers and Mothers,* 396.

57. Ibid., 371. Alternatively, Johnston, echoing in certain respects a New Left critique of progressivism, sees Curt Muller as someone embodying small proprietor values of a competitive capitalist order who fell victim to the reforming propensities of "corporate liberals" intent on driving them from the marketplace. Johnston, *Radical Middle Class,* 24–25. For the general argument, see James Weinstein, *The Corporate Ideal of the Liberal State, 1900–1918* (Boston: Beacon Press, 1968).

58. Hart, *Bound by Our Constitution,* 79, 104–7. See also Skocpol, *Protecting Soldiers and Mothers,* 401–17, and Kessler-Harris, *Out to Work,* 195–98. For a useful overview, see Nancy Woloch, *Muller v. Oregon: A Brief History with Documents* (Boston: Bedford, 1996), 21–40.

59. Lillian Wald and Florence Kelley to Florence Harriman, 1914, quoted in Kessler-Harris, *Out to Work,* 207.

60. Ibid., 202, 203.

61. Debates over the virtues of the family wage are discussed in Martha May, "Bread before Roses: American Workingmen, Labor Unions and the Family Wage," in *Women, Work and Protest: A Century of U.S. Women's Labor History,* ed. Ruth Milkman (Boston: Routledge, 1985), 1–21; see also Skocpol, *Protecting Soldiers and Mothers,* 408–12.

62. Maureen Flanagan, "Gender and Urban Political Reform: The City Club and the Woman's City Club of Chicago in the Progressive Era," *American Historical Re-*

view 95, no. 4 (October 1990): 1032–50, esp. 1047. For a more extended treatment of this argument, see Flanagan, *Seeing with Their Hearts,* 85–109. A study that finds less difference between women's and men's activism is Enstam, *Women and the Creation of Urban Life,* 145. For racial undercurrents in the debate about protectionism, see Newman, *White Women's Rights,* 95–101.

63. Flanagan, "Gender and Urban Political Reform," 1044, 1041, 1046. On similar class-bridging work of middle-class women in Boston, see Deutsch, *Women and the City,* 136–60. The distinctive role that women played in municipal reform was not limited to large cities or elite civic organizations. John Cumbler found striking differences between charity organizations led by men and women in smaller industrial cities. See John T. Cumbler, "The Politics of Charity: Gender and Class in Late 19th Century Charity Policy," *Journal of Social History* 14 (Fall 1980): 99–111.

64. Nancy Schrom Dye, "Creating a Feminist Alliance: Sisterhood and Class Conflict in the New York Women's Trade Union League, 1903–1914," *Feminist Studies* 2, no. 2/3 (1975): 24–38, quote from 25. For an interpretation that stresses the viability of cross-class alliances in the Chicago WTUL, see Flanagan, *Seeing with Their Hearts,* 109–14.

65. *Weekly Bulletin of the Clothing Trades* (1905), quoted in Dye, *As Equals and Sisters,* 39, 41–42.

66. Dye, *As Equals and Sisters,* 16–17. Deutsch, *Women and the City,* 161–218, esp. 190. Other important works on the WTUL are Dye, "Creating a Feminist Alliance"; Tax, *Rising of the Women;* Jacoby, "Women's Trade Union League," 203–24; Colette A. Hyman, "Labor Organizing and Female Institution-Building: The Chicago Women's Trade Union League, 1904–24," in *Women, Work and Protest: A Century of U.S. Women's Labor History,* ed. Ruth Milkman (Boston: Routledge, 1985), 22–41; Elizabeth Anne Payne, *Reform, Labor and Feminism: Margaret Dreier Robins and the Women's Trade Union League* (Urbana: University of Illinois Press, 1988); Ellen Carol DuBois, "Harriot Stanton Blatch and the Transformation of Class Relations among Woman Suffragists," in *Gender, Class, Race and Reform in the Progressive Era,* ed. Noralee Frankel and Nancy S. Dye (Lexington: University Press of Kentucky, 1991), 162–79; Ellen Carol DuBois, "Working Women, Class Relations, and Suffrage Militance: Harriot Stanton Blatch and the New York Woman Suffrage Movement, 1894–1909," *Journal of American History* 74 (June 1987): 34–58; and Kessler-Harris, *Out to Work,* 165–66, 203–14.

67. Dye, *As Sisters and Equals,* 40–41, 43–46. Dorr, *What Eighty Million Women Want,* quoted in Dye, *As Sisters and Equals,* 46.

68. Dye, *As Sisters and Equals,* 52–53. Mary van Kleeck, "Daily Record," September 27, 1905, Van Kleeck Papers.

69. Laura Elliot to Leonora O'Reilly, March 1911, quoted in Dye, *As Sisters and Equals,* 54.

70. Scudder quoted in *Life and Labor* (1911), in Dye, *As Sisters and Equals,* 55. Scudder wrote a novel based on her own experience, *A Listener in Babel: Being a Series of*

Imaginary Conversations Held at the Close of the Last Century (Boston: Houghton Mifflin, 1903), in which, as Sarah Deutsch shows, she crosses class boundaries and in so doing invents the city as new women's space for reform activism. Deutsch, *Women and the City,* 8–13.

71. Dye, *As Sisters and Equals,* 55.

72. Minutes of NYWTUL executive board, January 25, 1906, cited in Annalise Orleck, *Common Sense and a Little Fire: Women and Working Class Politics in the United States, 1900–1965* (Chapel Hill: University of North Carolina Press, 1995), 43–44.

73. Leonora O'Reilly to Executive Board, WTUL, December 1905, Reel 4, f. 765, Leonora O'Reilly Papers, Papers of the WTUL and Its Principal Leaders, 1855–1964, microfilm series (Woodbridge, Conn.: Research Publications, 1981). An account that stresses the role of O'Reilly in the early WTUL is Tax, *Rising of the Women,* 95–124.

74. Orleck, *Common Sense and a Little Fire,* 43, 46.

75. Minutes, Executive Board, NYWTUL, March 1906, quoted in Dye, *As Sisters and Equals,* 65.

76. Ibid., 68–69, 78–86.

77. Alice Kessler-Harris, "Organizing the Unorganizable: Three Jewish Women and Their Union," in *Class, Sex, and the Woman Worker,* ed. Bruce Laurie and Milton Cantor (Westport, Conn.: Greenwood Press, 1977), 149, 153.

78. Orleck, *Common Sense and a Little Fire,* 62.

79. Dye, *As Sisters and Equals,* 94.

80. Secretary's Report, NYWTUL, August 22, 1912, cited in ibid., 100, 97–100.

81. Steve Fraser, *Labor Will Rule: Sidney Hillman and the Rise of American Labor* (New York: Free Press, 1991), 46, 58, 60. Again, see Flanagan, *Seeing with Their Hearts,* 109–12, for an account of the strike that contrasts the cross-class solidarity shown by reforming women with the male reform and business communities. See Deutsch, *Women in the City,* on the more volatile interactions between middle- and working-class activists in Boston, 192–94.

82. Fraser, *Labor Will Rule,* 61.

83. Ardis Cameron, *Radicals of the Worst Sort: Laboring Women in Lawrence, Massachusetts, 1860–1912* (Urbana: University of Illinois Press, 1993), 125–26, 140–41, 149. See also Deutsch, *Women in the City,* 195–96.

84. Sue Ainslie Clark to Margaret Dreier Robins, April 1912, quoted in Dye, *As Sisters and Equals,* 105–6.

85. Kessler-Harris, "Organizing the Unorganizable," 149–50, 152–55; Orleck, *Common Sense and a Little Fire,* 43–44, 48–50.

86. Secretary's Report to the NYWTUL Executive Board (1911), quoted in Orleck, *Common Sense and a Little Fire,* 67–68.

87. Pauline Newman to Rose Schneiderman, n.d., quoted in Dye, *As Equals and Sisters,* 117.

88. Rose Schneiderman to Paul, Alice, Florence, Hilda, and Maud, n.d., quoted in Orleck, *Common Sense and a Little Fire,* 129.

89. See Dye, *As Sisters and Equals*, 118–21. See also Dye, "Creating a Feminist Alliance," 36. On the revolt of the laborers, see David Montgomery, *The Fall of the House of Labor: The Workplace, the State, and American Labor Activism, 1865–1925* (New York: Cambridge University Press, 1987), and chapter 7 of this book.

90. DuBois, "Working Women, Class Relations, and Suffrage Militance," 36–40. See also Tax, *Rising of the Women*.

91. DuBois, "Working Women, Class Relations and Suffrage Militance," 47–50.

92. B. Borrman Wells, "The Militant Movement for Woman Suffrage," quoted in ibid., 57.

93. Scudder, *On Journey*, 164–65.

94. DuBois, "Working Women, Class Relations, and Suffrage Militance," 58. For a parallel account, see also Ellen Carol DuBois, "Harriet Stanton Blatch and the Transformation of Class Relations among Woman Suffragists," in *Gender, Class, Race and Reform in the Progressive Era*, ed. Nora Lee Frankel and Nancy Schrom Dye (Lexington: University Press of Kentucky, 1991), 162–79.

Chapter 6: The Boundaries of Difference

1. Simon Patten, "The Theory of Social Forces" (1896), quoted in Dorothy Ross, *The Origins of American Social Science* (New York: Cambridge University Press, 1991), 148. W. E. B. Du Bois, "The Souls of White Folk," *Independent* 69 (August 18, 1910): 340.

2. Optimistic and pessimistic versions of this racial consciousness vied for dominance in Progressive Era America. See, for instance, Horace M. Kallen, "Democracy versus the Melting-Pot: A Study of American Nationality," pts. 1 and 2, *Nation*, February 18, 1915, 190–94, and February 25, 1915, 217–20; and Madison Grant, *The Passing of the Great Race; or the Racial Bias of European History* (New York: Charles Scribner, 1916). For an overview, see Philip Gleason, "American Identity and Americanization," in *The Harvard Encyclopedia of American Ethnic Groups*, ed. Stephan Thernstrom (Cambridge, Mass.: Belknap Press, 1980), 31–58.

3. On the progressive roots of the Dunning School of Reconstruction historiography, see Eric Foner, *Reconstruction: America's Unfinished Revolution, 1863–1877* (New York: Harper and Row, 1988), xix–xx. John R. Commons, *Races and Immigrants in America* (New York: Macmillan, 1908), 41–43.

4. See David Roediger, *Towards the Abolition of Whiteness: Essays on Race, Politics, and Working-Class History* (London: Verso, 1994); James R. Barrett and David Roediger, "Inbetween Peoples: Race, Nationality and the New Immigrant Working Class," in *American Exceptionalism? U.S. Working-Class Formation in an International Context*, ed. Rick Halpern and Jonathan Morris (London: Macmillan, 1997), 181–220; and, most important, David Roediger, *Working Toward Whiteness: How America's Immigrants Became White: The Strange Journey from Ellis Island to the Suburbs* (New York: Basic Books, 2005).

5. Mark Haller, *Eugenics: Hereditarian Attitudes in American Thought* (New Bruns-

wick, N.J.: Rutgers University Press, 1963), 40–57, 144–59. Linda Gordon, *Woman's Body, Woman's Right: A Social History of Birth Control in America* (New York: Viking, 1976), 126–35, discusses the ambiguities of eugenist thinking for birth-control advocates and feminists. See also Frank Dikötter, "Race Culture: Recent Perspectives on the History of Eugenics," *American Historical Review* 103, no. 2 (April 1998): 467–78.

6. Mary E. Richmond, "The Inter-relation of Social Movements," Report of the Committee on Families and Neighborhoods, *Proceedings of the National Conference of Charities and Corrections* (hereafter cited as *Proceedings of the NCCC*), St. Louis, Missouri, 1910 (Ft. Wayne, Ind.: Archer Printing, 1910), 212–13, and Jane Addams, "Report of the Committee on Immigrants," *Proceedings of the NCCC*, Buffalo, 1909 (Fort Wayne Ind.: Fort Wayne Printing, 1909), 215.

7. On northern and southern perceptions of conditions in the post–Civil War South, see Foner, *Reconstruction*, 497–99, and C. Vann Woodward, *Origins of the New South, 1877–1913* (Baton Rouge: Louisiana State University Press, 1951), 51–74. See also Robert Dykstra, *Bright Radical Star: Black Freedom and White Supremacy on the Hawkeye Frontier* (Cambridge, Mass.: Harvard University Press, 1993), 149–92, 216–70, on the attitudes of Iowans toward the enfranchisement of blacks. Longstanding racial constructions of black identity are discussed in George M. Fredrickson, *The Black Image in the White Mind: The Debate on Afro-American Character and Destiny* (New York: Harper and Row, 1971), 97–129; Joel Williamson, *The Crucible of Race: Black/White Relations in the American South since Emancipation* (New York: Oxford University Press, 1984); and, for northern working men, David Roediger, *The Wages of Whiteness: Race and the Making of the American Working Class* (London: Verso Press, 1991). For an argument that stresses the material roots of socially constructed racial identities, see Barbara Fields's essay, "Ideology and Race in American History," in *Region, Race and Reconstruction: Essays in Honor of C. Vann Woodward*, ed. J. Morgan Kousser and James McPherson (New York: Oxford University Press, 1982), 143–77.

8. The early development of nativism is traced in John Higham, *Strangers in the Land: Patterns of American Nativism, 1860–1925* (New York: Atheneum, 1963), 12–34. See also Tyler G. Anbinder, *Nativism and Slavery: The Northern Know-Nothings and the Politics of the 1850s* (New York: Oxford University Press, 1992).

9. On racial and ethnic fragmentation of the nineteenth-century working class, see Alexander Saxton, *The Indispensible Enemy: Labor and the Anti-Chinese Movement in California* (Berkeley: University of California Press, 1971); and Alexander Saxton, *The Rise and Fall of the White Republic: Class, Politics and Mass Culture in Nineteenth-Century America* (London: Verso, 1990); on the tensions between race and class, see Peter Rachleff, *Black Labor in Richmond, 1865–1890* (Urbana: University of Illinois Press, 1988).

10. Foner, *Reconstruction*, 222–23, 289; Leon F. Litwack, *Trouble in Mind: Black Southerns in the Age of Jim Crow* (New York: Alfred A. Knopf, 1998), 214–15.

11. Washington Gladden, "Moral Reconstruction" (1875), quoted in Ralph Luker,

The Social Gospel in Black and White: American Racial Reform, 1885–1912 (Chapel Hill: University of North Carolina Press, 1991), 14–15; see Luker, *Social Gospel*, 74–75, 140, 203, 212, 215–16, for a discussion of Gladden's evolving views. See also the very insightful discussion by Gary J. Dorrien, *The Making of American Liberal Theology: Imagining Progressive Religion, 1805–1900* (Louisville, Ky.: Westminster John Knox Press, 2001), 326–29.

12. See C. Vann Woodward, *Tom Watson: Agrarian Rebel* (New York: Macmillan, 1938); and Bryant Simon, *A Fabric of Defeat: The Politics of South Carolina Millhands, 1910–1948* (Chapel Hill: University of North Carolina Press, 1998).

13. No historian has so effectively analyzed the racial dynamics of southern politics in the 1890s as C. Vann Woodward in his *Origins of the New South, 1877–1913; The Strange Career of Jim Crow* (New York: Oxford University Press, 1957); and *Tom Watson*. See also Litwack, *Trouble in Mind*. On Booker T. Washington, see Louis R. Harlan, *Booker T. Washington: The Making of a Black Leader, 1856–1901* (New York: Oxford University Press, 1972). See also Washington's collected speeches, especially the rightly famous address to the Atlanta Exposition in 1895, in Booker T. Washington, *Up from Slavery: An Autobiography* (New York: Doubleday, 1901), 218–25. On his relationship with Progressive reformers, especially Theodore Roosevelt, see Thomas G. Dyer, *Theodore Roosevelt and the Idea of Race* (Baton Rouge: Louisiana State University Press, 1980), 105. On the dominance of the Tuskegee machine and its racial vision, see David Levering Lewis, *W. E. B. Du Bois: Biography of a Race, 1868–1919* (New York: Henry Holt, 1993).

14. *Proceedings of the Conference of Charities* (1876), and *Congressional Record,* 48 Cong., quoted in Higham, *Strangers in the Land,* 44, 48.

15. See Saxton, *Indispensible Enemy,* 138–201; Sucheng Chan, *Entry Denied: Exclusion and the Chinese Community in America, 1882–1943* (Philadelphia: Temple University Press, 1991); and Charles J. McClain, *In Search of Equality: The Chinese Struggle Against Discrimination in Nineteenth-Century America* (Berkeley: University of California Press, 1994), 147–53.

16. See Litwack, *Trouble in Mind,* 217–79. On the imposition of Jim Crow in the 1890s, see Woodward, *Origins of the New South,* 321–49, and Howard Rabinowitz, *Race Relations in the Urban South, 1865–1890* (New York: Oxford University Press, 1978), 282–328. See also Jack T. Kirby, *Darkness at Dawning: Race and Reform in the Progressive South* (Philadelphia: Lippincott, 1972); John Dittmer, *Black Georgia in the Progressive Era, 1900–1920* (Urbana: University of Illinois Press, 1977); Dewey W. Grantham, *Southern Progressivism: The Reconciliation of Progress and Tradition* (Knoxville: University of Tennessee Press, 1983); J. Morgan Kousser, *The Shaping of Southern Politics: Suffrage Restriction and the Establishment of the One-Party South, 1880–1910* (New Haven, Conn.: Yale University Press, 1974); and Michael Perman: *Struggle for Mastery: Disfranchisement in the South, 1888–1908* (Chapel Hill: University of North Carolina Press, 2001). For the ways in which Progressive reformers ra-

tionalized the existence of Jim Crow, see Ray Stannard Baker, *Following the Color Line: An Account of Negro Citizenship in the American Democracy* (New York: Doubleday, 1908). Also important is Fredrickson, *Black Image in the White Mind*.

17. Thomas F. Gossett, *Race: The History of an Idea in America* (Dallas: Southern Methodist University Press, 1963), 160–75, esp. 163–64. On Lamarck's biological theories, see "Lamarck, Chevalier De, Jean-Baptiste," in *The Encyclopedia of the Social Sciences*, vol. 9, ed. Edwin R. A. Seligman (New York: Macmillan, 1933), 21–22. Useful accounts of the pervasiveness of Lamarckian ideas among Progressive Era social scientists may be found in George W. Stocking Jr., "Lamarckianism in American Social Science, 1890–1915," in *Race, Culture, and Evolution: Essays in the History of Anthropology,* by George W. Stocking Jr. (New York: 1968), 234–69, and Dyer, *Theodore Roosevelt and the Idea of Race,* 37–44.

18. Franklin Giddings, *The Principles of Sociology* (1902), cited in Fredrickson, *The Black Image in the White Mind,* 313–14.

19. Commons, *Races and Immigrants in America,* 5, 12.

20. Ibid., 7, 41, 42, 45.

21. Ibid., 231. See also Douglas C. Baynton, "Disability and the Justification of Inequality in American History," in *The New Disability History: American Perspectives,* ed. Paul K. Longmore and Lauri Umansky (New York: New York University Press, 2001), 33–57.

22. See Fredrickson, *Black Image in the White Mind,* 314, 292–93, 299, 303–4; Walter Rauschenbusch, "The Problem of the Black Man" (1914), quoted in Fredrickson, *Black Image in the White Mind,* 304. Gary J. Dorrien, *The Making of American Liberal Theology: Idealism, Realism, and Modernity* (Louisville, Ky.: Westminster John Knox Press, 2003), 95–96, 145–46, discusses the racial chauvinism of the social gospelers and Walter Rauschenbusch in particular.

23. Edgar Gardner Murphy, *The Basis of Ascendancy* (1909) quoted in Fredrickson, *Black Image in the White Mind,* 310–11.

24. Ray Stannard Baker, *Following the Color Line: An Account of Negro Citizenship in the American Democracy* (New York: Doubleday, 1908), 44, 3. See also Lewis, *W. E. B. Du Bois,* 363–65.

25. Elisabeth Lasch-Quinn, *Black Neighbors: Race and the Limits of Reform in the American Settlement House Movement, 1890–1945* (Chapel Hill: University of North Carolina Press, 1993), 14.

26. Lewis, *W. E. B. Du Bois,* 363–65.

27. Baker, *Following the Color Line,* 302–3.

28. Ibid., 304, 305, 307.

29. Theodore Roosevelt to Owen Wister, April 27, 1906, quoted in Gary Gerstle, *American Crucible: Race and Nation in the Twentieth Century* (Princeton, N.J.: Princeton University Press, 2001), 65. Gerstle uses the terms "racial nationalism" and "civic nationalism" to describe Roosevelt's intersecting values.

30. Grace Abbott, *The Immigrant and the Community* (New York: Century, 1917), 278–79; Rivka Lissak, *Pluralism and Progressives: Hull House and the New Immigrants, 1890–1919* (Chicago: University of Chicago Press, 1989), 143.

31. Jane Addams, *Twenty Years at Hull-House* (New York: Macmillan, 1910), 172.

32. Simon N. Patten, *The New Basis of Civilization* (1907; reprint, Boston: Belknap Press, 1968), 71, 69. Theodore Roosevelt also shared this commitment to individual Americanization and distrust of "old world" ways. See Gerstle, *American Crucible,* 53–55.

33. Robert E. Park, "Racial Assimilation in Secondary Groups" (1913), in Robert E. Park, *Race and Culture* (Glencoe, Ill.: Free Press, 1950), 205.

34. Kallen, "Democracy versus the Melting-Pot," pt. 1, 193. See also Desmond King, *Making Americans: Immigration, Race, and the Origins of the Diverse Democracy* (Cambridge, Mass.: Harvard University Press, 2000), 27–31.

35. Ibid., 194, and pt. 2, 217, 219.

36. Ibid., pt. 2, 219–20.

37. John Dewey to Horace Kallen (1915), quoted in Lissak, *Pluralism and Progressives,* 151; on Kallen's "romantic racialism," see Gleason, "American Identity and Americanization," 31–58. The racial pessimists are represented especially by Madison Grant, *The Passing of the Great Race; or the Racial Bias of European History* (New York: Charles Scribner, 1916), and Lothrop Stoddard, *The Rising Tide of Color Against White World Supremacy* (New York: Scribner's, 1920).

38. Josiah Strong, *Our Country: Its Possible Future and Present Crisis* (1885), quoted in Walter A. McDougall, *Promised Land, Crusader State: The American Encounter with the World since 1776* (New York: Houghton Mifflin, 1997), 105. Washington Gladden shared with Strong a commitment to this racialized civilizing mission, a "righteous empire"; see Dorrien, *Making of American Liberal Theology: Imagining Progressive Religion,* 324–26. See also Alan Dawley, *Changing the World: American Progressives in War and Revolution* (Princeton, N.J.: Princeton University Press, 2003), 76–83.

39. "The Real Issue," *Outlook* 64 (June 9, 1900): 337.

40. McKinley's recollection quoted in Tony Smith, *America's Mission: The United States and the Worldwide Struggle for Democracy in the Twentieth Century* (Princeton, N.J.: Princeton University Press, 1994), 41.

41. "Expansion but Not Imperialism," *Outlook* 64 (March 24, 1900): 663.

42. "The Meaning of the Election," *Outlook* 66 (November 10, 1900): 633; "The Danger of Imperialism," *Outlook,* August 11, 1900, 857; "Which Is Imperialism?" *Outlook,* September 29, 1900, 249.

43. Howard Gillette Jr., "The Military Occupation of Cuba, 1899–1902: Workshop for American Progressivism," *American Quarterly* 25 (October 1973): 410–25, quotes on 414, 424. Military occupation in Puerto Rico provided an environment conducive to economic transformation of the cigar industry at the hands of the American Tobacco Company; see Arturo Bird-Carmona, "Between the Insular Road and San Juan Bay: The Cigar World of Puerta de Tierra" (Ph.D. diss., University of Iowa, 1998).

44. William Howard Taft is quoted in Smith, *America's Mission*, 43; the "U.S. observer" in Puerto Rico is quoted in Walter LaFeber, *The American Search for Opportunity, 1865–1917*, Cambridge History of American Foreign Relations, vol. 2 (New York: Cambridge University Press, 1993), 154.

45. "Danger of Imperialism," 857–58.

46. H. Bonis, "Imperial Republicanism Historically Considered," *Arena* 23, no. 3 (March 1900): 329–30; J. C. Guffin, "Evolution vs. Imperialism," *Arena* 23, no. 2 (February 1900): 145.

47. The *New York World*, quoted in Robert L. Beisner, *Twelve Against Empire: The Anti-imperialists, 1898–1900* (New York: McGraw Hill, 1968), 219; see also McDougall, *Promised Land, Crusader State*, 113. Freeman Stewart, "Preservation of the Republic: The Giant Issue of 1900," *Arena* 23, no. 6 (June 1900): 572. See also Louise Michele Newman, *White Women's Rights: The Racial Origins of Feminism in the United States* (New York: Oxford University Press, 1999), 14–16.

48. "Mr. Bryan's Letter of Acceptance: Imperialism," *Outlook* 66 (September 29, 1900): 939–40.

49. Jeremiah W. Jenks and W. Jett Lauck, *The Immigration Problem: A Study of American Immigration Conditions and Needs* (New York: Funk and Wagnalls, 1913), 2–5.

50. See Philip Taylor, *The Distant Magnet: European Emigration to the USA* (New York: Harper and Row, 1971), 103, for annual data on European immigration to the United States.

51. "The Making of Americans," *Survey* 23 (January 1, 1910): 436.

52. See, for instance, "Our Responsibility for Immigrants after Landing," *Survey* 24 (April 9, 1910): 75–76, and "Judge Mack on Immigration" (Immigrants' Protective League of Chicago), *Survey* 25 (March 18, 1911): 992.

53. Jane Addams, "Immigrants," *Survey* 22 (June 26, 1909): 453–54.

54. Allen F. Davis, *Spearheads for Reform: The Social Settlements and the Progressive Movement, 1890–1914* (New York: Oxford University Press, 1967), 93–94.

55. "New York League to Protect Immigrants," *Survey* 23 (January 1, 1910): 436–37.

56. "Must Know Ourselves to Teach Immigrants," *Survey* 24 (June 4, 1910): 360; Edward A. Steiner, *On the Trail of the Immigrant* (Chicago: F. H. Revell, 1906), 13–14, 363.

57. For an analysis of Jane Addams's views on Americanization, see Lissak, *Pluralism and Progressives*, 28–33.

58. "Can Jonah Swallow the Whale?" (Joseph Lee letter), *Survey* 24 (July 9, 1910): 598.

59. "Making of Americans," 436; William S. Bennett, "The Immigration Commission," *Survey* 23 (March 12, 1910): 924.

60. H. Parker Willis, "The Findings of the Immigration Commission," *Survey* 25 (January 7, 1911): 571–78, quotations from 572–73, 575.

61. W. Jett Lauck, "Industrial Communities," *Survey* 25 (January 7, 1911): 579–86, quotations from 585–86.

62. "Recommendations of the United States Immigration Commission," *Survey*

25 (January 7, 1911): 603–4. Desmond King argues that the Dillingham Commission reified an implicitly racial classification of "old" and "new" immigration as the basis of subsequent restrictive immigration policy; see *Making Americans*, 79–81. On the Dillingham commission, see also Robert F. Zeidel, *Immigrants, Progressives and Exclusion Politics: The Dillingham Commission, 1900–1927* (DeKalb: Northern Illinois University Press, 2004).

63. Simon Patten saw the opportunity for racial uplift in the growth of immigration; see his "Construction vs. Distribution," *Survey* 25 (February 18, 1911): 866.

64. "The Spirit of Internationalism" (Arthur Mayer), *Survey* 25 (February 18, 1911): 867–68, and Grace Abbott, "Adjustment—Not Restriction," *Survey* 25 (January 7, 1911): 527–29.

65. The Editor, "The Selection of Immigrants," *Survey* 25 (February 4, 1911): 715–16.

66. Paul U. Kellogg, "An Immigrant Labor Tariff," *Survey* 25 (January 7, 1911): 529–31.

67. Jenks and Lauck, *Immigration Problem*, 372–73.

68. Ibid., 285.

69. Addams, "Immigrants," 453, and Abbott, "Adjustment—Not Restriction," 529.

70. Lissak, *Pluralism and Progressives*, 4–5. See also Addams, *Twenty Years at Hull-House*, 169–85.

71. Davis, *Spearheads for Reform*, 92–93; Lissak, *Pluralism and Progressives*, 7–8, 30–33.

72. Robert E. Park and Herbert A. Miller, *Old World Traits Transplanted* (New York: Harper, 1921), 269–71, 286; Sophonisba P. Breckinridge and Edith Abbott, *Delinquent Child and the Home* (1912), quoted in Lissak, *Pluralism and Progressives*, 26–27.

73. Jane Addams, *Democracy and Social Ethics* (New York: Macmillan, 1902), 11; Rivka Lissak, *Pluralism and Progressives*, 27.

74. Lissak, *Pluralism and Progressives*, discusses the antipathy of Hull-House reformers towards ethnic community leaders, 36–45; quote from John Dewey, "The School as a Social Center," on 45.

75. Ibid., 143 (also 38–40); Dewey, "Nationalizing Education," quoted in Lissak, *Pluralism and Progressives*, 143. See also Robert Westbrook, *John Dewey and American Democracy* (Ithaca, N.Y.: Cornell University Press, 1991), 213–14.

76. Lissak, *Pluralism and Progressives*, 51–52, 53–55; Addams, "The Public School and the Immigrant Child," quoted in Lissak, *Pluralism and Progressives*, 54.

77. Davis, *Spearheads for Reform*, 88–89; Lissak, *Pluralism and Progressives*, 36–37. One of the best accounts of the ways in which such a stratum within immigrant communities was drawn into the life and culture of the houses is Hilda Satt Polacheck, *I Came a Stranger: The Story of a Hull-House Girl* (Urbana: University of Illinois Press, 1989), esp. 61–80.

78. Lissak, *Pluralism and Progressives*, 167, 162–63.

79. Thomas Lee Philpott, *The Slum and the Ghetto: Neighborhood Deterioration and the Middle-Class Reform, Chicago, 1880–1930* (New York: Oxford University Press, 1978), 297, 298.

80. Frances Kellor, "The Criminal Negro: A Sociological Study" (1901), as quoted in Lasch-Quinn, *Black Neighbors*, 18–19.

81. Ruth Crocker, *Social Work and Social Order: The Settlement Movement in Two Industrial Cities, 1889–1930* (Urbana: University of Illinois Press, 1992), 69–71.

82. Fannie Barrier Williams, "The Frederick Douglass Center" (1906), quoted in Philpott, *Slum and the Ghetto*, 318; see 315–20. See also Steven J. Diner, "Chicago Social Workers and Blacks in the Progressive Era," *Social Service Review* 44, no. 4 (December 1970): 393–410.

83. Crocker, *Social Work and Social Order*, 73, 83–84.

84. Ibid., 92.

85. Ibid, 92–93. On the pervasive ideology of "uplift" among black elites, see Kevin Gaines, *Uplifting the Race: Black Leadership, Politics and Culture in the Twentieth Century* (Chapel Hill: University of North Carolina Press, 1996), quotations from xiv–xv.

86. Elisabeth Lasch-Quinn has provided the most complete and insightful account of an alternative "settlement" movement in black communities that grew from unique institutional sources, largely outside the influence of the mainstream movement. See *Black Neighbors*, 7–8, 56–66, 74–81, 100–5, 115–26.

87. Presidential address, WCTU, 1893, quoted in Ruth Bordin, *Frances Willard: A Biography* (Chapel Hill: University of North Carolina Press, 1986), 216.

88. For a full account of the controversy, see Patricia Ann Schechter, *Ida B. Wells-Barnett and American Reform, 1880–1930* (Chapel Hill: University of North Carolina Press, 2001), 102, 108, 110–12.

89. The definitive account of the circumstances leading up to the Atlanta Exposition speech is Harlan, *Booker T. Washington*, 210–26, esp. 218–19.

90. Ibid., 218–27, esp. 218–19.

91. Lewis, *W. E. B. Du Bois*, 198–201.

92. W. E. B. Du Bois, "Credo" (1904), quoted in ibid., 313.

93. On Washington's Committee of Twelve and Du Bois Niagara gathering, see Lewis, *W. E. B. Du Bois*, 304–11, 315–22. See also Manning Marable, *W. E. B. Du Bois: Black Radical Democrat* (Boston: Twayne, 1986), 52–57.

94. William Stueck, "Progressivism and the Negro: White Liberals and the Early NAACP," *Historian* 38, no. 1 (November 1975): 75; Diner, "Chicago Social Workers and Blacks," 394–95; Alvin B. Kogut, "The Negro and the Charity Organization Society in the Progressive Era," *Social Service Review* 44, no. 1 (March 1970): 12.

95. Ibid., 14–19.

96. Graham Taylor, "The Riot in Lincoln's City" (1908), quoted in Diner, "Chicago Social Workers and Blacks," 401–5; Lewis, *W. E. B. Du Bois*, 471.

97. "The Niagara Movement: Address to the Country," in *W. E. B. DuBois: A Reader*, ed. David Levering Lewis (New York: Henry Holt, 1995), 368–69.

98. Mary White Ovington, *Black and White Sat Down Together: The Reminiscences of an NAACP Founder*, ed. Ralph E. Luker (1932–33; reprint, New York: Feminist Press, 1995), 55–57; also quoted in Lewis, *W. E. B. Du Bois*, 388–89. Leon Fink, "Joining the

People: William English Walling and the Specter of the Intellectual Class," in *Progressive Intellectuals and the Dilemmas of Democratic Commitment*, by Leon Fink (Cambridge, Mass.: Harvard University Press, 1997), 126–27, 322–23 n. 33, notes that Walling was particularly disturbed by the participation of "common people" in the Springfield riot.

99. Mary White Ovington, *And the Walls Came Tumbling Down* (1947; reprint, New York: Arno, 1969), 102–7; Charles Flint Kellogg, *NAACP: A History of the National Association for the Advancement of Colored People*, vol. 1, *1909–1920* (Baltimore: Johns Hopkins, 1967), 12–16, 297–99.

100. This account of the opening days of the conference is especially indebted to Lewis, *W. E. B. Du Bois*, 391–93; see also Kellogg, *NAACP*, 19–21; W. E. Burghardt Du Bois, "National Committee of the Negro," *Survey*, June 12, 1909, 407–9.

101. Lewis, *W. E. B. Du Bois*, 393.

102. Du Bois, "National Committee of the Negro," 408. See Schechter, *Ida B. Wells-Barnett*, 135–37, for an account that emphasizes the tension between Wells-Barnett and Du Bois; also Lewis, *W. E. B. Du Bois*, 394.

103. Du Bois, "National Committee of the Negro," 409, also quoted in Lewis, *W. E. B. Du Bois*, 395.

104. Ovington, *Walls Came Tumbling Down*, 106–7.

105. Lewis, *W. E. B. Du Bois*, 400–401, 405–7.

106. [W. E. B. Du Bois], "Social Equality," *Crisis* 2 (September 1911): 197. See also Philpott, *Slum and the Ghetto*, 299–300, and Lewis, *W. E. B. Du Bois*, 477–78.

107. The most thorough and insightful discussion of the way the race issued played out in the founding convention of the Progressive Party is John A. Gable, *The Bull Moose Years: Theodore Roosevelt and the Progressive Party* (Port Washington, N.Y.: Kennikat Press, 1978), 60–74. Gable sees the issue as more divisive between Roosevelt and the Progressives than I do.

108. These challenges are reminiscent of the efforts of the Mississippi Freedom Democratic Party to unseat the lily-white Mississippi Democrats from their place at the 1964 Democratic convention. See John Dittmer, *Local People: The Struggle for Civil Rights in Mississippi* (Urbana: University of Illinois Press, 1994).

109. Gable, *Bull Moose Years*, 61–63; Theodore Roosevelt to Jane Addams, October 31, 1911, quoted in Melanie S. Gustafson, "Partisan Women: Gender, Politics and the Progressive Party of 1912" (Ph.D. diss., New York University, 1993), 231.

110. Dewey W. Grantham Jr., "The Progressive Movement and the Negro," *South Atlantic Quarterly* 54 (October 1955): 469–70; Theodore Roosevelt to Rev. Bradley Gilman, July 24, 1912, quoted in Gable, *Bull Moose Years*, 64.

111. For the Du Bois–authored resolution, see the *Crisis* 4, no. 5 (September 1912): 236. For the redrafted resolution and its fate in committee, see Gable, *Bull Moose Years*, 72.

112. Gustafson, "Partisan Women," 232–33, 235–36.

113. This appeal represented a poignant reversal of the predicament suffragists faced with the adoption of the Fourteenth Amendment, which guaranteed voting rights only to men.

114. Gable, *Bull Moose Years*, 73; Jane Addams, *The Second Twenty Years at Hull-House, September 1909 to September 1929* (New York: Macmillan, 1930), 34–35.

115. *New York Evening Post*, quoted in *Crisis* 4, no. 5 (September 1912): 226; "Editorial: Mr. Roosevelt," *Crisis* 4, no. 5 (September 1912): 236.

116. "Opinion: The Negro in Politics," *Crisis* 5, no. 1 (November 1912): 19.

117. On the Hull-House meeting in October, see also Gustafson, "Partisan Women," 236. Jean Bethke Elshtain, *Jane Addams and the Dream of American Democracy* (New York: Basic Books, 2002), 193–94, 200, fails to engage the contradictions in Addams's position with respect to the race issue and the Progressive Party.

118. Jane Addams, "The Progressive Party and the Negro," *Crisis* 5, no. 1 (November 1912): 30–31.

119. It is remarkable how Addams's rationalizations follow those of Theodore Roosevelt himself. See Gerstle, *American Crucible*, 76–79.

120. "Editorial: A Philosophy for 1913," *Crisis* 5, no. 3 (January 1913): 127.

121. Elliot Rudwick and August Meier, "The Rise of the Black Secretariat in the NAACP, 1909–35," in *Along the Color Line: Explorations in the Black Experience* (Urbana: University of Illinois Press, 1976), 94–127, esp. 98–105, charts the tensions over black leadership of the NAACP in its early history.

122. David Levering Lewis details the growing tensions between Du Bois and the white board members in *W. E. B. Du Bois,* 496–97, 469, quotations on 476. Ovington also discusses the reasons, in her view, the organization was dominated by whites in its earliest years: "Few colored people were trained to take such executive positions as we had to offer, and also few had the leisure of our volunteer white workers." Ovington, *Walls Came Tumbling Down,* 111. See also Meier and Rudwick, "Rise of the Black Secretariat," 100–104.

123. Lewis, *W. E. B. Du Bois,* 478; Meier and Rudwick, "Rise of the Black Secretariat," 100.

124. August Meier and John H. Bracey Jr., "The NAACP as a Reform Movement, 1909–1965: 'To Reach the Conscience of America,'" *Journal of Southern History* 59, no. 1 (February 1993): 10–11. On Du Bois's developing race consciousness, see Marable, *W. E. B. Du Bois,* 80–81, 90–94. On the intellectual foundations of race consciousness, see Alain LeRoy Locke, *Race Contacts and Interracial Relations: Lectures on the Theory and Practice of Race* (Washington, D.C.: Howard University Press, 1992).

125. These conclusions benefited enormously from discussions with my colleague Ken Cmiel.

126. W. E. B. Du Bois, *The Souls of Black Folk* (1903; reprint, New York: Fawcett, 1961), 41.

Chapter 7: Class Wars and the Crisis of Progressivism

1. L. A. Halbert to Frank Walsh, June 13, 1913, and Boyd Fisher to Frank Walsh, June 27, 1913; see also F. W. to L. A. Halbert, June 14, 1913, all in Box 33, File 68, Frank P. Walsh Papers, Manuscripts and Archives Division, New York Public Library (hereafter cited as Walsh Papers).

2. The comments by Harris Weinstock, a business representative on the U.S. Commission on Industrial Relations, and Walsh's own views quoted at the opening of this chapter suggest the polarization that developed within the USCIR. See *New York Times,* August 18, 1915, p. 1, and Frank Walsh, "To Urge Recommendations on Congress," *United Mine Workers Journal,* November 11, 1915, 6–7.

3. Allen F. Davis, "The Campaign for the Industrial Relations Commission, 1911–1913," *Mid-America* 45, no. 4 (October 1963): 211–28.

4. Frank Walsh to Edward J. Ward, April 29, 1915, and Frank Walsh to William Marion Reedy, April 17, 1915, Box 33, File 39, Walsh Papers.

5. See United States Commission on Industrial Relations, *Final Reports and Testimony,* 64th Cong., 1st sess., Senate Documents (Washington, D.C.: GPO, 1916), 1:415. For commentary, see "Industrial Conflict: Four Articles on the Reports of the Industrial Relations Commission," *New Republic* 4 (August 28, 1915): 89–92, and "Mr. Manley Takes Issue," *New Republic* 4 (September 18, 1915): 183–84. The most useful treatments of the divisions within the USCIR are Leon Fink, who emphasizes divisions between "agitators" and "engineers," in his essay "Expert Advice: Progressive Intellectuals and the Unraveling of Labor Reform, 1912–1915," in *Intellectuals and Public Life: Between Radicalism and Reform,* ed. Leon Fink, Stephen T. Leonard, and Donald M. Reid (Ithaca, N.Y.: Cornell University Press, 1996), 183, 193, 210; Joseph A. McCartin, *Labor's Great War: The Struggle for Industrial Democracy and the Origins of Modern American Labor Relations, 1912–21* (Chapel Hill: University of North Carolina Press, 1998), 12–14, 18–30; and Graham Adams Jr., *Age of Industrial Violence, 1910–1915: The Activities and Findings of the United States Commission on Industrial Relations* (New York: Columbia University Press, 1966). See also Clarence Wunderlin, *Visions of a New Industrial Order: Social Science and Labor Theory in America's Progressive Era* (New York: Columbia University Press, 1992). For the formative influences on the USCIR, see Davis, "Campaign for the Industrial Relations Commission," 211–28.

6. Walsh, "To Urge Recommendations on Congress," 1. See chapter 3 for further discussion of the surviving "producerist" tradition within progressivism, especially in the arena of municipal labor and socialist politics. This subject is also treated in a preliminary comparative context in Shelton Stromquist, "Imagining Labor's City: The Limits and Possibilities of Municipal Socialism in Comparative Perspective," unpublished paper, Social Science History Association, November 14, 2003.

7. Davis, "Campaign for the Industrial Relations Commission," 220–21; "The Industrial Platform of the New Party," *Survey,* August 24, 1912, 668–70; Allen F. Davis, "The Social Workers and the Progressive Party, 1912–1916," *American Historical Review* 69, no. 3 (April 1964): 674–75.

8. On the endemic character of class conflict in the Rocky Mountain West, see Melvyn Dubofsky, "The Origins of Western Working-Class Radicalism," in *Labor History Reader,* ed. Daniel Leab (Urbana: University of Illinois Press, 1985), 230–53, and Melvyn Dubofsky, *We Shall Be All: A History of the Industrial Workers of the World* (Chicago: Quadrangle Books, 1969). On the developing pattern of labor conflict after the economic downturn of 1907, see David Montgomery, *The Fall of the House of Labor: The Workplace, the State, and American Labor Activism, 1865–1925* (New York: Cambridge University Press, 1987), 288–89, and his influential essay, "The 'New Unionism' and the Transformation of Workers' Consciousness in America, 1909–22," in *Workers Control in America: Studies in the History of Work, Technology, and Labor Struggles,* by David Montgomery (New York: Cambridge University Press, 1979), 91–112.

9. Montgomery, "New Unionism," 93–94; see also David Brody, *Steelworkers in America: The Nonunion Era* (New York: Harper and Row, 1969).

10. See George Barnett, *Chapters on Machinery and Labor* (Cambridge, Mass.: Harvard University Press, 1926), 139–61, and Leo Wolman, *The Growth of American Trade Unionism, 1880–1920* (New York: NBER, 1924), 110–19, 120–23, on union membership statistics.

11. See accounts of the Pressed Steel Car strike in Dubofsky, *We Shall Be All,* 198–209, and Philip S. Foner, *History of the Labor Movement in the United States* (New York: International Publishers, 1965), 4:281–95.

12. See the discussion of the shirtwaist makers' strikes in chapter 5.

13. The literature on the "uprising of the 20,000" is enormous. See Foner, *History of the Labor Movement* 5:226–39; Meredith Tax, *The Rising of the Women: Feminist Solidarity and Class Conflict, 1880–1917* (New York: Monthly Review Press, 1980), 205–40; and Annalise Orleck, *Common Sense and a Little Fire: Women and Working-Class Politics, 1900–1965* (Chapel Hill: University of North Carolina Press, 1995), 53–86.

14. *Outlook* 94 (March 1910); Foner, *History of the Labor Movement* 5:143–63.

15. Rhodri Jeffreys-Jones has argued, not altogether convincingly, that levels of industrial violence in the United States have been wildly exaggerated, most notably during the Progressive Era, in the interests of producing a more favorable political climate for reform. Rhodri Jeffreys-Jones, *Violence and Reform in American History* (New York: New Viewpoints Press, 1978), 8–30, 155–76. Incomplete though his data are, they actually suggest higher levels of strike-related violence between 1900 and 1905–6 than his analysis acknowledges.

16. Daniel Swinarski, "Statistical Characteristics of Violent Strikes, 1908–1914," unpublished essay, University of Iowa, 1991, 5, in author's possession.

17. Ibid., 25–28. Swinarski constructed an intensity index to account for different levels of violence in strikes. The category of "extreme" violence reflected a level of intensity that usually involved multiple incidents in which fatalities, injuries, and "riots" occurred. The nine strikes in this category were "the 1909 IWW strike in McKees Rocks, Pennsylvania; the 1910 Street Railway strike in Philadelphia; the 1910

Bridge and Structural Iron strike in Los Angeles; the 1910 Garment Workers strike in Chicago; the 1913 United Mine Workers Strike in Mucklow, West Virginia; the 1913 IWW strike in Paterson, New Jersey; the 1913 Western Federation of Miners strike in Calumet, Michigan; and the 1914 United Mine Workers strikes in Trinidad and Forbes, Colorado" (27–28).

18. Paul Kellogg, "Conservation and Industrial War," *Survey* 27 (December 30, 1911): 1412.

19. "Larger Bearings of the McNamara Case," *Survey* 27 (December 30, 1911): 1413–29, esp. 1414, 1417, 1419–20.

20. Ardis Cameron, *Radicals of the Worst Sort: Laboring Women in Lawrence, Massachusetts, 1860–1912* (Urbana: University of Illinois Press, 1993), 12.

21. "Two Hours, Reduced Wages, and a Strike," *Survey* 27 (January 27, 1912): 1633.

22. "A Needless Labor War," *Outlook* 100 (January 27, 1912): 151–52.

23. "The Real Question," *Outlook* 100 (February 24, 1912): 385.

24. W. Jett Lauck, "The Significance of the Situation at Lawrence: The Condition of the New England Woolen Mill Operative," *Survey* 27 (February 17, 1912): 1772–74.

25. Robert A. Woods, "The Clod Stirs," *Survey* 27 (March 16, 1912): 1929.

26. "Anarchy: From Below and from Above," *Survey* 28 (June 1, 1912): 351–52.

27. Vida Scudder, "For Justice Sake," *Survey* 28 (April 6, 1912): 79. For an account of the mixed sentiments of Boston reformers during the Lawrence strike, see Sarah Deutsch, *Women and the City: Gender, Space, and Power in Boston, 1870–1940* (New York: Oxford University Press, 2000), 195–97.

28. John D. Adams, "Clod or Brother?" *Survey* 27 (March 30, 1912): 2014–15.

29. F. S. Boyd, "An Unmet Responsibility," *Survey* 27 (February 17, 1912): 1786.

30. These views have not always been treated explicitly. Compare the responses of Florence Kelley and Jane Addams to the Pullman strike; see Katherine Kish Sklar, *Florence Kelley and the Nation's Work: The Rise of Women's Political Culture, 1830–1900* (New Haven, Conn.: Yale University Press, 1995), 286–74, and Jane Addams, *Twenty Years at Hull-House* (New York: Macmillan, 1910). See also Vida Scudder, *On Journey* (New York: E. P. Dutton, 1937), 154–57, 184–89, and Clarke A. Chambers, *Paul U. Kellogg and the Survey: Voices of Social Welfare and Social Justice* (Minneapolis: University of Minnesota Press, 1971), 49–50, 216–18.

31. The early campaign for an investigating commission is best covered in Davis, "Campaign for the Industrial Relations Commission," 214–15.

32. "Petition to the President for a Federal Commission on Industrial Relations," *Survey* 27 (December 30, 1911): 1430–31.

33. Davis, "Campaign for the Industrial Relations Commission," 218–22.

34. Jeffreys-Jones, *Violence and Reform in American History*, 161–76, suggests, I think mistakenly, that the campaign for the USCIR was a calculated, even cynical, effort to inflate in the public mind the threat of class conflict in order to promote a specific reform and legislative agenda. My own view, indeed the central argument of this book, suggests that the reformers pursued these goals out of sincerely held

conviction and that their concern for the social threat posed by class conflict lay at the very foundation of the Progressive movement as far back as the 1890s.

35. "They Don't Suit the 'Intellectuals,'" *American Federationist* 20 (February 1913): 128–32.

36. Davis, "Campaign for the Industrial Relations Commission," 222–25; Florence Harriman, *From Pinafores to Politics* (New York: Henry Holt, 1923), 133; the nomination of the chairman is surrounded by conflicting accounts. John R. Commons claimed to have been the first choice and turned it down because he could not absent himself further from the University of Wisconsin (John R. Commons, *Myself* [Madison: University of Wisconsin Press, 1963], 166–67), whereas Harriman asserted that Wilson had first offered the position to Louis Brandeis before turning to Walsh (133). But a number of sources indicate Walsh's supporters were influential in putting his name forward early in the selection process. L. A. Halbert to Frank Walsh, June 13, 1913, Box 33, File 68, Walsh Papers. Walsh, according to Harriman, had swung his support to Wilson in July 1912 because, after meeting with Wilson, he was "convinced that Mr. Wilson's progressiveness was more progressive than the Colonel's." Harriman, *From Pinafores to Politics,* 131–32.

37. Dante Barton, "Frank P. Walsh: The Man Chosen by President Wilson to Lead the Commission on Industrial Relations," *Harper's Weekly* 58 (September 27, 1913): 24.

38. Graham Adams Jr., "Francis Patrick Walsh," *Concise Dictionary of American Biography* (New York: Scribner's, 1980), 691; George Creel, "Why Industrial War?" *Collier's,* October 18, 1913, 5–6; George Creel, *Rebel at Large* (New York: G. P. Putnam, 1947), 55–57; and McCartin, *Labor's Great War,* 16–19.

39. Creel, "Why Industrial War?" 6. The article is actually based on an "interview" invented by Creel for the purpose of introducing Walsh and his ideas to the public. See Frank Walsh to George Creel, August 18, 1913, September 9, 1912, Box 33, Files 40 and 52, Walsh Papers.

40. L. A. Halbert to Frank Walsh, June 13, 1913, and Frank Walsh to L. A. Halbert, June 14, 1913; also Frank Walsh to Boyd Fisher, June 24, 1913, all in Box 33, File 68, Walsh Papers.

41. Boyd Fisher to Frank Walsh, September 13, 1913, and Frank Walsh to Boyd Fisher, September 20, 1913, Box 33, File 52, Walsh Papers.

42. Frank Walsh to Boyd Fisher, June 30, 1913, Paul Kellogg to Frank Walsh, July 18, 1913, Frank Walsh to Paul Kellogg, July 31, 1913, and Frank Walsh to Stephen S. Wise, September 15, October 18, 1913, all in Walsh Papers; see also Commons, *Myself,* 165–66.

43. Paul U. Kellogg, "The Government, the People and the Labor Problem," *American Review of Reviews,* September 1913, 344–45; "The Constructive Work before the Industrial Relations Commission: A Symposium with Introduction by Paul Kellogg," *Survey* 30 (August 2, 1913): 571–88, esp. 571.

44. Commons, *Myself,* 171–72.

45. John R. Commons to Frank Walsh, n.d. [presumably November 1913], telegram, Box 33, File 60; Maurice Dower to Frank Walsh, December 22, 1913, Box

33, File 38; Frank Walsh to John R. Commons, January 17, 1914, Box 33, File 64, Walsh Papers. Testimony of Charles McCarthy, *Reports of the United States Commission on Industrial Relations* (Washington, D.C.: GPO, 1916), 1:377–90.

46. See Adams, *Age of Industrial Violence,* 146–75; George P. West, *Report on the Colorado Strike* (Washington, D.C.: GPO, 1915); Montgomery, *Fall of the House of Labor,* 343–47.

47. Testimony of Charles McCarthy, 377–80; see also Wunderlin, *Visions of a New Industrial Order,* on the work of the U.S. Industrial Commission, 25–36, and on Commons's "corporatist synthesis," 113–29.

48. Charles McCarthy to Frank Walsh, April 21, 1914, Box 6, File 2, Charles McCarthy Papers, State Historical Society of Wisconsin, Madison (hereafter cited as McCarthy Papers).

49. Frank Walsh to W. Jett Lauck, January 10, 1913, and Florence J. Harriman to Frank Walsh, January 14, 1913, Box 33, File 64, Walsh Papers; Mark Perlman, *Labor Union Theories in America: Background and Development* (Evanston, Ill.: Row, Peterson, 1958), 284–85; USCIR, Reports, vol. 1.

50. Charles McCarthy to Frank Walsh, May 29, 1913, Box 6, File 3, McCarthy Papers. Marion Casey misses McCarthy's disingenuousness in his pursuit of the appointment; see *Charles McCarthy: Librarianship and Reform* (Chicago: American Library Association, 1981), 105–6.

51. Frank Walsh to Charles McCarthy, June 1, 2, 3, 1913, Box 6, File 4, McCarthy Papers.

52. Frank Walsh to Charles McCarthy, September 1, 1914; William Leiserson to Charles McCarthy, September 4, 14, 1914, 7/2; Charles McCarthy to Luke Grant, September 28, 1914; and Frank Walsh to Charles McCarthy, October 2, 1914, Box 7, File 3, all in McCarthy Papers.

53. W. Jett Lauck to Charles McCarthy, October 3, 1914, Box 7, File 3, McCarthy Papers.

54. Previous scholarship has focused on the divisions within the commission without situating those divisions within the wider ideological splits among Progressives. See Adams, *Age of Industrial Violence;* Wunderlin, *Visions of a New Industrial Order;* Perlman, *Labor Union Theories in America;* Casey, *Charles McCarthy;* Jeffreys-Jones, *Violence and Reform in American History;* and Fink, "Expert Advice."

55. Paul Kellogg to Charles McCarthy, October 7, 1914, Box 7, File 4, McCarthy Papers; "Editorials," *Survey* 33 (October 10, 1914): 54.

56. *Survey* 33 (October 10, 1914): 53–55.

57. Frank Walsh to Charles McCarthy, October 8, 1914, Charles McCarthy to Jerome Greene, October 8, 1914, Charles McCarthy to John Murdock, October 9, 1914, all in Box 7, File 4, McCarthy Papers.

58. Charles McCarthy to Frank Walsh, October 8, 1914.

59. Frank Walsh to Paul Kellogg, October 19, 1914, Box 33, File 39, Walsh Papers.

60. "Editorials," *Survey* 33 (November 14, 1914): 175–81; George P. West, "Industrial Relations," *Survey* 33 (December 12, 1914): 303–4.

61. *New York Times,* November 26, 1914, p. 17, col. 3, and December 3, 1914, p. 14, col. 3; Basil M. Manley to Frank Walsh, December 3, 1914, Box 33, File 38, Walsh Papers.

62. The New York hearings were extensively reported in the *New York Times.* See, for instance, January 21, 1915, p. 1, col. 3; January 26, 1915, p. 1, col. 1; January 31, 1915, sec. 2, p. 1, col. 3; and February 6, 1915, p. 1, col. 1. See also John A. Fitch, "The Absentee Ownership of Industry on the Stand in New York," *Survey* 33 (January 30, 1915): 467–69; "The Rockefeller Interests in Industry and Philanthropy," *Survey* 33 (February 6, 1915): 477–80; and "Ludlow, Chrome, Homestead and Wall Street in the Melting Pot," *Survey* 33 (February 13, 1915): 531–34.

63. "Great Foundations and the Industrial Unrest," *Survey* 33 (January 23, 1915): 437–38.

64. Much of the discussion of conflicts within the commission has focused, mistakenly I think, on differences in style and methods of Walsh and McCarthy/Commons rather than their substantive differences over the causes of industrial unrest and the appropriate remedies. See, for instance, Casey, *Charles McCarthy,* 104–5, 120–23, but also Fink, "Expert Advice," 196–97, 210.

65. George Creel, "How 'Tainted' Money Taints," *Pearson's Magazine,* March 1915, 289–97; "Letting George Do It," *Survey,* February 13, 1915, 541–42; see also exchange of letters, Paul Kellogg to Frank Walsh, February 5, 1915, and Frank Walsh to Paul Kellogg, February 6, March 4, 1915, Walsh Papers.

66. McCarthy's friendship with Rockefeller stemmed from their time as classmates at Brown and Rockefeller's admiration of McCarthy, a much-revered football star. Rockefeller served the football team as a lowly assistant manager. See Fink, "Expert Advice," 189, and Casey, *Charles McCarthy,* 9–13.

67. The financial predicament of the commission is discussed in William Leiserson, "Memorandum of Meeting, Sunday, Feb. 28, 1915," Box 8, File 7, McCarthy Papers; for McCarthy's own defense of his relations with Rockefeller, see Charles McCarthy to Frank Walsh, February 15, 1915; for Walsh's view of the controversy, see Frank Walsh to William Marion Reedy, March 3, 1915, Walsh Papers; see also Adams, *Age of Industrial Violence,* 161–68.

68. Charles McCarthy to Redmond S. Brennan, March 1, 1915, Charles McCarthy to John Fitch, March 1, 1915, Box 8, File 7, McCarthy Papers; John A. Fitch, "Field Investigations of the Industrial Relations Commission," *Survey,* February 27, 1915, 578–82. See also Charles McCarthy to John R. Commons (with comments by William Leiserson), March 1, 1915, Box 8, File 7, McCarthy Papers.

69. Walsh to Reedy, April 17, 1915.

70. Frank Walsh to Dante Barton, May 24, 1915, Walsh Papers, also quoted in Adams, *Age of Industrial Violence,* 171. Adams has a useful account of Walsh's interrogation of Rockefeller and the public's response on 164–73. For a different view, more criti-

cal of Walsh and sympathetic to Rockefeller and his adviser Mackenzie King, see H. M. Gitelman, *Legacy of the Ludlow Massacre: A Chapter in American Industrial Relations* (Philadelphia: University of Pennsylvania Press, 1988), 148–54, 159–61.

71. Quoted in Perlman, *Labor Union Theories in America*, 290–91.

72. The best general accounts of the commission's final reports are Perlman, *Labor Union Theories in America*, and Adams, *Age of Industrial Violence*.

73. "Industrial Conflict," 89. "Supplemental Statement of Chairman Frank P. Walsh," *Final Report and Testimony, Commission on Industrial Relations*, 1:153.

74. "Manly Report," Final Report and Testimony; see also Perlman, *Labor Union Theories in America*, 292–93, and Adams, *Age of Industrial Violence*, 215–17.

75. "Supplemental Statement of Chairman Frank P. Walsh," Final Report and Testimony, 153–57.

76. Wunderlin, *Visions of a New Industrial Order*, 124–29, quotation on 127; Perlman, *Labor Union Theories in America*, 295–98; Commons Report, U.S. Commission on Industrial Relations, *Final Reports and Testimony*, 1:207, also quoted in Wunderlin, *Visions of a New Industrial Order*.

77. Commons Report, 186, 195.

78. "Industrial Conflict," 89–90.

79. *New Republic*, August 28, 1915, 91–92. Not surprisingly, the *Survey* also continued its close coverage of the commission through a critical evaluation of its final reports. John A. Fitch, "Probing the Causes of Industrial Unrest: A Series of Three Installments Reviewing the Reports Issued by the United States Commission on Industrial Relations," *Survey* 35 (December 18, 1915) and (January 1, 8, 1916): 317–33, 395–402, 432–34. The first two reports analyzed the Manly and Commons Reports; the last singled out the staff report on the "Tactics of Violence," written by Luke Grant on the structural iron industry and the McNamara bombing, for detailed attention.

80. "Report of President John McLennan, Colorado State Federation of Labor," *United Mine Workers Journal*, September 30, 1915, 8.

81. Mabel LaRue Germer, "Governor of Colorado and Frank P. Walsh," *United Mine Workers Journal*, September 2, 1915, 16.

82. "Undisputed Facts for All the People," *United Mine Workers Journal*, September 30, 1915, 7.

83. "Who Is This Man Walsh?—Sketch of the Two-fisted Irishman of Missouri Who Has Been Catechizing Capitalists," *Current Opinion* 59 (August 1915): 90–92.

84. Frank Walsh to Austin Garretson, November 2, 1915, Dante Barton to Frank Walsh, November 11, 12, 1915, Committee on Industrial Relations, introductory letter, n.d., all in Box 34, Walsh Papers. "Support Needed and Deserved," November 11, 1915, 4, and "From Committee on Industrial Relations," *United Mine Workers Journal*, November 25, 1915, 4. See also Adams, *Age of Industrial Violence*, 220–21.

85. Basil M. Manly to Frank Walsh, August 24, 1914 [*sic;* letter should have been dated August 24, 1915], Box 33, File 39, Walsh Papers.

86. The schisms within the Progressive movement induced by the war are discussed

in David Kennedy, *Over Here: The First World War and American Society* (New York: Oxford University Press, 1980), 45–92; Eugene M. Tobin, *Organize or Perish: America's Independent Progressives, 1913–1933* (Westport, Conn.: Greenwood Press, 1986), 57–61; and Adams, *Age of Industrial Violence,* 222–26. On the meanings of "industrial democracy," see Steve Fraser, *Labor Will Rule: Sidney Hillman and the Rise of American Labor* (New York: Free Press, 1991), 114–15, 124–27, 136–39; Milton Derber, "The Idea of Industrial Democracy in America, 1898–1915," *Labor History* (Fall 1966): 262–65.

Conclusion

1. Walter Lippman, *Drift and Mastery: An Attempt to Diagnose the Current Unrest* (1914; reprint, Englewood Cliffs, N.J.: Prentice Hall, 1961), 141–42, is a pivotal text of the new liberalism. See Gary Gerstle, "The Protean Character of American Liberalism," *American Historical Review* 99, no. 4 (October 1994): 1049–56, for a useful discussion of the new liberal (progressive) critique of classical liberalism. See also Leonard Williams, *American Liberalism and Ideological Change* (DeKalb: Northern Illinois University Press, 1997), 41–49; Alan Brinkley, *The End of Reform: New Deal Liberalism in Recession and War* (New York: Random House, 1995), 8–11; and Charles Forcey, *The Crossroads of Liberalism: Croly, Weyl, Lippmann, and the Progressive Era, 1900–1925* (New York: Oxford University Press, 1961), xiii–xxix. The liberal project, as the descendants of progressivism understood it, was influentially articulated in Louis Hartz, *The Liberal Tradition in America: An Interpretation of American Political Thought since the Revolution* (New York: Harcourt Brace, 1955).

2. John Dewey, *Liberalism and Social Action* (New York: G. P. Putnam's Sons, 1935), 90–91.

3. Arthur S. Link, "What Happened to the Progressive Movement in the 1920s?" *American Historical Review* 64 (July 1959): 833–51, esp. 836–42, and Richard L. McCormick and Arthur S. Link, *Progressivism* (Arlington Heights, Ill.: Harlan Davidson, 1983), 110–13, stress divisions within the movement accentuated by the war as primary factors contributing to decline.

4. For a review of the conventional narrative, see Allen F. Davis, "Welfare, Reform and World War I," *American Quarterly* 19, no. 3 (Fall 1967): 516–17. See also David Kennedy, *Over Here: The First World War and American Society* (New York: Oxford University Press, 1980), 30–92. This view also finds its way into Graham Adams, *The Age of Industrial Violence, 1910–1915: The Activities and Findings of the United States Commission on Industrial Relations* (New York: Columbia University Press), 222; see also Robert H. Zieger, *America's Great War: World War I and the American Experience* (Lanham, Md: Rowman and Littlefield, 2000), 2–3, 235–36, for a distinction between the fate of "liberal" and "control" progressive reform agendas.

5. Eldon J. Eisenach, *The Lost Promise of Progressivism* (Lincoln: University of Nebraska Press, 1994), 243–48. John Higham's study of American nativism remains one of the most compelling portraits of the jingoism of wartime that infected Progres-

sives and non-Progressives alike. See *Strangers in the Land: Patterns of American Nativism, 1860–1925* (New York: Atheneum, 1963).

6. Alan Dawley, *Struggles for Justice: Social Responsibility and the Liberal State* (Cambridge, Mass.: Harvard University Press, 1991), 237–43; *New Republic*, July 19, 1919, quoted in Dawley, *Struggles for Justice*, 239.

7. On the new organizing in basic industry, see David Montgomery, *The Fall of the House of Labor: The Workplace, the State, and American Labor Activism, 1865–1925* (New York: Cambridge University Press, 1987); see also David Montgomery, "The New Unionism and the Transformation of Workers' Consciousness in America, 1909–1922," in *Workers Control in America: Studies in the History of Work, Technology, and Labor Struggles*, by David Montgomery (New York: Cambridge University Press, 1979), 91–112; Joseph A. McCartin, *Labor's Great War: The Struggle for Industrial Democracy and the Origins of Modern American Labor Relations, 1913–1921* (Chapel Hill: University of North Carolina Press, 1998); James R. Barrett, *Work and Community in the Jungle: Chicago's Packinghouse Workers, 1894–1922* (Urbana: University of Illinois Press, 1987); David Brody, *Steelworkers in America: The Nonunion Era* (Cambridge, Mass.: Harvard University Press, 1960); and Cecelia Bucki, *Bridgeport's Socialist New Deal, 1915–1936* (Urbana: University of Illinois Press, 2001). The war also saw the growth of interest in scientific management. Louis Brandeis had become a proponent of scientific management, properly used; see his *Scientific Management and the Railroads* (New York: Engineering Magazine, 1912). For discussion of his views on labor-management relations, see Philippa Strum, *Brandeis: Beyond Progressivism* (Lawrence: University of Kansas Press, 1993), 24–48, and Lewis J. Paper, *Brandeis* (Englewood Cliffs, N.J.: Prentice Hall, 1983), 135–60. Another model for many Progressives was the "protocols of peace" in the garment industry, in the construction of which Brandeis also participated, which sought to rationalize the relations between labor and management. See also Steve Fraser, *Labor Will Rule: Sidney Hillman and the Rise of American Labor* (New York: Free Press, 1991), 68, 79–83.

8. Ronald Steel, *Walter Lippmann and the American Century* (New York: Vintage, 1980), 72–73.

9. The optimistic spirit of Progressives that crested in 1914 is evident in a number of texts: Benjamin DeWitt, *The Progressive Movement* (New York: Macmillan, 1915); Lippmann, *Drift and Mastery;* Herbert Croly, *Progressive Democracy* (New York: Macmillan, 1914); and Walter Weyl, *The New Democracy* (New York: Macmillan, 1912). See also John Dewey, *Democracy and Education* (New York: Macmillan, 1916). For a socialist vision that comported well with certain strains of progressivism, see William English Walling, *Progressivism—and After* (New York: Macmillan, 1914).

10. Steel, *Walter Lippmann*, 77–78.

11. Ibid., 65, 79–80.

12. Ibid., 78–79.

13. The most comprehensive treatment of Dewey's development as an intellectual Progressive is Robert Westbrook, *John Dewey and American Democracy* (Ithaca, N.Y.:

Cornell University Press, 1991); for the war years, see especially 195–227. The war as a period in which "time became compressed" is a phrase from Alan Cywar, "John Dewey: Toward Domestic Reconstruction, 1915–1920," *Journal of the History of Ideas* 30 (1969): 387.

14. Cywar, "John Dewey," 386, 388, 390.

15. John Dewey, "Nationalizing Education (1916)," in *The Middle Works, 1899–1924,* vol. 10, *1916–17,* ed. Jo Ann Boydston (Carbondale: Southern Illinois University Press, 1980), 203, 207, 209; John Dewey, "The New Paternalism," in *The Middle Works, 1899–1924,* vol. 11, *1918–19,* 117, 120. These essays are also cited in Cywar, "John Dewey," 393, 394.

16. John Dewey, "What Are We Fighting For?" in *The Middle Works, 1899–1924,* vol. 11, *1918–19,* ed. Jo Ann Boydston (Carbondale: Southern Illinois University Press, 1982), 98–106, esp. 103, 104–5. This essay is also cited in Cywar, "John Dewey," 400.

17. Walter Lippman, "The World Conflict in Relation to American Democracy" (1917), quoted in Kennedy, *Over Here,* 39.

18. On the intellectual foundations for "a liberal war," see Forcey, *Crossroads of Liberalism,* 242–86; Westbrook, *John Dewey and American Democracy,* 202–12, 223–27; and Alan Cywar, "John Dewey in World War I: Patriotism and International Progressivism," *American Quarterly* 21, no. 3 (Fall 1969): 578–94. Dawley, *Struggles for Justice,* 184–203, provides a useful summary of the dynamics of mobilization for "total war." See also John McClymer, *War and Welfare: Social Engineering in America, 1890–1925* (Westport, Conn.: Greenwood Press, 1980).

19. Randolph Bourne, "The War and the Intellectuals," in *War and the Intellectuals: Collected Essays, 1915–1919,* ed. Carl Resek (New York: Harper and Row, 1964), 13.

20. Jane Addams, *The Second Twenty Years at Hull-House, September 1909 to September 1929* (New York: Macmillan, 1930), 145, 142.

21. An important document reflecting the sentiments of antiwar social reformers is Addams's *Second Twenty Years;* see also Allen F. Davis, "Welfare, Reform and World War I," and Eugene M. Tobin, *Organize or Perish: America's Independent Progressives, 1913–1933* (Westport, Conn.: Greenwood Press, 1986).

22. Addams, *Second Twenty Years.*

23. Bourne, "War and the Intellectuals," 9–10; see also Bourne's October 1917 powerful attack on Dewey in "Twilight of the Idols," in *War and the Intellectuals: Collected Essays, 1915–1919,* ed. Carl Resek (New York: Harper and Row, 1964), 53–64. On the Bourne-Dewey debate, see Westbrook, *John Dewey and American Democracy,* 202–12; Cywar, "John Dewey"; Christopher Lasch, *The New Radicalism in America, 1889–1963: The Intellectual as a Social Type* (New York: Knopf, 1965), 205–13; Bruce Clayton, *Forgotten Prophet: The Life of Randolph Bourne* (Baton Rouge: Louisiana State University Press, 1984), 203–30; and David Kennedy, *Over Here,* 49–53.

24. New studies have provided a more precise accounting of this campaign for industrial democracy. See especially McCartin, *Labor's Great War,* 8–10, 199–210, and Julie Greene, *Pure and Simple Politics: The American Federation of Labor, 1881–1917*

(New York: Cambridge University Press, 1998), 242–73. Fraser, *Labor Will Rule*, includes an insightful discussion of the contested meanings of industrial democracy on 114–18, 124–28, and 136–40. See essays by David Montgomery, Howell John Harris, and Joseph A. McCartin in *Industrial Democracy in America: The Ambiguous Promise*, ed. Nelson Lichtenstein and Howell John Harris (New York: Cambridge University Press, 1993), 20–42, 43–66, 67–86; see also Milton Derber, *The American Idea of Industrial Democracy, 1865–1965* (Urbana: University of Illinois Press, 1970).

25. William P. Harvey to Frank P. Walsh, August 2, 1917, Box 5, General Correspondence, Walsh Papers.

26. George Creel to Frank Walsh, September 1, 1917, and FPW to George Creel, September 10, 1917, Box 5, General Correspondence, Walsh Papers.

27. Scott Nearing to FPW, September 6, 1917, Box 5, General Correspondence, Walsh Papers.

28. FPW to Louis S. Irvin, July 6, 1918, Box 6, General Correspondence, Walsh Papers.

29. Montgomery, "New Unionism," 91–112. For an important account of conflicting currents in the labor movement during the war years, see also Montgomery, *Fall of the House of Labor*, 370–464; on Walsh's support for Tom Mooney, see McCartin, *Labor's Great War*, 70–71.

30. McCartin, "'An American Feeling': Workers, Managers, and the Struggle over Industrial Democracy in the World War I Era," in *Industrial Democracy in America: The Ambiguous Promise*, ed. Nelson Lichtenstein and Howell John Harris (New York: Cambridge University Press, 1993), 79.

31. John A. Fitch, "The War Labor Board: A Wartime Experiment with Compulsory Arbitration," *Survey* 2 (May 3, 1919): 195.

32. See Montgomery, *Fall of the House of Labor*. A nice summary of immediate postwar developments is provided by McCartin, "American Feeling," 78–86.

33. Forcey, *Crossroads of Liberalism*, 277–306.

34. McCartin, *Labor's Great War*, 395–423; Fraser, *Labor Will Rule*, 160–77, 205–21, 282–84. On the shape of a new labor relations in the 1920s, see Colin Gordon, *New Deals: Business, Labor, and Politics, 1920–1935* (New York: Cambridge University Press, 1994), 87–127. And for different views on the origins and impact of welfare capitalism, see Lizabeth Cohen, *Making a New Deal: Industrial Workers in Chicago, 1919–1939* (New York: Cambridge University Press, 1990), 159–211, and David Brody, "The Rise and Decline of Welfare Capitalism," in Brody, *Workers in Industrial America: Essays on the Twentieth Century Struggle* (New York: Oxford University Press, 1980), 48–81.

35. See Colin Davis, *Power at Odds: The 1922 National Railroad Shopmen's Strike* (Urbana: University of Illinois Press, 1997), 43–51, on the struggle for continued government ownership of railroads and the organizing of the shop trades. See also Montgomery, *Fall of the House of Labor*, 400–407.

36. On the postwar battles of labor Progressives, see Montgomery, *Fall of the House of Labor*, 399–410; James Weinstein, *The Decline of Socialism in America, 1912–1925*

(New York: Monthly Review Press, 1967), 177–257; Melvyn Dubofsky and Warren Van Tine, *John L. Lewis: A Biography* (New York: Quadrangle, 1977), 43–94; Davis, *Power at Odds*, 43–47; and Fraser, *Labor Will Rule*, 148–70. A fascinating account of the collapse of a radical labor movement and its vision of a cooperative postwar social order is Dana Frank, *Purchasing Power: Consumer Organizing, Gender, and the Seattle Labor Movement, 1919–1929* (New York: Cambridge University Press, 1994). Also for an insightful contemporary analysis of the state of the labor movement in the 1920s, see J. B. S. Hardman, *American Labor Dynamics in Light of Postwar Developments* (New York: Harcourt, Brace, 1928). See also James R. Barrett, *William Z. Foster and the Tragedy of American Radicalism* (Urbana: University of Illinois Press, 1999).

37. Kim E. Nielsen, *Un-American Womanhood: Antiracialism, Antifeminism, and the First Red Scare* (Columbus: Ohio State University Press, 2001). See also Nancy F. Cott, *The Grounding of Modern Feminism* (New Haven, Conn.: Yale University Press, 1987), 424–67.

38. Clarke A. Chambers, *Seedtime of Reform: American Social Service and Social Action, 1918–1933* (Minneapolis: University of Minnesota Press, 1963). Eugene M. Tobin, *Organize or Perish: America's Independent Progressives, 1913–1933* (Westport, Conn.: Greenwood Press, 1986), 11, stresses the intense but largely ineffective organizational activity of Progressives during the 1920s, noting that they were "few in number, organizationally inept, and politically impotent. Were this a study of liberal triumphs, it would be a very short one."

39. Dawley, *Struggles for Justice*, 239, 243, argues that Progressives' failure to maintain their reform momentum lay in the collapse of ties between "the broad middle class and industrial wage earners." He adds, "The consequence of disrupting cross-class alliances was to remove the necessary condition for progressive social reform." Such ties, even in the prewar period, should not be exaggerated, however.

40. Steve Fraser, "The 'Labor Question,'" in *The Rise and Fall of the New Deal Order, 1930–1980,* ed. Steve Fraser and Gary Gerstle (Princeton, N.J.: Princeton University Press, 1989), 62.

41. Dewey, *Liberalism and Social Action,* 79, 48–49.

42. While communists and socialists offered valuable organizing skills to the struggles of the unemployed and to the formation of the CIO, their embrace of the New Deal, especially after 1935, led them to a Popular Front discourse within which a class critique of the New Deal reform agenda was largely abandoned or submerged in a new rhetoric of "the people." For a cultural critique of that process, see Warren I. Susman, *Culture as History: The Transformation of American Society in the Twentieth Century* (New York: Pantheon, 1973), esp. chapters 9 and 10, "The Culture of the Thirties" and "Culture and Commitment." Michael Denning, *The Cultural Front: The Laboring of American Culture in the Twentieth Century* (New York: Verso, 1997) offers a more comprehensive and sympathetic analysis of Popular Front culture and its impact.

43. Fraser, "'Labor Question,'" 56.

44. On the limits of New Deal liberalism, see essays in *The Rise and Fall of the New*

Deal Order, 1930–1980, ed. Steve Fraser and Gary Gerstle (Princeton, N.J.: Princeton University Press, 1989); see also Gordon, *New Deals,* 280–305, and Brinkley, *End of Reform,* 9–10, 38–42. An older study that emphasizes the limited nature of New Deal and Great Society responses to the problem of unemployment and liberals' stake in the existing social order is Frances Fox Piven and Richard Cloward, *Regulating the Poor: The Functions of Public Welfare* (New York: Vintage, 1971). For a generally positive assessment of the influence of progressivism on twentieth-century liberalism, see Sidney M. Milkis and Jerome M. Mileur, eds., *Progressivism and the New Democracy* (Amherst: University of Massachusetts Press, 1999), especially Sidney M. Milkis, "Introduction: Progressivism, Then and Now," 1–39.

45. Such a comparison of reform in the 1930s and 1960s is indebted to Piven and Cloward, *Regulating the Poor,* and Frances Fox Piven and Richard Cloward, *Poor Peoples' Movements: Why They Succeed, and How They Fail* (New York: Vintage, 1979).

46. See Mary Dudziak, *Cold War Civil Rights: Race and the Image of American Democracy* (Princeton, N.J.: Princeton University Press, 2000).

47. For a useful discussion of this shift in twentieth-century liberalism from economic to race concerns, see Gerstle, "Protean Character of American Liberalism," 1043–73, esp. 1059–72.

48. Ironically, it fell to a former conservative theoretician of the "emerging Republican majority" to articulate one of the more compelling cases for the continuing relevance of class to American politics. See Kevin Phillips, *The Politics of Rich and Poor: Wealth and the American Electorate in the Reagan Aftermath* (New York: Random House, 1990), and Kevin Phillips, *American Dynasty: Aristocracy, Fortune and the Politics of Deceit in the House of Bush* (New York: Viking, 2004).

Index

SHELTON STROMQUIST is a professor of history and a collegiate fellow of the College of Liberal Arts and Sciences at the University of Iowa. He is the author of *A Generation of Boomers: The Pattern of Railroad Labor Conflict in Nineteenth-Century America* and *Solidarity and Survival: An Oral History of Iowa Labor in the Twentieth Century.* He coedited *The Pullman Strike and the Crisis of the 1890s* and several other volumes.

The University of Illinois Press
is a founding member of the
Association of American University Presses.

Composed in 10.5/13 Adobe Minion
with Meta display
by Type One, LLC
for the University of Illinois Press
Manufactured by Sheridan Books, Inc.

University of Illinois Press
1325 South Oak Street
Champaign, IL 61820-6903
www.press.uillinois.edu